Handbook of Management Accounting Research

Volume 3

Handbook of Management Accounting Research
Volume 3

Edited by

CHRISTOPHER S. CHAPMAN
Imperial College London, UK

ANTHONY G. HOPWOOD
University of Oxford, UK

MICHAEL D. SHIELDS
Michigan State University, USA

ELSEVIER

AMSTERDAM – BOSTON – HEIDELBERG – LONDON – NEW YORK – OXFORD
PARIS – SAN DIEGO – SAN FRANCISCO – SINGAPORE – SYDNEY – TOKYO

Elsevier
The Boulevard, Langford Lane, Kidlington, Oxford OX5 1GB, UK

First edition 2009

British Library Cataloguing in Publication Data
A catalogue record for this book is available from the British Library

Library of Congress Cataloging-in-Publication Data
A catalog record for this book is available from the Library of Congress

ISBN: 978-0-08-055450-1 (Volume 3)
ISBN: 978-0-08-087929-1 (Volumes 1, 2 and 3)

Printed and bound UK

09 10 11 12 13 10 9 8 7 6 5 4 3 2 1

Contents

MANAGEMENT ACCOUNTING AROUND THE WORLD

Contributors to Volume 3

Robert H. Chenhall
Mark A. Covaleski
Antonio Davila
Mark W. Dirsmith
David A. Dittman
George Foster
James J. Gong
James W. Hesford
Christopher D. Ittner
Sanjay Kallapur
Robert S. Kaplan
Ranjani Krishnan
Liisa Kurunmäki
David F. Larcker
Gordon Potter
Sajay Samuel
Tobias Scheytt
Kim Soin
James E. Sorensen
Wim A. Van der Stede
S. Mark Young

Preface

Varying across time, space and area of application, management accounting is fortunate to have maintained a research tradition that is characterized by a diversity of both intellectual perspectives and modes of inquiry. As the systematic reviews in Volumes 1 and 2 made clear, research in the area has utilized the conceptual and theoretical frameworks of many of the human and social sciences, as well as using historical inquiries to map out the emergence and development of the subject. The full range of approaches to research in the social sciences has also been called upon to aid our understanding of the functioning of the craft. Indeed, at the present time there is most probably a greater investment in research method diversity than ever before, as field studies, analytical inquiries, experiments, surveys and historical investigations are all called upon to give insights into the complexities of the design and functioning of management accounting systems in action.

For an applied subject, such diversity is important. With the task of trying to understand the effective functioning of existing practices and the design of new ones that can facilitate organizational decision-making and control, management accounting needs to call on bodies of knowledge that can illuminate the requirements of rational economic action; the politics of organizational resource allocation and decision-making; the links to other managerial bodies of knowledge; the organizational strategies, structures and processes that are implicated in its use and impacts; the ways in which management accounting knowledge has been intertwined with the development of particular occupational structures; and the historical processes of the emergence of specific forms and emphases. No one approach to research can do all of this. Agency theoretic understandings certainly cannot, but neither can contingency formulations, social psychological insights or historical analyses on their own. Because the focus of attention is given—the design and use of forms of economic calculation and control within the organization—its understanding and advance necessitates appeals to a wide range of quite different bodies of knowledge.

As is clear from the range of perspectives and approaches reviewed in Volume 1, so far management accounting research has indeed been tolerant of the diversity of approaches that are needed to make sense of its organizational functioning. In this respect it is certainly different from the research tradition that has emerged in financial accounting in the US. That also invested in a variety of different approaches at one time, ranging from income theoretic and other economic perspectives, through historical inquiries and technical analyses, to economically informed statistical and econometric investigations. But at least in the US that diversity was challenged by the specializations of elite institutions and journals and the resultant isomorphic pressures that this created, with the result that what is now regarded as the "mainstream" of financial accounting research has a narrow focus, intolerant of other theoretical perspectives and research approaches and, as a consequence, only partial in the insights it gives into financial accounting in practice. That management accounting research has so far avoided this constrained conformity should itself be the subject of some investigation, not least as there are some emergent pressures that might seek to challenge that status quo. Residing outside the financial accounting mainstream in North American business schools has helped to maintain diversity both directly, insofar as this might have given a degree of autonomy to the subject, and indirectly because this autonomy has increased the influence of less constrained non-North American perspectives. In most countries management accounting research has a history of interacting with a wider array of other social sciences and business disciplines.

Moving on from theoretical perspectives and research methods, Volume 2 also provided a review of research into a variety of areas of management accounting practice including costing, budgeting, transfer pricing and capital budgeting. Additional consideration was given to reviewing the research that has been conducted into the important relationships that management accounting has with operations management, the overall strategy of an organization, and the design and implementation of wider control and information systems. While contingent understandings of management accounting (Chenhall, 2007) have recognized that the contexts in which its practices are employed can influence their design and use, the adaptation of practice to circumstance is still a relatively underdeveloped area. The reviews in Volume 2 attempted to give some insights into what could be involved in more contingent analyses of management accounting by looking at the research literatures on its application in healthcare, the manufacturing sector and in the increasingly significant interorganizational sphere. Moreover, quite explicit recognition was given to the ways in which both management accounting practice and research vary in different national and regional contexts.

It is the continuation of these important themes that provide the focus for this, the third volume of the *Handbook of Management Accounting Research*. First of all, consideration is given to research in three further areas of management accounting practice—the newly labelled balanced scorecard, the increasing extension of management accounting into the area of nonfinancial measures, and management accounting across the organization rather than up and down the organizational hierarchy, as has been more usually the case until relatively recently. All these represent important new areas of management accounting that have emerged or been developed within the last decade or so. Also included in the category of research on practice is a review of the literature on management accountants themselves, in this instance as they operate in the US. Until relatively recently the practitioners of the craft have represented a black box for research in the area, rarely seen as being problematic let alone capable of influencing the functioning and consequences of the practices. Of course there have been some distinguished exceptions (for example Simon et al., 1954; Loft, 1990), but at a time when the practitioners and their practices have been subject to a great deal of change, it is important to recognize the role that serious research can play in probing into the occupational structures and behaviours that are associated with the practice of management accounting.

It is equally important to encourage research on the design and functioning of management accounting in particular areas of application, be they sectoral or national. Exploring the detailed involvement of practices in the contexts of their use is a complex and time-consuming task that has difficulty attracting the attention of either academic researchers or management consultants. The academics have concerns about the sheer amount of time involved and possibly also the lower status that such grounded inquiries seem to attract, at least in some national academic settings. The consultants are also bothered by the costly investment that the construction of more specific understandings involves and, as a result, usually continue to propagate and sell more abstract and generalized understandings and approaches, whatever the difficulties these have in relating to specific settings and however much has to be spent subsequently on adapting them to their new contexts. Be that as it may, for those concerned with the effective functioning of management accounting in practice, insights into its operation in a variety of sectoral and national contexts are of very real importance. To this end, Volume 3 provides reviews of the emergent literatures on governmental and non-profit accounting in the US, the involvement of management accounting in entrepreneurial activities and new venture creation, and the role which economic calculation and management accounting play in one important component of the media and entertainment sector, namely the US motion picture industry. Consideration is also given to management accounting in the hospitality industry and the financial services sector. Finally there is a review of research on the involvement of accounting in the reforms that have constituted the New Public Management.

Although preliminary in nature, the sectoral reviews are nevertheless of some importance. Until very recently, and perhaps still in many institutions, instruction and research in management accounting invariably assumed a manufacturing context. Even in the recent case of activity-based costing this was often so. But, as important as manufacturing might be, in many of the countries where management accounting teaching and research takes place it is now a minority activity. The sum total of the economic activity in the sectors discussed in Volume 3, namely financial services, media and entertainment, and hospitality, is substantially ahead of that in the manufacturing sector even without adding the public sector. If the latter were to be included, the comparison would be even more extreme. Yet all these sectors have been relatively neglected by the management accounting research community, as have other services and the retail sector.

The reasons for this are not well understood, but might include the fact that until relatively recently management accounting itself was not well represented in sectors outside of manufacturing and local government. For many years management accounting's role in manufacturing had much to do with the control of labour costs in particular, and costs more generally, in what used to be a competitive sector of the economy where profit management had to be more dependent on cost reduction than price enhancement. In local government, management accounting was implicated for many years in facilitating effective management within the constraints set by central government and political circumstances. And in many other sectors what economic calculation there was, was seen as being a component of mainstream operations management rather than necessarily the preserve of a separate accounting activity. That certainly was the case in retailing, the hospitality sector and many financial services. But such institutional characteristics can and do change. In many areas of manufacturing quasi-monopolistic price enhancement started to become a more significant instrument of strategy than cost management. But, equally, the growth of competition in the service sector, in retailing and between financial institutions encouraged an investment in management accounting in these sectors. Still, however, we know far too little about the application of accounting practices in the management of many significant sectors of the economy.

Consider, for example, the rise of a new sector of the US economy in and around what is now known as Silicon Valley, or the rise of the pharmaceutical, healthcare and bio-tech industries around universities and research institutes with expertise in the life sciences. Fascinating as these developments were and still are, until very recently they have failed to capture the imagination and interest of management accounting researchers, at least until a few very recent examples. While anthropologists, organizational scholars and sociologists have shown some interest, accountants have not. Whether this is because they have such a generalized view of their subject that they genuinely think that the emergence of such new contexts is not relevant is not clear. Could it be because their sense of curiosity is relatively poorly developed, too many accounting researchers having too technical a training in accounting rather than a more intellectual one? Or is it even that the encroachment of the uniformity of the mainstream makes them very cautious about exploring such new areas? As of now we do not know. But what is clear is that, despite the fascination with the likes of Google and eBay, they have failed to attract inquiries into the mobilization of economic calculation and accounting in their internal operations. The review provided by Davila & Foster in this volume starts to open up this type of area for further investigation, and this is to be welcomed.

The final chapter in this volume provides further insight into the geographical spread of management accounting. While Volume 2 provided some understanding of management accounting practice and research in China, Volume 3 now adds India, thereby enabling a more informed insight into economic management in two of the most significant generators of economic development in Asia and indeed the world.

Many of the chapters in Volume 3 illustrate the constantly changing nature of management accounting practice and knowledge. Rarely stable, they adjust to changing circumstances and understandings of their role in organizational management. That alone provides a reason for continuing to invest in a diversity of research perspectives, because no one will ever know which will prove to be useful next as new agendas for both practice and research will continue to emerge. Advances in technology will continue to change the underlying cost structures of organizations. Organizational collaboration is likely to develop further, creating an intensification of interest in lateral forms of information mobilization and provision. The application of project forms of management is likely to develop further, possibly creating more interest in organizing financial information around products, product variants and groupings of retail outlets, for instance, as well as across time. The probability is that lifecycle costing will thereby become more important, not least in an era when lifecycles have been getting progressively shorter. Finally, at a time when issues related to climate change are becoming ever more significant, the incorporation of environmental and sustainability indicators and information into management accounts is likely to become a more important issue. With the development of carbon markets and the associated rise of new categories of cost, with greater emphasis being placed on the environmental management of supply chains and with increasing levels of investment in emission reduction and the constrained use of finite resources, a new interdependency of the economic and the environmental is likely to emerge. For all these reasons we can look forward to a continuing process of knowledge development and accumulation in management accounting practice and research.

Finally, we would like to thank the chapter authors who have made this additional volume possible. They have all put in an enormous amount of work despite having to operate to very tight deadlines. We also would like to thank Takamasa Fujioka for all his help in producing the manuscript.

Christopher S. Chapman
Imperial College London
Anthony G. Hopwood
University of Oxford
Michael D. Shields
Michigan State University

References

Chenhall, R. H. (2007). Theorising contingencies in management control systems research. In: C. C. Chapman, A. G. Hopwood, & M. D. Shields (Eds), *Handbook of Management Accounting Research*. Amsterdam, The Netherlands: Elsevier.

Loft, A. (1990). *Coming into the light: a study of the development of a professional association for cost accountants in Britain in the wake of World War 1*. London, UK: Chartered Institute of Management Accountants.

Simon, H. A., Guetzkow, H., Kozmetsky, G. & Tyndall, G. (1954). *Centralization vs. decentralization in organizing the Controller's Department*. New York, NY: The Controllership Foundation.

Management Accounting Practices

Handbook of Management Accounting Research
Edited by Christopher S. Chapman, Anthony G. Hopwood and Michael D. Shields

Accounting for the Horizontal Organization

Robert H. Chenhall

Monash University, Australia

Abstract: There have been many approaches that have sought to identify the principles of best practice organizational management. The horizontal organization (HO) has been proposed as a method that draws on ideas from marketing, production, organizational behaviour and human resource management. It identifies specific value propositions with a customer-oriented focus and then develops process efficiency and continuous improvements, flattened structures with a team-based focus, human resource policies concerned with empowerment, and a supportive and committed culture to help institutionalize change. The key distinguishing feature is to move away from traditional vertical, functional structures to lateral structures, processes and information to support the HO. This chapter reviews three approaches which, when taken together, distil the key elements of the HO. These are Ostroff (1999) *The Horizontal Organization*, New York, Oxford University Press; Schonberger (1996) *World Class Manufacturing: The Next Decade*, New York, The Free Press; and Galbraith (2005) *Designing the Customer-centric Organization: a Guide to Strategy, Structure and Process*, San Francisco, Jossey-Bass. How these authors envisage a role for management accounting in the design and application of the HO is of particular interest. The chapter will review the essence of HO and critically examine the extent to which there have been complementary developments in management accounting, and how effective practice and research have been in developing a horizontal dimension to management accounting. It is concluded that innovations in management accounting, such as activity-based accounting and holistic performance measurement like balanced scorecards, have not had any significant effects on those developing ideas related to HO. Reasons why this is so are canvassed and areas where accounting innovations may provide valuable input to implementing the HO are discussed. Recent developments in management practices that elaborate on HO and implications for a horizontal dimension to accounting are examined.

1. Introduction

Over recent years there have been a variety of schemes to develop best practice approaches to managing organizations. Many approaches such as just-in-time (JIT) and total quality management (TQM) that were originally focused on improving production processes have become more holistic, incorporating explicit consideration of managing customers and suppliers and improving practices related to production processes and human resources. A central emerging theme is a focus on how organizations integrate activities across the value chain to support strategy that is customer-focused. This approach is encapsulated in the idea of the horizontal organization (HO). While different viewpoints stress various aspects of management, a common approach includes identifying specific strategic priorities or value propositions with a customer-oriented focus, and then developing process efficiency and continuous improvements, flattened structures with a team-based focus, human resource policies concerned with empowerment and a supportive and committed culture to help institutionalize change. A key issue is to move away from traditional vertical, functional structures to horizontal structures and processes to support the HO.

2. Historical Context of the Horizontal Organization

HO is essentially about structural forms and organizational arrangements that enable a lateral integration of strategies, processes, structures and people to deliver value to customers. The origins of HO can be found in the 1960s with the advent of matrix structures developed to help facilitate project-focused management for subcontractors to the US government (Kingdon, 1973). The intention was to ensure that representatives of the US agencies would have a project manager dedicated to the contract responsible for managing costs and deadlines,

DOI: 10.1016/S1751-3243(07)03001-5

rather than having to negotiate with a number of departmental heads who were only partially responsible for parts of the project.

In preference to abandoning existing functional groupings and organizing wholly around contracts, the subcontracting organizations superimposed a project focus on top of the existing functional structures, thereby creating matrix organizations. The functional structure allowed preservation of critical mass around functions which enabled subsequent development of expertise, while the project focus satisfied customer needs for personalized service and performance (Marquis, 1969). As organizations became involved in increasingly complex projects, particularly in the aerospace industry, matrix structures with their emphasis on more organic, direct contacts were seen to provide more flexibility to respond to complexities. Galbraith (1973) was the first to stress that increased complexity caused existing information processing capacity to become overloaded. He suggested several responses that involved working with traditional vertical structures, creating slack resources and increasing vertical information systems. Other suggestions recognized the role of horizontal or lateral relations. These involved creating self-contained tasks or sub-units with a purely project focus. He stressed the importance to lateral coordination of arrangements that involved direct interfunctional contacts at operational levels. These were presented as involving increasing degrees of lateral process: direct contact between managers; liaison roles; temporary task forces; permanent interdepartmental teams; creating an integrating role and transforming this role into a linking–managerial function.

Matrix organizations involve horizontal flows of resources and information, drawing on functional expertise. This creates the possibility of conflict between the authority of project heads and of functional managers, with possible consequences of stress and costs of ensuring coordination between functional and project concerns. Knight (1976, pp. 126–127) suggested that conflict and ambiguity should be addressed by careful planning of the matrix organization, including definition of organizational roles, setting up guidelines and rules of operation. In addition, given the novelty of matrix structures, training and development and supportive management systems are needed. Knight (1976, p. 130) provides examples of systems that are consistent with matrix organizations, most of which fall within a broad definition of management accounting: project planning; personnel reviews; corporate planning; economic evaluation and profit reporting. In addition he notes the importance of mangement by objectives (MBO) and personnel reviews.

There was some early acknowledgement in accounting of the importance of the horizontal dimension specified in the matrix organization. Hopwood (1977) explicated the design of information systems for matrix organizations, warning of the possibilities that the application of information based on functional structures can frustrate the effectiveness of implementing matrix organizations. He suggested that information systems for matrix organizations should distinguish between information for control and decision-making, with a functional emphasis on resource utilization and a project emphasis for end results. Importantly, he notes that functional controls tend to draw their power from the vertical structure, while the project-oriented information systems for project decisions and control depend on the more fragile patterns of lateral relations. As such, project-focused information needs to be as visible and as well-articulated as functional control information.

Project management represents a development that occurred as a recognized approach to management about the same time as matrix structures were being refined, and is also important to understanding the origins of the HO. Project management involves structuring around projects that are managed by a project manager, who puts together a team and ensures the integration and communication of the workflow that occurs horizontally across different departments. Originally, in the 1960s, project management had an engineering orientation with techniques being proposed for project scheduling involving critical path methods developed by Dupont and Remington, PERT as developed by Booz-Allen and Hamilton for the US Polaris submarine programme, Gantt charts and critical chain project management (CCPM). They provided quantitative approaches to managing projects that quickly spread into many private enterprises. The approaches involved selecting critical steps and milestones for project progress, the sequence of activities, network diagrams, timing of activities, critical paths and use of charts to monitor and adjust projects. Throughout the 1970s project management gained in popularity, retaining its technical planning and control elements. A study by Cook & Granger (1976) on the status of project management instruction in US tertiary institutions indicated that project management courses tended to be taught in engineering departments, also being included as a topic in courses within business departments. The authors concluded that human relations and communication areas were under-represented in courses and recommended a stronger emphasis on these aspects.

More recently, project management has been developed to incorporate wider aspects of management. Kerzner (2001) sees project management as a way to manage or control company resources on a given activity within time, within cost and within technology constraints, and with good customer relations. The potential benefits are:

- identification of functional responsibilities to ensure that all activities are accounted for (regardless of personnel turnover);

- minimization of the need for continuous reporting;
- identification of time limits for scheduling;
- a methodology for trade-off analysis;
- measurement of accomplishment against plans;
- early identification of problems so that corrective action can be taken;
- improved estimating capability for future planning and assessing when objectives cannot be met or will be exceeded.

(See also recent approaches that stress the way project management should be focused on customer needs and human resource (HR) concerns that relate to project manager leadership and the composition and dynamics of the project team (e.g., Graham & England, 2004; Frame, 2003).) Project management has had a considerable impact in management circles, with the formation of the International Project Management Association (IPMA) in 1967 and the Project Management Institute (PMI) in 1969. These were formed to serve the interests of the emerging project management profession. In 1981, the PMI board of directors authorized the development of what has become a guide to project management. This is the *Project Management Body of Knowledge* (PMBOK) and it contains the standards and practice guidelines that are widely used throughout the profession. Project management is important historically as it demonstrates the advantages of focusing business activity laterally on specific customers, a central theme developed in the HO. It also encompasses many attributes that are part of management accounting, such as resource planning, trade-off analysis and performance measurement, while building controls into processes to avoid continuous reporting. It is curious that ideas from project management, with its emphasis on horizontal flows of information and accounting, were not incorporated within mainstream management accounting.

During the 1970s deregulation and improved transport, infrastructure and communications triggered increased global competition and the multinational nature of organizations. It was widely believed that Western industrial countries were suffering a decline, due in part to the increased competitiveness of Japanese firms on both cost and quality. Japanese firms had developed advanced manufacturing techniques from studying and developing innovations in US production techniques and statistical quality controls by Ishikawa, Deming and Juran. This produced approaches such as the Toyota Production Systems (a precursor to JIT), quality circles and cellular manufacturing (Suzaki, 1987). The new manufacturing technologies were seen by many Western managers as a way to improve their company's competitive position. Early attempts to implement these new approaches failed, as the basic principles were not understood and they were not integrated into complete systems. By the 1980s some firms were achieving success and this promoted the growth of campaigns such as world-class manufacturing, continuous flow manufacturing and lean manufacturing, all of which stressed the importance of managing horizontal flows of resources and information (Womack, Jones & Roos, 1991). These were supported and promoted by consultants. For improved manufacturing practices to work within Western organizations, attention had to be paid to Western HR issues. Advanced manufacturing stressed the importance of both efficient production throughput and HR to consider how individuals could be motivated to work towards goals of achieving effectiveness of interdependent workflows, rather than only their own performance. HO emerged from recognizing that satisfying demanding customers and improving the efficiency and effectiveness of production required processes that would allow for the lateral flow of resources and information along the value chain, and structural and HR practices that would develop a workforce committed to the lateral dimension.

During this period management accounting had responded to the advent of advanced manufacturing by way of activity accounting and performance measurement systems that moved away from financials, incorporating nonfinancial measures sometimes integrated with financials. While these approaches provided data for managing elements of the HO, there were few linkages made between management accounting and the HO. In the main, the recommendations focused on relating the accounting to the technical aspects of advanced manufacturing operating within vertically-structured organizations. They did not embrace the essence of accounting for highly decentralized organizations where competitive advantage involved efficiently managing the horizontal dimension.

Hopwood (1996) drew attention to the limited conception of autonomy implied in developments in management accounting. He noted that, as a consequence of new production arrangements, local managers were faced with integrating and coordinating tasks both within the organization and between organizations, with a requirement for information related to the lateral dimension. He voiced disappointment that there was little management accounting research into inter- and intra-organizational interdependencies, noting in particular that there had been little or no consideration of the implications for accounting of matrix structures and project-oriented structural forms. Picking up on this theme, two articles provided early insights into lateral issues. Frances & Garnsey (1996) showed how information technology promoted the growth in dominance of large UK supermarkets by enabling efficient integration between these supermarkets and their suppliers and customers. This provided the supermarkets with considerable power over suppliers and ultimately competitive advantage, by facilitating smaller timelier ordering, assessing performance of suppliers, improving forecasting, monitoring goods from source to checkout, and improved price and market control. Gietzman (1996) examined Japanese subcontracting arrangements to analyze the benefits and costs of different forms of outsourcing, and consequent costs of governance and accounting. This paper is important as it brought attention to alternatives to market-based competitive subcontracting decisions, such as multi-year supplier arrangements with specialist subcontractors. This decision involves analysis of both market-determined costs and the cost and benefits of alternative long-term relationships, together with an assessment of inherent governance arrangements and associated costs. Since these papers there has been growing interest in how accounting is implicated in organizational relationships with suppliers and customers (see Anderson, 2007, pp. 490–493).

3. The Elements of the Horizontal Organization: an Overview

The starting point for this chapter is to review the essence of the HO. Three approaches which, when taken together, distil the key elements of the HO, are *The Horizontal Organization* by Ostroff (1999); *World Class Manufacturing: The Next Decade* by Schonberger (1996); and *Designing the Customer-centric Organization: a Guide to Strategy, Structure and Process* by Galbraith (2005). How these authors envisage a role for management accounting in the HO is of particular interest. This chapter will review the essence of HO and critically examine the extent to which there have been complementary developments in management accounting and HO, and how effective practice and research has been in encouraging a horizontal dimension to management accounting. To date, ideas that have had the greatest impact on thinking about HO have come from disciplines other than management accounting. However, developments in management accounting, such as activity accounting and integrated performance measures, have considered issues related to horizontal flows of resources and information. This chapter considers the extent to which these ideas have provided a useful contribution towards issues considered important in developing HO. Additionally, a selection of recent ideas that are pertinent to developing HO which could enhance the application of a horizontal dimension to accounting are identified.

In its most general sense horizontal accounting refers to approaches to management accounting that are consistent with the intent of HO. Horizontal accounting is sometimes referred to as lateral accounting, network accounting or value chain accounting. Management accounting practices that have elements of the horizontal include approaches to strategic management accounting (SMA) such as activity-based cost management (ABCM) (Kaplan & Cooper, 1998), and elaborations including target costing (Ansari, Bell & Okano, 2007); strategic performance management, such as balanced scorecards (BSC) (Kaplan & Norton, 1996, 2000, 2004) and activity-based profitability analysis (ABPA) (Meyer, 2002). It would be incorrect to claim that these approaches are consistent with the intent of HO, as they are typically conceived as being applied within vertically structured organizations and do not encompass all facets of HO. However, they are important to an evaluation of how effective management accounting has been in assisting in the implementation of HO, as they were developed over the same time period that saw the popularization of the HO. Moreover, proponents of these approaches claim that they provide a focus on managing across the value chain and identifying cause–effect linkages between strategy and operations. The extent to which these ideas have been (or could be) employed in contributing to organizing horizontally is of interest. There have also been attempts to extend management accounting beyond its traditional concern with production processes to suppliers (Dekker, 2003) and customers (Foster & Gupta, 1994), although these do not examine all aspects of managing the value chain.

Traditional approaches to capital budgeting and operational budgets, when designed to consider resource flows across the organizations, can also be considered to be horizontal. The key to horizontal accounting is the intent to incorporate accounting thinking into organizational change programmes that are based on aligning work and structural arrangements laterally with a customer focus. In this chapter the practices of ABCM and BSC are used, in the main, to illustrate the extent to which management accounting thinking has contributed to the development of the HO.

The three books to be considered were selected because together they represent the essential aspects of the HO. The remainder of this section provides a review of the key elements of the HO. While all three authors consider similar aspects of the HO, their emphases differ. Ostroff (1999) provides the most general appreciation considering all key areas, but with a strong HR emphasis. Schonberger (1996) has long been regarded as a seminal writer on world-class manufacturing with an emphasis on the production process aspects of the HO. Galbraith's (2005) work has a particular focus on developing a customer-driven organization with consequent challenges in managing interdependencies. In reviewing these works the chapter aims to determine the extent to which management accounting has developed a horizontal dimension that has helped inform the advancement of the HO. The distinctive characteristics of HO are classified as relating to strategy including the decision to adopt HO and product and customer mix planning, and processes, structures and human resources.

3.1. Strategy

While strategy is important to the HO the approach is very specific, being targeted on customers and how the organization delivers value to customers by way of its processes and people. Ostroff (pp. 10–11) provides a list of fundamental principles for the HO. However strategy, as such, is not explicitly included in these principles which are focused on how to organize around processes and teams, integrate with customers and suppliers, develop employee skills, measure end-of-process performance objectives, use information technology (IT) to help managers undertake work and build a value-adding culture. It is not until advice is given on implementing the HO that strategy is explicitly considered. Ostroff (p. 153) provides a conventional approach. He sees the decision to develop a HO as a major strategic transformation. It requires senior managers to identify the company's "winning value proposition" and then to assess whether a HO should be implemented and, if so, what type of HO should be developed. Value propositions indicate what the organization can do to create and deliver value to its customers and are often encapsulated by specific mission statements and credos. Once this is established, managers must then undertake an audit of factors to identify if the elements of the HO will assist in delivering on the value propositions, whether there are impediments to future progress and then if the organization has sufficient capabilities to succeed in its area of business. Next, strategic planning is recommended with the customary considerations for rational strategy formulation and implementation (Chapter 10).

Schonberger is unenthusiastic in his support for conventional planning and the contribution of accounting and finance to organizational design and the practice of organizing horizontally. He sees formal, top-down conventional planning as an impediment to developing world-class manufacturing. Finance-oriented top managers who manage by financial metrics are singled out as ineffective (p. 91). Strategy is best understood as being related to manufacturing, marketing, performance measurement, product design and development, supplier relations and human resource management (p. 14). Poor strategy and practices in these areas are identified as the causes of business decline. To Schonberger, strategy involves "management by principles" where the principles are "customer-focused, employee driven, data (fact)-based" and these are intended to be "broadly effective, robust and enduring" (pp. 20–21). Management by principles is to be preferred to management by edict, procedures and policies. These latter approaches are not sufficiently responsive, do not cover all contingencies and are wasteful of human talent within the organization. (pp. 20–21). Formal strategic plans are included in the approach, however, the details are not elaborated apart from an HR recommendation that front line teams of associates are involved in strategic planning (p. 33).

Galbraith identifies strategy in the "customer-centric organization" as providing the best solution to the customer's needs. This involves a customized and personalized package of reliable products, services, support, education and consulting to make the customer more effective (p. 17). The "customer relationship" is the firm's most valued asset. The price of a customer solution is not the sum of the prices of the products and services that constitute the solution, but is the savings and improvements that the customer experiences. As with other approaches to HO, the initial strategic decision is whether a customer-centric approach will be an advantage to the business. This will require an assessment as to whether HO will enable the business to become customer-centric. Considerations include the number and types of different products that are combined into a customer solution and the degree of integration between products; are they independent or do they represent an integrated set of products? Many interdependent products create greater integration problems for the organization than stand-alone products. Different structures will be required to manage greater interdependencies, and this involves decisions on the number of organizational units and lateral networking capabilities to draw together different products, functions and perhaps countries to service the customer solution. The key strategy is determining competitive advantage when choosing solutions and comparative advantage when choosing customers (p. 151). Strategy implementation is about leading change, comprehensive roll out, managing conflict and linking processes (Chapter 8).

3.2. Processes, Structures and Human Resources

All three approaches to HO stress that production processes should be structured around customers and HR initiatives that encourage a motivated and committed workforce. These are seen as mutually reinforcing and lack of attention to any aspect will jeopardize the successful implementation of the HO. Only Schonberger provides details of principles for production improvements, using a variety of contemporary advanced manufacturing practices that elaborate on TQM and JIT. These cover aspects such as continuous improvement in quality, response time, flexibility and value (removing non-value adding waste to keep costs down); reducing components and suppliers; cutting flow time, start-ups and changeovers; producing at average demand; reducing variation and mishaps; improving present facilities before considering new equipment; employing flexible equipment (pp. 30–36, 39, 43, 44). These are not novel to HO and neither Ostroff nor Galbraith includes extensive discussion of these types of initiatives. Rather they recognize the role of advanced manufacturing, but are concerned with aligning these improvements in processes, structures and people around customers. Schonberger's approach is not entirely related to improvements in production processes. He also recommends organizing around products or customers and he stresses the need for the continual enhancement of human resources.[1] Ostroff (p. 10) aims to achieve alignment and lateral efficiencies with a blend of structural recommendations and HR initiatives. The structural redesign includes:

- organize around cross-functional processes, not tasks or functions;
- install process owners who will take responsibility for core processes in their entirety;
- structure around teams not individuals;
- decrease hierarchy and incorporate decisions into teams that relate to their activities;
- integrate with customers and suppliers;
- redesign functional departments as partners in process performance.

Galbraith also stresses aligning structure and processes around customers and employing HR to support the new structures. The approach to structure and process starts with customer relationship management and customer solutions development. The idea is to identify those customers who will be receptive to having their need for products and services supplied by the firm. These customers are grouped into segments and are served by customer teams. The aim is to find and deliver the best combination of products for the customer (some of which may not be those of the firm) and expand the proportion of the customer needs that the firm can serve. The most powerful people in the organization are the relationship managers who aim to ensure repeat business, which flows from a close knowledge of the customer's needs. Galbraith sees control problems occurring due to difficulties in integrating across products that are provided to customers. The greater the number of products and the greater the difference in the products the more difficult is the integration. Integration drives the type of structure used to achieve appropriate lateral networking. These mechanisms are designed to cope with increasing levels of complexity in integration (pp. 33–41). These are, in order of increasing complexity: voluntary or informal groups; e-coordination; formal groups (simple or multidimensional and hierarchical); integrator (full-time, by roles or department); matrix organization (units within product lines dedicated to particular customers) and separate customer line organizational units. Power and authority related to the integrative devices increase from the more voluntary approaches to customer-dedicated units.

HR is particularly important to HO as it aims to embed the change processes required to implement the HO. Ostroff (p. 12) identifies HR as a way of keeping process performance on track to meet objectives. He suggests empowering people by providing them with tools, skills, motivation and authority to make decisions essential to the team's performance; emphasizing multiple competencies; promoting multi-skilling and creative thinking and responding to challenges within the team. The aim is to build a corporate culture of openness, cooperation, and collaboration; develop a focus on continuous performance improvement; ensure employee empowerment, responsibility and well-being.

Schonberger sees conventional HR as being at odds with customer-focused principles and devotes a chapter to "Remaking Human Resource Management" (Chapter 9). HR initiatives interlink with other elements of the HO and occur in concert. In essence, they involve front line employees being engaged in change and strategic planning, enhancement of human resources by cross training, job and career-path rotation, and improvements in health, safety and security. Part of the HR function is to ensure that the customer-focused structure works. That is, teams are aligned with customers, they become multifunctional and self-managed. Managers from former hierarchical structures become facilitators. Teamsmanship, shaped by customer-focused principles, replaces "inspirational leadership."

For Galbraith, HR issues involve moving to a situation where the most powerful people are relationship managers serving the most important customers. Training is designed to develop managers who serve an account, not salespeople to market products. Developing in-depth knowledge of a customer requires skills related to customer relationship management. Galbraith captures the "solution culture" of the customer-centric organization

[1]In related works, Schonberger (1990) and Schonberger and Knod (1994) stress the need for the organization to identify ways to provide for customer wants with the HO aspect being stressed by the aim of developing a customer-driven chain of action. Schonberger (2001) provides updated guidelines to "fix manufacturing" where standards have diminished and profits eroded due to low cost start-ups from emerging economies such as China, the Near East and Latin America. Continuous improvement, with a focus on the human side of performance measurement, is stressed with a four part formula to combat competition: developing or acquiring new products; eliminating manufacturing waste; simplifying and standardizing production; moving production abroad for high-volume manufacturing. Clearly, a strong emphasis on production processes is apparent.

as one that is organized around the customer, involving solution strategies, customer profit centres, customer relationship management, customer share and retention rewards systems, and selecting and developing relationship managers (pp. 22–23). HR processes involve hiring and firing individuals based on who can work without hierarchy (pp. 57–58). The active participation of leaders in organizational design and HR processes includes conflict resolution. Other HR initiatives involve recruitment and training of employees into new customer-focused businesses (p. 157). The organization should aim to achieve a job–people match and people–team match by assigning individuals to work situations that suit them best.

In summary, HO draws on a variety of "best practice" management initiatives to provide an integrated approach to management that operates within a structural form that will allow the organization to focus the business in ways that will deliver value to its customers. It is concerned with ensuring that advanced manufacturing practices, such as TQM and JIT initiatives, involve a cross-functional, integrated approach that aligns work with customer-focused goals. The approach operates "horizontally" using structures where teams, not individuals, are responsible for delivering customer value in ways that ensure continuous performance improvement within a culture of employee empowerment, responsibility and well-being. Functional expertise can be provided by vertical structures, but authority lies with teams and functions are to provide service to teams.

4. Management Accounting and the Horizontal Organization

This section examines the extent to which management accounting has assisted in the development of the HO. Consideration is given to the extent to which innovations in management accounting may be characterized as horizontal accounting, in the sense that the accounting systems are consistent with the intent of HO. In doing this the chapter examines contemporary developments in management accounting that adopt a more holistic approach to connect strategy, processes, structure and HR. Notably, innovations that can be characterized as strategic management accounting (SMA) have characteristics related to aspects of HO, as they aim to connect strategy to the value chain and link activities across the organization that relate to cost objectives. These practices include activity-based cost management (ABCM) and integrated cost systems (Kaplan & Cooper, 1998) and elaborations such as target costing (Ansari, Bell & Okano, 2007) and lifecycle costing (Berliner & Brinson, 1988); strategic performance management systems such as balanced scorecards (BSC) (Kaplan & Norton, 1996, 2000, 2004) and activity-based profitability analysis (Meyer, 2002). Innovations that adopt a lateral perspective, such as quality costing (Atkinson et al., 1991), theory of constraints (Goldratt & Cox, 1992), customer-focused accounting (Foster & Sjoblom, 1996), supply chain management (Dekker, 2003) and open-book accounting (Carr & Ng, 1995), while relevant to parts of the value chain do not encompass the whole value chain. This chapter focuses, mainly, on the role of ABCM and BSC in the adoption and implementation of HO, as these are the most prevalent illustrations of SCM that include a lateral dimension to accounting. The following section will consider the extent to which management accounting has been drawn upon to assist in the strategic decision to adopt an HO and decisions concerning planning product or customer mix within HO, and operational control including structural and HR arrangements and performance measurement.

4.1. Management Accounting and Strategic Decisions within Horizontal Organizations

Holistic approaches that consider horizontal aspects of the value chain are not novel to management accounting. SMA practices such as ABCM and BSC moved management accounting from an emphasis on planning and control, as related to the concerns of middle and operational managers, to strategic issues including the integration of customers, processes, HR and financials (for reviews of the development of SCM see Lord, 1996; Roslender & Hart, 2003; Jones & Dugdale, 2002; Anderson, 2007; Gosselin, 2007). Jones & Dugdale (2002) provide a history of ABCM, pointing out its development from a costing technique to a management philosophy with an emphasis on identifying value-adding activities and eliminating non-value-adding activities. ABC has, as its primary focus, the calculation of costs by linking expenditure to activities. ABCM identifies both cost and value drivers with the aim of assisting managers to manage both costs and value-creating activities to achieve the desired outcomes of the organization.

Perhaps the most comprehensive treatment of ABCM is provided by Kaplan & Cooper (1998). Their approach to ABCM is concerned with managing activities across the value chain and, as such, appears to have relevance to elements of the HO. Kaplan & Cooper (1998, p. 287) claim that ABCM enables organizations to achieve their outcomes at lower total cost. ABCM distinguishes operational controls from a strategic use of ABCM to assess resource usage across the value chain, which can be related to products, customers or other cost objects. The strategic issues involve assessing resource usage, which can be related to product design, product and customer mix, supplier relations, customer relations (pricing, order size, delivery, packaging), market segmentation and distribution channels. Once strategy is established operational controls can be enhanced by using activity management, business process reengineering, total quality and performance measurement. ABCM systems are intended to be incorporated into thinking about strategic and operational issues and are intended to become part of the fabric of the organization being linked to product and customer mix decisions, budgeting and transfer pricing and, in very sophisticated systems, to financial accounting (Kaplan & Cooper, 1998, p. 301).

While ABCM considers the lateral dimension of managing organizations, the focus is firmly on the financial impact of process, structural and HR innovations. That is, improvement initiatives such as TQM and JIT or structural arrangements, such as teams and profit centres, should be assessed by their impact on financial considerations, either at the cost level or overall profits from products, customers or profit centres. While there is less emphasis on the details of manufacturing improvements, structural and HR innovations, the main message is that all change initiatives and consequent expenditure of resources are to be related to how operations generate value to customers, and that ABCM is a way of understanding these connections and their financial impact. As will be pointed out below, it is this primary focus on the financial impact of HO initiatives that presents difficulties for advocates of HO.

There has been a variety of developments in performance measurement systems (PMS) that are strategic and horizontal in that they aim to provide an integrated approach, relating various aspects of operations to customers and corporate vision. These have included performance pyramids and hierarchies (Dixon, Nanni & Vollmann, 1990; McNair, Lynch & Cross, 1990; Hronec, 1993; Lynch & Cross, 1995), balanced scorecards (BSC) (Kaplan & Norton, 1996, 2000) and the intangible asset scorecard (Sveiby, 1997). BSC have been popularized and developed as a strategic performance management system that can accommodate a lateral dimension to managing the organization (Kaplan & Norton, 1996, 2000). A distinctive feature of BSC is that they are designed to present managers with financial and nonfinancial measures covering different perspectives which, in combination, provide a way of translating strategy into action by way of a coherent set of performance measures. The perspectives that are relevant to profit-orientated companies most often include financial, customers, internal processes and long-term innovation. It is claimed that this system of associated measures has the potential to identify the cause–effect linkages that describe the way operations are related to the organization's strategy and the way they interconnect across the value chain.

In summary, the aim of management accounting practices such as ABCM and BSC is to provide approaches to strategic management that are holistic, and to integrate operations with strategy and objectives. This is consistent with many aspects of the HO. Given this apparent alignment of purpose between management accounting innovations, such as ABCM and BSC, and HO, to what extent have developments in HO been informed by management accounting?

In the main, proponents of HO do not see management accounting and its approach to the analysis of strategy as playing a significant role. While it is recognized that there is a need for the organization to operate profitably there is suspicion towards accounting frameworks that provide economic models to consider the costs and benefits of configuring the HO. There is indifference or opposition to innovations in management accounting that aim to develop improved costing to translate the elements of HO into economically viable options, and performance measurement systems that focus attention on cause–effect relationships between strategy and operations and between elements of operational value chains. This is not to say that financials are totally ignored. There is acknowledgement of the need to calculate profit and costs related to products, but overall there is lack of attention to debates that occur within management accounting on holistic resource management. There is little cross-referencing to contemporary deliberations found in management accounting on issues that, arguably, are relevant to designing and operating horizontally.

Schonberger (p. 92) provides the most detailed assessment of the role of management accounting in the HO. He claims that financial numbers are mainly for managing cash flow by way of budgets. In addition, financial numbers are recommended for spotting potential problems or opportunities having long-term significance (p. 92). He sees a role for management accounting in "improvement, product development and competitive decisions" that must be taken within the HO, and devotes a chapter to "Value and Valuation" (Chapter 5). For decisions on product development and competitive analysis, target costing and more accurate cost information are singled out for recommendation. These decisions are made infrequently, so cost data are required only on a needs basis. Regular cost reporting is unnecessary and wasteful. For improvement decisions, real-time customer and root cause-oriented performance measures are required (p. 96). Schonberger notes that ABC has potential to assist in product line decisions, but these systems are not helpful for cost management which requires more direct manufacturing-oriented controls, such as wall charts, to track causes on the spot. Moreover, Schonberger (p. 104) cautions on the use of ABC. ABC is seen as problematic as it does not balance requirements other than cost, such as time-to-market and high quality. Furthermore, it is difficult to get the optimal number of cost drivers, too few and costing will be inaccurate, too many and the system is overly complex.[2] ABC systems are inflexible and do not accommodate the dynamics of changing drivers. He argues that ABC can have symbolic benefits to emphasize the monetary effects of undertaking process improvements. Also, by demonstrating effects on costs, managers wedded to financial numbers can be encouraged to examine process improvement (p. 106). In essence Schonberger sees costing (ABC) as relevant for as-need-be product cost analysis, but management accounting is not relevant for control of processes; what is needed are process controls based on customers and root cause effects.

Galbraith is more positive about management accounting, recognizing a fundamental need to evaluate profitability of organizational segments structured around customers. However, the calculation of costs and their allocation to customer-focused units is not seen as problematic and issues associated with ABCM are not examined. He also recognizes that budgets have a role in planning, but these must be organized laterally, around either products or customers. Apart from strategic planning techniques, Ostroff is silent on the potential usefulness of management accounting practices, such as ABCM and BSC, or any coordinative budgetary processes. This is emblematic of the lack of close engagement that many advocates of HO have with innovations in management accounting.

The lack of serious consideration of debates in management accounting that could relate to designing and planning HO is unfortunate, as many management accounting innovations aim to address issues concerning the meaning and measurement of elements of HO, notably concerns with valuing both tangible and intangible assets and lateral implications of costing and performance measurement. When designing an HO the starting point is to identify customer-focused strategies and then conceive the organizational space so that processes, structures and people are aligned to deliver value to these customers. Stressing the importance of the economics of restructuring, some accounting commentators have noted that management accounting practices, such as capital budgeting and ABCM, can have an important influence on how processes and structures are designed within an HO. This occurs by way of these practices having a role in evaluating plans to establish a HO. Mouritsen & Hansen (2006, pp. 275–277) argue that management accounting defines the space of the HO before it is put in place and occurs independently of operations management. Here the important point is that a financial assessment of HO initiatives may well provide information for the final choice on how to design a particular HO. While this is true, in most organizations the financial analysis will be based on strategic, operational, structural and HR parameters provided by the HO designers. That is, the HO space will be defined by the HO designers and typically the accountants will provide the economic analysis on these attributes. Ideally, if the option is not economically viable the design team will reconfigure the space until it becomes economically viable or the initiative is abandoned. Thus, the financial analysis will help select between different HO spaces defined by the HO designers. In this sense the management accountant will be an important player on the design team. This, of course, is the essence of target costing which involves a design team of operational and financial managers. Given the potentially important role of management accounting as part of the HO design team, it is perplexing that there is little elaboration of this role by advocates of HO (note, however, that Schonberger recommends target costing, but does not discuss how this would work within his proposed approach).

One of the difficulties in determining the value of HO is that many of the assets are "soft" and aim to encourage managers to learn and develop how managing the organizational whole and its lateral dimension adds value. Management accounting has much to offer in examining how investment in change programmes can generate value by way of knowledge and intellectual capital. Advocates of HO could well find merit in areas such as intangible assets (Grojer, 2001), knowledge-based organizations (Ditillo, 2004), intellectual capital (Andriessen, 2004), using intellectual capital for managing knowledge (Mouritsen, Larsen & Pukh, 2001) and for mobilizing change (Johanson, Martensson & Skoog, 2001). Links between intellectual capital and the design of management accounting systems are examined by Widener (2004) and ways of including intangibles benefits in financial analysis are reviewed by Davila & Wouters (2007, p. 839).

It is possible that indifference by advocates of HO to the role of management accounting in assisting strategic decision-making is due to their enthusiasm for highly visible and comprehensible outcomes from improvements that focus on the customer, and operations that serve these customers. There is a sense that the associated financials have less proximity to these centres of attention. In addition, there are concerns that accounting approaches obscure events, as the data are too opaque and incomprehensible and they are not timely.

[2]Schonberger (pp. 111–113) provides suggestions for an ABC type cost model. It involves splitting overheads into technical support (e.g., set-ups, engineering) and production and inventory support (e.g., scheduling, dispatching). Computer information systems are split into support for factory and administration. Production and inventory controls and computer information support are allocated on the basis of manufacturing cycle time derived from a monthly audit of cycle times. Technical support is allocated on machine hours.

There is also uneasiness about management accounting that derives from a lack of confidence in the accuracy of costing and the usefulness of financial measures for evaluating the effectiveness of the HO and its components. There appears to be concern that, once introduced, a financial perspective may dominate thinking with negative effects on the ethos of the HO.

In summary, it seems clear that innovations in management accounting, such as ABCM and BSC, have had a considerable impact, at least in management accounting circles, in terms of consulting campaigns, management accounting text books and practitioner articles, business education programmes and endorsements by management accounting profession bodies (Jones & Dugdale, 2002). Much of the appeal has been to provide management accounting systems that are strategic zand relate to improving the efficiency of the value chain to deliver on strategic priorities. Writings on the HO also recognize a need to show the cost or profit implications of various initiatives related to achieving "winning strategies." The approaches share common ground on the need for financial analysis to indicate which products or customers are likely to be profitable and the usefulness of nonfinancial measures and perhaps BSC (at least as a way of moving away from financials). However, approaches to HO do not seem as concerned about building a cost-consciousness as are the proponents of ABCM. Cost-consciousness is seen to lead to distraction and a myopic vision of the organization. To the advocates of HO, accounting may improve understanding of product costs, although this is by no means certain and is likely to be useful only for those products that have relatively routine activities. There is a view that it is unlikely that ABCM could provide accurate strategic costing for the reorganization of processes, structures and HR that form part of the assessment of whether and how to implement a HO. Only Galbraith acknowledges a central role for financial analysis as an important part of assessing profit centres with a focus on customer profitability (p. 40). However, this is seen as not problematic, with little attention to the practices of ABCM and management accounting innovations in performance measurement to assist in determining profitability.

4.2. Management Accounting for Control, Structure and Lateral Integration in Horizontal Organizations

A primary aim of the HO is to enable managers to integrate highly interdependent processes around delivering customer value. In flattening the organizational structure conventional differentiation, or segmentation, gives way to lateral structures by way of teams that connect customers to operations. In these structures, people are critical to achieving integrative effort and they must be trained to make the lateral dimension their focus, rather than their own immediate work tasks. Functional structure is still relevant, but its role is to provide a service to the structural units. There is still a need for some hierarchy to consider the whole organization and senior managers will be required to develop value propositions, develop road maps for business development and organizational change, and oversee the redefinition of cross-functional processes (Ostroff, p. 63). Apart from these strategic issues, senior managers develop capabilities in others, discover new resources, and look for opportunities for continuous improvement and innovative ways to deliver value. All three advocates of HO are clear on the crucial role of people in achieving lateral coordination within the HO and they employ HR practices to achieve this. As such, control and lateral integration are achieved, primarily, by HR policies ensuring that people work within integrative team structures that provide connections across the value chain.

Ostroff (p. 85) sees the HO as the most efficient way for people to control the products and processes of the organization. This is done by having them work at various points along the value chain in ways that develop close relationships with customers. The way in which this operates forms an important part of the HO; specifically, core process groups are delegated the task to integrate the production processes with the support of functional groups such as HR for training and the finance function that supplies resources needed by the core process group (Ostroff, p. 188). Given the lateral flows involved in the HO, conventional accounting controls such as profit and functional budgets are seen as inappropriate. For Ostroff, structure is based on a separation of work roles, decision rights and obligations that flow from an analysis of work processes and their interconnectedness. Steering committees of senior stakeholders hold people accountable based on strong lines of communication. It is of interest that information technology (IT), not management accounting, is seen to have a critical role in supporting the alignment of structural delegation and integration. The emphasis is on real-time to monitor performance on nonfinancials, to identify problems and track progress in solving them. These processes provide updated best practice information to the work groups, and open avenues for collaborative effort in a timely way (pp. 213–214). Again, for Ostroff, while IT is important, management accounting is not seen as particularly relevant for controlling the HO, rather it is a support function for resourcing. Ostroff recognizes that performance measures can be useful in assessing the extent of coordination and the effectiveness of structural units such as teams, but these are seen as firmly in the area of IT (p. 211).

Some accounting commentators have alluded to the role of IT in areas that have typically been the domain of management accounting. The role of IT as a substitute for management accounting is noted by Shank (2006, p. 362). He claimed that developments in IT with common data architectures, client–server based transaction processing systems and relational databases for information management have created accounting as a by-product of IT systems with a consequence that accounting has a diminished impact. Dechow, Ganland & Mourisen (2007, p. 634) also note that IT is often designed to automate many control functions and user-friendly accounting tools, such as budgets, and that this may mean that line managers can use IT directly for control. It may be speculated that, in some organizations, the providers of IT are seen increasingly as deriving their rationale from supplying information useful for managers at the operational level, while management accountants are perceived as being instruments of top management influence and control. The role of IT as a provider of information for management accounting or as a substitute for the role of management accounting is an important area for further investigation (see Dechow et al., 2007, for a discussion of these issues). Notwithstanding the potential role of IT, for Ostroff employees are crucial for coordination and control. He states no matter how important IT is in assisting coordination, it can never take the place of employees committed to cooperation with each other across functional boundaries in order to deliver the best products to solve any customer problems (p. 220).

For Galbraith the essence of control is managing lateral relations, a theme that he introduced in earlier work (Galbraith, 1973, 2002). In designing the HO, Galbraith provides extensive treatment of managing lateral relationships. He recommends that the back end production function and the customer front end need to be combined by management processes, compensation and HR that aligns the organization with strategy (p. 116). As indicated above, for Galbraith, the greater the number of products and the greater the difference in the products the more difficult it is to achieve integration across the value chain. Integrative mechanisms are designed to cope with increasing levels of complexity. These are, in order of increasing complexity: voluntary or informal groups; e-coordination, formal groups (simple or multidimensional and hierarchical); integrator (full-time, by roles or department); matrix organization (units within product lines dedicated to particular customers) and separate customer line organizational units. Assessing the profitability of product lines and customers is important, but the potential pitfalls from these calculations, derived from an elaboration of management accounting issues, are not discussed.

Schonberger's view is that accounting is poor data, too far removed and it has a wrong emphasis. He stresses that control is best achieved by means of operational controls (control of root causes of cost and performance) (p. 41) and real-time, nonfinancial performance indicators in the areas of quality, response time, flexibility and value (p. 41). In addition, operational management is responsible for cutting flow time, distance, start-up and change-over times along the chain of customers and this applies to administrative processes (purchasing, invoicing, etc.) (p. 34). To ensure this occurs training is provided on process improvements and job skills. Front line teams translate strategy into numeric goals and self-monitor. Schonberger holds negative views as to the role of accounting in this process. He states: "Let the redundancy and inadequacy of monthly aggregated numbers cause the old system (accounting) to atrophy and sink under its own weight" (p. 107).

Some supporters of accounting data within HOs have noted that while those proposing HO are reluctant to recommend accounting data for operational controls, there is evidence that top managers may want to have operational data in financial terms for issues of longer-term accountability and viability of innovations on the shop floor (Mouritsen & Hansen, 2006, p. 276). However, the evidence provided to support this appears to be based on organizations with significant vertical structures where top managers are still dominant in controlling the organization's activities. While senior managers' preferences for accounting control data may well be evident in vertically structured organizations, advocates of HO do not envisage structures where top managers are involved in extensive vertical control. Rather control, including strategic issues and performance measures to assess coordination, is embedded within the team-based, empowered workforce. While this might be unrealistic for many organizations, it helps explain why proponents of HO are wary of the use of financials by top managers to sustain elements of traditional vertical control. Vertical hierarchy may be apparent in the HO, but its role is to provide a service to empowered employees and it must work in concert with them.

While vertical structure is downplayed in the HO, these organizations are not totally devoid of vertical structures. Strategic decisions, innovation and learning at the team level need to be coordinated and made explicit and this is best achieved by senior managers. There is also a role for senior managers to consider organizational-wide strategic issues, monitor the external environment and be alert to medium- to long-term opportunities and threats and their impact, both in operational and financial terms. Useful ideas in considering how HO structures based on teams can be combined with hierarchy in the context of developing learning and knowledge are presented in Romme (1996). Romme suggests that teams appear to be the key learning units which are indispensable for producing and understanding novel information, and a senior manager's role within hierarchies is indispensable for processing and storing important learning results. The trade-off between teams and hierarchy can be solved by emphasizing the idea of circularity, involving the ability to switch between teams and hierarchies as complementary information systems in the context of organizational learning.

In sum, for advocates of HO, there is limited support for using management accounting. In particular, while innovations in accounting may provide useful costing information for customer and supplier analysis and for product mix decisions, it is not appropriate for evaluating the economic viability of different configurations of HO. Schonberger, who explicitly considers ABCM, is concerned that the financial orientation of ABCM is inappropriate for HO as its calculations cannot be trusted. However, there is little discussion of debates in management accounting that relate to the pros and cons of ABCM systems. It would seem that much could be added to thinking about HO if advocates of HO drew on accounting deliberations that examine the potential benefits and pitfalls of ABCM, at least for strategic decisions concerning designing and implementing the HO, and to elaborate on the financial implications of product- and customer-mix decisions.

4.3. The Role of Performance Evaluation for Control in Horizontal Organizations

Performance measurement is another area of management accounting that would seem to have much to offer in the design and implementation of the HO. In recent years management accounting has recognized the potential importance of nonfinancial measures, as well as financials, to plan and control organizations. Balanced scorecards (BSC) are the most popular exemplar of this approach (Kaplan & Norton, 1998, 2000, 2004). It is claimed that BSC provide a system of associated measures that has the potential to identify the cause–effect linkages that describe the way operations are related to the organization's strategy. The aim is to provide a rational framework to formulate and implement strategies. While BSC may be developed within traditional structures, their appeal to designing the HO is their potential to connect measures that relate operations and HR to customers and to show the financial implications.

Performance measures are also an essential aspect of managing the HO. All three authors include performance measurement within the principles of designing and managing the HO. The emphasis is on multiple nonfinancial measures, often subjective assessments, although it is recognized that the financial implications of initiatives need to be assessed. While performance measurement is important, the idea of using performance measures to model cause–effect relationships to achieve overall strategy is not considered. There is little enthusiasm for the use of financial performance measures to assist in operational control.

Ostroff (p. 24) 2006 discusses the need to measure end-of-process performance objectives (driven by value propositions) as well as customer satisfaction, employee satisfaction and financial contribution. He claims that precise, quantified measures bring clarity and focus to the front line and help senior managers make informed decisions about investments in the transformation process (p. 157). Performance measures are more important in institutionalizing the HO than at the design stage (p. 207). It is noted that BSC provide multiple measures (pp. 21–22), however, how they might assist in managing the HO is not elaborated.

For Schonberger, performance measurement should entail a basket of measures, but importantly these are connected to the science of process improvement and to customers. Schonberger provides suggestions for performance measurement and rewards that include: recognition, pay and celebration; involvement of front line employees in change and strategic planning. He has specific recommendations on performance appraisal and rewards. They include: tracking of customer-oriented metrics and measures on processes with ownership by front line employees; public achievements; and a focus on teams results. He recommends involvement of suppliers and customers in performance assessment. Multiple rewards are to be used to overcome the potential negative effects of limited approaches (p. 190). Where multiple measures are used it will be likely that some measures will have information value that can overcome other measures that may have potential negative effects if used on their own. Schonberger (pp. 228–229) identifies the BSC as a management accounting innovation that some firms claim is useful. However, following his general concern for using accounting for control due to its distance from operations, he suggests that BSC are not useful for operational management but can be valuable to show managers how business processes work outside their own areas. BSC can also help wean executives off an overly financial focus. He is suspicious of performance measures that have shareholder value as a first order result, as this may lead to decisions to cut in ways that might improve shareholder value but negatively affect quality, customer satisfaction and human resources, which he sees as the drivers of long-term value.

For Galbraith, performance measures are about customers and people. He quotes Narver & Slater (1998) to support a relationship between market-driven firms and profitability, sales growth and new product success. The most profitable customers are existing loyal customers (Reicheld, 1996; Seybold, 1998). Customer-centricity builds customer loyalty. Consequently, performance measures are customer-oriented. Customer measures are built into rewards with measures such as share of customer's business, customer satisfaction, lifetime value of a customer and customer retention. Reward systems are built around customer satisfaction, share of the most valuable customer's product needs, lifetime value of a customer and retention metrics. If commissions are paid they are given one year after the sale and are related to the customer's satisfaction with the sales. HR measures are also important, being based on competencies, group discussions and 360-degree approaches. Galbraith recognizes a need for financial viability and stresses a role for customer profitability analysis as a basis to organize around profitable customers. However, any problems in measuring customer profitability or measuring and allocating costs are not discussed. Here management accounting would appear to have relevance to clarify and refine profit measures. Galbraith also includes variable compensation using stock options and stock grants. The assignment of options is based on a person's contribution to the company, which is determined by value delivered to customers, and subjective assessments of aspects such as teamwork and effective interactions with colleagues (pp. 111–112).

In summary, performance measurement is part of contemporary management accounting and it has potential to encourage managers to think strategically about how their activities fit with other parts of the organization. They can also help relate the performance dimensions of operations and HR to financial outcomes. BSC seem to have captured the imagination of scholars in many disciplines, with particular BSC being proposed across disciplines such as HR (Becher, Huselid & Ulrich, 2001) and production (Neely, Adams & Kennerley, 2002), as well as strategy (Kaplan & Norton, 2000). It is also possible that BSC holds promise to help coordinate ideas on the development of performance measures across disciplines, particularly between those promoting HO and those stressing a horizontal dimension to management accounting (Chenhall & Langfield-Smith, 2007). However, as with other aspects of management accounting, proponents of HO are reluctant to embrace performance measurement innovations such as BSC. One concern is that the use of financials as a first order measure can result in dysfunctional effects, such as short-termism, and a relegating of priorities related to critical improvements, such as quality and customer satisfaction, to secondary consideration. BSC may help in sensitizing managers to the role of nonfinancial measures and they may be useful for communication, but they are problematic for performance evaluation. Meyer (2002), an advocate of the use of activity-based methods to determine profitability of customers, proposes the use of activity-based profitability analysis (ABPA) for planning, but not for evaluating managers. Like proponents of the HO, Meyer (2002) sees lateral decentralized structures providing the basis for connections between customers, activities and costs, and the means to decentralize strategizing. Profitability provides coarse grained performance appraisal for contributions to customer profitability, but shop floor control and managerial evaluation occurs elsewhere. Unlike Kaplan & Norton's BSC, Meyer does not see the BSC as providing an integrated approach to strategy; employing combinations of measures across the categories is sufficient. This follows as it is difficult to combine different types of measures into an overall assessment. If a formula is used this encourages game playing, if it is subjective then this creates uncertainty in the fairness of the performance measures and undermines motivation (see also Ittner, Larcker & Meyer, 2003). Thus BSC-type performance measurement should be used to monitor progress towards strategic objectives, not to appraise and compensate performance (Meyer, p. 108). These issues help explain the reluctance of those advocating HO to accept BSC as a means to evaluate the effectiveness of managers in achieving their goals in ways that are laterally coordinated.

5. The Contribution of Management Accounting to Horizontal Organizations

Most of the support for the universal benefits of HO, and aspects of management accounting, derives from prescriptions drawing on selected success stories for the suggested approaches. Do we have evidence from rigorous research, which may be generalized, on the level of take up of accounting innovations in organizations employing HO, and the positive benefits from these practices to the application of HO? This is difficult to assess as the level of empirical research that examines how management accounting practices might assist HO is limited. Furthermore, HO and management accounting innovations have not been articulated carefully as constructs. Practices like ABCM and BSC cover "practice defined" variables that have changed their meaning over time. Consequently, research is specific to the conceptualization of the practices at a particular point in time. It is therefore difficult to draw on this work to build theory and to generalize findings (Lord, 1996; Jones & Dugdale, 2002; Roslender & Hart, 2003; Anderson, 2007). For example, in considered ABC, Jones & Dugdale (2002, p. 159) suggest "the term ABC now covers a melange of competing, and often contradictory, ideas and practices that may appear to be without authors, or authors so multiple that no clear guiding intelligence can be identified." Similarly for BSC, while there is some support for growing BSC implementation (Chenhall & Langfield-Smith, 1998; Ittner & Larcker, 1998; Silk, 1998; Hoque & James, 2000), the characteristics or information dimensions of BSC are not examined in these studies. It seems clear that there is wide variation in the meaning of BSC, ranging from combinations of financial and nonfinancial measures to more comprehensive systems linking operations to various perspectives and to strategy (Ittner & Larcker, 1998b; Hoque & James, 2000; Ittner et al., 2003). Likewise, HO is a practice-defined variable, being a composite of elements from advanced manufacturing practices such as TQM and JIT, HR and marketing. Advocates of HO see defining the precise nature of the attributes of HO as less important than the processes of combining the various elements in ways that are mutually reinforcing. Thus, generalizing across studies is difficult, as the research evidence we have relates to specific aspects of accounting and elements of HO which are defined in different ways across a variety of studies.

Several accounting commentators have reviewed the role of management accounting to assist in achieving the aims of organizations that have restructured around ways consistent with aspects of HO (Anderson, 2007; Hanson & Mouritsen, 2007; Mouritsen & Hanson, 2006; Shank, 2006). Anderson (2007) concludes that advances in management accounting have been made in the area of executional cost management (cost effective execution of strategy), but that little is known about structural cost management (a more horizontal form of accounting) that involves building cost structures that are coherent with strategy which requires consideration of organizational, product and process design. In general, she is somewhat pessimistic about the contribution of management accounting to areas of product and process development, advanced manufacturing practices, learning, costing for low cost and exit strategies, supplier and alliance partners, customer relations, sustainability and enterprise risk management. She sees the broader management literature providing the lead in these areas. Hansen & Mouritsen (2007, p. 747) consider research into the role of performance measures in integrated manufacturing and pose a variety of potentially problematic issues that arise from conventional budgeting and standard setting. For example, in the context of organizations seeking production policies of variability reduction and continuous improvement, they pose the question "are budgeting and standard setting inconsistent with the flexibility needed to implement these policies and will these accounting practices encourage game playing?" These issues may also translate to ABCM and BSC when they are used for standard setting and performance evaluation within HO, if they also lack flexibility. The authors emphasize the need for accounting to focus on ways to provide incentives for coordination, stressing that integrated manufacturing systems often directly tie rewards to simple performance measures, including subjective evaluations, without the need for accounting. These propositions are consistent with proposals for performance evaluation of those advocating HO. Hansen & Mouritsen (2007) suggest that these areas should be researched further in management accounting.

6. Reasons why it is Difficult for Management Accounting to Contribute to Horizontal Organizations

In the main, advocates of HO have not employed management accounting practices as a framework to assess the economic viability of HO. There is limited support for using techniques such as ABCM to assess the financial benefits of particular products and customers within a HO. However, there is little engagement with arguments in the accounting literature that address the potential benefits and difficulties of designing and implementing these systems. While coordination across the value chain and performance measurement is central to HO, management accounting is not seen as a significant contributor to these endeavours. In this section a variety of reasons are identified for this reluctance, from advocates of HO, to engage in a discourse with management accounting. Additionally, recent developments in the literature that relate to aspects of HO and a horizontal dimension to accounting are identified. Developments in these areas might assist in providing ideas to progress research and practice in the way HO and management accounting can develop in complementary ways.

6.1. The Accounting Numbers are not Believable

The target managers for the three approaches to HO considered in this chapter are those who are likely to be familiar with other models of best practice management, such as TQM, reengineering, teams and empowerment. The aim of HO is to integrate and make use of the best ideas from these initiatives and to coordinate effort across the value chain to deliver value to customers. Inasmuch as approaches to management accounting also draw on these core ideas, their incremental value to those familiar with HO is in translating proposed changes into financial numbers. Authorities on HO, and perhaps many nonfinancial managers who are their target audience, believe that financials obscure understanding of the actual activities that underlie management innovations. Certainly many managers would see large-scale restructuring, such as HO, as being highly complex with uncertain outcomes. In such situations it is plausible that there is reluctance to believe that accounting is (or could be) sufficiently well-developed to capture the way in which value is created by combining, laterally, a customer-focused strategy, processes improvements, restructuring and empowering of the workforce.

Advocates of HO are not alone in being circumspect about the ability of accounting innovations to provide reliable data. Some accountants also believe that it is disingenuous to think that ABCM could provide a believable figure that assesses, in financial terms, all of the innovations that are necessary to develop the integration required for configurations of HO based on different customers and products (see Gosselin, 2007, pp. 61–663, for a review of literature examining the lack of success of ABCM; and Banker & Johnston, 2007, for a discussion of the difficulties of using ABCM when reformulating strategy). Some of the costs related to structuring the HO around different customers and products may be likened to sustaining expenses, such as research and development, which in contemporary ABCM should not be allocated as they are investments in the future. Guidelines on when not to drive costs to cost objects are given by Kaplan & Cooper (1998, pp. 258–259): "When no quantity measure exists for such an assignment, so that the only remaining method would be to use percentages unrelated to the supply of services to the next level of the organization." A sizable part of expenditures related to developing HO is likely to relate to implementing structures and HR practices which do not have quantity measures for assigning costs to different configurations of HO based on alternative products or customers.

Similarly, some who are critical of BSC doubt that they can identify cause–effect relationships that lie at the heart of BSC modelling (Nørreklit, 2000). Nørreklit suggests that BSC show logical, not causal, relationships between various measures. She does not see BSC as being valid for strategic planning as they do not provide for coherence between means and ends. She concludes that causal models tend to be unrealistic in terms of capturing change between means and ends that occur through time and become more difficult to understand as levels of uncertainty increase. Given this assessment it is difficult to have confidence that BSC could clarify the links between the elements of HO and financial returns.

If proponents of HO are sceptical about the likelihood of an accounting system providing financial models or figures that are believable, how do they ensure that the initiatives will achieve satisfactory financial outcomes? It appears that it becomes a matter of faith that the HO initiatives will be successful. The proponents of HO are management gurus and present HO in ways which suggest that their approaches are the embodiment of "best practice" when implemented effectively and in their entirety. The focus is on achieving highly visible outcomes related to customer effectiveness, process improvements and coordination, and committed employees. It seems that any manifest problems in designing these aspects of an HO will be clearly identified in operational terms when the potential benefits are assessed at the outset. Getting the parts of the HO right will ensure that effective strategic, operational and people outcomes will occur and these will lead to improved financial returns. Schonberger (pp. 96–97) claims that good managers following principles of HO will gravitate towards correct decisions without the need for backup cost data, and quotes from Thomas Johnson that even for product line decisions cost diverts attention from competitive essentials, which, for Schonberger, are expressed in terms of his principles for implementing an HO. These sentiments are not unusual and there is evidence that financial appraisals are often "adapted" to support preferred innovative approaches to manufacturing and organizational restructuring (see Davila & Wouters, 2007, pp. 840–841).

The uncritical adoption of new administrative innovations, such as HO, that may not survive careful economic analysis has been explained by fads and fashion where organizations adopt innovations because others do so (Malmi, 1999). In addition, competitive bandwagon effects encourage adoption as mangers want to avoid potential problems of losing competitive advantage that are assumed to derive from innovations (Malmi, 1999; Abrahamson & Rosenkopf, 1993; see Gosselin, 2007, pp. 663–665 for a discussion of these effects). The role of gurus and the promotion of rhetoric around management innovations have been discussed by Nørreklit (2003). She suggests that innovations may achieve popularity due to a reputation for the innovations being helpful, and may be used in a flexible way to generate discussion and to think about change, in general; they may challenge old ways of doing things and promote ideologies for change; they may promote images of managers as rational and being effective and up-to-date; they promote an attractive way to manage, i.e., they provide for "performance art"; they legitimize the roles of managers, consultants and the academic community as they promote a network of people who have reputations for knowing how to get things done.

Notwithstanding technical problems in developing "perfect" costing and resource allocation models, management accountants might argue that advances in ABCM and BSC, and a sensitivity to the problems identified by critiques of early approaches, means that there is a good case that management accounting can assist in understanding the economics of the HO. The accounting practices can translate the intuition concerning costs and benefits of HO into harder financials, or a range of "what if" scenarios with bottom line implications. This could direct attention to initiatives that appear to be effective, but will possibly be too costly. These potential benefits would seem to provide the gurus of management accounting innovations with ample reasons to believe that they should achieve high reputation effects in the management literature at large. How is it that the "accounting" gurus proposing these potentially beneficial aspects of management accounting have not had a significant impact on those promoting HO? Even given that there is a market for competing ideas, there does not seem to have been an exchange of ideas whereby a particular view could dominate. Rather, debates within management accounting seem, simply, to have been largely ignored by advocates of HO.

6.2. Lack of Acceptance of a Strategic Role for Management Accountants

HO advocates are not alone in cautioning on the use of management accounting techniques for more strategic concerns. In assessing the evolving role of ABCM, Armstrong (2002) argues the use of ACBM is really about cost reduction and control, and not about enhancing the value to customers (Armstrong, 2002, p. 108). He claims that ABCM can lead to a degradation of functions where the direct links between activities and costs are unclear, as is the case in many staff functions. For example, activities involving a dialogue across functions often cannot be related to costs or immediate outcomes and could be candidates for downsizing or removal. This is inconsistent with the strategic approach taken in HO which recognizes a need for structures and HR considerations that relate to developing possibilities for advantage, but which may not readily be related to products. These expenditures are part of the transformation process from traditional management to HO. Certainly cost cutting is one potential application of ABCM. However, while ABCM emphasizes cost efficiency, it is also targeted on identifying value drivers. The emphasis on cost cutting and the targeting of staff functions for downsizing is consistent with the commonly held view of accountants as myopic bean counters preoccupied with cost cutting. This may help explain why many management accountants have poor reputations among proponents of HO for not being able to influence managerial thinking at the strategic level, where innovation in product and customer development is seen as critical, with economic evaluation a necessary adjunct.

Shank (2006), an early proponent of ABCM, reported a gloomy view on the lack of take-up of ABCM, despite strong advocacy by many academics and consultants. He claimed that most management accountants do not report to senior strategists. He suggested that this lack of penetration of ABCM is partly due to an education system that does not train management accountants to apply accounting practices as business tools. If this is so then there is a possibility that information relevant to strategy and organizational change will not be driven by management accountants, as they lack perspectives consistent with HO. Other reasons, suggested by Shank, that have militated against a strategically influential role for management accountants include lack of support from professional bodies (in the US) for a strategic dimension. Moreover, Shank suggested that some senior managers guard their own position as strategy managers. These managers are hostile to any management accountants who challenge traditional finance in favour of a multifunctional approach which empowers line managers to take the lead in strategic analysis. He claimed that to be effective management accountants must understand the business context of organizations and the linkages across functional silos and across business boundaries with customers and suppliers. He complained that management accounting too often focuses on decision settings, but not on the business circumstances for the decision or the strategic context of the business. In other words, Shank is suggesting that to be effective management accountants must understand the lateral dimension and that, in the main, they do not. Clearly, to be effective in contributing to the HO management accountants need to be familiar with contemporary developments in management that are relevant to making the HO work. A variety of recent ideas from management that relate to various aspects of the HO are referenced in the discussions below.

6.3. Management Accounting Lacks Relevance to the Process of Strategy

The techniques of both management accounting and HO are prescriptive, functional approaches. While it is recognized that the establishment of both HO and management accounting innovations may be complex, the approach is to follow a prescribed approach informed by rationality. HO authors tend to provide precise principles to direct the development and implementation of HO. Management accounting practices such as ABCM provide a practical guide on how ABCM can increase organizational profitability and performance (Kaplan & Cooper, 1998, p. vii) with recommendations and blueprints (Kaplan & Cooper, 1998, p. 300). There is little recognition that mangers are often faced with problems and opportunities that cannot be defined objectively and that are open to interpretation from many different angles. There is no consideration that strategic problems are "wicked problems" and managers who are designing and implementing management accounting innovations or HO are likely to face issues that are complicated, uncertain, ambiguous and conflicting. Thus, while the strategy to adopt management accounting practices or HO may involve intended rationality, this process is likely to involve interpretation of decision issues that have high levels of subjectivity and complex behavioural responses. An examination of the literature on the process of strategy reveals that strategy often does not follow a rational planned approach (Chenhall, 2005, p. 24). In the prescriptions of HO and management accounting innovations there is little concern for understanding the dynamic relationships between strategic position, resources, value chain and outcomes. These processes do not always follow a neat, rational, logical approach, despite the best intentions of planners. Rather they involve ill-structured ideas emerging from ongoing operations, with initiatives being partly conceived that need considerable reflection to develop and become viable. Does a lack of consideration of the dynamic processes of how management accounting and HO interact limit understanding of the way accounting may help inform the design and application of HO?

Recent work on organizational dynamics provides helpful ideas that may advance understanding of the way management accounting relates to the processes involved in designing and implementing HO. For example, rational approaches employing proactive managerial initiatives can be contrasted with organizational inheritance (group think and strategic drift that can constrain new developments and strategic initiatives) (Tidd & Trewella, 1997). In addition, there is a need to consider how strategy and ideas are formulated by either exploration (the pursuit of new knowledge) or exploitation (the use of past knowledge) and consideration of which should go first (Gupta, Smith & Shalley, 2006). Innovation and creativity are particularly important outcomes for HO, as most firms recognize the importance of new ideas to be focused on customers in highly competitive markets. Recent work in management accounting has considered how accounting may be used to help generate innovation (Bisbe & Otley, 2004) and to assist in developing capabilities leading to strategic choices (i.e., market orientation, entrepreneurship, innovativeness and organizational learning) (Henri, 2006). It is notable that there has been little research examining management accounting and individual creativity. Research is needed on how management accounting may help provide a platform for creativity at the individual level, and how creativity links to innovation (Von Oetinger, 2004). Research in the area of resource development and renewal could be informed by examining the processes of developing resources and knowledge by way of dynamic capabilities (Teece, Pisano & Shuen, 1997; Winter, 2003), and a dynamic resource-based view or capability lifecycles (Helfat & Peteraf, 2003). Work on the dynamics of strategic fit also provides guidelines to model the changes in strategic fit (Zajac, Kraatz & Bresser, 2000). This is particularly important to help understand how accounting and HO can be designed to suit particular contexts as the context changes.

How organizations manage different types of change scenarios has significant implications for changes involving HO and management accounting innovations. Important considerations here are to understand different modes of change, such as whether organizations are facing "chaos or control" (predictable or unpredictable), "continuous or discontinuous," "revolutionary or evolutionary," "rational or unpredictable," and "incremental or comprehensive." Given that adopting a HO will involve movement between different ways of managing the organization, the speed or velocity of change will probably have an impact on effective design and implementation. Literature on strategic decision speed, such as speed of decision-making (Baum & Wally, 2003) and presumptive adaptation (fast or gradual) (Szulanski & Jensen, 2006) may be helpful.

6.4. Management Accounting Does Not Relate Well to Operations

An important aspect of HO is the application of advanced manufacturing practices in ways that integrate best practice operations with customer-focused strategies and structures that are designed laterally with supporting HR and IT initiatives. Proponents of ABCM and BSC claim that these techniques are particularly suited to settings such as TQM and JIT, where both cost and value drivers are being sought. There has been considerable research that provides evidence on how management accounting is implicated in methods such as TQM, JIT and flexible manufacturing. Extensive reviews of this literature include Young & Selto (1991), Anderson (2007, pp. 486–493), Chenhall (2006, pp. 176–179), Davila & Wouters (2007) and Hansen & Mouritsen (2007). While it is difficult to draw conclusions from this research because of varying definitions of constructs and their measurement, in the main the evidence suggests that the advent of advanced management has had an influence on the application of innovative accounting practices. However, our understanding of these connections remains elusive. The evidence tends to be specific to particular aspects of advanced manufacturing, including TQM, JIT and supplier and customer relationships (for a review, see Anderson, 2007, pp. 490–493). There is a considerable body of evidence from accounting researchers to support the idea that nonfinancial measures are particularly useful in advanced manufacturing (Ittner & Larcker, 1995; Chenhall, 1997; Fullerton & McWatters, 2002). Interestingly, some studies have shown that technologies such as JIT and TQM may provide for operational controls and as such support the views of proponents of HO that there is less need for accounting to coordinate and control operations (Hoque, 2000; Davila & Wouter 2007, p. 843). Anderson (2007) suggests that insights into the innovative analysis of costs, particularly structural cost management, are found in areas other than accounting, such as marketing, strategy, finance, economics and operations management.

There are no studies that have addressed, directly, how management accounting practices have been employed to help configure HO to achieve lateral coordination focused on customers or how they are implicated in decisions within HO. Chenhall & Langfield-Smith (1998) link performance with combinations of various contemporary and traditional management accounting techniques and a selection of management practices, however the study is not focused on all the elements of HO. A recent study has shown how the association between ABC and performance (unit manufacturing cost, cycle time and product quality) is mediated by world-class manufacturing (WCM) (Banker, Indranil, Bardhan & Chen, 2007). The study shows that ABC can be an enabler of WCM. The WCM construct is a summation of JIT, TQM, Kanban, continuous improvement, competitive benchmarking and self-directed teams, while the precise meaning of ABC is not specified.

Issues related to the type of performance measures to employ to assess operations are important to HO. In general, advocates of HO criticize accounting measures, and financials in particular, as being too obscure and removed from operational reality. There is a preference for multiple measures with an emphasis on nonfinancial and subjective measures. While accounting research has supported the idea that nonfinancials are employed in advanced manufacturing, their impact on performance is equivocal. It seems likely that effects depend on the specific context of the organization, such as the predictability of the technology and the uncertainty in the operating environment (Chenhall, 2006). Multiple measures, or a basket of measures, are recommended in HO. However, accounting research has shown that problems can occur in terms of combining measures and in weighting their relative importance (Chenhall, 2006, p.109). Some commentators have questioned the claim that nonfinancials are to be preferred to financials as they are more real (Mouritsen & Hansen, 2006, pp. 283–284). For example, some constructs such as quality, flexibility and customer value can have a variety of meanings which makes their reliable measurement problematic. Certainly, accounting research suggests that nonfinancial indicators require careful definition and measurement before they can be used across the organization (Chenhall, 2006). Subjective measures are recommended in HO, however, recent accounting research has shown that these may be the source of bias and be seen as unreliable with potential negative effects (Moers, 2005). Ittner, Larcker & Meyer (2003) found that high level of subjectivity in the weighting of different dimensions of BSC used in reward systems led managers to complain about favouritism in bonus awards and uncertainty in the criteria being used to determine rewards. This led to the abandonment of the approach in favour of a formula-based scorecard.

Research in HR provides potentially useful avenues to understand ways of combining multiple performance measures and to link them to specific desired outcomes such as improved productivity or cohesiveness. Multiple-attribute utility analysis (MAU) is an approach that attempts to assess how the multiple facets of job performance combine to achieve desired outcomes (Boudreau, 1991; Roth & Bobko, 1997). The innovation of 360-degree performance ratings provides a way of gaining insight into an individual's performance from a variety of sources, such as supervisors, peers, subordinates, customers and suppliers (Hazucha, Hezlett & Schneider, 1993). The provision of information from a wide set of individuals who have close working relationships with the employee provides multiple perspectives of the individual's performance. This approach is favoured by advocates of HO. The potential pitfalls of this approach include a lack of understanding between assessors of the same performance criteria and how to ensure consistency in measuring the performance criteria. It is also important to assess if additional measures provide incremental information beyond the ratings from a single source (Borman, 1997).

Recent research in operations management provides an elaboration of how the objectives of HO may be achieved, with implications to explore how management accounting may relate to these innovations. For example, recent advances in agile manufacturing highlight the development of dynamic capabilities by stressing the need for a strategic use of new technologies, the integration of strategies and operations, customer satisfaction through new forms of interfirm cooperation and knowledge management (Gunasekaran & Yusuf, 2002). Work done in management accounting on intellectual capital and knowledge management would seem particularly suited to help inform in this area with its focus on dynamic capabilities. Agile project management is based on an approach where the project is seen as a series of relatively small tasks conceived and executed as the situation demands in an adaptive manner, rather than as a completely preplanned process (Highsmith, 2004). Modularization has focused on building products from smaller subsystems that can be designed independently, yet function together as a whole (Baldwin & Clark, 1997). Valuation of modules may be assisted by the application of ABCM. Six Sigma as an organization-wide approach has refined issues concerning minimizing defects by stressing the need for cultural change to achieve high levels of manufacturing efficiency across the value chain, with implications for management accounting in project reviews and performance tracking (Antony & Banuelas, 2001).

Network perspectives provide powerful frameworks for studying issues of coordination within HO and the role of accounting (see Hakansson & Lind, 2007, pp. 897–898). Work on networks has helped reinforce the main message of HO that parts of the organization need to cooperate and share information with other organizations to achieve their end purposes (both internally across operations and externally with other organizations). From a network perspective the role of management accounting can be important as it helps to clarify who is in the network and how network partners interrelate. Mouritsen & Thrane (2006) argue that networks become formalized and exist beyond the partners who can be expelled if they do not play by the rules, and accounting helps contribute to these rules. Network rules can be defined from the outcomes of management accounting practices. For example, Mouritsen & Thane (2006) suggest the following examples of network defining rules: transfer pricing rules, fees to the centre, intellectual capital statements, competency accounts, peer review of network partners and geographical segmentation in defining network arrangements. Jones & Dugdale (2002) also discuss the integrating role of ABCM from an actor–network perspective, where actors and networks mutually form and reform each other, and how this can help explain the evolution of ABC. Briers & Chua (2001) provide an example of how ABC helped in organizational change by developing networks and boundary spanning. The involvement of parties interested in ABC helped sustain organizational change. These parties reinforced the implementation by using "boundary objects" such as common databases for different parties to draw on, and visionary beliefs as to the usefulness of ABC that all parties could believe in. More general elaborations of networks can be found in Oliver & Ebers (1998) and Grandori & Soda (1995). A useful integrating theory is provided by Das & Teng (2000) which involves a balancing strategy for networks between three pairs of competing forces: cooperation versus competition; rigidity versus flexibility; long-term versus short-term orientations.

Other ideas that draw on networks show how networks that cross organizations can blur organizational boundaries. "Strategic communities" and their integration focus on how strategies that add value can emerge from inter-organizational networks as collaborative action can increase knowledge, create innovation and markets, and develop virtual teams between various organizations (Kodoma, 2005, 2006). Ideas of combining external networks with an internal resource-based view also provide a way of connecting the external setting with internal capabilities (Choonwoo, Kyungmook & Pennings, 2001).

6.5. Management Accounting Does Not Support Horizontal Organization's Structural and Human Resources Initiatives

Traditionally, management accounting has been concerned with designing control systems to suit organizations with conventional structures based on vertical hierarchies. There have been deliberations on the extent to which aggregate numbers such as return on investment (ROI), in contrast to nonfinancials, are suitable for decentralized segments (Hemmer, 1996; Feltham & Xie, 1994). Issues of traceability and controllability are discussed (Merchant, 1987). These matters are relevant when considering the effectiveness of managing profit centres, even when they are based laterally around customers or products. Advocates of HO recommend that profit should be used to assess profit centres based on products and customers but, in the main, this is for planning purposes. Only Galbraith envisages profit centres for managerial evaluation, however, issues of traceability and controllability are not discussed. Of more importance to advocates of HO are team-based structures and there is considerable attention given to how HR policies are to be used to ensure that coordination is achieved between teams. Performance measures are important to motivate employees and assess progress, including the effectiveness of lateral coordination; but again there is little emphasis on using financial measures, and the potential for innovations such as BSC in these settings is unexplored. Where BSC are discussed the inclusion of financials is seen to introduce elements of short-termism. At best BSC can assist in indicating the effect of individual work on others across the value chain and weaning managers off financials (Schonberger, p. 228).

In management accounting there is some research suggesting ways in which performance measures can be useful within team-based structures. Evidence has shown that to be effective performance measures within teams need to be set participatively (Scott & Tiessen, 1999; Chalos & Poon, 2000); rewards should be based on group incentives (Drake et al., 1999) and formal measures may be inconsistent with achieving trust within teams (Chenhall & Langfield-Smith, 2003). These outcomes are consistent with the thrust of HO that team-based control and lateral coordination should be embedded within the team, that this should be based on socializing individuals to work towards a collaborative culture and rewards should focus on the team (Ostroff, p. 226).

A variety of approaches to studying teams has emerged in the management literature that has relevance to management accounting and HO. Teams can be studied from a dynamic perspective. Social network theory has been applied to small group research studying the emergence and change of informal structures and patterns of relations (Burt, 1978). The role of teams that cross organizational boundaries has received attention. Virtual teams involve structural teams, but people work independently across geographic boundaries using IT as a source of rich media (DeRosa, Hantula, Kock & D'Arcy, 2004). Clusters provide another HO dimension where clusters of organizations are formed to establish high trust relations among companies within a cluster, with the aim of exploiting joint purchasing services, as well as sharing dedicated facilities (Van de Ven, 1991). An important issue for firms combining teams with some hierarchal structure is how teams and hierarchy are combined (Romme, 1996).

There have been considerable advances in ideas related to organizational structuring that are consistent with the quest for lateral coordination that may provide useful leads for investigating the role of management accounting within HO. New modes of organizing to achieve lateral efficiencies emphasize business unit reconfiguration (Karim, 2006). The concerns are with what organizations do rather than what they have (i.e., the dynamics of restructuring) and there are strong links to dynamic capabilities and resources. The dynamics of restructuring are concerned with understanding changing structural relationships that entail aligning resources with needs. For example, patching involves remapping structure (add, combine, split and exit chunks of the business) to match resources with turbulent conditions (Eisenhardt & Brown, 1999). Organizational modularity emphasizes flexibility to link structure to modular product systems, altering responsibilities and reusing resources between work units (Helfat & Eisenhardt, 2004). Developing management accounting to suit these highly flexible structural arrangements presents many challenges.

Leadership is important to HO, although the role of traditional leaders is down-played. A personal or consideration style is recommended that aims to derive commitment from employees to the aspirations of the HO. For Schonberger (p. 191) traditional leadership becomes less important. Teamsmanship is required and is based on a willingness of senior managers to share knowledge, egalitarian communication talents, common sense, consideration, empathy and kindness. Galbraith (pp. 171–172) sees leadership as being effected through the company's management processes. This involves confronting and resolving the flow of contentious issues by way of discussion, debate and resolution. Contentious issues arise from decisions on product and customer plans, product portfolio and opportunity management. Ostroff (p. 67) considers successful leaders to be demanding and aspiration-driven. What is required is a willingness and the follow-through to plan thoughtfully and develop capabilities in others to be empowered and held accountable for meeting performance goals.

In HR, leadership has recently been considered as the process of transformational leadership (see the work of B. M. Bass in Zaccaro & Banks, 2004). This approach seems particularly suited to understanding the role of leadership in organizations undergoing change towards a focus on customer-based strategies. The aim is to develop strategic flexibility that involves organizational visioning and an ability to manage change. Effective transformational leadership is associated with trust, commitment, self- and team-efficacy (Arnold, Barling & Kelloway, 2001). Other issues that appear to be important include changing mental models, facilitating collaboration, attracting and selecting employees.

Governance has become an important aspect of control, aiming to ensure that individuals undertake their tasks in ways consistent with doing business sanctioned to achieve organizational beliefs. Relationship governance has been raised as important to managing the way lateral relationships are to be performed within the organization (Meer-Kooistra & Scapens, 2004; cited in Scapens, 2006, p. 346). In HO, governance takes place in situations with high interdependencies between organizational units. Consequently, governance needs to be firm but flexible; trust is encouraged when structure mitigates risks of cooperation between individuals with different interests. Guiding considerations are information-sharing and knowledge exchange, cooperation and competition, flexibility and standardization, sharing and shifting of leadership roles to suit changing structures.

Culture is central to the HO, yet its meaning is not defined, apart from reference to the strategic intent of HO. Ostroff (p. 206) says that corporate culture is about openness, cooperation, collaboration; a culture that focuses on continuous performance improvement and values employee empowerment, responsibility and well-being. For Schonberger (p. 21), HO culture is about customer-focused, employee-driven, data-based performance (customers, processes, competitors, best practices). Galbraith (p. 1) sees culture as concerning customer relationships, i.e., searching for increased customer needs to satisfy. All three authors use aspirational statements that do not tease out the meaning of culture in the HO. In accounting, the notion of organizational culture is not well-developed. Henri (2006) used survey methods to study accounting and culture using a culture with "control and flexibility" as the competing values. The research showed that firms with flexible values tended to integrate performance measures into their organizational processes and used more performance indicators than firms with control values. Ahrens & Mollona (2007) provide an ethnographic study that examined culture. They argued that subcultures at the shop floor level were constituted in practices of control which enabled organizational members to pursue diverse objectives that were related to their various cultural aspirations. Given that culture affects the way individuals see the organization, its importance to management accounting's role in the HO would seem central. In studying culture a distinction needs to be made between organizational culture and climate. Culture is organizational while climate is at the individual level. Organizational culture is a pattern of knowledge, belief and behaviour that includes social forms. Culture circumscribes and includes organizational structure: it is the form, beliefs, norms, social patterns, the way things are done, the symbols and rituals (Ravasi & Schultz, 2006; Tagiuri & Litwin, 1968). Psychological climate is a set of global perceptions held by individuals about their organization's internal environment, feelings about actual events based on the interaction between actual events and the perception of those events (James & Jones, 1974). It has been measured along dimensions such as: disengagement, hindrance, esprit, intimacy, aloofness, production emphasis, trust and consideration. Understanding how management accounting can be used within HO would best be informed by understanding the way climate and culture are connected.

Finally, many of the initiatives from HR within HO are designed to encourage employees to contribute to strategic decisions and to take responsibility for operations. The extent to which individuals interact with each other within the organization and with those in other organizations is likely to be facilitated by trust and commitment to commonly held goals. While trust and commitment are implicit in the HO, there is considerable research across a variety of disciplines, including management accounting, that has clarified and explored how information and accounting are implicated in trust (e.g., Barney & Hansen. 1994; Creed & Miles, 1996; Lane 1998; Tomkins, 2001; Busco, Riccaboni & Scapens, 2006; Johansson & Baldvinsdottir, 2003) and commitment (Allen & Meyer, 1990; Mowday, Steers & Porter, 1979; Nouri, 1994; Nouri & Parker, 1998). As the HO aims to encourage individuals to act as team players and to cooperate with others across the value chain, how they trust others and their commitment to the organization would seem to be important. The way in which management accounting can assist, or hinder, the generation of trust and commitment is also clearly an important consideration.

7. Conclusion

In this chapter the essential attributes of HO are seen to have emerged in the context of the development of the matrix organization (Knight, 1976; Hopwood, 1977), in approaches to project management (Cook & Granger, 1976) and to Japanese-inspired production practices to compete in increasingly competitive international market conditions (Susaki, 1987). The works of Ostroff, Schonberger and Galbraith, when taken together, provide a description of the HO. From these authors the HO is concerned with seeking competitive advantage for organizations by structuring the organization around customers and employing best practice production processes. Additionally, HR policies are used to encourage employee commitment to the efficient management of interdependencies involved in the HO. The approach operates within structures where teams, not individuals, are responsible for delivering customer value in ways that ensure continuous performance improvement within a culture of employee empowerment, responsibility and well-being. Functional expertise can be provided by vertical structures, but authority lies with teams and functions are to provide service to teams.

In this chapter it is suggested that management accountants can learn from understanding the thinking underpinning the HO and that advocates of HO can also learn from complementary ideas and research offered from management accounting. If there is to be a productive conversation between parties advocating HO and those advancing management accounting innovations, then both need to understand the basic assumptions, values and viewpoints that lie behind each of the approaches. Moreover, progress is likely to be made if both understand the contribution that can be made from contemporary developments in related disciplines.

Concerning strategy, the three authors reviewed in this chapter see the adoption of HO as the key strategic decision. This involves a careful assessment of the extent to which the principles proposed by the various authors can be implemented. Here instructions are provided on structural change, production improvements and HR initiatives to establish the HO. While all three authors have much to say in each of these areas, there are differences in emphases with Ostroff stressing HR considerations, Schonberger production processes and Galbraith the management of interdependencies caused by aligning the organization around customers. A key concern to this chapter is the extent to which management accounting has developed in ways that have contributed to a horizontal dimension, and whether the ideas of the three authors were informed by innovations in management accounting. ABCM and BSC were used as popular exemplars of emerging strategic approaches that aim to help manage, in a cost-effective way, complexity between parts of the organization. Do these practices fully embrace the horizontal?

A key aspect of the HO is the replacement of vertical structures with horizontal forms that includes functional specialization to be used by teams when needed. The tools of ABCM and BSC are envisaged to be strategic and used by senior managers for planning and controlling within conventional vertical structures. However, within a decentralized structure such as that proposed by HO, presumably, these tools could be provided to teams when needed. ABCM can be used in supplier and customer decision-making as they emphasize not only cost, but also collaborative approaches that provide for delivery, quality and flexibility. Again, this might be useful information for teams operating horizontally. However, the accounting systems are not horizontal in the sense that they focus on the full resource implications of delivering value to a customer group which involves conventional investments in material, labour and equipment, but also in soft assets such as HR, structural change and complex integrative mechanisms. Certainly, advocates of HO do not see ABCM or BSC as providing useful information on the viability of organizing horizontally. It seems there is little confidence that accounting systems can capture the complexities involved in adopting HO. However, there is support from Galbraith, and reluctantly from Schonberger, that accounting has a role in calculating product and customer profitability. This would seem to provide for useful applications of ABCM or target costing, at least for costing and product profitability analysis, if not for comprehensive horizontal accounting. Issues that are of concern to accountants about overhead allocations and cost driver analysis do not rate as critical aspects of decision-making by advocates of HO. Ostroff and Galbraith do not discuss the implications of issues related to the reliability of cost and profit calculations. Schonberger provides his own, somewhat simplified, ABC-type costing system. This trivial treatment of the costing debate signifies the lack of engagement between advocates of HO and those exploring innovations in management accounting. Somewhat dispiriting explanations for this are a lack of political influence of management accountants, management accountants do not understand the philosophy of the HO (including the precursors of matrix and project management forms), a lack of trust in accounting data, and more generally the persistent stereotyping of accountants as myopic bean-counters.

Regarding control, all three authors have detailed recommendations on how to develop production controls and assess individuals' performance. None believes that management accounting has a useful role in evaluation and control at the operational level, including BSC. Any emphasis on financial figures is seen to be unreliable because it clouds events and may distract individuals from managing horizontally. Rather, advocates of HO rely on operational controls and HR performance evaluation techniques. The concern with multiple performance measures (and multiple assessors) and qualitative measures provides challenges for highly innovative approaches to performance evaluation. It is encouraging that recent research in management accounting has begun to explore the effectiveness of these types of measures. This would seem to be an area where much could be gained by a closer interchange of ideas between management accountants and proponents of HO on how to assess the effectiveness of operations and individuals within a HO.

The chapter has reviewed the thinking that has been employed by those recommending HO. Much of the content of HO is not new, having been proposed by those in operations management, marketing and HR. What is novel is the lateral structuring of the organization to combine the best ideas from the core disciplines. Recent developments in operations, marketing and HR also stress the need to become more holistic and examine where their disciplines' boundaries interface with others. It seems that advocates of HO have not seriously embraced ideas and debates about value and performance measurement from management accounting. This seems unfortunate as many of these ideas could help illuminate various issues concerning economic value and performance measurement that are pertinent to aspects of HO. Even if there are difficulties in the calculation of value and the integration of performance measures in ways consistent with horizontal structures and processes, much could be gained by a dialogue between the enthusiasts of HO and those proposing management accounting innovation.

An issue remains as to how management accounting can become more horizontal. Techniques such as ABCM and BSC can provide ways of thinking about cost, value and performance that connect parts of the value chain. The practices are not without difficulties and many would not see them as horizontal while they are constrained by applications within vertically structured organizations. To be effective, accounting innovation such as ABCM and BSC would have to be used in a multi-dimensional way, as suggested by Hopwood (1977). That is, one use of the accounting innovations would be for organizational-wide issues, such as the economic viability of the HO, or strategic shifts; while the other use would be dedicated to managing the horizontal aspects of doing business. Of course this requires attention to developing an organizational culture that supports accounting that relates to the HO. It is possible that the complexities in many HO will defy any approach to overlay confused and uncertain activities and structures with highly formalized economic modelling. However, elaborations of approaches such as target costing or whole-of-life costing have provided management accountants with ways of working with others to help define what is needed to launch projects. It would seem that much could be gained by an interchange of ideas with others developing contemporary project management, using the term "project" in ways focused on customers and potential products to satisfy these customers. Considering the complexities of coordination that can occur within the HO, accounting could benefit from examining lateral coordination mechanisms, such as those suggested by Galbraith. As indicated earlier these approaches range from informal groups, e-coordination, formal groups, integrators, matrix organizations and separate customer line organizational units. Within each of these approaches there are implications for information and accounting practices and processes.

Finally in this chapter, it is suggested that for progress to be made in developing horizontal accounting a closer dialogue between management accountants and proponents of HO is required. It is recognized that this presents challenges and several commentators have noted the lack of cross-fertilization of ideas between management accounting and other disciplines. Merchant, Van der Stede & Zheng (2003) observe the apparent limited awareness that accounting researchers have of developments and insights into other disciplines. Mensah, Hwang & Wu (2004) also claim that there is limited cross-fertilization of ideas and findings with a decreasing incidence of citations of management accounting in other disciplines. These observations can be applied to the poor communications between those proposing HO and those offering management accounting as a complementary or ancillary approach. To ensure that a productive dialogue takes place, management accountants must become familiar with HO and developments that extend the philosophy of the approach. Those promoting HO should also be receptive to work done in accounting and elsewhere that can inform on aspects of the HO and the debate that surrounds these practices. It is hoped that this chapter provides a contribution by stimulating this debate and suggesting areas where both HO and management accounting can have productive dialogue. Certainly there are many challenges for management accounting if it is to provide a more horizontal dimension.

Acknowledgement

I gratefully acknowledge Anthony Hopwood for his helpful suggestions and comments.

References

Abrahamson, E. & Rosennkopf, L. (1993). Institutional and competitive bandwagons: using mathematical modelling as a tool to explore innovation diffusion. *Academy of Management Review*, **18**, 498–517.

Ahrens, T. & Mollana, M. (2007). Organisational control as cultural practice: A shop floor ethnography of a Sheffield steel mill. *Accounting, Organizations and Society*, **32**(4–5), 305–331.

Allen, N. J. & Meyer, J. P. (1990). The measurement and antecedents of affective continuance and normative commitment to the organization. *Journal of Occupational Psychology*, **63**, 1–18.

Anderson, S. W. (2007). Managing costs and cost structure throughout the value chain: research on strategic cost management. In: C. S. Chapman, A. G. Hopwood, & M. D. Shields (Eds), *Handbook of Management Accounting Research*, (Vol. 2). Amsterdam, The Netherlands: Elsevier, pp. 481–506.

Andreessen, D. (2004). *Making Sense of Intellectual Capital: Designing a Method for the Valuation of Intangibles*. Boston, MA: Butterworth Heinemann.

Ansari, S., Bell, J. & Okano, H. (2007). Target costing: uncharted research territory. In: C. S. Chapman, A. G. Hopwood, & M. D. Shields (Eds), *Handbook of Management Accounting Research*, (Vol. 2). Amsterdam, The Netherlands: Elsevier, pp. 507–530.

Antony, J. & Banuelas, R. (2001). A strategy for survival. *Manufacturing Engineer*, **80**(3), 119–121.

Arnold, K. A., Barling, J. & Kelloway, E. K. (2001). Transformational leadership or the iron cage which predicts trust, commitment, and team efficacy. *Leadership and Organizational Development Journal*, **22**(7), 315–320.

Atkinson, J. H., Hohner, G., Mundt, B., Troxel, B. & Winchell, W. (1991). *Current trends in cost of quality: linking the cost of quality and continuous improvement*. Montvale, NJ: National Association of Accountants.

Armstrong, P. (2002). The costs of activity-based management. *Accounting, Organizations and Society*, **27**, 99–120.

Baldwin, C. Y. & Clark, K. B. (1997). Managing in an age of modularity. *Harvard Business Review*, **September–October**, 84–93.

Banker, R. D., Bardhan, I. R. & Chen, T-Y. (2008). The role of manufacturing practices in mediating the impact of activity-based costing on plant performance. *Accounting, Organizations and Society*, **31**(1), 1–19.

Banker, R. D. & Johnson, H. H. (2007). Cost and profit driver research. In: C. S. Chapman, A. G. Hopwood, & M. D. Shields (Eds), *Handbook of Management Accounting Research*, (Vol. 2). Amsterdam, The Netherlands: Elsevier, pp. 531–556.

Barney, J. B. & Hansen, M. H. (1994). Trustworthiness as a source of competitive advantage. *Strategic Management Journal*, **15**, 175–190.

Baum, R. & Wally, S. (2003). Strategic decision speed and firm performance. *Strategic Management Journal*, **24**(11), 1107–1129.

Becher, B. E., Huselid, M. A. & Ulrich, D. (2001). *The HR Scorecard: Linking People, Strategy and Performance*. Boston, MA: Harvard Business School Press.

Berliner, A. & Brimson, J. A. (1988). *Cost Management for Today's Advanced Manufacturing—The CAM-I Conceptual Design*. Boston, MA: Harvard Business School Press.

Bisbe, J. & Otley, D. (2004). The effects of an interactive use of control systems on product innovation. *Accounting, Organizations and Society*, **29**, 709–737.

Borman, W. C. (1997). 360-Degree ratings: an analysis of assumptions and a research agenda for evaluating their validity. *Human Resource Management Review*, **6**(3), 299–315.

Boudreau, J. W. (1991). Utility Analysis and Decisions in Human Resource Management. In: M. D. Dunnette, & L. M. Hough (Eds), *Handbook of Industrial and Organizational Psychology*, (Vol. 2).Palo Alto, CA: Consulting Psychologists Press, pp. 621–745.

Briers, M. & Chua, W. F. (2001). The role of actor-networks and boundary objects in management accounting change: a filed study of an implementation of activity-based costing. *Accounting, Organizations and Society*, **26**(3), 237–269.

Burt, R. (1978). Cohesion versus structural equivalence as a basis for network sub-groups. *Sociological Methods and Research*, **7**, 189–212.

Busco, C., Riccaboni, A. & Scapens, R. W. (2006). Trust for accounting and accounting for trust. *Management Accounting Research*, **17**(1), 11–41.

Carr, C. & Ng, J. (1995). Total cost control: Nissan and its UK supplier partnerships. *Management Accounting Research*, **6**, 347–365.

Chalos, P. & Poon, M. C. C. (2000). Participation and performance in capital budgeting teams. *Behavioral Research in Accounting*, **12**, 199–229.

Chenhall, R. H. (1997). Reliance on manufacturing performance measures, total quality management and organizational performance. *Management Accounting Research*, **8**, 187–206.

Chenhall, R. H. (2005). Content and process approaches to studying strategy and management control systems. In: C. S. Chapman (Ed.), *Controlling Strategy: Management, Accounting and Performance Measurement*. Oxford, UK: Oxford University Press, pp. 10–36.

Chenhall, R. H. (2006). The contingent design of performance measures. In: A. Bhimani (Ed.), *Contemporary Issues in Management Accounting*. Oxford, UK: Oxford University Press, pp. 92–1160.

Chenhall, R. H. & Langfield-Smith, K. (1998). Adoption and benefits of management accounting practices: An Australian study. *Management Accounting Research*, **9**, 1–19.

Chenhall, R. H. & Langfield-Smith, K. (2003). The role of employee pay in sustaining organisational change. *Journal of Management Accounting Research*, **15**, 117–143.

Chenhall, R. H. & Langfield-Smith, K. (2007). Multiple Perspectives in Performance Measures. *European Journal Management*, **September**, 266–282.

Choonwoo, L., Kyungmook, L. & Pennings, J. M. (2001). Internal capabilities, external networks, and performance: a study on technology-based ventures 3. *Strategic Management Journal*, **22**(6–7), 615–640.

Cook, D. L. & Granger, J. G. (1976). Current status of project management instruction in American colleges and universities. *Academy of Management Journal*, **19**(2), 223–328.

Creed, W. E. D. & Miles, R. E. (1996). Trust in organizations: A conceptual framework linking organizational forms, managerial philosophies and the opportunity cost of controls. In: R. M. Kramer, & T. R. Tyler (Eds), *Trust in Organizations: Frontiers of Theory and Research*. Thousand Oaks, CA: Sage Publications, pp. 16–38.

Das, T. K. & Teng, B. (2000). Instabilities of strategic alliances: an internal tensions perspective. *Organization Science*, **11**(1), 77–101.

Davila, T. & Wouters, M. (2007). Management accounting in the manufacturing sector: managing costs at the design and production stages. In: C. S. Chapman, A. G. Hopwood, & M. D. Shields (Eds), *Handbook of Management Accounting Research*, (Vol. 2). Amsterdam, The Netherlands: Elsevier, pp. 831–858.

Dechow, N., Granlund, M. & Mouritsen, J. (2007). Management control of the complex organization: relationship between management accounting and information technology. In: C. S. Chapman, A. G. Hopwood, & M. D. Shields (Eds), *Handbook of Management Accounting Research*, (Vol. 2). Amsterdam, The Netherlands: Elsevier, pp. 625–640.

Dekker, H. C. (2003). Value chain analysis in interfirm relationships: a field study. *Management Accounting Research*, **14**(1), 1–23.

Derosa, D. M., Hantula, D. A., Kock, N. & D'Arcy, J. (2004). Trust and leadership in virtual teamwork: a media naturalness perspective. *Human Resource Management*, **43**(2–3), 219–232.

Ditillo, A. (2004). Dealing with uncertainty in knowledge-intensive firms: the role of management control systems as knowledge integration mechanisms. *Accounting, Organizations and Society*, **29**(3–4), 401–421.

Dixon, J. R., Nanni, A. J. & Vollmann, T. E. (1990). *The new performance challenge: measuring operations for world-class competition*. Homewood, IL: Dow Jones-Irwin.

Drake, A. R., Haka, S. F. & Ravenscroft, S. P. (1999). Cost system and incentive structure effects on innovation, efficiency and profitability in teams. *The Accounting Review*, **74**(3), 323–345.

Eisenhardt, K. M. & Brown, S. L. (1999). Patching: restitching business portfolios in dynamic markets. *Harvard Business Review*, **77**(3), 71–82.

Feltham, G. & Xie, J. (1994). Performance measure congruity and diversity in multi-task principal/agent relations. *The Accounting Review*, **69**, 429–453.

Foster, G. & Gupta, M. (1994). Marketing cost, management and management accounting. *Journal of Management Accounting Research*, **6**(3), 43–77.

Foster, G. & Sjoblom, L. (1996). Quality improvement drivers in the electronics industry. *Journal of Management Accounting Research*, **8**, 55–86.

Frame, J. D. (2003). *Managing projects in organizations: how to make best use of time, techniques and people*. San Francisco, CA: Jossey-Bass.

Frances, J. & Garnsey, E. (1996). Supermarkets and suppliers in the United Kingdom: systems integration information and control. *Accounting, Organizations and Society*, **21**(6), 591–610.

Fullerton, R. R. & McWatters, C. S. (2002). The role of performance measures and incentive systems in relation to the degree of JIT implementation. *Accounting, Organizations and Society*, **27**(8), 735–771.

Galbraith, J. (1973). *Designing complex organizations.* USA: Addison Wesley Publishing Company.

Galbraith, J. (2002). *Designing Organizations: An Executive Briefing on Strategy, Structure, and Process.* San Francisco, CA: Jossey-Bass.

Galbraith, J. (2005). *Designing the Customer-centric Organization, A guide to Strategy, Structure, and Process.* San Francisco, CA: Jossey-Bass.

Gietzmann, M. B. (1996). Incomplete contracts and the make or buy decision: governance design and attainable flexibility. *Accounting, Organizations and Society*, **21**(6), 611–622.

Goldratt, E. M. & Cox, J. (1992). *The goal: a process of ongoing improvement.* Great Barrington, MA: North River Press.

Gosselin, M. (2007). A review of activity-based-costing: techniques, implementation and consequences. In: C. S. Chapman, A. G. Hopwood, & M. D. Shields (Eds), *Handbook of Management Accounting Research*, (Vol. 2). Amsterdam, The Netherlands: Elsevier, pp. 641–671.

Graham, R. J. & England, R. J. (2004). *Creating an environment for successful projects.* San Francisco, CA: Jossey-Bass.

Grojer, J-E. (2001). Intangibles and accounting classifications: in search of a classification strategy. *Accounting, Organizations and Society*, **26**(7–8), 695–713.

Grandori, A. & Soda, G. (1995). Inter-firm networks: antecedents, mechanisms and forms. *Organization Studies*, **16**(2), 183–214.

Gupta, A. K., Smith, K. G. & Shalley, C. E. (2006). The interplay between exploration and exploitation. *Academy of Management Journal*, **49**, 693–706.

Gunasekaran, A. & Yusuf, Y. (2002). Agile manufacturing: a taxonomy of strategic and technological imperatives. *International Journal of Production Research*, **40**(6), 1357–1385.

Hakansson, H. & Lind, K. (2007). Accounting in inter-organizational settings. In: C. S. Chapman, A. G. Hopwood, & M. D. Shields (Eds), *Handbook of Management Accounting Research*, (Vol. 2). Amsterdam, The Netherlands: Elsevier, pp. 885–902.

Hansen, A. & Mouritsen, J. (2007). Management accounting and operations management: understanding the challenges from integrated manufacturing. In: C. S. Chapman, A. G. Hopwood, & M. D. Shields (Eds), *Handbook of Management Accounting Research*, (Vol. 2). Amsterdam, The Netherlands: Elsevier, pp. 729–752.

Hazucha, J. F., Hezlett, S. A. & Schneider, R. J. (1993). The impact of 360° feedback on managerial skill development. *Human Resource Management*, **32**, 325–351.

Helfat, C. E. & Eisenhardt, K. M. (2004). Inter-temporal economies of scope, organizational modularity, and the dynamics of diversification. *Strategic Management Journal*, **25**(13), 1217–1232.

Helfat, C. E. & Peteraf, M. (2003). The dynamic resource-based view: capability lifecycles. *Strategic Management Journal*, **24**(10), 997–1010.

Hemmer, T. (1996). On the design and choice of "modern" management accounting measures. *Journal of Management Accounting*, **8**, 87–116.

Henri, J-P. (2006). Organizational culture and performance measurement systems. *Accounting, Organizations and Society*, **31**(1), 77–103.

Henri, J-P. (2006). Management control systems and strategy: a resource-based perspective. *Accounting, Organizations and Society*, **31**(6), 529–559.

Highsmith, J. (2004). *Agile Project Management: Creating Innovative Products.* Boston, MA: Addison Wesley Professional.

Hopwood, A. G. (1977). The design of information systems for matrix organizations. In: K. Knight (Ed.), *Matrix management.* Farnborough, Hants, UK: Gower Press, pp. 195–208.

Hopwood, A. G. (1996). Looking across rather than up and down: on the need to explore the lateral processing of information. *Accounting, Organizations and Society*, **21**(6), 589–590.

Hoque, Z. & James, W. (2000). Linking balanced scorecard measures to size and market factors: impact on organizational performance. *Journal of Management Accounting Research*, **12**, 1–17.

Hronec, S. M. (1993). *Vital Signs.* New York, NY: Arthur Anderson and Co.

Ittner, C. D. & Larcker, D. F. (1995). Total quality management and the choice of information and reward systems. *Journal of Accounting Research*, **33**(Supplement), 1–34.

Ittner, C. D. & Larcker, D. F. (1998). Innovations in performance measurement: trends and research implications. *Journal of Management Accounting Research*, **10**, 205–238.

Ittner, C. D., Larcker, D. F. & Meyer, M. W. (2003). Subjectivity and the weighting of performance measures: evidence from a balanced scorecard. *The Accounting Review*, **78**(3), 725–758.

Ittner, C. D., Larcker, D. F. & Randell, T. (2003). Performance implications of strategic performance measurement in financial services firms. *Accounting, Organizations and Society*, **28**(7–8), 715–741.

James, L. R. & Jones, A. P. (1974). Organizational climate: A review of theory and research. *Psychological Bulletin*, **81**, 1096–1112.

Johansson, I-L. & Baldvinsdottir, G. (2003). Accounting for trust: some empirical evidence. *Management Accounting Research*, **14**(3), 219–234.

Johanson, U., Martensson, M. & Skoog, M. (2001). Mobilizing change through the control of intangibles. *Accounting, Organizations and Society*, **26**(7–8), 715–733.

Jones, C. T. & Dugdale, D. (2002). The ABC bandwagon and the juggernaut of modernity. *Accounting, Organizations and Society*, **27**(1), 121–163.

Kaplan, R. S. & Cooper, R. (1998). *Cost and Effect: Using integrated cost systems to drive profitability and performance*. Boston, MA: Harvard University Press.

Kaplan, R. S. & Norton, D. P. (1996). *The Balanced Scorecard – Translating Strategy into Action*. Boston, MA: Harvard Business School Press.

Kaplan, R. S. & Norton, D. P. (2000). *The Strategy Focused Organization: How Balanced Scorecard Companies Thrive in the New Business Environment*. Boston, MA: Harvard Business School Press.

Kaplan, R. S. & Norton, D. P. (2004). *Strategy Maps–Converting Intangible Assets into Tangible Outcomes*. Boston, MA: Harvard Business School Press.

Karim, S. (2006). Modularity in organizational structure: the reconfiguration of internally developed and acquired business units. *Strategic Management Review*, **27**, 799–823.

Kerzner, H. (2001). *Project Management: A Systems Approach to Planning, Scheduling and Controlling*. New York, NY: John Wiley.

Kingdon, D. R. (1973). *Matrix Organization*. London, UK: Tavistock.

Knight, K. (1976). Matrix organization: a review. *Journal of Management Studies*, **13**, 111–130.

Kodama, M. (2005). Knowledge creation through networked strategic communities. *Long Range Planning*, **38**(1), 27–49.

Kodama, M. (2006). Strategic community: foundation of knowledge creation. *Research Technology Management*, **49**(5), 49–58.

Lane, C. (1998). Introduction: theories and issues in the study of trust. In: C. Lane, & R. Bachmann (Eds), *Trust within Organizations and Between Organizations*. Oxford, UK: Oxford University Press, pp. 1–30.

Lord, B. R. (1996). Strategic management accounting: the emperor's new clothes. *Management Accounting Research*, **7**(3), 346–366.

Lynch, R. L. & Cross, K. F. (1995). *Measure up! Yardsticks for Continuous Improvement*. Cambridge, MA: Basil Blackwell Inc.

Malmi, T. (1999). Activity based costing diffusion across organizations: an exploratory empirical analysis of Finnish firms. *Accounting, Organizations and Society*, **24**, 649–672.

Marquis, D. (1969). Ways of organizing projects. *Innovation*, **5**, 26–33.

Meer-Kooistra, J. van der & Scapens, R. (2004). The governance of lateral relations between and within organizations. Paper presented at the *Annual Congress of the European Accounting Association*, Prague.

McNair, C. J., Lynch, R. L. & Cross, K. F. (1990). Do financial and nonfinancial performance measures have to agree?. *Management Accounting (USA)*, **November**, 28–36.

Mensah, Y. M., Hwang, N. R. & Wu, D. (2004). Does managerial accounting research contribute to related disciplines? An examination using citation analysis. *Journal of Management Accounting Research*, **16**, 163–182.

Merchant, K. (1987). How and why firms disregard the controllability principle. In: W. J. Bruns, & R. S. Kaplan (Eds), *Accounting and Management: Field Study Perspectives*. Boston, MA: Harvard Business School Press, pp. 316–338.

Merchant, K. S. A., Van der Stede, W. & Zheng, L. (2003). Disciplinary constraints in the advancement of knowledge: the case of organizational incentive systems. *Accounting, Organizations and Society*, **28**(2–3), 251–286.

Meyer, M. W. (2002). *Rethinking performance measurement: beyond the balanced scorecard*. Cambridge, UK: Cambridge University Press.

Moers, F. (2005). Discretion and bias in performance evaluation: the impact of diversity and subjectivity. *Accounting, Organizations and Society*, **30**(1), 67–80.

Mouritsen, J. & Hansen, A. (2006). Management accounting, operations and network relations: debating the lateral dimension. In: A. Bhimani (Ed.), *Contemporary Issues in Management Accounting*. Oxford, UK: Oxford University Press, pp. 266–290.

Mouritsen, J., Larsen, H. T. & Pukh, P. N. D. (2001). Intellectual capital and the "capable firm" narrating, visualizing and numbering for managing knowledge. *Accounting, Organizations and Society*, **26**(7–8), 735–767.

Mouritsen, J. & Thrane, S. (2006). Accounting, network complementarities and the development of interorganisational relations. *Accounting, Organizations and Society*, **31**(3), 241–275.

Mowday, R. T., Steers, R. M. & Porter, L. W. (1979). The measurement of organizational commitment. *Journal of Vocational Behavior*, **14**, 224–247.

Narver, J. C. & Slater, S. F. (1990). The effect of a market orientation on business profitability. *Journal of Marketing*, **54**, 20–35.

Neely, A., Adams, C. & Kennerley, K. (2002). *The Performance Prism: The Scorecard for Measuring and Managing Business Success*. London, UK: Financial Times Prentice Hall.

Nouri, H. (1994). Using organizational commitment and job involvement to predict budgetary slack: A research note. *Accounting, Organizations and Society*, **19**(3), 289–295.

Nouri, H. & Parker, R. J. (1998). The relationship between budget participation and job performance: The roles of budget adequacy and organizational commitment. *Accounting, Organizations and Society*, **23**(5–6), 467–483.

Nørreklit, H. (2000). The balance on the balanced scorecard a critical analysis of some of its assumptions. *Management Accounting Research*, **11**(1), 65–88.

Nørreklit, H. (2003). The Balanced Scorecard: what is the score? A rhetorical analysis of the Balanced Scorecard. *Accounting, Organizations and Society*, **28**(6), 591–619.

Oliver, A. L. & Ebers, M. (1998). Networking network studies: an analysis of conceptual configurations in the study of inter-organisational relationships. *Organisation Studies*, **19**(4), 549–583.

Ostroff, F. (1999). *The Horizontal Organization*. New York, NY: Oxford University Press.

Ravasi, D. & Schultz, M. (2006). Responding to organizational identity threats: exploring the role of organizational culture. *Academy of Management Journal*, **49**(3), 433–458.

Reichheld, F. F. (1996). *The Loyalty Effect: The Hidden Force behind Growth, Profits and Lasting Value*. Boston, MA: Harvard Business School Press.

Romme, G. L. (1996). A note on the hierarchy-team debate. *Strategic Management Journal*, **17**(5), 411–417.

Roslender, R. & Hart, S. J. (2003). In search of strategic management accounting: theoretical and filed study perspectives. *Management Accounting Research*, **14**(3), 255–279.

Roth, P. L. & Bobko, P. (1997). A research agenda for multi-attribute utility analysis. human resources management. *Human Resource Management Review*, **7**(3), 341–368.

Seybold, P. (1998). *Customer.com*. New York, NY: Times Books.

Scapens, R. (2006). Changing times: management accounting research and practice from a UK perspective. In: A. Bhimani (Ed.), *Contemporary Issues in Management Accounting*. Oxford, UK: Oxford University Press, pp. 329–354.

Schonberger, R. J. (1990). *Building a Chain of Customers: Linking Business Functions to Create a World Class Company*. New York, NY: The Free Press.

Schonberger, R. J. (1996). *World Class Manufacturing: The Next Decade*. New York, NY: The Free Press.

Schonberger, R. J. (2001). *Let's fix it, overcoming the crisis in manufacturing*. New York, NY: The Free Press.

Schonberger, R. J. & Knod, E. M. Jr. (1994). *SynchroService! An Innovative way to Build a Dynasty of Customers*. New York, NY: Richard Irwin.

Scott, T. W. & Tiessen, P. (1999). Performance measurement and managerial teams. *Accounting, Organizations and Society*, **24**(3), 107–125.

Shank, J. K. (2006). Strategic cost management: upsizing, downsizing, and right (?) sizing. In: A. Bhimani (Ed.), *Contemporary Issues in Management Accounting*. Oxford, UK: Oxford University Press, pp. 355–379.

Silk, S. (1998). Automating the balanced scorecard. *Management Accounting*, **78**(11), 38–42.

Suzaki, K. (1987). *The New Manufacturing Challenge: Techniques for Continuous Improvement*. London, UK: The Free Press.

Sveiby, K. E. (1997). *The New Organizational Wealth*. San Francisco, CA: Berrett-Koehler Publishers, Inc.

Szulanski, G. & Jensen, R. J. (2006). Presumptive adaptation and the effectiveness of knowledge transfer. *Strategic Management Journal*, **27**(10), 937–957.

Tagiuri, R. & Litwin, G. H. (1968). Organizational culture: A key to financial performance. In: B. Schneider (Ed.), *Organizational Climate and Culture*. San Francisco, CA: Jossey-Bass.

Teece, D. J., Pisano, G. & Shuen, A. (1997). Dynamic capabilities and strategic management. *Strategic Management Journal*, **18**(7), 509–533.

Tidd, J. & Trewhella, M. J. (1997). Organizational and technological antecedents for knowledge acquisition and learning. *R and D Management*, **27**(4), 359–375.

Tomkins, C. (2001). Interdependencies, trust and information in relationships, alliances and networks. *Accounting, Organizations and Society*, **26**(2), 161–191.

Van de Ven, A. (1991). The development of an infrastructure for entrepreneurship. *Journal of Business Venturing*, **8**, 211–230.

Von Oetinger, B. (2004). From ideas to innovation: making creativity real. *Journal of Business Strategy*, **15**(5), 35–41.

Widener, S. K. (2004). An empirical investigation of the relation between the use of strategic human capital and the design of management control system. *Accounting, Organizations and Society*, **29**(3–4), 377–399.

Winter, S. (2003). Understanding dynamic capabilities. *Strategic Management Journal*, **24**(10), 991–995.

Womack, J. P., Jones, D. & Roos, D. (1991). *The Machine that Changed the World*. New York, NY: Harper Perennial.

Young, S. M. & Selto, F. H. (1991). New manufacturing practices and cost management: a review of the literature and directions for future research. *Journal of Accounting Literature*, **10**, 265–298.

Zaccaro, S. & Banks, D. (2004). Leader visioning and adaptability: bridging the gap between research and practice on developing the ability to manage. *Human Resource Management*, **43**(3), 367.

Zajac, E. J., Matthew, S., Kraatz, R. K. & Bresser, F. (2000). Modelling the dynamics of strategic fit: a normative approach to strategic change. *Strategic Management Journal*, **21**(4), 429–453.

Handbook of Management Accounting Research
Edited by Christopher S. Chapman, Anthony G. Hopwood and Michael D. Shields

Extending the Boundaries: Nonfinancial Performance Measures

Christopher D. Ittner[1] and David F. Larcker[2]

[1]*The Wharton School, University of Pennsylvania, USA*
[2]*Graduate School of Business, Stanford University, USA*

Abstract: Consistent with the growing use of nonfinancial performance measures by public and private sector organizations, researchers are placing increasing emphasis on the choice, use and performance consequences of these measures. Although this emphasis has produced a variety of informative studies using a diverse set of research designs, researchers face the ongoing challenge of determining how to significantly extend studies on nonfinancial measures in order to prevent stagnation in this research stream, increase our understanding of measurement practices and benefits, and respond to the emerging performance measurement issues facing organizations.

Our objective is to examine some of the means available to extend the boundaries of research on nonfinancial performance measures. These include both advances in research designs and the examination of new research topics. Although our discussion primarily focuses on quantitative empirical studies, the research issues and emerging topics we cover are equally applicable to qualitative, experimental and theoretical research on nonfinancial performance measurement.

We begin by providing a broad overview of existing empirical studies on the three primary research topics examined in this literature:

1. the association between nonfinancial performance and current or future economic returns;
2. the factors influencing the choice of nonfinancial performance measures and the relative emphasis placed on financial and nonfinancial measures;
3. the performance effects of nonfinancial performance measurement systems. In conducting this overview, we highlight opportunities to improve or extend research on these traditional topics.

We then discuss several emerging research areas that have received relatively little emphasis in the management accounting literature. These topics include the evolution in firms' nonfinancial performance measurement practices, the use of nonfinancial measures for risk management purposes, the roles of these measures in corporate governance, and the links between the internal use of nonfinancial measures and the external disclosure of this information (the latter of which we consider an important component of management control systems).

1. The Association between Nonfinancial Measures and Economic Performance

A substantial body of literature has examined the claim that nonfinancial measures are leading indicators of economic performance that provide incremental information beyond that provided by current financial measures (see Wyatt, 2008, for a review). These studies take two general forms. Cross-sectional value-relevance studies typically investigate whether firms' stock market values are associated with nonfinancial information, after controlling for the accounting book values of assets and liabilities and other financial measures such as past earnings. The assumptions underlying these tests are that the market value of the firm is based on the expected net present value of future cash flows, that nonfinancial measures are a potential source of incremental information on future cash flows, that market participants have access to the information contained in the nonfinancial measures used by the researcher, and that the market correctly impounds this information into stock price. If these assumptions

DOI: 10.1016/S1751-3243(07)03002-7

are not true, then the resulting empirical results will be unreliable.

A smaller number of value-relevance studies attempt to provide stronger tests of the market implications of nonfinancial information by examining whether the release of new information on nonfinancial performance affects short-term stock returns or whether hedge portfolios formed on the basis of nonfinancial performance can beat stock market returns in the future. The vast majority of both types of value-relevance studies find that information on nonfinancial performance provides incremental information to the stock market.

A second set of tests examines the relationship between nonfinancial measures and current or future accounting performance (i.e., costs, revenues, or profits) using either publicly-available or firm-specific data. As with the value-relevance studies, this research generally reports significant positive associations between nonfinancial measures and financial performance. However, the time lag between changes in nonfinancial performance and financial performance in these studies is often quite short. Ittner & Larcker (1997b) find that customer satisfaction is reflected in financial performance, with a one quarter to one year lag in the banking and telecommunications firms in their samples. Banker et al. (2000) find a six month lag between customer satisfaction and financial performance in a hotel chain. Nagar & Rajan's (2001) examination of quality measures in a manufacturing firm finds that changes in these measures are reflected in revenue changes in three quarters or less. While the short lags in these studies may be unique to certain types of nonfinancial measures or competitive settings, they raise important questions about the validity of claims that nonfinancial measures (in general) are beneficial because they contain information on long-term performance that is not captured in short-term accounting measures.

A number of studies also find that the relationship between nonfinancial measures and financial performance can be quite complex. Ittner's (1993) analysis indicates that the indirect effects of nonfinancial quality measures on manufacturing plant productivity (through their impact on inventory levels and schedule realization) greatly exceed their direct effects, with the indirect effects not captured by the firm's financial quality cost measurement system. Nagar & Rajan's (2005) study in the banking industry finds that individual financial and nonfinancial measures have no direct association with future earnings, but that these measures collectively interact to influence subsequent financial performance. Ittner & Larcker (1997b, 2005) identify non-linearities in the relationship between customer satisfaction measures and economic outcomes in both service and manufacturing firms.

Ryan et al. (1995), Sedatole (2003) and others provide further evidence that different methods for measuring the same nonfinancial attribute (e.g., the functional form used to determine whether a product is defective, the specific questions or issues covered in a survey, the number of survey scale points, etc.) can have dramatically different abilities to predict financial performance, suggesting that the appropriate nonfinancial measurement methodology in one situation may not be suitable in another. The results from these studies imply that the relationship between nonfinancial performance and economic returns is likely to depend not only on factors such as the organization's strategy and competitive environment, but also on its specific measurement methods (among many other factors), highlighting an important research design challenge for large sample, cross-sectional studies.

In sum, the bulk of evidence on the relationship between nonfinancial performance and financial results indicates that nonfinancial measures can provide incremental information on future performance (often in complex ways). However, this evidence provides little or no support for claims that nonfinancial measures as a group are better indicators of long-term performance than short-term financial measures.

While it is highly likely that researchers can identify other contingencies or measurement attributes that influence the ability of nonfinancial measures to predict future financial performance, we believe that the greatest advances in this research stream will be made by understanding how (or if) organizations attempt to assess how their nonfinancial measures are expected to improve financial performance, and whether organizations try to validate whether the expected relationships actually occur.

Despite calls for firms to develop "causal business models" or "strategy maps" that explicitly lay out how changes in nonfinancial performance are expected to yield improvements in economic performance (e.g., Kaplan & Norton, 1996), surveys indicate that the majority of firms do not develop these models when choosing performance measures (Gates, 1999; Ittner & Larcker, 2003; Ittner et al., 2003). Instead, the expected relationships are frequently based on unarticulated heuristics or intuition. While heuristics and intuition are clearly necessary for decision-making, they may be inappropriate when they are based on past experience that is no longer applicable or are based on flawed assumptions, reducing their effectiveness in choosing performance measures.

When causal business models are developed, the resulting models can exhibit quite different relationships depending upon the methods and managers used to elicit the expected cause-and-effect relationships. For example, the beliefs about these relationships by individual participants within the same firm need not be consistent. Carr & Ponemon (1992) survey key managers in eleven high-technology firms on their perceptions of the effects of quality investments on financial performance. They find that controllers and marketing managers believe that prevention costs increase and failure costs decline as quality improves, while production and general managers believe that both types of costs decline with quality improvements. This evidence suggests that various players within the same firm can have very different (often unarticulated) beliefs regarding the relationship between certain nonfinancial measures (such as quality improvements) and financial consequences.

Similarly, the methods used to elicit the causal relationships can yield different expectations. For example, Abernethy et al. (2005) use multiple approaches, including computerized analysis of interview data, ethnographic analysis and interactive mapping by participants, to develop causal models in a hospital. Although the models identified using the various methods are clearly related, each exhibits some unique and distinctly different relationships, again suggesting that beliefs regarding the relationship between nonfinancial measures and economic performance can vary significantly within organizations.

Given the potential differences in internal beliefs about the relationship between nonfinancial measures and financial performance within the same firm, together with the competing causal models found within many firms, an important issue is how organizations resolve these differences.[1] One recommendation offered in the performance measurement literature is for companies to validate the expected relationship in a manner similar to the empirical tests used by researchers to examine which measures are leading indicators. Kaplan & Norton (1996), for example, argue that the causal relations in the business models (or "strategy maps") are merely hypotheses that need to be tested.[2] However, surveys indicate that even in cases where explicit business models are developed, relatively few companies actually attempt to validate the links, and even fewer are able to do so when they try (Ittner & Larcker, 2003). As a result, the majority of companies studied by Ittner & Larcker (2005) make decisions based on unarticulated or unvalidated business models. When these researchers test the underlying heuristics or intuition in these companies, the organization's assumptions often prove wrong.

Future research can build on these studies to examine how formal or informal causal business models are developed and updated (if at all), and whether certain methods for developing and testing business models and choosing performance measures yield more valid and reliable nonfinancial measures. For example, advances in analytic techniques such as data mining and system dynamics modelling offer the promise of enhanced ability to identify and test relationships between (and among) nonfinancial measures and economic performance. Akkermans & van Oorschot (2005) and Laitinen (2006) demonstrate the use of system dynamics and simulation analysis for developing balanced scorecard measures in a Dutch insurer and Nokia, respectively. Similar studies can examine how these and other advanced analytic techniques influence organizations' understanding of causal relations between financial and nonfinancial measures, and whether these techniques influence performance measurement practices.

2. The Choice and Use of Nonfinancial Performance Measures

A second major research stream examines the factors influencing the choice and use of nonfinancial performance measures. Much of this research is motivated by contingency theories or principal–agent models which argue that the choice of performance measures should be a function of the informativeness of alternative performance measures and the measures' alignment with organizational objectives. Empirical studies generally support these theories, finding that organizations tend to make greater use of, or place more weight on, nonfinancial measures when pursuing a "prospector," "build," or "innovation" strategy or facing greater perceived environmental uncertainty (see Langfield-Smith, 1997, 2005, for reviews), having larger growth opportunities, employing operational strategies such as just-in-time production, flexible manufacturing systems and total quality management (e.g., Banker et al., 1993; Abernethy & Lillis, 1995; Ittner & Larcker, 1995, 1997), having longer product development cycles (e.g., Bushman et al., 1996; Said et al., 2003), operating in regulated industries (e.g., Bushman et al., 1996; Ittner et al., 1997; Said et al., 2003), and having financial measures with greater "noise" and lower sensitivity and precision (e.g., Ittner et al., 1997; Moers, 2007).

The majority of these studies use an aggregate proxy for the overall use of nonfinancial measures (e.g., the overall percentage weight placed on nonfinancial measures of any kind or survey responses on the use of various types of nonfinancial measures aggregated to form a single index) or for the use of a specific type of measure

[1]Another important research issue raised by these studies is the validity of surveys of performance measurement practices that use a single respondent. If different organizational participants in a given company differ in their views of the importance of the surveyed performance attributes or performance measures, using a single survey respondent can lead to biased answers and research results.

[2]Several experimental studies have identified potential benefits from identifying or providing employees with causal models when using nonfinancial measures (e.g., Banker et al., 2004; Oz et al., 2007; Wong-On-Wing et al., 2007). However, the use of causal business models has not been universally embraced in the performance measurement literature. See, for example, Nørreklit's (2000, 2003) critiques of cause-and-effect relations in the balanced scorecard.

(e.g., similar proxies for the emphasis on quality or flexibility measures) without considering the other measures used by the organization. However, nonfinancial measures (as well as financial measures[3]) are not monolithic. Even within a given performance category, different measures can be measured in various dimensions (e.g., percentages, survey scales, times, achievement of milestones) or assessed at different units of analysis (e.g., individual, team, business unit or firm),[4] can be objective or subjective, can capture different attributes of the same broad construct (e.g., manufacturing-related quality problems within a manufacturing plant versus engineering-related quality failures in the field) and can have different measurement properties (e.g., sensitivity, precision and verifiability). Since the factors affecting the choices among these nonfinancial measurement differences are likely to vary, advances in our understanding of performance measurement practices require researchers to take these differences into consideration not only for individual measures or types of measures, but also as part of a portfolio of measurement choices.

Even though most studies assume that measures that are not traditional short-term financial metrics such as accounting profits or returns must be nonfinancial, individual measures within many common categories that researchers define as "nonfinancial" can be either financial or nonfinancial (e.g., defect rates versus quality costs, customer satisfaction versus customer profitability, brand awareness versus brand value). However, surveys typically ask about the use of customer, employee, operational or other measures without asking whether these categories are assessed using financial or nonfinancial metrics. As a result, it is difficult to determine whether it is the measurement of nontraditional performance categories or the use of nonfinancial measures that is being investigated.

More importantly, different nonfinancial measures can have different measurement properties. Table 1 illustrates one of the problems that can arise when aggregating proxies for different types of nonfinancial measures into a single construct. The table reports Pearson correlations between the sensitivity, precision and verifiability of financial, internal nonfinancial and external nonfinancial measures using survey data gathered for Moers, (2006) study of the effects of measurement properties on performance measurement choices in 105 units belonging to six Dutch companies. Moers' survey defines financial measures as "traditional" aggregate financial measures (e.g., ROA or net income), internal nonfinancial measures as those directly related to task performance (e.g., productivity or project implementation), and external nonfinancial measures as those reflecting performance in the market (e.g., customer satisfaction, market share or market growth). Three measurement properties (sensitivity, precision and verifiability) are assessed for each of these categories. These properties relate to the extent to which performance measures in each category are influenced by:

1. the managers actions;
2. factors outside the managers control; and
3. the measurement process itself.

As discussed by Moers (2006), principal–agent theory suggests that differences in these measurement properties should influence the weights placed on different performance measures.

The correlations in Table 1 indicate that in this setting the measurement properties of external nonfinancial measures are more closely related to the measurement properties of financial measures than to those of internal nonfinancial measures. For example, the correlation is 0.373 ($p < 0.01$) between the sensitivities of financial and external nonfinancial measures, but the correlation between the sensitivities of internal and external nonfinancial measures is only 0.246 ($p < 0.05$). In addition, some of the measurement properties are not significantly correlated across the two nonfinancial categories in a number of the individual comparisons (e.g., between sensitivity in one nonfinancial category and precision in the other), but are significantly correlated within a given category of measures (e.g., between the sensitivity and precision of external nonfinancial measures). Consequently, if the internal and external nonfinancial measurement categories are lumped into a single construct, the resulting statistical inferences may be biased.

[3]See Bouwens & van Lent (2007) for a study examining the factors influencing different types of financial performance measures in organizations.

[4]For example, in a survey of US firms we conducted with PricewaterhouseCoopers, 70% of the respondents with balanced scorecards implemented these systems at the corporate level, 90% at the business unit level, 40% at the product or market segment level, and 33% at the department, plant, or office level. When asked whether they used common or individually tailored scorecard measures, 15% stated that they used all common measures, 35% used mostly common measures, 17% used mostly tailored measures, and 3% used all individually tailored measures. The extent to which scorecards were used for incentive compensation also varied by level, with 87% of the scorecards used for senior management incentives, 84% for middle management incentives and 48% for lower management incentives. These results indicate that researchers must be very careful in specifying the organizational level or manager being examined. They also highlight opportunities to investigate the factors affecting the use of similar or different measures at different organizational levels, the choice between individual or tailored measures, and the use of scorecard measures for compensation decisions.

Table 1. Pearson correlations among measurement properties for financial, internal nonfinancial and external nonfinancial measures from Moers (2007) survey of 105 units belonging to six Dutch firms.

	Financial			***Internal Nonfinancial***			***External Nonfinancial***		
	Sensitivity	Precision	Verifiability	Sensitivity	Precision	Verifiability	Sensitivity	Precision	Verifiability
Financial									
Sensitivity	1								
Precision	−0.061	1							
Verifiability	0.212**	−0.131	1						
Internal nonfinancial									
Sensitivity	0.184*	−0.091	−0.84	1					
Precision	−0.136	0.389***	0.119	−0.094	1				
Verifiability	0.165*	−0.058	0.212**	0.262***	−0.087	1			
External nonfinancial									
Sensitivity	0.373***	−0.260***	0.155	0.246**	−0.123	0.204**	1		
Precision	−0.114	0.669***	0.020	−0.142	0.525***	0.001	−0.264***	1	
Verifiability	0.244**	−0.029	0.375***	0.176	0.030	0.378***	0.373***	0.004	1

***, **, * = statistically significant at the 1%, 5% and 10% levels respectively

Financial measures are defined as "traditional" aggregate financial measures (e.g., ROA, net income), internal nonfinancial measures are defined as those directly related to tasks performed (e.g., productivity, project implementation), and external nonfinancial measures are defined as those reflecting performance in the market (e.g., customer satisfaction, market share, market growth). Sensitivity, precision and verifiability refer to the extent to which each type of performance measure is influenced by the manager's actions, factors outside the manager's control and the measurement process, respectively. See Moers (2007) for the specific survey questions and construct development.

The benefits from specific types of nonfinancial measures may also differ depending upon the organization's measurement objectives. For example, the majority of compensation studies assume that the primary goal of these systems is improving incentives for employees to take the actions desired by the firm's owners. This assumption is consistent with agency models, but ignores other potential goals such as the use of performance appraisals for career development or the use of compensation plans to foster teamwork, link bonuses more closely to the firm's ability to pay, enhance communication of business objectives or improve the firm's ability to attract and retain key employees.

Prendergast's (1999) agency model demonstrates that these alternative objectives have major implications for the design of performance measurement and compensation plans. Consistent with this prediction, Ittner & Larcker's (2001) study of worker incentive plans finds the performance measures in these plans to be significantly influenced by the plans' objectives. Using cluster analysis, they identify three configurations of measurement choices:

1. profit-based plans focused almost exclusively on accounting profits;
2. plans focused on a mix of financial and nonfinancial business unit or facility-level measures such as cost, volume and quality;
3. plans focused on nonfinancial worker-related or behavioural measures such as safety, attendance, and productivity.

In many cases, the influence of plan objectives on the plan's cluster differs from the objectives influencing the use of aggregate financial versus nonfinancial measures. In addition, the factors influencing the choice of specific types of measures within the individual clusters (e.g., cost control, volume and quality within their business unit cluster) also vary, with the goal of linking bonuses more closely to the firm's ability to pay, positively associated with the use of profit, cost control, volume and quality measures, and negatively associated with productivity and safety measures; organizational change goals positively associated with cost, quality, productivity and safety measures, but negatively associated with attendance; and workforce enhancement goals positively associated with attendance measures, but negatively associated with cost, quality, productivity and safety measures.

Campbell's (2007) examination of store managers in a fast food chain adds that nonfinancial measures play a greater role in promotion decisions (the primary source of significant pay raises for most middle managers) in his research site, while financial measures play a greater role in determining bonuses in the manager's current job. Campbell's results again suggest that a general question on the use of nonfinancial measures for evaluating managerial performance is likely to be incomplete, and emphasize the need for researchers to be very specific when articulating the study's decision context to research participants and readers, even when examining a relatively narrow issue such as compensation and performance evaluation.

Empirical studies motivated by economic and contingency theories typically overlook organizational and psychological influences on the choice and use of performance measures. In contrast, Waggoner et al.'s (1999) interdisciplinary review of the performance measurement literature notes that organizations are "political arenas" in which divergent constituencies attempt to institutionalize performance criteria that serve their interests. The potential conflicts that arise as various constituencies and stakeholder groups try to promote self-interested performance measures are resolved through the use of power and bargaining. Their review suggests that internal politics and the participation of different stakeholder groups in incentive plan design can influence the performance measures included in the plan, independent of the measures ability to motivate or assess worker performance.

Experiments (e.g., Lipe & Salterio, 2000) and archival research (e.g., Ittner et al., 2003) indicate that psychological biases can also influence the weights organizational participants place on different types of financial and nonfinancial measures, and have started to identify various mechanisms that appear to reduce these biases (e.g., Banker et al., 2004; Oz et al., 2007). Only when empirical studies begin to assess these multiple perspectives and mechanisms will we fully understand the determinants of performance measure selection and use.

Finally, greater attention needs to be paid to the use of nonfinancial measures for purposes other than managerial performance evaluation and compensation, such as capital justification, operational improvement decisions and cultural or strategic change initiatives. Ittner & Larcker (2003) provide evidence that the importance of nonfinancial performance measures for one purpose often differs from their importance for another. Future studies can examine the factors influencing the use of nonfinancial measures for these other purposes, as well as those influencing the consistency (or lack of consistency) of nonfinancial measurement use across various purposes.[5]

[5]For example, experimental studies suggest that participants use different measures for evaluating the business unit than for evaluating the unit's manager, with participants favouring nonfinanical measures for managerial performance evaluation and financial measures for business unit evaluation. Similarly, agency models show that it may be optimal to use different criteria to evaluate business units and their managers since the factors useful in determining the value of the firm need not be the same as those useful for determining whether the agent took the actions desired by the principal.

3. Performance Implications of Nonfinancial Measures

A third major research stream in the nonfinancial measurement literature examines whether the use of these measures (or performance measurement frameworks, such as the balanced scorecard, that emphasize their use) is associated with measurement system satisfaction or organizational performance. These studies take two general forms:

1. large-sample, cross-sectional studies investigating whether firms making greater use of nonfinancial measures for decision-making or compensation purposes are associated with higher satisfaction or perceived organizational performance, or with actual accounting and stock returns;
2. quasi-experimental, company-level analyses examining whether accounting performance improved after the adoption of measurement systems with greater emphasis on nonfinancial measures.

Cross-sectional studies examine whether firms making greater or more appropriate use of nonfinancial measures or measurement techniques, such as the balanced scorecard, achieve higher performance. Two research design choices are extremely important in this literature:

1. the method used to evaluate the use of nonfinancial measures;
2. the use of perceptual or actual outcome variables.

Ittner et al. (2003) discuss three primary approaches for assessing the use of nonfinancial measures in cross-sectional studies. The simplest approach assesses the diversity in the types of financial and nonfinancial measures used by the organization (i.e., more measures are nonfinancial versus financial or more categories of nonfinancial measures are used), with no information on the different measures' relative importance. A second approach examines the relative importance or weights placed on the various measures. The most sophisticated approach draws on contingency and agency theories to assess the "match" or "fit" between the organization's use of nonfinancial measures and its strategy, value drivers and competitive environment.

Cross-sectional studies can assess performance using perceptual measures (such as satisfaction with the measurement system or perceived organizational performance relative to internal targets or competitors) or using actual accounting or stock market performance (either self-reported by survey respondents or from public sources). Company-specific, quasi-experimental studies, on the other hand, compare actual accounting performance before and after the implementation of the nonfinancial performance measures, with a sample of non-adopters often used to control for time series trends and other common factors that potentially influence performance in all of the units, but are unrelated to the new measures.

Literature reviews by Franco & Bourne (2004) and Ittner (2008) indicate that the majority of published performance studies find significant, positive associations between the use of nonfinancial measures and measurement system satisfaction or organizational performance, particularly when the emphasis on nonfinancial measures is aligned with the organization's sources of competitive advantage. But the two reviews also indicate that the strength of these associations declines as the sophistication of the analyses increases, emphasizing the importance of research design choices when assessing the performance benefits from nonfinancial performance measures. The vast majority of cross-sectional studies using satisfaction or perceived performance as outcome variables report significant positive associations, but results are mixed in cross-sectional studies when actual economic performance is used to assess performance effects (particularly with respect to balanced scorecard usage). Results are even more mixed in the small number of quasi-experimental, company-level performance studies (e.g., Banker et al., 2000; Davis & Albright, 2004; Neely, 2007; Griffith & Neely, 2007).

The weaker results in studies using more sophisticated research designs raise important questions regarding the advantages and disadvantages of these various designs. Cross-sectional studies using perceptual outcome measures have the advantage of allowing the researcher to assess economic performance effects in settings where actual outcome measures are not accessible (due to the lack of publicly-available data or survey respondents' reluctance or inability to provide actual performance results) and where improvements in nonfinancial performance only produce economic performance gains with some lag.

However, perceptual outcome measures have a number of limitations. First, having a single respondent answer survey questions about both performance measurement system characteristics and outcomes (as is generally the case) can lead to common method biases that increase the likelihood that a significant, positive association is found (Podakoff et al., 2003). Secondly, surveys commonly ask respondents to rate performance relative to competitors or internal expectations on a scale such as 1 = "significantly below" to 5 = "significantly above," but differences in the choice of competitive peers, internal targets, or the interpretation of "significant" can lead to substantially different responses. Thirdly, the outcome measures often relate to unspecified "overall" performance or are based on aggregated performance on multiple financial and nonfinancial dimensions (with the relative weights placed on different categories of financial and nonfinancial measures varying with the respondents perceptions about their relative weighting or importance, which often differ across studies). However, research indicates that improvements in nonfinancial performance dimensions do not always translate into improved economic results (e.g., Ittner & Larcker, 2005). Consequently, higher perceived nonfinancial performance does not necessarily mean that these improvements will yield higher actual economic performance.

Cross-sectional studies using actual accounting or stock market performance as outcome variables overcome possible common method biases, and the outcome measures may be more verifiable and more closely linked to the economic returns that are the ultimate goals of most performance measurement initiatives. However, the use of actual financial outcome measures may not pick up interim improvements in nonfinancial performance dimensions that have not yet yielded financial improvements and (in the case of publicly-available performance data) may lack direct correspondence between the units of analysis used for the surveyed measurement practices and the outcome measures (e.g., survey participants may respond with respect to their business units, but publicly-available performance data may only be available at the firm level).

Regardless of their use of perceptual or actual outcome variables, cross-sectional performance studies face the problem of assessing complex performance measurement practices using surveys or public disclosures without the ability to directly evaluate these measurement practices. As discussed earlier, measurement choices include not only the aggregate use of financial or nonfinancial measures and their relative importance, but also the specific types of measures or techniques used to measure nonfinancial performance dimensions (e.g., customer or employee measures; measures based on survey responses, counts, percentages or time-based measures; quantitative or qualitative measures; relative or absolute measures; etc.).

A simple example of the interpretation problems that can arise when finer distinctions in measurement practices are not taken into account is presented in Table 2.

Table 2. OLS regressions of measurement system satisfaction on different proxies for nonfinancial performance measure use in 157 US firms.

	(1)	(2)	(3)
Intercept	2.140***	1.932***	3.120***
Model	0.134*	0.111	0.159**
Test	−0.083	−0.82	−0.065
ACCT	−0.049	−0.054	−0.091
NF	0.301**		
Customer		0.200***	
Employee		0.026	
Efficiency		0.119	
Quality		−0.001	
Alliance		−0.086	
Innovation		−0.015	
Community/environment		−0.099	
BSC			0.281*
Adj. R^2	0.121	0.149	0.102
F-statistic	5.833***	3.474***	5.042***

***, **, * = statistically significant at the 1%, 5% and 10% levels (two-tailed), respectively

Model equals the extent to which the company has developed formal causal business models or maps (from 1 = not at all to 5 = completely) and Test equals the extent to which the company has attempted to test whether nonfinancial performance is related from future accounting or stock market performance (from 1 = not attempted to 4 = to a great extent). ACCT equals the extent to which current accounting results are used to make evaluations and management decisions (from 1 = to no extent to 5 = a great extent). Similarly, Customer, Employee, Efficiency, Quality, Alliance, Innovation and Community/Environment equal the extent to which nonfinancial measures in these categories are used to make evaluations and management decisions (from 1 = to no extent to 5 = a great extent). NF is the equally-weighted average response for the seven nonfinancial measurement categories. BSC is an indicator variable for the use of a balanced scorecard.

The table reports regressions of measurement system satisfaction (obtained from a survey of a diverse sample of US firms we conducted with PricewaterhouseCoopers) on three sets of variables that are commonly used to capture measurement practices. The first model regresses measurement system satisfaction on the use of short-term accounting measures and an aggregate measure of nonfinancial measurement use (assessed using the equally-weighted importance placed on seven categories of nonfinancial measures). The second model regresses satisfaction on the accounting usage variable and individual usage variables for the seven nonfinancial measurement categories. The third model replaces the nonfinancial performance measurement variables with an indicator variable for the use of a balanced scorecard. To control for other potential determinants of measurement system satisfaction, each model also includes variables for the extent to which the firm has developed causal business models and has tested the hypothesized links in the business models.

When an aggregate measure for the use of nonfinancial measures or an indicator for the reported use of a balanced scorecard are included in the models, the coefficients on the aggregate and balanced scorecard measures are positive and significant, suggesting that these practices improve measurement system satisfaction. However, when separate variables for the use of the seven individual nonfinancial measurement categories are included in the model, the adjusted R^2 increases and only the use of customer measures is statistically significant, suggesting that it is the use of customer measures rather than the use of other types of nonfinancial measures, nonfinancial measures in general, or a balanced scorecard that drives measurement system satisfaction. Moreover, the use of business modelling is no longer significant when the individual categories are included in the model.[6]

While these simple tests are clearly open to criticism, they point out the need to move beyond aggregate proxies for measurement practices in performance tests. In addition, other measurement practices, such as the targets set for the measures, the use of causal business models for choosing and validating measures, factors such as the amount of pay at risk and the presence of performance hurdles or payout caps in compensation studies, the other management control systems used by the organization, as well as other organizational and strategic changes that are implemented at the same time as the measurement system, are likely to have significant effects on the performance consequences of different measurement practices.[7] These distinctions in measurement practices (either individually or interacting as elements of an integrated measurement system) need to be incorporated into performance tests if our understanding of the performance implications of nonfinancial performance measures is to be complete.

Potential lags may also exist between measurement system implementation and any resulting performance effects. As a result, it can be difficult for cross-sectional tests to identify performance benefits from nonfinancial measures if researchers do not know how long the measurement system has been in place and/or the lag between nonfinancial performance improvements and any economic consequences (particularly in diverse samples where these lags can vary significantly). At a minimum, researchers should attempt to ascertain how long the current performance measures have been in place and include this information in their performance tests.

An alternative to the use of large sample cross-sectional research designs is the use of quasi-experimental studies using company-specific time series data. In these studies, performance is compared before and after the implementation of nonfinancial measures, with a sample of non-adopters frequently used to further control for time series trends and other common factors that influence performance in both adopting and non-adopting units, but that are unrelated to the new systems.

Although small sample, quasi-experimental studies using data from a single company may not generalize to broader samples, they offer some of the most powerful tests of the claimed benefits from nonfinancial performance measurement. This power comes from the researcher's ability to determine the actual implementation date and to control for many potential confounding factors by comparing performance before and after implementation. Even greater power is achieved when a sample of non-adopters in the same company is used to control for time series trends and other factors that are unrelated to the new systems. Banker et al. (2000), for example, examine the implementation of an incentive system containing nonfinancial measures in a hotel chain. The authors use franchisees of the hotel chain (which did not implement the new system) to control for other factors that may impact all members of the chain (e.g., advertising campaigns). Similarly, Griffith & Neely (2007) use a matched

[6]Low variance inflation factor scores indicate that these differing results are not due to multicollinearity.

[7]See Ittner (2008), for a review of studies on the performance implications of causal business models. Implementation practices are another important issue that has not received sufficient attention in performance tests. Qualitative and perceptual studies suggest that technical and organizational barriers can have a significant impact on measurement system use and effectiveness. See Bourne et al. (2003), and Franco-Santos & Bourne (2004) for reviews.

sample of branches belonging to two divisions of a heating and plumbing distributor, one division an adopter and the other a non-adopter of a balanced scorecard incentive plan. The use of pre- and post-implementation tests and matched samples of non-adopters provide much stronger tests of causality and better controls for confounding factors than are generally available in cross-sectional studies.

Small sample performance studies also allow researchers to determine the specific measurement practices being adopted (i.e., measures, weights, targets, uses, etc.) and other organizational practices and changes surrounding the implementation. The intimate knowledge of measurement practices and other organizational issues available from quasi-experimental studies of a single firm allows researchers to incorporate this knowledge into their statistical models and their interpretation of the statistical results. For example, the new incentive plan in Banker et al.'s (2000) research site included greater variable pay, as well as the introduction of nonfinancial measures, and the authors are careful not to ascribe the observed performance effects from the new plan to the nonfinancial measures alone. This distinction would not be made in a cross-sectional study that only addresses the types of measures used by the organization.

Researchers conducting performance tests must weigh the advantages and disadvantages of the various research designs and attempt to minimize the limitations in their chosen design. With respect to cross-sectional studies, we believe that advances in nonfinancial performance studies require researchers to place greater emphasis on actual outcome variables (both financial and nonfinancial, as well as other objective measures such as system termination due to poor results) rather than satisfaction with the system or subjective assessments of system or organizational success. In addition, greater use of more objective measures of performance measurement practices (e.g., the actual number of measures or their weights in incentive contracts rather than subjective assessments of their use on Likert scales) can increase the credibility of performance tests. Finally, we encourage the use of small sample performance studies that incorporate both quantitative and qualitative analyses. Although these studies may lack the generalizability of large sample cross-sectional studies, they generally provide a better mechanism for obtaining the detailed knowledge of performance effects and their determinants that are critical for extending our understanding of measurement practices and outcomes.

4. Emerging Research Topics

Advances in the traditional topics discussed above are not the only means for extending the boundaries of research on nonfinancial performance measurement. In this section, we discuss four emerging topics that offer significant opportunities for future research: the dynamic aspects of performance measurement; nonfinancial measures and risk management; the role of nonfinancial measures in corporate governance; and the interplay between the use of nonfinancial measures for internal and external purposes.

4.1. Dynamic Aspects of Performance Measurement

One issue with major implications for our understanding of performance measurement choices and outcomes is the evolutionary nature of performance measurement practices. Empirical studies indicate that firms often make significant changes in the number, types and relative weights of nonfinancial measures over fairly short time periods. HassabElnaby et al. (2005), for example, find that 31.8% of US firms using nonfinancial measures for executive compensation dropped these measures within two years. Their quantitative and qualitative analyses identify a variety of explanations for the abandonment, including poor short-term financial returns, lack of "fit" between the measures and the organization's characteristics, CEO changes and changes in regulation. Ittner et al. (2003) describe how one financial services firm made significant changes in its branch manager bonus plan over five years, with the initial formula-based plan becoming increasingly complex as the organization attempted to prevent gaming, and was subsequently replaced by a subjective plan that experienced continual evolution in the weights placed on various financial and nonfinancial measures. Bol & Moers (2006) document a continual evolution in nonfinancial measurement in another bank. Malina & Selto's (2004) study of a manufacturer's distributor measurement system examines the factors influencing the extensive changes in performance measures and weights over a four year period.

Rapidly changing performance measurement systems offer both challenges and opportunities for researchers. On the one hand, assessing the performance implications of nonfinancial measures becomes difficult. If performance measures and weights are rapidly changing, it is difficult to determine the appropriate performance measures and weights to use in the study since survey responses or archival data for a given period may not apply in the next period. This is especially problematic if (as is likely) there is a lag between the implementation of a system and subsequent performance changes.

On the other hand, the rapid and ongoing evolution in nonfinancial performance measurement provides an interesting setting to examine the influence of economic, behavioural and political factors on measurement choices. A number of theories, for example, suggest that the evolution in performance measures is a function of organizational knowledge and learning. Dye (2004), for instance, develops a principal–agent model in which managers must choose a performance measurement system and strategic actions when the firm's profit drivers are uncertain. His results indicate that the firm's preferred performance measurement system is likely to change over time as experimentation leads management to revise their priors about what drives value. This finding is consistent with claims in the performance measurement literature that "feedback loops," "double-loop learning" and "strategic data analysis" are critical components in the effective use and evolution of strategic measurement systems (Kaplan & Norton, 1996; Ittner & Larcker, 2005).

Operations management researchers (e.g., Hayes et al., 1988; Carnegie Mellon, 1994; Ittner et al., 2001) argue that performance measurement choices are a function of the organization's stage of process knowledge and capability. The learning process begins by identifying the need for specific improvements. As the process progresses the level of required information becomes progressively higher as attempts are made to characterize the process, uncover the sources of normal and abnormal variation and understand how different variables and their interactions affect performance. In the early stages of process knowledge, operational performance measures range from nonexistent to random. As knowledge increases, the measures change from simple bottom-line metrics to families of metrics. Only at very high levels of knowledge and capability are the refined and interrelated metrics called for by causal modelling advocates implemented.

Courty & Marschke (2004) examine a different attribute of learning on measurement choices. They develop an evolutionary agency model of how organizations manage performance measures as knowledge of dysfunctional and unintended responses (or gaming) are revealed over time. Their model indicates that selecting measures based on their correlation with the firm's objectives will be flawed when gaming plays an important role and that the choice of performance measures must be experimental and dynamic in these settings.

Meyer & Gupta (1994), in turn, posit that measures "run down" over time as managerial actions cause the variance in the measures to shrink, reducing the measures' ability to discriminate good performance from bad. As a result, the authors argue that new measures that are orthogonal to existing measures emerge in their place.

In contrast to learning theories of performance measure evolution, Waggoner et al.'s (1999) review suggests that internal politics and power issues can also influence measurement changes. Consistent with this argument, Ittner & Larcker's (2003) field research finds that the number of performance measures often increases dramatically over time as self-interested managers attempt to get their measures included on balanced scorecards in order to increase the visibility of their operations (and themselves).

All of these theories are likely to hold to some extent. Researchers can attempt to discern the relative importance of these explanations in different settings, their influence on the specific measures and practices used over time and the performance implications of the different dynamic models.

4.2. Nonfinancial Measures and Risk Management

Recent crises, scandals and regulatory requirements, such as the Sarbanes-Oxley Act in the US and the Basel II requirements for financial service firms, have brought the issue of risk management and measurement to the fore. The Committee of Sponsoring Organizations of the Treadway Commission (COSO, 2004) defines risk as the possibility that an event will occur and adversely affect the achievement of objectives, and enterprise risk management (ERM) as a process applied to strategy setting and across the organization to identify potential risk events, manage the risks within the organization's risk appetite and provide reasonable assurance regarding the achievement of the organization's objectives.

COSO's ERM framework consists of eight interrelated components: the entities' internal environment with respect to risk; objective setting; event identification; risk assessment; risk response; control activities; information and communication; and monitoring. The risk management literature argues that nonfinancial measures can play important roles in several of these categories. For example, during event identification, analysis of internal and external measures can help the organization identify current and future risks, as well as each event's threshold value for triggering management action. The identification and reporting of nonfinancial "key risk indicators" (KRIs) and the development of models linking these indicators to predicted loss events can provide leading information for communication, control and monitoring purposes.

Two major challenges confronting the use of nonfinancial risk measures are selecting KRIs that are predictive of risk problems and estimating the relationships between these measures and the pattern of financial losses (Taylor & Davies, 2003). This is especially true for infrequent events (such as major fraud cases in banks) that firms may not have experienced in the past. To assist in modelling the probability distributions of infrequent risk events and losses some companies are relying on external data from third-party data providers such as FitchRisk, and others are beginning to share data on infrequent events. Researchers can assist these efforts by estimating the relationships between nonfinancial KPIs, actual events and financial losses from these events.

Another potential topic is examining how regulatory requirements, organizational and governance structure, the risks confronting the organization, risk appetite, and the overall enterprise risk management process influence the types and uses of risk measures and the impact of these choices on risk mitigation.

The interaction between risk measurement and other performance measurement practices may also be important.

A global survey of financial service firms by Deloitte (2004) finds that 20% of these firms used balanced scorecards for measuring risk, and more than 50% expected to do so in the future. In addition, McWhorter et al. (2006) find that firms reporting that they employ strategic performance measurement systems also report stronger risk management practices, leading the authors to conclude that strategic measurement practices improve risk management. Researchers can examine whether communication, monitoring and loss prevention are enhanced when risk measurement becomes a key element of the overall performance measurement system.

4.3. The Use of Nonfinancial Measures for Corporate Governance

In the principal–agent theories that underlie most economics-based management accounting studies, the goal of performance measurement and control systems is aligning the goals of the agent with those of the principal. As the representatives of shareholders (or other "owners" in non-profit settings), boards of directors act as principals who (theoretically) are responsible for motivating and evaluating the performance of agents, such as the organization's executives.

Considerable accounting research has focused on the corporate governance provided by boards of directors (see Larcker et al., 2007, for a review of studies linking governance and organizational performance). However, few studies have examined the types of measures used by boards to assess managerial or organizational performance. To the extent that nonfinancial measures provide information on managerial actions or organizational performance that is not captured in current financial measures, the use of nonfinancial measures by boards of directors may improve corporate governance.

Despite the potential governance benefits from nonfinancial measures, surveys indicate that significant disconnects often exist between the measures used by managers and the measures provided to the board. Ambler (2000), for example, finds no statistical relationship between the marketing measures used by managers and the marketing measures reaching the board. More importantly, the perceived importance of various nonfinancial performance categories to long-term value creation and the provision of measures related to these categories to board members often differ. Table 3 reports some of the results from a global survey of board-level measurement practices conducted by Deloitte (2007). Panel A of the table provides information on whether respondents believe the different financial and nonfinancial performance categories are key drivers of success, whether the board should monitor and/or take responsibility for performance on those dimensions (either individually or together with senior management), whether these measures are among the three performance categories receiving their greatest attention and the perceived quality of information on these dimensions given to the board.

The panel reveals some large differences between perceptions regarding the key nonfinancial success drivers and measurement quality and use. For example, 52% of respondents view customer performance to be a key driver of success (the highest percentage of any nonfinancial measure), but only 48% think it should be monitored by the board, 31.8% think the board should take responsibility, 34.3% rank customer measures among the three performance categories receiving their greatest attention, and only 23.1% rate the quality of customer information going to the board as "excellent." In contrast, only 5.4% state that performance related to society and the environment is a key driver of success, but more than three-quarters believe that boards should monitor and take responsibility for this performance dimension.

Panel B and C in Table 3 list the perceived barriers to effective use of nonfinancial measures by these board members and the leading triggers that would spur organizations to reassess their measurement practices. Many of the responses are consistent with the broader research topics discussed earlier. Among the various barriers to the use of nonfinancial measures are undeveloped analysis tools and scepticism that the measures are directly related to the bottom line, together with lack of accountability for and familiarity with these measures. In line with these results, the primary trigger that would lead organizations to reassess their measurement practices is greater understanding of how to measure nonfinancial performance, followed by a decline in customer performance, greater internal and external accountability demands and major compliance failures.

This evidence suggests a number of potential research topics. The most obvious is whether board use of nonfinancial measures is associated with firm performance. In one of the few studies examining this issue, Ittner & Larcker (1997a) find mixed evidence that the provision of quality measures to the board of directors influences performance, either directly or interacting with the organization's quality strategy. In the automotive industry, greater provision of quality information interacts positively with quality strategy to improve ROA and sales growth. However, the provision of quality information to the board has significant negative main effects on computer industry accounting returns and no interaction effect. Future studies can update and refine these analyses. For instance, how closely must the board's emphasis on various performance measurement dimensions match the overall perceived importance of these dimensions to firm value? Is it necessary for board members to both monitor and be accountable for these dimensions? Does the quality of performance information influence the board's ability to monitormanagers and improve firm

Table 3. The use of nonfinancial measures by boards of directors.

Panel A: Perceived importance, use and quality of performance measures.

	Key driver of success[a] %	Board should monitor[b] %	Board should take responsibility[b] %	Given greatest attention[c] %	Quality of information given to board[d] %
Financial	64.6	85.5	51.2	70.3	67.8
Governance and management	21.1	87.7	78.0	36.6	27.8
Employees	23.4	38.6	29.2	25.1	12.1
Customers	52.0	48.0	31.8	34.3	23.1
Operational performance	37.7	48.8	31.0	44.0	29.9
Quality	30.9	38.2	28.9	28.0	25.9
Innovation	28.0	61.4	48.8	19.4	19.2
External stakeholders	15.4	56.6	50.6	15.4	17.9
Society and environment	5.7	84.2	78.2	7.4	17.2
Brand strength	12.6	68.2	51.8	9.1	26.4

Panel B: Leading barriers to effective use of nonfinancial performance measures.[e]

	%
Undeveloped tools for analyzing such measures	55.5
Scepticism that these measures are directly related to the bottom line	48.0
Low levels of accountability for these aspects of performance	44.0
Lack of familiarity with these measures on part of management	41.1
Lack of familiarity with these measures on part of board members	40.1

Panel C: Leading triggers that are likely to spur the organization to reassess how it measures and monitors performance.[e]

	%
Greater understanding of how to measure nonfinancial drivers of performance	53.7
Sharp decline in customer satisfaction/retention	44.6
Board members or the CEO demand greater visibility and accountability	43.4
Competition for capital dictates expanded reporting and more stringent control	21.7
Major compliance failure	21.1

Source: Adapted from Deloitte Touche Tomatsu (2007)
[a]Percentage of respondents agreeing with the statement
[b]Percentage agreeing that the board of directors, either by itself or together with senior management, should monitor or take responsibility for this performance category
[c]Percentage placing this performance category among the top three areas they give the greatest attention
[d]Percentage ranking this performance category "excellent" instead of "average," "poor," or "don't know"
[e]The top five reasons receiving affirmative responses; respondents were allowed to select up to three reasons

performance? Research on topics such as these can make a significant contribution not only to the performance measurement literature, but also to the broader corporate governance literature.

4.4. The Interplay between Internal and External Uses of Nonfinancial Measures

Related to the issue of corporate governance is the external disclosure of performance information to shareholders and other stakeholders. By providing shareholders (i.e., principals) with information on managers' (i.e., agents') performance, external disclosures play a role in the management control process. External disclosure represents a major accounting research stream, and the disclosure of nonfinancial information has received some attention in this literature. As discussed earlier, a number of studies have examined the markets valuation of, or response to, the release of nonfinancial information, and other studies have examined the voluntary disclosure of nonfinancial information (e.g., Cerbioni & Parbonetti, 2007).

Table 4. OLS regressions linking external disclosure of performance measures in different categories to the measures perceived importance to long-term shareholder value, internal use for performance evaluation and decisions and perceived use by investors when evaluating the firm.

	ACCT	Customer	Employee	Efficiency	Quality	Alliance	Innovation	Community involvement
Intercept	1.240**	−0.339	−0.085	−0.261	−0.682	0.602**	0.141	0.008
Importance	−0.177	−0.113	−0.013	−0.127	−0.273**	0.076	−0.176	0.028
Internal use	0.074	0.304***	0.085	0.390***	0.628***	0.046	0.046	0.231***
Analyst use	0.656***	0.807***	0.910***	0.736***	0.703***	0.670***	0.670***	0.754***
Adj. R^2	0.283	0.533	0.596	0.564	0.550	0.462	0.462	0.666
F-test	15.353	41.692	52.134	46.700	44.217	31.286	46.373	70.042

***, **, * = statistically significant at the 1%, 5% and 10% levels (two-tailed), respectively

The dependent variables are the self-reported extent to which 157 US firms disclose information on short-term accounting performance (not required by GAAP), customer satisfaction and loyalty, employee satisfaction and turnover, operational efficiency, product and service quality, alliances, innovation, community involvement and environmental performance, respectively. Importance equals the perceived importance of that measurement category to long-term shareholder returns (from 1 = not at all important to 5 = extremely important), Internal use equals the self-reported use of that measurement category for internal evaluations and decision-making (from 1 = no extent to 5 = a great extent), and Analyst use equals the perceived extent to which analysts and investors consider the firms performance on that dimension when evaluating the firm.

What these studies have not examined is the interplay between the internal use of nonfinancial measures and external disclosure. Some authors claim that knowledge of the causal, nonfinancial drivers of firm value should influence not only the choice of internal performance measures, but also external disclosures (e.g., Black et al., 1998; Eccles et al., 2001; Gates, 1999). The argument behind this claim is that the same "value driver" measures that allow the organization to communicate strategic objectives, motivate behaviour against strategic goals and assess performance, also provide useful information that shareholders, potential investors and other stakeholders can use to assess firm value and monitor managerial actions.

These authors conclude that the measures disclosed by firms should be positively associated with the firm's perceived value drivers and the measures used for internal purposes. However, our examination of survey data on performance measurement practices in US firms indicates that the disclosure of information on various performance dimensions is associated more with the firms' beliefs about the measures considered by analysts and investors than by respondents beliefs that these performance dimensions are important determinants of long-term shareholder returns, or the internal use of measures for these dimensions for internal evaluations and management decisions.[8] The OLS regressions reported in Table 4 investigate the extent to which respondents disclose information on short-term accounting performance (not required under generally-accepted accounting principles) and seven categories of nonfinancial performance. In every case, the disclosure of information on a given performance dimension is positively and significantly associated with the perceived use of information on that dimension by analysts and investors. The extent to which customer, employee, quality, and community and environment measures are used for internal purposes are also positively associated with the extent to which information on these dimensions is disclosed (though the coefficients and significance levels suggest that the internal use of these measures has less influence on external disclosure than their perceived use by analysts and investors), but the importance of employee, alliance and innovation performance are not associated with disclosure of these measures. In contrast, the extent of external disclosure does not have a significant positive association with the perceived importance of any of the performance dimensions, and has a significant negative association with the perceived importance of product and service quality to the firms long-term shareholder returns.[9]

This evidence suggests that the majority of US firms do not align their disclosure practices with their perceived value drivers, and internal and external performance reporting is only related for a subset of performance dimensions. When a subsample of respondents who reported making limited disclosures on all or most of the

[8]The survey was conducted in conjunction with Pricewaterhouse-Coopers.

[9]Low VIF scores indicate that these results are not driven by multicollinearity. Results are similar when the three independent variables are entered into the model individually.

performance dimensions they claim to be important value drivers were asked why, the leading response was that competitors might use the information against them, followed by the market not understanding the information, the information not being sufficiently reliable to put on the market and the firm not yet completely understanding its value drivers.

Some of these issues are similar to those confronting the internal use of nonfinancial performance measures and the use of these measures by boards of directors. Studies can extend the boundaries of research on nonfinancial measures by investigating the factors influencing whether firms use similar or different measures for internal and external purposes, and whether greater alignment between the firms' value drivers and external disclosures and/or between internal and external measurement influence the organizations' cost of capital (the primary outcome examined in the economics-based disclosure literature) or other desired outcomes (such as minimizing pressure for greater emphasis on nonfinancial dimensions from institutional investors, government entities or other stakeholder groups).

5. Conclusions

Despite the large body of existing empirical research on nonfinancial performance measures, significant opportunities exist to extend the boundaries of this research. Though far from a comprehensive review of the literature, our overview of research on the links between nonfinancial measures and future financial performance, the determinants of measurement practices and the performance effects of nonfinancial measures, identifies a number of opportunities to improve on and extend studies on these traditional topics. Furthermore, a number of emerging topics provide exciting opportunities to expand the focus of nonfinancial performance measurement studies to governance, risk management and external disclosure issues that have largely been ignored in this literature. By expanding the boundaries of nonfinancial measurement studies, researchers can prevent stagnation in this research stream, increase our understanding of measurement practices and benefits, and respond to the emerging performance measurement issues facing organizations.

Acknowledgement

We thank Frank Moers for providing access to his survey data and PricewaterhouseCoopers for joint survey research. The financial support of Ernst & Young is greatly appreciated.

References

Abernethy, M. & Lillis, A. (1995). The impact of manufacturing flexibility on management control system design. *Accounting, Organizations and Society*, **20**, 241–258.

Abernethy, M., Home, M., Lillis, A., Malina, M. A. & Selto, F. H. (2005). A multi-method approach to building causal performance maps from expert knowledge. *Management Accounting Research*, **16**, 135–155.

Akkermans, H. & van Oorschot, K. (2005). Relevance assumed: a case study of balanced scorecard development using systems dynamics. *Journal of the Operational Research Society*, **56**, 931–941.

Ambler, T. (2000). *Marketing and the Bottom Line*. London, UK: FT Prentice Hall.

Banker, R., Chang, H. & Pizzini, M. (2004). The balanced scorecard: judgmental effects of performance measures linked to strategy. *The Accounting Review*, **79**, 1–23.

Banker, R., Potter, G. & Schroeder, R. (1993). Reporting manufacturing performance measures to workers: an empirical study. *Journal of Management Accounting Research*, **5**, 35–55.

Banker, R., Potter, G. & Srinivasan, D. (2000). An empirical investigation of an incentive plan that includes nonfinancial performance measures. *The Accounting Review*, **75**(1), 67–92.

Black, A., Wright, J., Bachman, J., Makall, M. & Wright, P. (1998). *In Search of Shareholder Value: Managing the Drivers of Performance*. London, UK: Pitman Publishing.

Bol, J. & Moers, F. (2006). The cost-benefit trade-off in adopting performance-based incentives: early vs. late adopters. Working paper. IESE Business School and Maastricht University.

Bourne, M., Kennerley, M. & Franco-Santos, M. (2005). Managing through measures: a study of impact on performance. *Journal of Manufacturing Technology Management*, **16**, 373–395.

Bourne, M., Neely, A., Mills, J. & Platts, K. (2003). Implementing performance measurement systems: a literature review. *International Journal of Business Performance Management*, **5**, 1–24.

Bouwens, J. & van Lent, L. (2007). Assessing the performance of business unit managers. *Journal of Accounting Research*, **45**, 667–697.

Bushman, R., Indjejikian, R. & Smith, A. (1996). Aggregate performance measures in business unit compensation: the role of intrafirm interdependencies. *Journal of Accounting Research*, **33**, 101–128.

Campbell, D. (2007). Nonfinancial performance measures and promotion-based incentives. Working paper. Harvard University.

Carnegie Mellon (1994). *Capability Maturity Model: Guidelines for Improving the Software Process*. Carnegie Mellon University Software Engineering Institute.

Carr, L. & Ponemon, L. (1992). Managers' perceptions about quality costs. *Journal of Cost Management*, **7**, 38–58.

Cerbioni, F. & Parbonetti, A. (2007). Exploring the effects of corporate governance on intellectual capital disclosure: and analysis of European biotechnology companies. *European Accounting Review*, **16**, 791–826.

COSO (2004). *Enterprise Risk Management–Integrated Framework: Executive Summary Framework.* New York, NY: Committee of Sponsoring Organizations of the Treadway Commission.

Courty, P. & Marschke, G. (2004). Dynamics of performance measurement systems. *Oxford Review of Economic Policy*, **19**, 268–284.

Davis, S. & Albright, T. (2004). An investigation of the effect of balanced scorecard implementation on financial performance. *Management Accounting Research*, **15**, 135–153.

Deloitte (2004). *2004 Global Risk Management Survey.* New York, NY: Deloitte Touche Tomatsu.

Deloitte (2007). *In the Dark II: What Many Boards and Executives Still Don't Know About the Health of Their Businesses.* New York, NY: Deloitte Touche Tomatsu.

Dye, R. (2004). Strategy selection and performance measurement choice when profit drivers are unknown. *Management Science*, **50**, 1624–1637.

Eccles, R., Herz, R., Keegan, E. & Phillips, D. (2001). *The Value Reporting Revolution: Moving Beyond the Earnings Game.* New York, NY: John Wiley & Sons.

Franco, M. & Bourne, M. (2004). Are strategic performance measurement systems really effective: a closer look at the evidence. *Proceedings of the EurOMA Conference*, INSEAD, Paris, (Vol. 2), **June**, 163–174.

Franco-Santos, M. & Bourne, M. (2005). An examination of the literature relating to issues affecting how companies manage through measures. *Production Planning & Control*, **16**, 114–124.

Gates, S. (1999). *Aligning Strategic Performance Measures and Results.* New York, NY: The Conference Board.

Griffith, R. & Neely, A. (2007). Incentives and managerial experience in multi-task teams: evidence from within a firm. Working paper. Institute for Fiscal Studies and Cranfield School of Management.

HassabElnaby, H., Said, A. & Wier, B. (2005). The retention of nonfinancial performance measures in compensation contracts. *Journal of Management Accounting Research*, **17**, 23–42.

Hayes, R., Wheelwright, S. & Clark, K. (1988). *Dynamic Manufacturing: Creating the Learning Organization.* New York, NY: The Free Press.

Ittner, C. (1994). An examination of the indirect productivity gains from quality improvement. *Production and Operations Management*, **3**, 153–170.

Ittner, C. (2008). Does measuring intangibles for management purposes improve performance? A review of the evidence. *Accounting and Business Research*, forthcoming.

Ittner, C. & Larcker, D. (1995). Total quality management and the choice of information and reward systems. *Journal of Accounting Research*, **34**(Supplement), 1–34.

Ittner, C. & Larcker, D. (1997a). Quality strategy, strategic control systems, and organizational performance. *Accounting, Organizations and Society*, **22**, 293–314.

Ittner, C. & Larcker, D. (1997b). Are nonfinancial measures leading indicators of financial performance? An analysis of customer satisfaction. *Journal of Accounting Research*, **36**(Supplement), 1–35.

Ittner, C. & Larcker, D. (2002). Determinants of performance measure choices in worker incentive plans. *Journal of Labor Economics*, **20**, 58–90.

Ittner, C. & Larcker, D. (2003). Coming up short on nonfinancial performance measurement. *Harvard Business Review*, **81**(11), 88–95.

Ittner, C. & Larcker, D. (2005). Moving from strategic measurement to strategic data analysis. In: C. Chapman (Ed.), *Controlling Strategy*. Oxford, UK: Oxford University Press, pp. 86–105.

Ittner, C., Larcker, D. & Meyer, M. (2003). Subjectivity and the weighting of performance measures: evidence from a balanced scorecard. *The Accounting Review*, **78**, 725–758.

Ittner, C., Larcker, D. & Randall, T. (2003). Performance implications of strategic performance measurement in financial services firms. *Accounting, Organizations and Society*, **28**, 715–741.

Ittner, C., Larcker, D. & Rajan, M. (1997). The choice of performance measures in annual bonus contracts. *The Accounting Review*, **72**, 231–255.

Ittner, C., Nagar, V. & Rajan, M. (2001). An empirical examination of dynamic quality-based learning models. *Management Science*, **47**, 563–578.

Kaplan, R. & Norton, D. (1996). *The Balanced Scorecard: Translating Strategy into Action.* Boston, MA: Harvard Business School Press.

Laitinen, E. (2006). A constant growth model of the firm: empirical analysis of the balanced scorecard. *Review of Accounting and Finance*, **5**, 140–173.

Lipe, M. & Salterio, S. (2000). The balanced scorecard: judgemental effects of common and unique performance measures. *The Accounting Review*, **75**, 283–298.

Langfield-Smith, K. (1997). Management control systems and strategy: a critical review. *Accounting, Organizations and Society*, **22**(2), 207–232.

Langfield-Smith, K. (2005). What do we know about management control systems and strategy? In: C. Chapman (Ed.), *Controlling Strategy*. Oxford, UK: Oxford University Press, pp. 62–85.

Larcker, D., Richardson, S. & Tuna, I. (2007). Corporate governance, accounting outcomes, and organizational performance. *The Accounting Review*, **82**, 963–1008.

Malina, M. & Selto, F. (2001). Communicating and controlling strategy: and empirical study of the effectiveness of the balanced scorecard. *Journal of Management Accounting Research*, **13**, 47–90.

McWhorter, L., Matherly, M. & Frizzell, D. (2006). The connection between performance measurement and risk management. *Strategic Finance*, **February**, 50–55.

Meyer, M. & Gupta, V. (1994). The performance paradox. In: B. Staw & L. Cummings (Eds), *Research in Organizational Behavior*, **16**, 309–389.

Moers, F. (2006). Performance measure properties and delegation. *The Accounting Review*, **81**, 897–924.

Nagar, V. & Rajan, M. (2001). The revenue implications of financial and operational measures of product quality. *The Accounting Review*, **76**, 495–514.

Nagar, V. & Rajan, M. (2005). Measuring customer relationships: the case of the retail banking industry. *Management Science*, **51**, 904–919.

Neely, A. (2007). Does the balanced scorecard work: an empirical investigation. Working paper. Cranfield School of Management.

Norreklit, H. (2000). The balance on the balanced scorecard—a critical analysis of some of its assumptions. *Management Accounting Research*, **11**, 65–88.

Norreklit, H. (2003). The balanced scorecard: what is the score? A rhetorical analysis of the balanced scorecard. *Accounting, Organizations and Society*, **28**, 591–619.

Podsakoff, P., MacKenzie, S., Lee, J. & Podsakoff, N. (2003). Common method biases in behavioral research: a critical review of the literature and recommended remedies. *Journal of Applied Psychology*, **88**, 879–903.

Prendergast, C. (1999). The provision of incentives in firms. *Journal of Economic Literature*, **March**, 7–63.

Ryan, M., Buzas, T. & Ramaswamy, V. (1995). Making CSM a power tool. *Marketing Research*, **7**(3), 10–16.

Said, A., HassabElnaby, H. & Wier, B. (2003). An empirical investigation of the performance consequences of nonfinancial measures. *Journal of Management Accounting Research*, **15**, 193–223.

Sedatole, K. (2003). The effect of measurement alternatives on a nonfinancial quality measures forward-looking properties. *The Accounting Review*, **78**, 555–581.

Taylor, C. & Davies, J. (2003). Getting traction with KRIs: laying the groundwork. *The RMA Journal*, **November**, 58–62.

Waggoner, D., Neely, A. & Kennerley, M. (1999). The forces that shape organizational performance measurement systems: an interdisciplinary review. *International Journal of Production Economics*, **60**, 53–60.

Wong-On-Wing, B., Guo, L., Li, W. & Yang, D. (2007). Reducing conflict in balanced scorecard evaluations. *Accounting, Organizations, and Society*, **32**, 363–377.

Wyatt, A. (2008). What financial and non-financial information on intangibles is value-relevant? A review of the evidence. *Accounting and Business Research*, forthcoming.

Handbook of Management Accounting Research
Edited by Christopher S. Chapman, Anthony G. Hopwood and Michael D. Shields

Conceptual Foundations of the Balanced Scorecard

Robert S. Kaplan

Harvard Business School, Harvard University, USA

Abstract: David Norton and I introduced the balanced scorecard in a 1992 *Harvard Business Review* article (Kaplan & Norton, 1992). The article was based on a multi-company research project that studied performance measurement in companies whose intangible assets played a central role in value creation (Nolan & Norton, 1991). Our interest in measurement for driving performance improvements arose from a belief articulated more than a century earlier by a prominent British scientist, Lord Kelvin (1883):

> I often say that when you can measure what you are speaking about, and express it in numbers, you know something about it; but when you cannot measure it, when you cannot express it in numbers, your knowledge is of a meagre and unsatisfactory kind.
> If you can not measure it, you cannot improve it.

Norton and I believed that measurement was as fundamental to managers as it was for scientists. If companies were to improve the management of their intangible assets, they had to integrate the measurement of intangible assets into their management systems.

After publication of the 1992 *Harvard Business Review* article, several companies quickly adopted the balanced scorecard, giving us deeper and broader insights into its power and potential. During the next 15 years, as it was adopted by thousands of private, public and non-profit enterprises around the world, we extended and broadened the concept into a management tool for describing, communicating and implementing strategy. In this chapter, I describe the roots and motivation for the original balanced scorecard article, as well as the subsequent innovations that connected it to a larger management literature. The chapter uses the following structure for organizing the origin and subsequent development of the balanced scorecard:

1. Balanced Scorecard for Performance Measurement
2. Strategic Objectives and Strategy Maps
3. The Strategy Management System
4. Future Opportunities.

1. Balanced Scorecard for Performance Measurement

Figure 1 shows the original structure for the balanced scorecard (BSC). The BSC retains financial metrics as the ultimate outcome measures for company success, but supplements these with metrics from three additional perspectives (customer, internal process, and learning and growth) that we proposed as the drivers for creating long-term shareholder value.

1.1. Historical Roots: 1950–1980

The balanced scorecard, of course, was not original for advocating that nonfinancial measures be used to motivate, measure and evaluate company performance. In the 1950s, a General Electric corporate staff group conducted a project to develop performance measures for GE's decentralized business units (Lewis, 1955).[1] The project team recommended that divisional performance be measured by one financial and seven nonfinancial metrics.

1. profitability (measured by residual income);
2. market share;

[1]See also General Electric (A), Harvard Business School case study

DOI: 10.1016/S1751-3243(07)03003-9

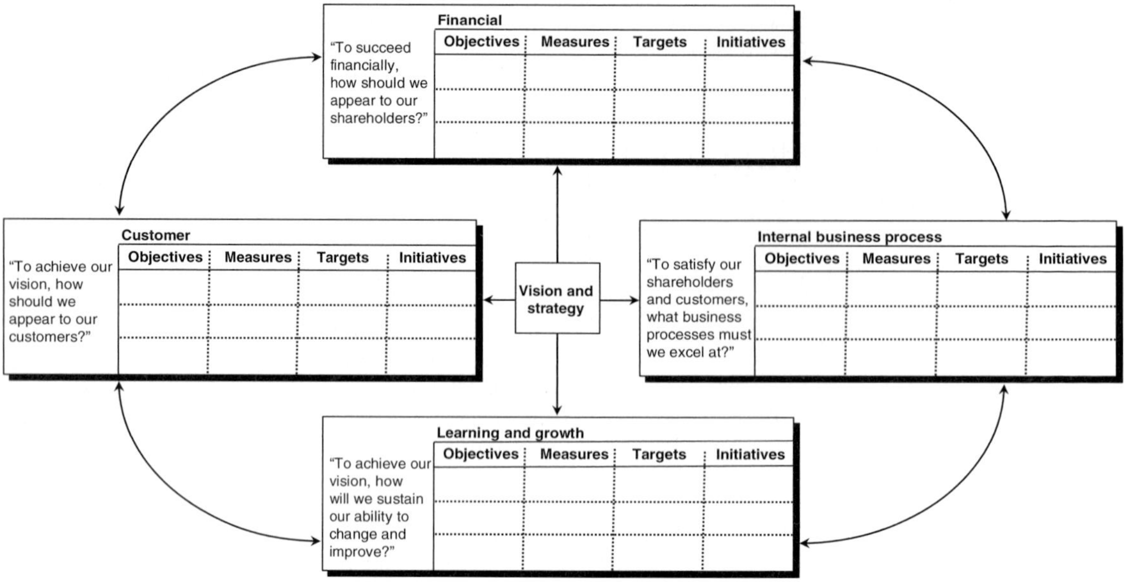

Figure 1. Translating vision and strategy: four perspectives.

3. productivity;
4. product leadership;
5. public responsibility (legal and ethical behaviour and responsibility to stakeholders including shareholders, vendors, dealers, distributors and communities);
6. personnel development;
7. employee attitudes;
8. balance between short-range and long-range objectives.

One can see the roots of the balanced scorecard in these eight objectives. The financial perspective is represented by the first GE metric, the customer perspective with the second, the process perspective with metrics 3–5, and the learning and growth perspective with metrics 6 and 7. The eighth metric captures the essence of the balanced scorecard, encouraging managers to achieve a proper balance between short- and long-range objectives. Unfortunately, the noble goals of the 1950s GE corporate project never became ingrained into the management system and incentive structure of GE's line business units. In fact, despite metrics 5 and 8 in the above list, several GE units were subsequently convicted of price-fixing schemes, with their managers claiming that corporate pressure for short-term profits led them to compromise long-term objectives and their public responsibilities.

At about the same time as the GE project, Herb Simon and several colleagues at the newly-formed Graduate School of Industrial Administration, Carnegie Institute of Technology (later Carnegie-Mellon University) identified several purposes for accounting information in organizations:

- *Scorecard questions*: "Am I doing well or badly?"
- *Attention-directing questions*: "What problems should I look into?"
- *Problem-solving questions*: "Of the several ways of doing the job, which is the best?"

Simon and his colleagues explored the role for financial and nonfinancial information to inform these three questions. This study was perhaps the first to introduce the term "scorecard" into the performance management discussion.

Peter Drucker introduced management by objectives in his classic 1954 book, *The Practice of Management*. Drucker argued that all employees should have personal performance objectives that aligned strongly to the company strategy:

> Each manager, from the "big boss" down to the production foreman or the chief clerk, needs clearly spelled-out objectives. These objectives should lay out what performance the man's (sic) own managerial unit is supposed to produce. They should lay out what contribution he and his unit is expected to make to help other units obtain their objectives. … These objectives should always derive from the goals of the business enterprise. … (M)anagers must understand that business results depend on a balance of efforts and results in a number of areas. … Every manager should responsibly participate in the development of the objectives of the higher unit of which his is a

> part.... He must know and understand the ultimate business goals, what is expected of him and why, what he will be measured against and how.
>
> Drucker, 1954, pp. 126–129

However, despite Drucker's insights and urgings management by objectives in the next half-century mostly became a somewhat bureaucratic exercise, administered by the human resources department, based on local goal-setting that was operational and tactical, and rarely informed by business-level strategies and objectives. Companies at Drucker's time and for many years thereafter lacked a clear way of describing and communicating top-level strategy in a way that middle managers and front line employees could understand and internalize.

In the mid-1960s, Robert Anthony, building upon the decade-earlier research by Simon et al., (1954) and on another article by Simon (1963) on programmed versus nonprogrammed decisions, proposed a comprehensive framework for planning and control systems. Anthony identified three different types of systems: strategic planning, management control and operational control. Strategic planning was defined as:

> ... the process of deciding upon objectives, on changes in these objectives, on the resources used to attain these objectives, and on the policies that are to govern the acquisition, use, and disposition of these resources.
>
> Anthony, 1965, p.16

Foreshadowing the subsequent development of strategy maps, Anthony claimed that strategic planning depends "on an estimate of a cause-and-effect relationship between a course of action and a desired outcome," but concluded that, because of the difficulty of predicting such a relationship, "strategic planning is an art, not a science." Further, Anthony noted that strategic planning is not accompanied by what we would today call strategic control, "Although strategic revision is important, top management spends relatively little time in this activity." Anthony also believed that information for strategic planning usually had a financial emphasis.

Anthony's second category, management control, concerned "the process by which managers assure that resources are obtained and used effectively and efficiently in the accomplishment of the organization's objectives" (Anthony, 1965, p. 17). He observed that management control systems, with rare exceptions, have an underlying financial structure; that is, plans and results are expressed in monetary units ... the only common denominator by means of which the heterogeneous elements of outputs and inputs can be combined and compared. He acknowledged, however:

> ... although management control systems have financial underpinnings, it does not follow that money is the only basis of measurement, or even that it is the most important basis. Other quantitative measurements, such as ... market share, yields, productivity measures, tonnage of output, and so on, are useful.
>
> Anthony, 1965, p. 42

Anthony described the third category, operational or task control, as "the process of assuring that specific tasks are carried out effectively and efficiently." He stated that information for operational control was mostly non-monetary, though some information could be denominated in monetary terms (presumably, frequent variance reports on labour, machine and materials quantity and cost variances).

Thus the roots of management planning and control systems encompassing both financial and nonfinancial measurement can be seen in these early writings of Simon, Drucker and Anthony. Despite the advocacy of these scholars, however, the primary management system for most companies, until the 1990s, used financial information almost exclusively and relied heavily on budgets to maintain focus on short-term performance.

1.2. The Japanese Management Movement: 1975–1990

During the 1970s and 1980s, innovations in quality and just-in-time production by Japanese companies challenged Western leadership in many important industries. Several authors argued that Western companies' narrow focus on short-term financial performance contributed to their complacency and their slow response to the Japanese threat. Johnson & Kaplan (1987) reviewed the history of management accounting and concluded that US corporations had become obsessed with short-term financial measures and had failed to adapt their management accounting and control systems to operational improvements from successful implementation of total quality and short cycle time management.

A Harvard Business School project on Council on Competitiveness (Porter, 1992) echoed these critiques when it identified the following systematic differences between investments made by US corporations versus those made in Japan and Germany:

> The US system is less supportive of investment overall because of its sensitivity to current returns ... combined with corporate goals that stress current stock price over long-term corporate value.
>
> The US system favors those forms of investment for which returns are most readily measurable.... This explains why the United States underinvests, on average, in intangible assets (n.b., product and process innovation, employee skills, customer satisfaction) where returns are more difficult to measure.
>
> The US system favors acquisitions, which involve assets that can be easily valued over internal development projects that are more difficult to value.
>
> Porter, 1992, pp. 72–73

Some accounting academics proposed methods by which a firm's spending to create intangible assets could be capitalized and placed as assets on the corporate balance sheet. During the 1970s there was a burst of interest in human resources accounting (Flamholtz, 1974; Caplan & Landekich, 1975; Grove et al., 1977). Subsequently, Baruch Lev and his doctoral students and colleagues proposed that financial reporting could be more relevant if companies capitalized their expenditures on intangible assets or found other methods by which these assets could be placed on corporate balance sheets. While such a treatment is consistent with Lord Kelvin's (and our) advocacy of measurement to improve understanding and management, none of these approaches gained traction in actual companies. Several factors led to the lack of adoption of placing values for intangible assets on corporate balance sheets.

First, the value from intangible assets is indirect. Assets such as knowledge and technology seldom have a direct impact on revenue and profit. Improvements in intangible assets affect financial outcomes through chains of cause-and-effect relationships involving two or three intermediate stages. For example, consider the linkages in the service management profit chain (Heskett et al., 1994; Heskett, Sasser & Schlesinger, 1997), a development done in parallel and consistent with our balanced scorecard approach:

- investments in employee training lead to improvements in service quality;
- better service quality leads to higher customer satisfaction;
- higher customer satisfaction leads to increased customer loyalty;
- increased customer loyalty generates increased revenues and margins.

Financial outcomes are separated causally and temporally from improving employees' capabilities. The complex linkages make it difficult, if not impossible, to place a financial value on an asset such as workforce capabilities or employee morale, much less to measure changes from period to period in such a financial value.

Secondly, the value from intangible assets depends on organizational context and strategy. This value cannot be separated from the organizational processes that transform intangibles into customer and financial outcomes. A corporate balance sheet is a linear, additive model. It records each class of asset separately and calculates the total by adding up each asset's recorded value. The value created from investing in individual intangible assets, however, is neither linear nor additive.

Senior investment bankers in a firm such as Goldman Sachs are immensely valuable because of their knowledge about complex financial products and their capabilities for managing relationships and developing trust with sophisticated customers. People with the same knowledge, experience and capabilities, however, are nearly worthless to a financial services company such as etrade.com that emphasizes operational efficiency, low cost and technology-based trading. The value of an intangible asset depends critically on the context (the organization, the strategy and other complementary assets) in which the intangible asset is deployed.

Intangible assets also seldom have value by themselves.[2] Generally, they must be bundled with other intangible and tangible assets to create value. For example, a new growth-oriented sales strategy could require new knowledge about customers, new training for sales employees, new databases, new information systems, a new organization structure and a new incentive compensation programme. Investing in just one of these capabilities, or in all of them but one, could cause the new sales strategy to fail. The value does not reside in any individual intangible asset. It arises from creating the entire set of assets along with a strategy that links them together. The value-creation process is multiplicative, not additive.

Rather than attempt a solution to the measurement and management of intangible assets within the financial reporting framework, several articles and books in the 1980s recommended that companies integrate non-financial indicators of their operating performance into their management accounting and control systems, e.g., Howell et al. (1987), Berliner & Brimson (1991), Kaplan (1990). Some authors went further when they urged that internal reporting of financial information to managers and employees, especially those tasked with improving operations by continuous improvement of quality, process yields and process cycle times, be abolished.

> Managing with information from financial accounting systems impedes business performance today because traditional cost accounting data do not track sources of competitiveness and profitability in the global economy. Cost information, per se, does not track sources of competitive advantage such as quality, flexibility and dependability.... Business needs information about activities, not accounting costs, to manage competitive operations and to identify profitable products.
>
> Johnson, 1989, pp. 44–45

Essentially, these authors argued that companies should focus on improving quality, reducing cycle times and improving companies' responsiveness to customers' demands. Doing these activities well, they believed, would lead naturally to improved financial performance.

[2]Brand names, which can be sold, are an exception.

In 1987 the US Government introduced the Malcolm Baldrige National Quality Award to promote quality awareness, recognize quality achievements and publicize successful quality strategies. The initial set of Baldrige criteria included financial metrics (profits per employee), customer-perceived quality metrics (market cycle time, late deliveries), internal process metrics (defects, total manufacturing time, order entry time, supplier defects) and employee metrics (training per employee, morale). However, in the early 1990s, several studies revealed that even businesses that had received the Baldrige Award for quality excellence could encounter financial difficulties, suggesting that the link assumed by the academic scholars quoted above between continuous process improvement and financial success was far from automatic.

During the late 1980s I wrote several case studies that described how some companies had integrated financial information with nonfinancial information on process quality and cycle times for front line employees. In an operating department of a large chemical company,[3] a chemical engineer department manager had introduced a daily income statement for the operators in his department. Even though the employees already had access (every 2–4 hours) to thousands of observations about operating parameters, throughput and quality, the new daily income statement proved a big hit, and helped the employees set production records for throughput and quality. The daily income statement helped employees quickly to assess the consequences from off-specification production or machine downtime, enabled them make trade-offs among conflicting demands on quality and throughput and guided and justified their decisions about spending to improve quality and throughput.

Another case described how a Big-3 automobile engine fabrication plant had made a deep commitment to total quality management principles. It provided decentralized work teams with continuous information about machine downtime and scrap to facilitate operational improvements at bottleneck machines and processes, and to eliminate the root causes of scrap and off-specification production. But, in addition to the daily information on machine downtime, throughput and scrap (all nonfinancial measures), the work teams received a daily report on their spending on indirect materials, such as supplies, tools, scrap and maintenance materials, plus a weekly report on total overhead expenses charged to their departments, including telephone, utilities, indirect labour and salaries of engineering and technical assistants. Plant management wanted the teams not only to improve quality and throughput, but also to make decisions that could directly influence the costs being incurred in their departments.[4] These two cases revealed the power of complementing nonfinancial information with financial information, even for front line production employees.

A third case about a semiconductor company, Analog Devices, described how executives at the top of the organization benefited from seeing nonfinancial information. Analog Devices, like the chemicals plant and the Big-3 automobile engine plant, had introduced a highly successful quality management system which included an innovative quality improvement metric.[5] In addition, Analog's vice president of quality and improvement, an experienced Baldrige Award examiner, had translated the Baldrige criteria into an internal corporate scorecard for his executive team. The corporate scorecard included some high-level financial metrics that the executive team had been accustomed to managing, but also the Baldrige quality metrics organized by three other perspectives:

- customer quality metrics, such as on-time delivery, lead time and customer-measured defects;
- manufacturing process metrics, such as yield, part-per-million defect rates and cycle times;
- employee metrics, such as absenteeism and lateness.

The Analog scorecard signalled that, to make quality improvement a senior executive focus, the measurement system should be expanded beyond financial indicators to include an array of quality metrics relating to customers, manufacturing processes and employees.

The three cases provided successful counter-examples to the various scholars and consultants who argued that front line employees need see only nonfinancial indicators, while senior management can and should focus only on financial ones. The cases showed how front line employees could benefit from seeing financial metrics, while senior executive teams benefited from supplementing their financial view of the world with metrics about customers, quality and employees. Thus the stage was set for thinking about a general framework by which both senior level executive teams and front line production workers would receive financial and nonfinancial information.

1.3. Shareholder Value and the Principal–Agent Framework

Not all academics, however, had been exposed to the recent advances in operations management. Many remained focused on economics and finance, especially the efficient

[3]"Texas Eastman Company," Harvard Business School Case #9-190-039.

[4]"Romeo Engine Plant," Harvard Business School Case #9-194-032.

[5]"Analog Devices: The Half-Life System," Harvard Business School Case #9-190061.

markets theory from the 1960s and early 1970s (Fama, 1971). Economists also introduced principal–agent theory (Jensen-Meckling, 1976; Harris-Raviv, 1979; Holmström, 1979; Grossman-Hart, 1983) to formalize the inherent conflict of interests between hired executive teams and the companies' dispersed shareholders (owners). The principal–agent adherents urged companies to provide more financial incentives to senior executive teams, especially incentives based on financial performance, the typical "outcome" measure assumed in principal–agent models. Efficient market research suggested that stock prices continually reflected all the relevant public information about companies' performance, and that executives' compensation could be better aligned with owners' interests through expanded use of stock options and other equity rewards (Jensen-Meckling, 1976; Fama-Jensen, 1983). In a similar vein, some argued for aligning compensation to better accounting surrogates of stock market performance, especially residual income under its new name, economic value added (Stewart, 1991).

The 1980s saw a huge increase in the link between executives' pay and incentives to financial performance. For the financial economists at the vanguard of this movement, the idea of senior executives paying attention to nonfinancial performance metrics was close to blasphemous. As Michael Jensen (2001), a leading financial economics scholar, has stated:

> Balanced scorecard theory is flawed because it presents managers with a scorecard which gives no score—that is no single-valued measure how they have performed. Thus managers evaluated with such a system … have no way to make principled or purposeful decisions.

I obviously agree with Jensen that managers cannot be paid by a set of unweighted performance metrics. Ultimately, if a company wants to set bonuses based on measured performance, it must reward based on a single measure (either a stock market or accounting-based metric) or provide a weighting among the multiple measures a manager has been instructed to improve. But linking performance to pay is only one component of a comprehensive management system.

Consider an airplane where passengers contract with the pilot for a safe and on time journey. One can imagine an airplane cockpit designed by a financial economist. It consists of a single instrument that displays the destination to be achieved and the desired time of arrival. Alternatively the pilot is given a more complex navigation instrument where the movement of the needle represented a weighted average of estimated time to arrival, fuel remaining, altitude, deviation from expected flight path and proximity to other airplanes. Few of us would feel comfortable flying in a plane guided only by the single instrument, even though the incentives of the pilot and the passengers for a safe, on time arrival are perfectly aligned. Incentives are important, but so also are information, communication and alignment.

1.4. Uncertainty and Multi-period Optimization

Many of the principal–agent models developed by economists and finance scholars are single-period, in which the firm's output is revealed at the end of the period and no further managerial (agent) actions are required. In these cases contracting on output, such as measured financial performance, can be optimal. Alternatively, if financial performance measured by end-of-period stock price or economic value added is a complete and sufficient statistic for the value managers have created during the period, then incentive contracts based on stock prices or economic value added can also be optimal. But many of the actions that managers take during a period (such as upgrading the skills and motivation of employees, advancing products through the research and development pipeline, improving the quality of processes and enhancing trusted relationships with customers and suppliers) are not revealed to public investors, so that their implications for firm value cannot be incorporated into end-of-period stock prices. While managers may know the amount they spent on enhancing their intangible assets, they may also have little idea, in the short-run, about how much value they have created. And, certainly, such value increases (or decreases if the expenditures do not generate future value in excess of the amount spent) do not get incorporated into the end-of-period stock price or residual value (economic value added) metric.

Dynamic programming teaches us that the optimal actions in the first period of a multi-period model are far from the optimal actions in the final period. Managers attempting to maximize total shareholder value over, say, a ten-year period cannot accomplish this goal by optimizing reported financial performance or stock price, period-by-period. The balanced scorecard recognizes the limitations of managing to financial targets alone in short-term horizons when managers are following a long-term strategy of enhancing the capabilities of their customer and supplier relationships, operating and innovation processes, human resources, information resources, and organizational climate and culture. But, because the links from process improvements and investments in intangible assets to customer and financial outcomes are uncertain (recall the financial problems of several of the early excellent quality companies), the balanced scorecard also includes the outcome metrics to signal when the long-term strategy appears to be delivering the expected and desired results.

1.5. Stakeholder Theory

Stakeholder theory offers another multi-dimensional approach for enterprise performance measurement.

Stakeholders are defined as the groups or individuals, inside or outside the enterprise, that have a stake or can influence the organization's performance. The theory generally identifies five stakeholder groups for a company: three of them, shareholders, customers and communities, define the external expectations of a company's performance; the other two, suppliers and employees, participate with the company to plan, design, implement and deliver the company's products and services to its customers (Atkinson et al., 1997, p. 27). Management control scholars who apply stakeholder theory to performance measurement believe "performance measurement design starts with stakeholders" (Neely & Adams, 2002). The stakeholder approach to performance measurement starts by defining objectives for what each stakeholder group expects from the corporation and how each group contributes to the success of the corporation. Once stakeholder expectations or even further, implicit and explicit contracts between the stakeholders and the corporation, are defined, the corporation then defines a strategy to meet these expectations and fulfil the contracts. Thus, while the balanced scorecard approach starts with strategy and then identifies the interrelationships and objectives for various stakeholders, the stakeholder approach starts with stakeholder objectives and, in a second step, defines a strategy to meet shareholder expectations.

Just as Chandler articulated that strategy precedes structure, I strongly believe that strategy also precedes stakeholders. The stakeholder movement probably developed to counter the narrow shareholder value maximization view articulated by Milton Friedman and, subsequently, financial economists such as Jensen. In this spirit, I believe the stakeholder helped us appreciate the value from nurturing multiple relationships that drive long-term and sustainable value creation. But stakeholder theory confuses means and ends, and therefore ends up less powerful, less actionable and, ultimately, less satisfying (at least to me) than the strategy map/balanced scorecard approach. We advocate selecting a strategy first, and only subsequently working out the relationship with stakeholders, as required by the strategy. I will illustrate my point of view with several examples.

First, let's take the example of Mobil's US Marketing and Refining, a well-documented balanced scorecard implementation.[6] Mobil learned, through marketing research, that its customers were heterogeneous. Some valued low price only, for them Mobil should offer the cheapest prices, matching or beating the prices of discount stations and the other major gasoline companies. Other customers, however, were not so price sensitive and were willing to pay a price premium, say up to $0.10–0.12 per gallon, if they could have a superior buying experience (rapid service, pay by credit card at the pump, clean rest rooms, friendly helpful employees, great convenience store, etc.). Stakeholder theory fails here. Which customers' expectations should Mobil satisfy? It could not be the best for both customer groups. Having larger gasoline stations with more pumps, equipped with self-pay mechanisms, better-paid and more trained and experienced employees and a full service convenience store, costs money and these costs would need to be covered by higher prices, thereby disappointing the price-sensitive customers. If Mobil offered the lowest prices, it could not afford to invest in the employees, the convenience store and the larger stations with more self-service and self-pay pumps, thereby disappointing the customers desiring a great buying experience.

Strategy is about choice. Companies cannot meet the expectations of all their possible customers. Wal-Mart meets the apparel needs of one market segment of customers (price-sensitive), Nordstrom meets the needs of another segment (customer relationships and solutions), and Armani and Ferragamo meet the expectations of a third segment (product-leading fashion, fabric and fit, price-insensitive). Similarly, customers of Southwest Airlines have different expectations of performance than the business and first class customers who fly British Airways. Strategy determines which customers the company has decided to serve and the value proposition that it will offer to win the loyalty of those customer segments. The determination of strategy must come before defining measures of customer satisfaction and loyalty. Otherwise, following the recommendations of the stakeholder theorists, the company would attempt to meet the expectations of all the existing and potential customers it could serve, getting stuck "in the middle," as described by Michael Porter, with both a high cost and a non-differentiated approach, a recipe for strategy failure.

A similar situation occurs for employees. The balanced scorecard deliberately did not label its fourth perspective the "employees" or "people" perspective, choosing a more generic name, "learning and growth," to signal that we were not taking a pure stakeholder approach. Under the BSC approach, employee objectives always appear (in the learning and growth perspective), but they get there because they are necessary for the strategy, not because someone has labelled them as a "stakeholder." Consider a pharmaceutical company in the early 1990s. One of its most important groups of employees (what we would subsequently call a strategic job family) is the chemists performing research to screen and identify new compounds to treat specific diseases. The stakeholder approach would interview these key employees to learn their career expectations and develop a strategy that would meet their

[6] "Mobil US Marketing and Refining (A)," Harvard Business School Case # 197-025.

expectations and strive to continually motivate and satisfy these employees.

During the 1990s, however, and continuing into this century, the key scientific discipline for new drug development shifted from chemistry to biology. The new key employees became molecular biologists and geneticists. Pharmaceutical companies shifted their strategies to adapt to the new technologies; the fate of their previous key stakeholders, PhD chemists, became more tenuous, especially if they did not acquire dramatic new capabilities and competencies so that they could contribute to new drug development. Again, the stakeholder view would lock the company into maintaining relationships with its soon-to-be-obsolete employee group and not moving swiftly enough to reflect that it needed entirely new employees to help it implement the new strategy.

Stakeholder theorists also criticize the balanced scorecard for not having a separate perspective for suppliers, one of their five essential stakeholder groups. However, as with employees suppliers feature on the scorecard (typically in the process perspective) when they are essential to the strategy. So companies, such as Wal-Mart, Nike and Toyota, for whom suppliers provide a critical component in creating sustainable competitive advantage, would certainly feature supplier performance in their strategy maps. But consider a company like Mobil US Marketing and Refining, whose main suppliers are petroleum exploration and production companies, providing a commodity such as crude oil, and construction companies, who build refineries and pipelines. These suppliers provide essential products and services, but don't provide any differentiation or support of Mobil's strategy. Similarly, a community bank following a customer intimacy strategy gets its raw material, money, from the US Federal Reserve system. Suppliers are not a critical component of its strategy. So Mobil US Marketing and Refining and the community bank may not feature suppliers on their scorecards because they don't contribute to the differentiation and sustainability of their strategies. Again, strategy precedes stakeholders and, in this case, may reveal that one of the stakeholder categories is not decisive for the strategy.

Finally, the balanced scorecard does include performance in communities as process perspective objectives when such performance does contribute to the differentiation in the strategy (Kaplan & Norton, 2003). This view agrees with that articulated by Michael Porter when he advocates that environmental and social performance should be aligned to, and support, the company strategy (Porter & Kramer, 1999, 2006). Occasionally companies do not want shareholder value to be the unifying paradigm for its strategy. That's ok; it's their choice. They don't have to abandon the balanced scorecard methodology and switch to the stakeholder view. They can use a strategy map and balanced scorecard to articulate their strategy that attempts to simultaneously create economic, environmental and social value, and to balance and manage the tensions among them. This is exactly the path taken by Amanco, a Latin American producer of water treatment solutions, whose founding shareholder believed deeply in triple bottom line performance.[7]

In summary, stakeholder theory was useful to articulate a broader company mission beyond a narrow, short-term shareholder value-maximizing model. It increased companies' sensitivity about how failure to incorporate stakeholder preferences and expectations can undermine an excessive focus on short-term financial results. The balanced scorecard, however, incorporates stakeholder interests endogenously, within a coherent strategy and value-creation framework, when outstanding performance with those stakeholders is critical for the success of the strategy. The converse is not true for stakeholder theory. It does not enable companies to develop a strategy when some of the existing "stakeholders" are no longer essential or even desirable in light of changes in the external environment and internal capabilities.

1.6. Integration and Summary

Dave Norton and I introduced the balanced scorecard to provide a missing component and bridge across these various, apparently conflicting, literatures that had been developed in complete isolation from each other: the literature on quality and lean management, which emphasized employees' continuous improvement activities to reduce waste and increase company responsiveness; the literature on financial economics, which placed heightened emphasis on financial performance measures; and the stakeholder theory where the firm was an intermediary attempting to forge contracts that satisfied all its different constituents. We attempted to retain the valuable insights from each. Employee and process performance are critical for current and future success. Financial metrics, ultimately, will increase if companies' performance improves. And to optimize long-term shareholder value, the firm had to internalize the preferences and expectations of its shareholders, customers, suppliers, employees and communities. The key was to have a more robust measurement and management system that included both operational metrics as leading indicators and financial metrics as lagging outcomes, along with several other metrics to measure a company's progress in driving future performance.

This insight became glaringly obvious to us during our initial 1990 multi-company research project when we invited the innovative vice president of quality and productivity at Analog Devices, Arthur Schneiderman,

[7]"Amanco: Developing the Sustainability Scorecard," Harvard Business School Case # 107-038.

to address our group. At the end of the presentation, in response to a question about how the company was doing with its quality improvement metric and corporate scorecard, he reported that every quality measure on its corporate scorecard had experienced dramatic improvements. He also noted, however, that the company's stock price had decreased by nearly 70% during the previous three years. The company had failed to translate its improved manufacturing and delivery performance into increased sales and margins, and the stock price reflected this shortcoming. The failure to include the link between quality improvements on Analog's quality scorecard to a customer value proposition or to any customer outcomes probably contributed to the loss of shareholder value. Norton and I recognized that any comprehensive measurement and management system had to link operational performance improvements to customer and financial performance. Our balanced scorecard, while incorporating Analog's operational improvement metrics, also incorporated metrics for innovation, employee capabilities, technology, organizational learning and customer success. And, unlike the stakeholder perspective, we did place shareholder value as the highest-level metric, with all the other stakeholders reflected in how they contributed to the company's success in maximizing long-term shareholder value.

2. Strategic Objectives and Strategy Maps

As Norton and I began working with the companies, after the initial *Harvard Business Review* article appeared, we faced the question about how to choose the metrics that would go on a balanced scorecard. We could have adopted the generic metrics that many companies were already using, such as customer satisfaction, customer retention, defect rates, yields, lead and process times, and employee satisfaction. But we and the client companies were dissatisfied with these metrics. They were too generic. By 1992, virtually all companies (airlines and dysfunctional companies, such as WorldCom, being notable exceptions) were attempting to increase customer satisfaction, improve process quality and motivate employee performance. As we probed this issue with executives, we quickly learned that creating a balanced scorecard should not start with selecting metrics.

Many companies, however, already had extensive measurements from their existing quality and performance improvement programmes and wanted to create a quick balanced scorecard by classifying each of their existing metrics into one of the four BSC perspectives. While having a structure for reporting their nonfinancial metrics was better than having no nonfinancial metrics, or simply a long list of them, this bottom-up process of classifying existing measurements was unlikely to capture the most important drivers of future success.

A second group of companies looked externally for their metrics and conducted benchmarking studies to learn the metrics used by the companies they admired most. Norton and I did not want the balanced scorecard to become a benchmarking exercise. We knew that even high-performing companies succeeded with strategies that were quite different from each other. The metrics used by a company following a low cost strategy (Wal-Mart, for example) should be distinct from those used by a company implementing a complete customer solutions strategy (e.g., Nordstrom) or a company with an innovative product leadership strategy (e.g., Armani and Ferragamo). Adopting metrics used by a company with a different strategy would confuse and distract the focus of employees and cause the strategy to fail.

Company executives continually told us that their highest priority was implementing their strategy. We came to recognize that before selecting metrics, companies should describe what they were attempting to achieve with their strategies and, further, that the four BSC perspectives provide a robust structure for companies to express their strategic objectives. The financial objective would include a high-level objective for sustained shareholder value creation and supporting sub-objectives for revenue growth, productivity and risk management. The customer perspective would include objectives for desired customer outcomes, such as to acquire, satisfy and retain targeted customers, and to build the share of their spending done with the company.

In addition to these somewhat generic lagging measures of customer performance, we recognized that companies needed to express objectives for the value proposition they offered customers. The value proposition, the unique combination of price, quality, availability, ease and speed of purchase, functionality, relationship and service, was the heart of the strategy, what differentiated the company from its competitors or what it intended to do better than its competitors for the targeted customers. Thus, companies following a low-cost strategy would offer low prices, defect-free products and speedy purchase. Product innovating companies offered products and services whose performance exceeded that of competitors along dimensions that targeted customers valued.

Objectives in the process perspective reflected how the company would create and deliver the differentiated value proposition and meet the financial objectives for productivity improvements. Objectives in the learning and growth perspectives described the goals for employees, information systems and organizational alignment.

Over the years, we learned new ways to write strategic objectives. Many companies now write their strategic objectives in quotes to reflect the voice of their customers and employees. For example, one medium-sized community bank that was shifting from its traditional product-push strategy to one that emphasized developing complete financial solutions for its targeted customers expressed its customer objectives as:

1. "Understand me and give me the right information and advice"
2. "Give me convenient access to the right products"
3. "Appreciate me and get things done easily, quickly and right."

Each of these customer objectives, once identified, could be easily measured, for example by the following list:

1. (a) number of customers profiled
   (b) number of customers with financial plans;
2. number of targeted customer using on-line channel for transactions;
3. customer survey responses on questions related to appreciation and ease of working with the bank.

Similarly, the learning and growth objectives, written in the voice of employees, included:

- "We hire, develop, retain and reward great people"
- "We are trained in the skills we need to succeed"
- "We understand the strategy and know what we need to do to implement it"
- "We have the information and tools we need to do our job."

As with the customer objectives, once the employee objectives had been selected and expressed, it was a simple task to select metrics that measured the performance for each of these strategic objectives. These metrics were more aligned to the strategy than generic metrics of employee morale and satisfaction.

Thus, while our initial article had a subtitle, "Measures that Drive Performance," we soon learned that we had to start not with measures, but with descriptions of what the company wanted to accomplish. It turned out that selection of measures was much simpler after company executives described their strategies through the multiple strategic objectives in the four BSC perspectives.

2.1. Strategy Maps

It soon became natural to describe the causal relationships between strategic objectives. For example, a simple causal chain of strategic objectives would be: employees better trained in quality management tools reduce process cycle times and process defects; the improved processes lead to shorter customer lead times, improved on-time delivery, and fewer defects experienced by customers; the quality improvements experienced by customers lead to higher satisfaction, retention and spending, which ultimately drives higher revenues and margins. All the objectives are linked in cause-and-effect relationships, starting with employees, continuing through processes and customers, and culminating in higher financial performance.

The idea of causal linkages among balanced scorecard objectives and measures led to the creation of a strategy map, articulated in a *Harvard Business Review* article and several books (Kaplan & Norton 2001, 2004). Figure 2 shows the current structure for a strategy map. Today, all BSC projects build a map of strategic objectives first and only afterwards select metrics for each objective.

We recognized that the weakest link in a strategy map and balanced scorecard was the learning and growth perspective. For many years, as one executive described it, the learning and growth perspective was "the black hole of the balanced scorecard." While companies had some generic measures for employees, such as employee satisfaction and morale, turnover, absenteeism and lateness (probably growing out of the stakeholder movement of the previous decade), none had metrics that linked their employee capabilities to the strategy. A few scholars had investigated the connection between improvements in human resources and improved financial performance (e.g., Huselid, 1995; Becker et al., 1998).

Dave Norton led a research project in 2002 and 2003 with senior HR professionals to explore how to better link the measurement of human resources to strategic objectives. From this work came the concepts of strategic human capital readiness and strategic job families and, by extension, the linkages to information capital and organizational capital. These important extensions to embed the capabilities of a company's most important intangible assets were described in a *Harvard Business Review* article and a book (Kaplan & Norton, 2004a,b).

2.2. Extending Balanced Scorecard to Non-profit and Public Sector Enterprises

While initially developed for private sector enterprises, the balanced scorecard was soon extended to non-profit and public sector enterprises (NPSEs). Prior to the development of the balanced scorecard, the performance reports of NPSEs focused only on financial measures, such as budgets, funds appropriated, donations, expenditures and operating expense ratios. Clearly, however, the performance of NPSEs cannot be measured by financial indicators. Their success has to be measured by their effectiveness in providing benefits to constituents. The balanced scorecard helps NPSEs select a coherent use of nonfinancial measures to assess their performance with constituents.

Since financial success is not their primary objective, NPSEs cannot use the standard architecture of the balanced scorecard strategy map, where financial objectives

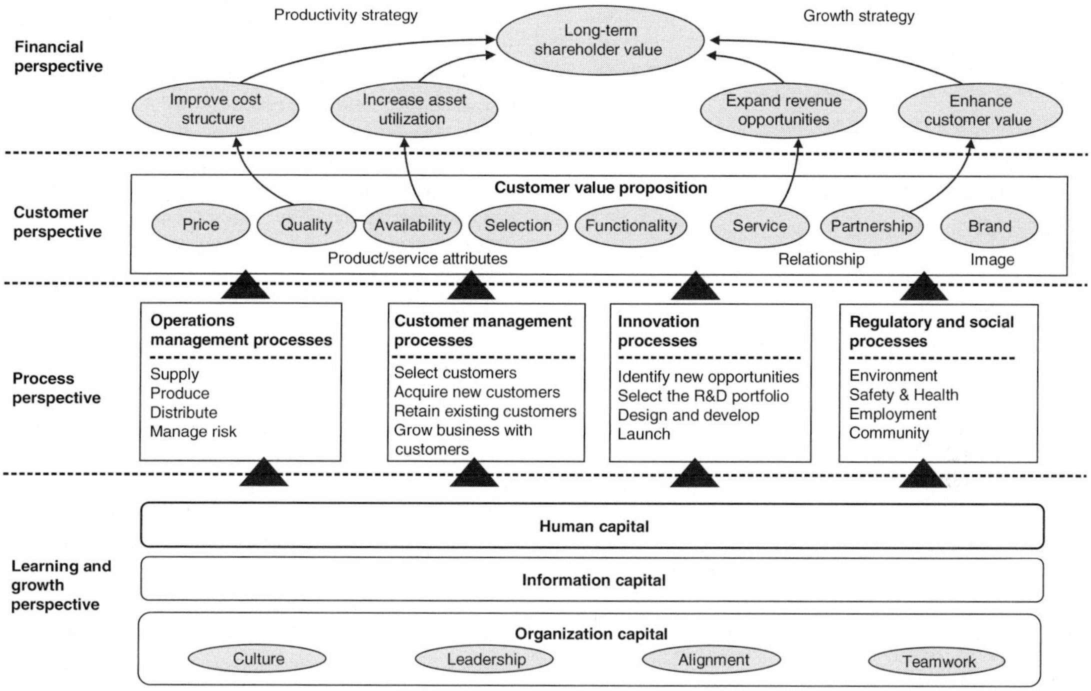

Figure 2. The strategy map links intangible assets and critical processes to the value proposition and customer and financial outcomes.

are the ultimate, high-level outcomes to be achieved. NPSEs generally place an objective related to their social impact and mission, such as reducing poverty, pollution, diseases or school dropout rates, or improving health, biodiversity, education and economic opportunities. A non-profit or public sector agency's mission represents the accountability between it and society, as well as the rationale for its existence and ongoing support. The measured improvement in an NPSEs social impact objective may take years to become noticeable, which is why the measures in the other perspectives provide the short- to intermediate-term targets and feedback necessary for year-to-year control and accountability.

One additional modification is required to expand the customer perspective. Donors or taxpayers provide the financial resources—they pay for the service—while another group, the citizens and beneficiaries, receive the service. Both constituents and resource suppliers should be the placed at the top of an NPSE strategy map.

3. The Strategy Management System

My Harvard Business School colleague, Robert Simons, developed the levers of control framework (Simons, 1995 a,b) at the same time that Norton and I were developing the balanced scorecard. Simons identified several types of management control systems that managers use to motivate, monitor and manage their strategies. The control systems included belief systems (mission, vision and values), boundary systems, internal control systems, diagnostic systems and interactive systems. As described at the beginning of this chapter, Norton and I originally envisioned the balanced scorecard as an enhanced performance measurement system, labelled by Simons as a diagnostic system. Our vision for the BSC was for managers to define and track performance among multiple financial and nonfinancial measures that were considered important for company success.

Several senior executives soon taught us that the balanced scorecard could operate in a far more powerful manner than its use as a management reporting and performance monitoring system. For example, Larry Brady, then President of the FMC Corporation, stated:[8]

> I think that it's important for companies not to approach the scorecard as the latest fad.... You hear about a good idea, several people on corporate staff work on it, probably with some expensive outside consultants, and you put in a system that's a bit different (incremental) from what existed before.

[8]Interview with Larry Brady in: R. S. Kaplan & D. P. Norton. (1993). "Putting the Balanced Scorecard to Work," *Harvard Business Review*, **September–October**, p. 147.

> It gets worse if you think of the scorecard as a new measurement system that eventually requires hundreds and thousands of measurements and a big, expensive executive information system. These companies lose sight of the essence of the scorecard: its focus, its simplicity, and its vision. The real benefit comes from making the scorecard the cornerstone of the way you run the business. It should be the core of the management system, not the measurement system. (It should become) the lever to streamline and focus strategy that can lead to breakthrough performance.

Brady and other early BSC implementation leaders (at Mobil US Marketing and Refining, Cigna Property and Casualty, and Chemical Retail Bank) adopted and used the scorecard to help them describe their strategies and implement a new strategy management system based on scorecard measurements. The new insights helped us formulate the fundamental structure for a generic strategy management system (Kaplan & Norton, 1996 a,b).

The development of the strategy management system transformed the balanced scorecard from being an extended diagnostic system to an interactive system, defined by Bob Simons as having the following characteristics (Simons 1995a, p. 97):

1. Information generated by the system is an important and recurring agenda addressed by the highest levels of management.
2. The interactive control system demands frequent and regular attention from operating managers at all levels of the organization.
3. Data generated by the system are interpreted and discussed in face-to-face meetings of superiors, subordinates and peers.
4. The system is a catalyst for the continual challenge and debate of underlying data, assumptions and action plans.

Simons' research indicated that CEOs selected an existing management system, such as the budget, the project management system or the revenue system, and operated it interactively. Our development of the strategy map and balanced scorecard turned out, serendipitously, to offer managers the framework for a generic interactive system. Managers could now design a customized interactive system based on their strategy and, following Brady's insight, use the strategy map and scorecard as the cornerstone of their management system for executing the strategy.[9]

For examples of the system's interactivity, two senior executives at Mobil US Marketing and Refining described how they used the balanced scorecard with their business unit and support unit managers. Bob McCool, CEO of the division stated:

> For a meeting with a BU manager, I have the manager plus representatives from various (support units), like supply, marketing, and convenience stores. And we have a conversation. In the past we were a bunch of controllers sitting around talking about variances. Now we discuss what's gone right, what's gone wrong. What should we keep doing, what should we stop doing? What resources do we need to get back on track, not explaining a negative variance due to some volume mix. The process enables me to see how the NBU managers think, plan and execute. I can see the gaps, and by understanding the manager's culture and mentality, I can develop customized programmes to make him, or her, a better manager.

Brian Baker, executive vice president of Mobil US Marketing and Refining, talked about his meetings:

> I went into these reviews thinking they would be long and arduous. I was pleasantly surprised how simple they were. Managers came in prepared. They were paying attention to their scorecards and using them in a very productive way—to drive their organization hard to achieve the targets. How they weighted their measures spoke clearly about their priorities of relative importance up and down the four perspectives.
>
> Basically, there's no way I can understand and supervise all the activities that report to me. I need a device like the scorecard where the business unit managers are measuring their own performance. My job is to keep adjusting the light I shine on their strategy and implementation, to monitor and guide their journeys, and see whether there are any potential storms on the horizon that we should address.

These managers had never seen Simons' description and definition of an interactive system, but their natural leadership style was to operate their scorecard system to question, probe, challenge and coach about the strategy and its implementation, an ideal example of Simons' description of an interactive system.

After studying the successful implementations of Mobil US Marketing and Refining and other early adopters, we proposed the following five leadership and management processes for successful strategy execution, helping to create "the strategy-focused organization" (SFO) (Kaplan & Norton 2001):

1. mobilize change through executive leadership;
2. translate the strategy;
3. align the organization to the strategy;

[9] Many academics, consultants and managers, however, continue to think erroneously of the scorecard as only a performance measurement system. Their knowledge and acquaintance with the scorecard is probably based only on reading the original 1992 *Harvard Business Revue* article or the first half of the initial balanced scorecard book.

The Enterprise Scorecard	Sources of enterprise derived value (Corporate themes)
Financial Synergies "How can we increase the shareholder value of our SBU portfolio?"	❑ *Internal capital management*—Create synergy through effective management of internal capital and labourmarkets. ❑ *Corporate brand*—Integrate a diverse set of businesses around a single brand, promoting common values or themes.
Customer Synergies "How can we share the customer Interface to increase total customer value?"	❑ *Cross-selling*—Create value by cross-selling a broad range of products/services from several business units. ❑ *Common value proposition*—Create a consistent buying experience, conforming to corporate standards at multiple outlets.
Internal Process Synergies "How can we manage SBU processes to achieve economies of scale or value chain integration?"	❑ *Shared services*—Create economies of scale by sharing the systems, facilities and personnel in critical support processes. ❑ *Value chain integration*—Create value by integrating contiguous processes in the industry value chain.
Learning & Growth Synergies "How can we develop and share our intangible assets?"	❑ *Intangible assets*—Share a competency around the development of human, information and organization capital. ❑ *Strategic themes*—Provide leadership in complex organizations through the management of strategic themes.

Figure 3. Sources of enterprise synergy.

4. motivate employees to make strategy their everyday job;
5. govern to make strategy a continual process.

This research completed the transformation of the balanced scorecard from a performance measurement system to an interactive management system for strategy execution.

Subsequent work, documented in additional books and *Harvard Business Review* articles, expanded upon this framework. Our third book, *Strategy Maps*, already mentioned, expanded upon Principle 2. Our fourth book, *Alignment*, expanded on Principle 3. We showed how strategy maps and scorecards could articulate the role for a corporate strategy that defined how a collection of business units could create more value than if each unit operated autonomously, as a standalone company (Kaplan & Norton, 2006a,b). We discovered that all the various corporate strategies for enhancing the value of their business units could be represented using the four balanced scorecard perspectives, as shown in Fig. 3.

Our most recent work has focused on Principle 5, in which companies link strategy and operations (Kaplan & Norton, 2008a,b). Figure 4 shows the architecture of a comprehensive six-stage closed-loop management system that links strategic planning with operational execution.

1. develop the strategy;
2. translate the strategy;
3. align the organization;
4. plan operations;
5. monitor and learn;
6. test and adapt the strategy.

In the sixth stage, managers use internal operational data and new external environmental and competitive data to test and update the strategy, which launches another loop around the integrated strategy and operational management system. This work integrates not only our prior work on strategy maps, alignment and employee motivation, but also quality management, dashboards, time-driven activity-based costing for resource capacity planning and strategy feedback (Kaplan & Anderson, 2004, 2007), strategy development and formulation tools, and analytics for testing and adapting the strategy.

This most recent development is about much more than just the balanced scorecard. It embeds the original balanced scorecard framework as a component within a comprehensive management system that integrates strategy

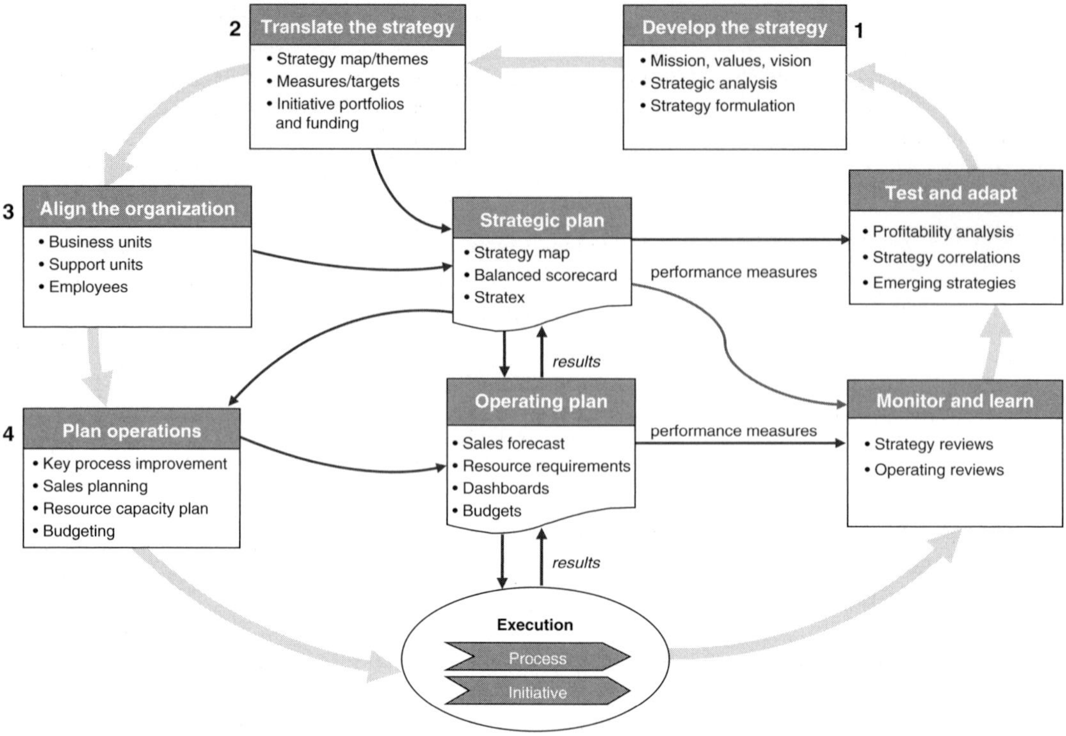

Figure 4. The management system: linking strategy to operations.

and operations. One can view the proposed management system as accomplishing the comprehensive framework advocated earlier by Herb Simon—for scorecarding, attention-directing and problem-solving—and Robert Anthony, for strategic planning, management control and operational control. Rather than have them as separate activities, as suggested by Simon and Anthony, we now have the various activities for strategy development, planning, alignment, operational planning, operational control and strategy control integrated within a closed-loop, comprehensive management system.

The integrated and comprehensive closed-loop management system has many moving parts and interrelationships, and requires simultaneous coordination among all organizational line and staff units. Existing processes that today are run by different parts of the organization—such as budgeting by finance, personal goals and communications by human resources, and process management by operations—must be modified and coordinated to create strategic alignment. They must work as a system, instead of a set of uncoordinated sub-systems as they do today. In addition, we have proposed some entirely new processes—such as creating strategy maps and scorecards that align organizational units and employees to the strategy. Because these processes are new to most organizations, they have no natural home within the existing structure. Clearly, organizations face a complex task to synchronize such an interrelated system.

We have identified the need for a new organizational function, which we call the office of strategy management (OSM), to be the process owner of the strategy execution system and its component processes (Kaplan & Norton, 2005). The OSM has ownership for the new processes that translate and cascade the strategy, link it to operations and organize the strategy review and strategy testing and adapting meetings. It also integrates and coordinates activities that align strategy and operations across functions and business units. The OSM, analogous to a military general's chief-of-staff, keeps all the diverse organizational players—executive team, business units, regional units, support units (finance, human resources, information technology), departments and, ultimately, the employees—aligned with each other, operating independently when appropriate, but also coming together, as needed, to execute the enterprise's strategy.

4. Future Opportunities

This article has documented the precursors of the balanced scorecard and its continued evolution, from its introduction in 1992 to recent developments in 2008, the time at which this chapter was written. Intensive and continual collaboration with innovating companies, public sector agencies and non-profit organizations have informed the enhancements and capabilities of the original balanced scorecard. Among these advances are the following:

- strategy maps of strategic objectives;
- extending the concept to non-profit and public sector enterprises;
- measurement of strategic readiness of intangible assets;
- role for executive leadership;
- creating synergies through alignment of business and support units to corporate strategy;
- using communication to create intrinsic motivation;
- deploying extrinsic motivation by aligning employees' personal objectives and compensation to strategic objectives;
- linking strategy and operations in a new closed-loop management system;
- creating the office of strategy management.

It's not easy to respond when questioned about what happens next. While each of these advances was a logical extension of previous work, each presented itself incrementally and opportunistically, not as part of a planned evolution of the concept over a 15-year period. While acknowledging a cloudy crystal ball, I can see several big opportunities for future work.

First, the early adopters of the BSC (Rockwater, FMC, Mobil, Chemical Bank, Cigna P&C, AT&T Canada, Wells Fargo Online Services, and the City of Charlotte) had superb leaders. Initially, perhaps, we took such leadership for granted. Subsequent experience revealed that when the balanced scorecard failed in organizations, we could usually trace the roots of failure back to lack of executive leadership, not to any particular inherent design flaw in strategy maps, scorecards or the four other strategy-focused organization principles. The failures occurred when staff groups or functional officers introduced the scorecard with the acquiescence, but not the leadership and commitment, of the CEO of the business unit. And the purpose for introducing the balanced scorecard was not for effective strategy execution, but for more tactical reasons, such as to change the compensation system, to reinforce a quality management system or to change the reporting system to give managers more access to information about their operations. All of these goals are laudable but none, by itself, can transform and align an organization for effective strategy execution, the principal deliverable, as it turned out, for balanced scorecard implementations.

Future research studies of BSC implementations could certainly benefit from measuring organizational leadership in each implementation and assessing this factor's role in creating success. Several authors have done limited testing about the environments in which the balanced scorecard has succeeded or failed. Most of these studies were ad hoc correlations of nonfinancial and financial variables. Few of the studies were informed by the concepts described in our writings on strategy-focused organization principles and the most recent work on integration of strategic planning and operational execution. The empirical evidence that Norton and I have seen and documented over the past 15 years identifies leadership as the most important variable explaining success or failure. To state a bold hypothesis, leadership may be both necessary and sufficient for success. It is necessary since, without it, the balanced scorecard will be just another ad hoc reporting system, and the gains from embedding the balanced scorecard in a system for effective strategy execution will not be realized. Leadership is required to translate strategy into the linked strategic objectives on a strategy map and then to use the map and the accompanying scorecard interactively, as described in this chapter. The more challenging claim is that it is also sufficient. This hypothesis emerges from the documented best practices, drawn from hundreds of successful implementations, on how to build and operate the new management system for strategy execution. Managers can apply this body of knowledge, which is referenced in this article, to implement the four strategy-focused organization principles other than leadership. But none of the four principles can be effectively mobilized and sustained without leadership at the top. Of course, such a strong claim about both necessity and sufficiency needs to be tested through careful research designs and instruments.

Research in leadership would start with measurement; there could be multiple forms of effective leadership but some aspects may be necessary or common across all leadership styles. Once leadership can be measured validly, then cross-sectional or longitudinal research can be performed to see its influence on explaining variation in the results delivered from following the five SFO principles.

Secondly, the emerging literature and practice on enterprise risk management needs to be more formally embedded in the strategy map and balanced scorecard. Many companies, especially financial services companies, have already specified risk management objectives in the scorecard's financial and process objectives. But these additions have been incremental and not part of an integrated risk management framework. Our generic strategy map template (see Fig. 2) emphasizes two primary financial sub-strategies, revenue growth and productivity, as the drivers of sustainable shareholder value creation. Surely, risk management must be introduced as a third pillar for financial performance, and perhaps an entirely new set of risk management processes should be included within the process perspective. Given the intense focus of companies around the world to improve their measurement and management of risk, we should expect important advances, over the next five years, to embed risk management objectives more centrally into the strategy execution framework.

Thirdly, strategy maps still represent a highly-aggregated view of causal relationships among strategic objectives. In order to make strategy maps more visually appealing to managers and employees, we have simplified the causal relationships assumed within the strategy map (one might even describe the generic strategy map as a "dumbed-down" representation of causal linkages). Norton and I, both trained as electrical engineers, have been aware from the outset that systems dynamics techniques could help produce a more detailed model that links both strategic and operational objectives in a more elaborate mapping exercise. A detailed systems dynamics model would incorporate causal linkages that have estimates of magnitude and time delay, as well as more complex feedback loops than are presently visualized in the generic strategy map. For an example of such a quantified linkage, analysts could estimate the percentage improvement in a lagging indicator that would be expected from, say, a 1% improvement in a leading indicator. The analysts would also estimate the time delay between a 1% improvement in a leading indicator and the expected response in a lagging indicator. And the causal linkages need not be uni-dimensional. The model could include multiple leading indicators and impacts that can be a combination of linear, multiplicative or even Boolean (no impact if the improvement is less than a given amount; a jump in impact once a threshold level of improvement has been achieved).

The statistical and modelling capabilities for constructing models of detailed causal relationships already exist. And many companies, particularly those operating hundreds or thousands of relatively similar decentralized units, generate sufficient data each month to estimate even complex models. The shortage seems to be how to marry analytic capabilities with companies that generate sufficient data and have a senior management team capable of understanding and using the dynamic, causal models effectively to guide their strategies and operations.

Thus, while much has been learned over the past 15 years, much interesting research can still be done. And with many private, public sector and non-profit enterprises around the world implementing new strategy execution systems based on the balanced scorecard framework, the opportunities for informed empirical research are great.

References

Anthony, R. N. (1965). *Planning and Control Systems: A Framework for Analysis.* Graduate School of Business Administration, Harvard Business School.

Atkinson, A., Waterhouse, J. & Wells, R. (1997). A stakeholder approach to strategic performance measurement. *Sloan Management Review*, **Spring**.

Becker, B. & Huselid, M. (1998). High performance work systems and firm performance: a synthesis of research and managerial implications. *Research in Personnel and Human Resources Management.* Greenwich, CT: JAI Press, pp. 53–101.

Berliner, C., & Brimson, J. (1991). CAM-I Study; R. Lynch and K. Cross, *Measure Up! Yardsticks for Continuous Improvement.* Cambridge, MA: Basil Blackwell.

Caplan, E. H. & Landekich, S. (1975). *Human Resource Accounting: Past, Present, and Future.* New York, NY: National Association of Accountants.

Drucker, P. (1954). *The Practice of Management.* New York, NY: HarperCollins.

Fama, E. F. (1970). Efficient capital markets: a review of theory and empirical work. *Journal of Finance*, **May**.

Fama, E. F. & Jensen, M. C. (1983). Separation of Ownership and Control. *Journal of Law and Economics*, **26**(2), June.

Flamholtz, E. (1974). *Human Resource Accounting.* Encino, CA: Dickenson Publishing.

Garvin, D. A. & Hayes, R. H. (1982). Managing as if tomorrow mattered. *Harvard Business Review*, **60**(3), 70–79.

Grossman, S. J. & Hart, O. D. (1983). An analysis of the principal-agent problem. *Econometrica*, **51**, 7–45.

Grove, H. D., Mock, T. J. & Ehrenreich, K. B. (1977). A review of human resource accounting measurement systems from a measurement theory perspective. *Accounting, Organizations and Society*, **2**(4), 219–236.

Harris, M. & Raviv, A. (1979). Optimal incentive contracts with imperfect information. *Journal of Economic Theory*, **20**(2), 231–259.

Hayes, R. H. & Abernathy, W. (1980). Managing our way to economic decline. *Harvard Business Review*, **58**(4), 67–77.

Heskett, J., Jones, T. O., Loveman, G. W., Earl Sasser, W. & Schlesinger, L. A. (1994). Putting the service-profit chain to work. *Harvard Business Review*, **72**(2), 164–174.

Heskett, J., Sasser, W. E. & Schlesinger, L. (1997). *The Service Profit Chain.* New York, NY: Free Press.

Holmstrom, B. (1979). Moral Hazard and Observability. *Bell Journal of Economics*, **10**(1), Spring 74–91.

Howell, R., Brown, J., Soucy, S. & Seed, A. (1987). *Management Accounting in the New Manufacturing Environment.* Montvale, NJ: National Assn. of Accountants and CAM-I.

Huselid, M. A. (1995). The impact of human resource management practices on turnover, productivity, and corporate financial performance. *Academy of Management Journal*, 635–672.

Jensen, M. (2001). Value maximization, stakeholder theory, and the corporate objective function. *Journal of Applied Corporate Finance*, **Fall**, 8–21.

Jensen, M. J. & Meckling, W. R. (1976). Theory of the firm: managerial behavior, agency cost, and ownership structure. *Journal of Financial Economics*, **3**, 305–360.

Johnson, H. T. (1989). Managing costs: an outmoded philosophy. *Manufacturing Engineering*, **May**.

Johnson, H. T. & Kaplan, R. S. (1987). *Relevance Lost: The Rise and Fall of Management Accounting*. Boston, MA: Harvard Business School Press.

Kaplan, R. S. (1990). *Measures for Manufacturing Excellence*. Boston, MA: Harvard Business School Press.

Kaplan, R. S. & Anderson, S. R. (2007). *Time-Driven Activity-Based Costing*. Boston, MA: Harvard Business School Press.

Kaplan, R. S. & Anderson, S. R. (2004). Time-driven activity-based costing. *Harvard Business Review*, **November**, 131–138.

Kaplan, R. S. & Norton, D. P. (2008a). Mastering the management system. *Harvard Business Review*, **January**, 57–62.

Kaplan, R. S. & Norton, D. P. (2008b). *The Execution Premium: Linking Strategy to Operations for Competitive Advantage*. Boston, MA: Harvard Business School Press.

Kaplan, R. S. & Norton, D. P. (2006a). *Alignment: Using the Balanced Scorecard to Create Corporate Synergies*. Boston, MA: Harvard Business School Press.

Kaplan, R. S. & Norton, D. P. (2006b). How to implement a new strategy without disrupting your organization. *Harvard Business Review*, **March**, 100–109.

Kaplan, R. S. & Norton, D. P. (2005). The office of strategy management. *Harvard Business Review*, **October**, 72–80.

Kaplan, R. S. & Norton, D. P. (2004a). *Strategy Maps: Converting Intangible Assets into Tangible Outcomes*. Boston, MA: Harvard Business School Press.

Kaplan, R. S. & Norton, D. P. (2004b). Measuring the Strategic Readiness of Intangible Assets. *Harvard Business Review*, **February**, 52–63.

Kaplan, R. S. & Norton, D. P. (2003). *Strategy Maps*. Boston, MA: Harvard Business School Press.

Kaplan, R. S. & Norton, D. P. (2001). *The Strategy-Focused Organization: How Balanced Scorecard Companies Thrive in the New Competitive Environment*. Boston, MA: Harvard Business School Press.

Kaplan, R. S. & Norton, D. P. (1996a). *The Balanced Scorecard: Translating Strategy into Action*. Boston, MA: Harvard Business School Press.

Kaplan, R. S. & Norton, D. P. (1996b). Using the Balanced Scorecard as a strategic management system. *Harvard Business Review*, **January–February**, 75–85.

Kaplan, R. S. & Norton, D. P. (1993). Putting the Balanced Scorecard to work. *Harvard Business Review*, **September–October**, 134–147.

Kaplan, R. S. & Norton, D. P. (1992). The Balanced Scorecard: measures that drive performance. *Harvard Business Review*, **January–February**, 71–79.

Kelvin, (1883). Electrical Units of Measurement, PLA, vol. 1, 1883–05–03.

Lewis, R.W. (1955). Measuring, reporting and appraising results of operations with reference to goals, plans and budgets. *Planning, Managing and Measuring the Business: A case study of management planning and control at General Electric Company*. New York, NY: Controllership Foundation.

Neely, A. & Adams, C. (2002). *Performance Prism: The Scorecard for Measuring and Managing Stakeholder Relationships*. London, UK: Financial Times/Prentice Hall.

Nolan Norton Institute. (1991). Measuring Performance in the Organization of the Future: A Research Study.

Porter, M. E. (1992). Capital Disadvantage: America's falling capital investment system. *Harvard Business Review*, **70**(5), September–October 65–82.

Porter, M. E. & Kramer, M. R. (1999). Philanthropy's new agenda: creating value. *Harvard Business Review*, **77**(6), November–December 121–130.

Porter, M. E. & Kramer, M. R. (2006). Strategy and society: the link between competitive advantage and corporate social responsibility. *Harvard Business Review*, **84**(12), December.

Simon, H. (1963). A Framework for Decision Making. *Proceedings of a Symposium on Decision Theory*, 1–9, 22–28.

Simon, H., Guetzkow, H., Kozmetsky, G. & Tyndall, G. (1954; reprinted 1978). *Centralization vs. Decentralization in Organizing the Controller's Department*. New York, NY: Controllership Foundation Scholars Book Co.

Simons, R. (1995a). *Levers of Control: How Managers Use Innovative Control Systems to Drive Strategic Renewal*. Boston, MA: Harvard Business School Press.

Simons, R. (1995b). Control in an age of empowerment. *Harvard Business Review*, **March–April**, 80–88.

Stewart, G. B. (1991). *The Quest for Value*. New York, NY: HarperCollins.

Handbook of Management Accounting Research
Edited by Christopher S. Chapman, Anthony G. Hopwood and Michael D. Shields

Management Accountants in the United States: Practitioner and Academic Views of Recent Developments[1]

James E. Sorensen

University of Denver, USA

Abstract: Management accountants (although not called management accountants in those days) can be traced back to the 1700s, but some of the exciting developments are in the late twentieth and early twenty-first centuries. In the past two decades management accountants have moved from data accumulators, financial reporters, data analysts, decision-supporters and business advisers to business partners. Top level management accountants are now emerging as members of the most important business decision-making groups guiding major organizational, operational and strategic choices. This chapter focuses on the recent and meteoric rise of management accountants. Research identifies the knowledge, skills and abilities (known also as KSAs) required for doing management accounting, along with transformations and trends changing at blistering rates. The stresses and strains of these new roles are apparent in the continuing educational requirements for current management accountants in transition, as well as the new collegiate entrants into the profession. Studies supported by both practitioner and academic sources identify major gaps between practice and the collegiate classroom. Trying to synchronize management accounting education with practice may require practitioner-driven curricular change and academic programmes willing to risk innovation. A few academics offer innovative approaches to teaching management accounting in an academic environment that is not particularly disposed to publications about teaching. Specific areas of management accounting research (especially empirical field studies, cases and surveys of practice) and education (especially curriculum models and classroom tested cases or simulations with appropriate assessments of effectiveness) justify future support and development. With a rapidly changing environment management accountants may need a possible change in name to reflect the key role they occupy in the finance function of organizations.

1. Introduction

The United States (US) Bureau of Labor Statistics reports that in 2005, 85% of the accountancy profession works inside organizations as accounting professionals and 15% of the profession works externally and performs public accounting services (Bureau of Labor Statistics, 2005). In other words, most accountants are management accountants, although some retain responsibility for internal auditing and financial reporting within the organization.

2. The Emergence of Management Accountants

2.1. *Historic Development of what Management Accountants do*

The history of management accounting development in the US, as well as many of the current issues of management accounting, are well documented in the second volume of the *Handbook of Management Accounting Research* by Chapman, Hopwood & Shields (2006). A comprehensive review of the history of accounting in the US is found in Previtts & Merino (1998). In outlining where management accountants are going, however, a brief summary of key historical developments (with

[1]This chapter is dedicated to the memory of Gary Siegel, Associate Professor of Accounting in the School of Accountancy, DePaul University, Chicago, IL. The author expresses his appreciation to Anthony Hopwood, Darius Fatemi and Lisa Victoravich for their reviews and thoughtful comments on this chapter.

DOI: 10.1016/S1751-3243(07)03004-0

appropriate references) is productive in viewing the evolution and current state of management accountants.

2.1.1. The Early Years

Management accounting in terms of purposeful costing is present in the US in the New England textile industry of the early 1800s (Fleischman & Tyson, 2006). Reports included comparative costing between different mills, different time periods and individual products and product lines. Mill owners and managers addressed issues such as make or buy, evaluating relative efficiency of mills, assessing if prices covered costs of production and deciding if production facilities should be expanded (Tyson, 1992, 1998). The reports were suboptimal, however, since the costing used simple averaging and allocation procedures and systematically ignored depreciation (Fleischman & Tyson, 2006, p. 1091). In the mid-1840s railroads used the ton-mile as a basic cost measure (Chandler 1997; Heier 2000) that became cost per ton, as developed by Andrew Carnegie of the Carnegie Steel Company (or what was to become US Steel). Still absent was attention to overhead costs and depreciation (Chandler, 1977, pp. 267–269; Fleischman, 1996, p. 131; Johnson and Kaplan, 1987, pp. 32–34). Pre-Civil War practices by the Springfield Armory saw the emergence of formal inspection of production and piece rates (Hoskin & Macve, 1996).

2.1.2. The Early to Mid-twentieth Century

While the precise origin of purposeful cost accounting is debated heatedly (namely, New England textiles, US railroading, West Point discipline of the Springfield Armory or the British Industrial Revolution from across the Atlantic), scientific management of the early 1900s is associated with standard costing and the analysis of variances between estimated and actual costs, although it was not actually widely used in practice even through World War II (Fleischman & Marquette, 2003). Decentralized corporations emerged in the 1920s and fostered return on investment (DuPont's famous ROI), forecasting, flexible budgeting and market-based transfer pricing (at General Motors) (Fleischman & Tyson, 2006, pp. 1093–1095). The Ford and GM competitive approaches are of special interest: Ford used price while GM focused on quality and functionality parameters that are the forerunners of lean accounting (Cooper, 1995). While glimmers of budgeting appeared earlier in business (see earlier reference to flexible budgeting at GM), budgeting appears to have been conveyed from government to business during the 1920s (Marquette & Fleischman, 1992). World War II, with an emphasis on actual cost, was a setback for standard costs (Kohler & Cooper, 1945).

2.1.3. The Latter Half of the Twentieth Century

Herbert Simon et al. (1954) observed accounting information was to support three distinct functions of controllership within a firm: (1) scorekeeping; (2) attention directing; and (3) problem solving. Simon's study helped to focus management accounting information on managerial decision-making. Direct (variable, marginal) costing and responsibility accounting (including the use of standard costs) emerged in the 1950s, along with heated discussions over absorption (full) costing (Previts & Merino, 1998). Cost and budgetary controls emerged during the 1960s, but this type of accounting was challenged in the 1970s with critical comments about the effectiveness of these approaches (Caplan, 1966; Hopwood, 1972). Other developments in the 1960s and 1970s included linear programming for profit maximization or cost minimization and planning, programming and budgeting system (PPBS). Programme evaluation and review techniques (PERT) emerged for planning and managing complex long-term projects, as well as zero-based budgeting (ZZB) (Fleischman & Tyson, 2006).

Starting in the 1970s, operations management through integrated manufacturing (namely, automation, just-in-time and total quality management) brought new dimensions to management accounting (Dean & Snell, 1991). This included decentralization, non-financial performance measures, cost calculations, standard setting and reward systems (Hansen & Mouritsen, 2006). Cost of quality posited a trade-off between the cost of failure and cost of conformance (Juran, 1979, 1951; Ittner, 1996; Ittner et al., 2001; Sedatole, 2003). Out of this environment emerged lean accounting (Womack & Jones, 1996; Kroll, 2004; van der Merwe & Thompson, 2007), theory of constraints (TOC) (Noreen et al., 1995; Kee, 1995; Kaplan & Cooper, 1998), lifecycle costing (Berliner & Brimson, 1988; Gupta & Gunasekaran, 2005) and continuous improvement or Kaizen (Kaplan & Cooper, 1998; Daniel & Reitsperger, 1992). The influence of operations management is still observed today, especially in approaches such as lean accounting (Johnson, 2005). Budgeting (one of the widely used tools in management accounting) continues to be one of the most extensively researched topics in management accounting, using theoretical perspectives of economics, psychology and sociology (Covaleski et al., 2003).

2.1.4. The Late Twentieth Century and the Early Twenty-first Century

As pressures to reduce costs increased in response to unrelenting global competition in the 1980s up until the recent 2000s, new costing approaches emerged.

Activity-based costing (ABC) appeared around the mid-1980s (Cooper, 1988a,b, 1989a,b; Cooper & Kaplan, 1988), appended with activity-based management (Jones & Dugdale, 2002) and a recently added time-driven version (Kaplan & Anderson, 2004). Before a quarter of a century of consideration and use, authors attempted to evaluate

ABCs success (Shields, 1995; Anderson & Young, 1999), utilization and contribution (Gosselin, 2006).

Target costing, as a strategic tool, emerged in the Western world in the mid-1990s and permeated the professional literature during the early 2000s (Brausch, 1994; Tayles, 1995; Shank & Fisher, 1999; Boer & Ettle, 1999; Cooper & Slagmulder, 2002; Ansari, Bell & Okano, 2006).

More recent developments reveal strategic cost management (including a value chain analysis) that purports to align the firm's cost structure with its strategy and pursues cost management decisions to deploy the strategy (Tomkins & Carr, 1996; Shank & Govindarajan, 1992, 1994; Kaplan & Norton, 1996, 2004; Anderson, 2006).

A major dimension of the strategic management focus has been the balanced scorecard (BSC) (Kaplan & Norton, 1966; Libby et al., 2004; Souissi & Ito, 2004) that is fashioned after the criteria for performance excellence (or Baldrige) (www.quality.nist.gov) and is often viewed as the gold standard for frameworks driving performance excellence. As one executive of a multinational firm observed, "The Baldrige Criteria for Performance Excellence provides the most capable … overall business system framework we have ever found …" (Baldrige National Quality Program, 2008, p. 2). The work in the BSC sets the stage for management accountants to be involved in multiple perspectives of performance measurement (Chenhall & Langfield-Smith, 2007).

2.1.5. Other Recent Descriptive Efforts

Boer offers a review of management accounting history from about 1919 to 2000 (Boer, 2000). Gupta & Gunasekaran (2005), while focusing on the recent developments of value-based costing and performance measurement systems (PMS), perform a useful background review of the development of management accounting (pp. 340–346). The review (while not in the same detail as contained in this chapter) highlights major topics from the 1850s to the early 2000s. In addition, Gupta & Gunasekaran (2005) add a useful perspective on the new (namely, virtual) enterprise faced by management accountants by identifying changes such as distributed operations management, global outsourcing, strategic alliances based on core competencies, information technology for an integrated supply chain management, enterprise resource planning systems, e-commerce and logistics value chain (p. 346). Lukka & Shields (1999) offer a focus on innovation in management accounting. Lillis & Mundy, (2005), attempt to close the gaps between surveys and case studies using cross-sectional field studies in management accounting.

3. Professional Associations of Management Accountants

3.1. The Early Professional Associations

The early ascendancy of cost accounting in professional associations is documented by Loft (1986) and the Institute of Cost and Works Accountants (ICWA) (Loft, 1990). Subsequent professional organizational developments in the US, such as a National Association of Cost Accountants (forerunner of the current Institute of Management Accountants or IMA) and the industry section of the American Institute of Certified Public Accountants (AICPA) are acknowledged by Fleischman & Tyson (2006).

3.2. Current Views of Professional Associations

Fleming conducted an interview with the top executives of three major accounting associations in 2005. Melancon (president of the AICPA, with over 150 000 members in business and industry) observed "(management accounting is) … the nerve centre of an organization" (Fleming, 2005, p. 67). Other chief executives of leading world accounting organizations representing 335 000 members around the globe who work in business and industry (C. Tilley, CEO of the Charted Institute of Management Accountants (CIMA) in London and S. F. Vieweg, president and CEO of the Certified Management Accountants of Canada (CMAC)) agreed that management accounting is the language of business (Tilley) and that management accounting has grown exponentially in recent times (Vieweg). Over 50% of US CPAs work in business and industry (Fleming, 2005).

Sharman, president and CEO of the IMA, with over 50 000 members worldwide, called for "… education and certification for entry-level professional that actually addresses the nature of the work they will be performing in industry (Sharman, 2007, p. 7)." Recently the IMA announced its involvement and funding of relevant, practitioner-based research to develop tools and methods for the profession (Wallin, 2003). The IMA now issues statements on management accounting (IMA, 2007).

Closely related to the work of management accountants who work in information technologies and internal controls are the Information Systems Audit and Control Association (ISACA) and the Institute of Internal Auditors (IIA). As management accountants move to the top side of an organization, new memberships in an organization such as the Financial Executives International (FEI) become possible. FEI has admission criteria such as minimum business size and organizational titles. As examples of the admission criteria, operating expenses must be \$20 million or the combined net worth and long-term debt must be \$15 million. The eligible positions include, for example, CFO, controller, treasurer, financial vice president or chief accounting officer.

These organizations all offer expanded continuing professional educational (CPE) programmes and these efforts are documented in their website offerings, cited below. In brief, key professional associations appear to be aware and supportive of the importance and the transformation of management accounting. The CPE development is too extensive and too dynamic to document here. The reader is encouraged to access the websites of these organizations, cited below,[2] to identify and to appreciate the CPE programming now offered by professional associations to management accountants. In addition, many other professional associations (for example, state societies of CPAs) offer continuing education programmes of interest to management accountants (for example, see California, Colorado, Florida, New York and Texas).

4. Recent Research on Management Accountants

4.1. Where do Management Accountants Work?

Most accounting graduates work inside organizations. The AICPA report, "The Supply of Accounting Graduates and the Demand for Public Accounting Recruits," indicates where accounting graduates begin their careers (AICPA, 2006). Table 1 includes data from the report and shows that more than 60% (62.56 % in Table 1) of accounting graduates in the US over the last five years immediately begin their careers in industry and other non-public accounting areas.[3] If an estimated cumulative turnover rate of 50%[4] is applied to total public accounting hirings staggered over the same five year period, the number of accounting graduates in industry and other careers grows to an average of 73%. If, as these statistics suggest, a large majority of accounting graduates begin, or quickly migrate to, careers outside of public accounting, the 85% cited earlier (Bureau of Labor Standards, 2005) seems quite achievable.

4.2. What do Management Accountants do?

The Practice Analysis of Management Accounting (Siegel et al., 1996) was the first national comprehensive practice analysis of management accounting. The Practice

Table 1. Analysis of accounting graduates entering industry or other careers from 2000 to 2004.

1 Year	2 Total Production (page 4)	3 Total PA Hires (page 24)	4 Industry and others Production (col 2–col 3)	5 Industry and others % (col 4–col 2)
1999–00	45 095	20 951	24 144	53.54
2000–01	46 555	16 370	30 185	64.84
2001–02	44 695	15 925	28 770	64.37
2002–03	49 665	16 825	32 840	66.12
2003–04	53 760	19 705	34 055	63.35
Total/%	239 770	89 776	149 994	**62.56**

Source: AICPA. (2006). The supply of accounting graduates and the demand for public accounting recruits—2005. American Institute of Certified Public Accountants, Inc. New York, NY

[2]Websites of selected current professional organizations (accessed November 9, 2007): American Institute of CPAs (AICPA): www.aicpa.org; Certified Management Accountants of Canada (CMA): www.cma-canada.org; Chartered Institute of Management Accountants (CIMA): www.cimaglobal.com; Financial Executives International (FEI): www.financialexecutives.org; Information Systems Audit and Control Association (ISACA): www.isaca.org; Institute of Internal Auditors (IAA): www.theiia.com; Institute of Management Accountants (IMA): www.imanet.org.

[3]The National Center for Education Statistics (NCES) reports accounting graduates in the Digest of Education Statistics 2005 Table 252: The bachelors, masters, and doctoral degrees by degree-granting institutions by sex of student and field of study 2003–2004 (see www.nces.ed.gov). The AICPA Supply and Demand reports 2003–2004 accounting graduates (bachelors 40 420 and masters 13 340) at 53 760 while the NCES reports 2003–2004 accounting graduates (bachelors 35 485 and masters 8022) at 43 507. The difference of 10 253 graduates cited by the AICPA Supply and Demand study is 23.5% higher than the total reported by NCES. The AICPA study reports (p. 38) the use of regression equations to estimate the accounting graduates from non-responding schools and similar procedures for the non-responding firms for each of the of the four firm-size categories (namely, more than 200 members, 50–200 members, 10–49 members and fewer than 10 members). Extensive follow-up procedures to secure the participation of the 17 largest firms were noted (p. 20).

[4]The AICPA Supply and Demand study (2006) reports an annual average of 12% turnover for all firms for the years 2000 to 2004 (p. 33), thus a five year cumulative percentage of 50% is conservative since five years at 12% would total 60%.

Analysis Project Committee consisted of representatives from the IMA, AICPA, FEI and IIA. The questionnaire was pretested, mailed to a proportionate sample of 4080 members of the IMA, AICPA, FEI and IIA, with a follow-up on non-respondents, and resulted in a response rate of 20%. The results were viewed as representative of the population since the non-respondents were similar to the respondents and since the quantitative results were supported by qualitative interviews. The mean of any given question could vary by 3.6% in either direction (Siegel et al., 1996, p. 130). One major finding was "the most frequently performed work activities" carried out by management accountants as shown in Fig. 1.

The numbers on the bars refer to the percentage of respondents who perform that work activity on a daily basis. The "percent" indicates the percentages of all respondents who identified that work activity, thus the total percentage exceeds 100 because respondents could name up to five work activities (Siegel et al., 1996, p. 9).

The frequency with which a work activity is performed is not necessarily an indicator of how critical the work is perceived to be. When confronted with a question of importance, a different set of "most critical work activities" for management accountants emerged as presented in Table 2.

As early as 1996 strategic planning, internal consulting, process improvement and customer and product profitability were appearing as critical activities on the work screen of management accountants (emphasis added in Table 2).

Table 2. Most critical work activities for management accountants.

Work Activity	%
Accounting systems and financial reporting	46
Long-term strategic planning (emphasis added)	**32**
Managing the accounting/finance function	29
Internal consulting (emphasis added)	**27**
Short-term budgeting process	25
Financial and economic analysis	25
Process improvement (emphasis added)	**24**
Computer systems and operations	21
Performance evaluation	21
Customer and product profitability (emphasis added)	**18**
Cost accounting systems	16
Internal auditing	14
Project accounting	13

Source: Gary Siegel et al., 1996. *The Practice Analysis of Management Accounting*. Institute of Management Accountants. Montvale, NJ, p. 9.

4.3. What are the Required Knowledge, Skills and Abilities?

Studies in the management accounting area provide several specific examples of knowledge, skills and abilities required for careers in management accounting. Two Institute of Management Accountants (IMA) studies (Siegel et al., 1996, p. 10; Siegel & Sorensen, 1999,

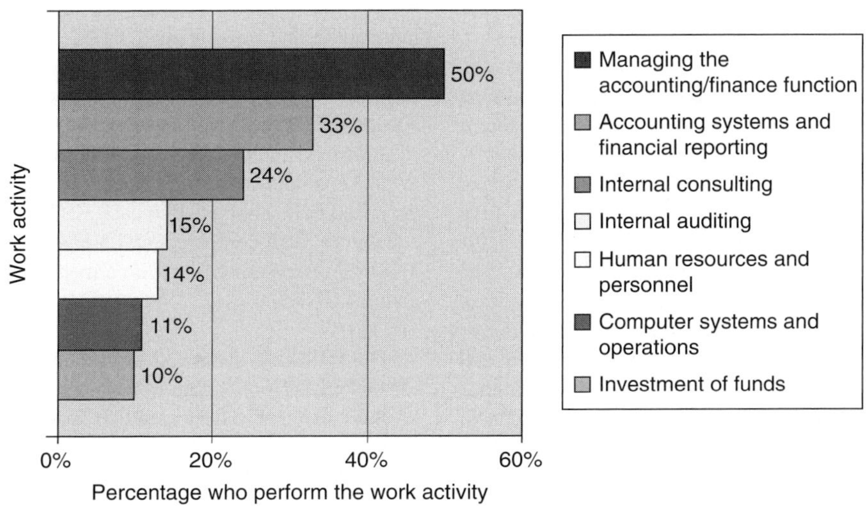

Figure 1. Most frequently performed work activities. *Source*: Gary Siegel et al. (1996). *The Practice Analysis of Management Accounting*. Montvale, NJ: Institute of Management Accountants, p. 8.

p. 13) revealed important information about the knowledge, skills and abilities (KSAs) required for success in accounting careers in corporate America. Rather than focus on knowledge, skills and abilities (KSAs) as separate and distinct classifications, Siegel et al. (1996, p. 44) recognized the overlap among them and considered KSAs as one bundle of necessary talent—as the competencies required for successful performance of the work activities. These competencies, or areas of proficiency, include an understanding of technical information, the ability to apply it in appropriate situations and an awareness of the limitation of technical information for solving problems. The KSAs also included the ability to recognize problems, to make sound decisions, to get along with people and to express ideas both orally and in writing (p. 44). A comprehensive list of over 1000 KSAs was reduced to 162 through qualitative research methods (Chapter 1). For survey instrumentation, the 162 items were classified into the following 12 categories (p. 45):

1. interpersonal and analytical skills;
2. management and cost accounting;
3 financial management;
4. income taxes;
5. computer systems and operations;
6. international (perspectives);
7. professional literature;
8. financial accounting;
9. internal auditing;
10. legal environment;
11. quantitative methods;
12. economics, marketing, management, operations and behavioural science.

Table 3. Most important knowledge, skill or ability (KSAs) for work as management accountants.

Knowledge, skill or ability	Mean
Work ethic	4.67
Analytical/problem-solving skills	4.66
Interpersonal skills	4.64
Listening skills	4.58
Use of computerized spreadsheets	4.51
Understanding the business	4.48
Understanding bottom-line implications of day-to-day business and accounting decisions	4.44
Writing skills	4.32
Familiarity with business processes	4.32
Relationship between balance sheet, income statement and cash flow statement	4.31
Leadership skills	4.30
Understanding/preparing financial statements	4.29
Accounting systems: the "books," cost flows, double entry, etc.	4.25
Use of computerized accounting systems	4.22
Interpreting or analyzing financial statements	4.19
Measurement, valuation and presentation of revenue and expenses	4.17
Accruals and deferrals, adjusting and closing entries	4.15
Speaking/presentation skills	4.11
Information needs of internal customers	4.03

Source: Gary Siegel et al., 1996. *The Practice Analysis of Management Accounting*. Institute of Management Accountants. Montvale, NJ, p. 10.

Respondents rated the importance of each KSA in relation to the competent performance of their work as a corporate accountant. On this scale, 1 equals not at all important and 5 equals very important. Table 3 summarizes respondents' ratings of KSAs with a mean score of 4.0 or higher, or the top 19 out of a list of 162 KSAs.

The highest-rated KSA is "work ethic;" it has an average importance rating of 4.67. Almost two-thirds (over 64%) of the respondents rated it with a score of 5 (the highest rating). Commitment to work in a management accounting/corporate environment appears highly critical. Another indicator of this commitment was respondents indicating an average (mean) 48 hour work week. In addition to the work ethic, the highest rated KSAs encompass problem-solving skills, interpersonal skills, communication (listening and writing) skills, understanding the business and the basics of accounting. Both the qualitative and quantitative results clearly indicate that management accountants are expected to have a thorough knowledge of basic accounting. Beyond these rock-solid accounting basics, management accountants need excellent communication and interpersonal skills, analytical skills and computer-related skills. These components of knowledge form the minimum requirement for work in management accounting (Siegel et al., 1996, p. 11).

A second major research question focused on entry-level accountants: "To what extent do entry-level accountants need to be competent in each KSA?" On this scale, 1 equals not at all competent and 5 equals very competent. Table 4 presents all KSAs with a mean competency score above 3.0 (Siegel et al., 1996, p. 11), or the top 26 out of 162 KSAs.

The following six KSAs are included in the 10 highest-ranked KSAs for both importance to work and entry-level competence. These could be viewed as the common ground for anyone working as a management accountant (Siegel et al., 1996, p. 12):

- work ethic;
- listening skills;

Table 4. Highest ranked KSA for entry-level competence as management accountants.

Knowledge, skill and ability (italics highlight non-accounting KSAs)	Mean
Work ethic	4.45
Listening skills	4.15
Accounting system: the "books," cost flows, double entry, etc.	4.04
Use of computerized spreadsheets	4.03
Analytical/problem-solving skills	3.98
Accruals and deferrals, adjusting and closing entries	3.97
Relationship between balance sheet, income statement, and cash flow statement	3.86
Interpersonal skills	3.82
Mathematics through college algebra	3.75
Understanding/preparing financial statements	3.70
Writing skills	3.69
Measurement, valuation and presentation of revenue and expenses	3.53
Use of computerized accounting systems	3.52
Codes of professional ethics	3.51
Measurement, valuation and presentation of assets and equities	3.41
Interpreting or analyzing financial statements	3.34
Communications processes; deterrents to effective communication	3.22
Information needs of external users of financial statements	3.20
Professional standards for accounting, auditing reporting, etc.	3.19
Measurement, valuation and presentation of cash flow statement	3.16
Purpose and use of management information systems in business	3.16
Speaking/presentation skills	3.13
Basic statistics: means; standard deviations; probability; sampling; hypothesis testing	3.08
Internal control systems	3.05
Understanding bottom-line implication of day-to-day business and accounting decisions	3.03
FASB statements	3.01

Source: Gary Siegel et al., 1996. *The Practice Analysis of Management Accounting*. Institute of Management Accountants. Montvale, NJ, p. 11.

- use of computerized spreadsheets;
- analytical/problem-solving skills;
- relationship between balance sheet, income statement and cash-flow statement;
- interpersonal skills.

Despite the rapid changes in the field, in all likelihood these common KSAs are still viable today, although the level of computer skills is likely to be more sophisticated. If communications and other non-accounting KSAs (in italics in Table 4) are ignored, the order of rank of only the accounting KSAs in Table 4 confirms that entry-level accountants need to be proficient in the fundamentals of accounting. The highest-ranking accounting KSAs are, in fact, the fundamentals of accounting (Siegel et al., 1996, p. 12).

What do these results mean? Accounting graduates need excellent communication skills, interpersonal skills, team building skills, analytical and computer-related skills. Fundamental skills include writing, speaking, presenting, listening, negotiating, persuading and influencing, along with the ability to work in teams using logical, diagnostic and reasoned approaches to business problems.

It is now thought that exposure to psychology and social psychology will help graduates understand how to motivate people and how to resolve conflict. Successful management of organizations requires exposure to theories and models from operations management, including the literature and tools embedded in the quality literature underlying process improvement. Contact with management approaches, such as strategic planning, value chains and enterprise systems, spotlight relevant frameworks for achieving performance excellence in an organization. Coverage of finance will bring to light relevant financial and economic analyses. An introduction to information technology will reveal approaches to computer information systems and internal controls. For accounting graduates to thrive, they will need to acquire a thorough understanding of the businesses in which they work. Without an understanding of the business, they cannot add value. Developing a student's sensitivity and heightened awareness to this requirement while in school is critical to his or her future success (Siegel et al., 2007).

What about accounting skills? Entry-level accountants must have solid accounting skills. Management accountants will need a comprehensive knowledge of accounting concepts and business entity tax laws (Combes, 2007). Their future work activities and areas of concentration will encompass the disciplines of accounting, finance, systems and decision support. To be effective in their roles, they need to be familiar with all functional areas of business (human resources, marketing, purchasing, production, etc.), the key organizational processes and how the processes support functional areas (Siegel et al., 2007).

Management accountants working in the finance function " … need to develop more finely honed business and technology skills—as opposed to technical accounting and finance skills—to take advantage of the time that streamlined processes and optimally deployed tools will afford them" (CFO Research Services 1996, p. 5).

4.4. Concerns from Industry and Corporate America

In the late 1980s and early 1990s, the IMA began hearing complaints from financial executives in organizations of many types indicating that entry-level accountants were not prepared for entry into the workforce. More specifically, these executives expressed concerns that students graduating from four-year accounting programmes did not have the skills necessary for success as an entry-level corporate accountant. Students did not appear to have an adequate understanding of topics such as corporate tax, budgeting or strategic planning, and they were unfamiliar with the role of accountants in a corporate environment. Further, the executives said that increasing competition in their industries made it difficult for them to invest one or two years in training to bring the entry-level accountants up to speed. They wanted their new hires to be able to "hit the ground running" and be productive as soon as they began employment.

IMAs approach to these concerns was to sponsor research that would be useful for the academic community. Together with the Financial Executives Institute (FEI), the IMA sponsored a research project entitled "What corporate America wants in entry level accountants" (Siegel & Sorensen, 1994). This research demonstrated that the complaints of top level financial executives were shared by a large majority of financial executives in US companies. The results of this research were posted on the IMA and AAA websites and were shared with accounting educators at multiple academic meetings in 1994 and 1995.

Following the release of the 1994 IMA/FEI sponsored study, another study helped answer the question "What should students be learning to better prepare them for a successful career as accounting professionals?" This question led to a 1996 IMA and AICPA sponsored study entitled the "Practice analysis of management accounting" (Siegel & Sorensen, 1996); the study documented the work activities performed by management accountants and the knowledge, skills and abilities needed for success as entry-level accountants. These results were shared with accounting educators at more than 50 academic meetings. Results were also posted on the IMA's website (www.imanet.org), and disseminated through articles in the *Strategic Finance* and *Journal of Accountancy* magazines (Siegel, Kulesza & Sorensen, 1997). The *Practice Analysis* also described the role that management accountants play in their organizations, the major changes in the nature of the work environment that were occurring in the early to mid-1990s, and the transition from a transactions-based focus to an emphasis on decision support, planning and control.

The discussion of the changes needed in accounting curricula (see Section 6, Gaps in Management Accounting Curricula) will refer back to these discussions to avoid a duplicate review of the specifics of the IMA studies (1996, 1999).

4.5. Changing Roles of Accounting Professionals

The nature of the work performed in public and private accounting practices evolved during the final decades of the twentieth century. Small businesses seeking to compete in an increasingly complex environment often relied extensively on their outside accountant for financial and business expertise. Auditing services were commonly viewed as a commodity and large public accounting firms focused on expanding their management advisory services practice to fuel continued growth. This process continued until financial excesses and frauds such as Enron and WorldCom ultimately resulted in the passage of the Sarbanes-Oxley Act of 2002 (Carpenter et al., 2004; Sinnett & Heffes, 2005; Parles, O'Sullivan & Shannon, 2007) to constrain inappropriate financial reporting and deceitful behaviour.

4.5.1. The early trends

In the study periods from 1995 to 1999 Siegel & Sorensen (1999) recognized several trends that received support by subsequent research, reported later in this chapter:

1. The *nature of management accounting work was changing* from collecting and compiling using standardized reports to interpreting information and involvement in decisions. "... Four out of five respondents say that compared to five years ago, they spend more time analyzing information and being involved in the decision-making process" (Siegel & Sorensen, 1999, p. 8).

   Compared to five years ago, the 1999 respondents believed they spent less time performing activities such as accounting and financial reporting, consolidations, accounting policy, short-term budgeting, project accounting and compliance accounting. Looking ahead three years, 1999 respondents expected to spend less time on these same activities (Siegel & Sorensen, 1999, p. 17).

   In a similar comparison of 1999 to five years earlier, respondents said they spent more time on internal consulting, long-term strategic planning, computer systems and operations, process improvement and financial and economic analysis. Looking ahead three years, respondents expected to spend more time on these same activities (Siegel & Sorensen, 1999, p. 17).
2. The *image of management accountants was shifting* (from five years ago) to where people outside the finance function believed that management accounts bring more value to the company (Siegel & Sorensen, 1999, p. 9).

3. The *work of management accountants was becoming more exciting*. Management accountants relished their new role as business partners (Siegel & Sorensen, 1999, p. 10). Respondents felt the most critical activities to their company's success (in three years from 1999) included long-term strategic planning, financial and economic analyses, customer and product profitability, computer systems and operations and process improvement (Siegel & Sorensen, 1999, p. 17).
4. The work of management accountants was moving to *more work in teams*. In 1955 less than half (48%) worked in teams, whereas in 1999 over 56% worked in teams. As the size of the finance function increased, it became more likely that management accountants would work in teams (Siegel & Sorensen, 1999, p. 11).
5. The *workplace of management accountants was changing* from exclusively central locations to sites outside the central location or in other departments (Siegel & Sorensen, 1999, p. 11). This change suggests a greater degree of integration with other business functions. Kimberly (2003) tried to extend workplace issues by examining alternative work arrangements, flexitime and telecommuting for management accountants through an experiment that did not reach conclusive results.
6. As a result of working in teams and fulfilling the role of internal consultant or business partner, *more time was spent in communicating with others*. About two-thirds of the respondents from finance organizations of varying sizes indicated more time was spent in sharing business information (in comparing 1995 to 1999). As part of the outlook for the next three years, management accountants would do less reporting of information and more planning and analysis, more partnering and consulting, more involvement with operations and more involvement in decision-making (Siegel & Sorensen, 1999, p. 17). As one respondent said, "We've got to be an integrated, expert business advisor to whoever (is) the equivalent of the CEO" (Siegel & Sorensen, 1999, p. 18).
7. The *definition of a management accountant was shifting*. Only one-third of the respondents defined themselves as "accountants." More frequently finance, decision support, business partner or some other term was used. Not one of the respondents used the term "management accountant" to describe him or herself (Siegel & Sorensen, 1999, p. 13).
8. The *rate of change* in the finance function was increasing. The rate of change over the past five years (1995–1999 compared to 1990–1995) was more rapid than in the prior five years, and the anticipated rate of change over the next three years (1999–2001) was expected to increase. Management accountants believed the change was driven by technology, the need for more rapid information, globalization and the competitive environment (Siegel & Sorensen, 1999, p. 15).

The trends noted above appear to be continuing through the 2000s. Other researchers, as noted below, are documenting the changing nature of the finance function.

4.5.2. The Later Trends

Within business organizations the roles management accountants were expected to perform also changed. Studies conducted by the FEI documented a transition of management accountants from "corporate cop" to "business partner" (Keating & Jablonsky, 1990). The term "business partner" is important, because it implies that management accountants are critical members of decision-making teams. As a business partner, management accountants have the authority and responsibility to tell an operating executive why particular types of information may or may not be relevant to decision-making and are expected to suggest ways to improve decision quality and to be a part of planning processes.

Ongoing changes in practice, along with other developments in the evolution of work in corporate America, prompted the IMA to conduct a follow-up study to the 1996 practice analysis (Siegel et al., 1996) entitled "Counting More, Counting Less: Transformations in the Management Accounting Profession" (Siegel & Sorensen, 1999). The 1999 study revealed that 80% of the respondents (practicing US accountants from entry-level positions through to the CFO) were spending more time interpreting information rather than preparing information. They were also more involved in decision-making than the study conducted five years earlier indicated (Siegel & Sorensen, 1994). They were perceived as adding value to the organization while spending more time communicating business information to non-accountants. Management accountants were becoming key players and, in many cases, leaders on cross-functional teams. The results indicated a significant percentage of respondents (80%) expected the trend toward more involvement with decision-making and key operational activities of the business to continue. These trends are confirmed in the KPMG international analysis of business finance functions where results showed " … new hires are expected to possess different capabilities focusing on softer skills such as communication, relationship management, change management and the ability to work in teams" (KPMG, 2006, p. 2). The KPMG study indicated that business finance professionals are also required to have more sophisticated analytical techniques and to be creative problem solvers.

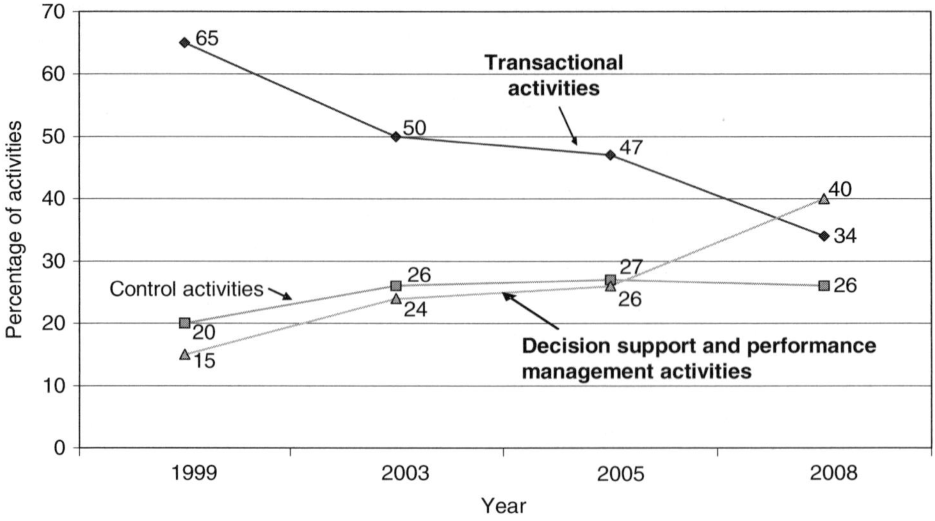

Figure 2. Finance's shifting workload distribution: 1999 to 2008. *Source*: IBM. (2005). The Agile CFO: A Study of 900 CFOs World Wide. CFO.com Webcast April 19, 2005, slide 11.

The results of "Counting More, Counting Less" (Siegel & Sorensen, 1999) were shared with the academic community in dozens of presentations at professional meetings. The report was posted on IMAs website and in articles in the IMA publication *Strategic Finance*. Shifts in the primary activities of the finance function over time (historical 1999 to projected 2008) are reported by IBM (2006), where transactional activities declined dramatically from 65% to 34%, control activities increased from 20% to 26% and decision support and performance management activities moved from 15% to the dominant activity at 40%, as shown in Fig. 2.

After "Counting More, Counting Less" the IMA conducted additional research on changes in the profession:

1. "How to Become a Business Partner," (2002) produced two articles in *Strategic Finance* (Siegel, Sorensen & Richtermeyer, 2003a,b).
2. "Impact of Sarbanes-Oxley on Management Accountants and Business Partners" (Siegel, Sorensen & Richtermeyer, 2007) was shared at several 2006 and 2007 academic conferences. The conclusions were similar to those reached by IBM (2006) and showed that agile finance organizations are moving to an enterprise-wide view that goes beyond measurement and reporting and are aspiring to insights about performance, growth and risk.

One key trend is the movement of the management accountant into the role of business partner. The earlier IMA studies (Siegel et al., 1996; Siegel & Sorensen, 1999) reveal that accountants were becoming business partners who do much more than accounting. Subsequent research (Siegel & Sorensen, 2002) supports this trend (Siegel, Sorensen & Richtermeyer, 2003a). They perform decision support, but go much beyond basic business support. They are business analysts, but do more than simply analyze. Management accountants may be internal consultants, but also have fiduciary responsibility over the company's assets. They are valued for their business savvy and financial insight, while being focused on improving business processes. Internally, they are becoming proactive and key players and leaders on teams. Rather than simply producing requested financial reports, business partners must first understand the nature of the business problem being addressed and the information that is most relevant for a decision, to address and to solve the problem. However, they have to foresee how company decisions and practices will affect accounting and tax reports (Siegel et al., 2003a). By analyzing successful business partners, transitioning strategies for becoming a business partner were suggested, including showing value-added analysis, gaining trust, showing balance among financial strategic and operational perspectives, giving high quality advice, helping users of financial information find solutions and understand financial information, promoting the value of financial advice and being involved in all stages of decision-making (Siegel et al., 2003b; Jarvenpaa, 2007). Not all researchers agree, however, about the emergence of management accountants as business partners. Byrne & Pierce (2007), for example, using a behavioural perspective on antecedents and characteristics related to the role of management accountants (including the push-back of Sarbanes-Oxley to control) suggest the consequences for their subjects (n = 38) argue the "... adoption of a 'business partner' model for (management accountants) ... to be ambiguous, conditional and uncertain" (p. 469). More specifically, the contingencies, conflicts (including role conflicts) and the nature of the interactions of management accountants and financial managers are key factors in the organizational movement toward more effective management control. The tantalizing research of Byrne & Pierce (2007) argues for more field studies (as is suggested later for a general research strategy for management accounting).

5. Response by the Academic Community

While a clearer picture of the practice of management accounting was emerging and a better specification of the KSAs needed to be a successful management accountant were documented, did the academic community respond with an improved synchronization between management accounting education and management accounting practice? Evidence reviewed in this section from both the academic and practice community suggests the answer is "no."

In 1984 the American Accounting Association (AAA) appointed a prestigious committee to consider the future of accounting education. In the Bedford Report, "Future Accounting Education: Preparing for the Expanding Profession" (AAA, 1986), the committee noted that while all professions change over time, the institutions that educate professionals frequently fail to evolve as rapidly as professional practice. The report described how professional accounting practice was changing in public accounting, government and industry. In a revealing fashion, the report noted that "there is little doubt that the current content of professional accounting education, which has remained substantially the same over the past 50 years, is generally inadequate for the future accounting professional." The report concluded that the accounting profession was expanding, but the state of accounting education (in 1986) was inadequate to meet the needs of the expanding profession. A key problem the committee identified was the "growing gap between what accountants do and what accounting educators teach."

As a follow-up to the Bedford Report, the AAA established the Accounting Education Change Commission (AECC) in 1989. The AECC issued several position statements. Statement Number 4, issued in April 1993 (AECC, 1993), noted that several research studies concluded that accounting graduates were poorly prepared for work in their first jobs. Study results showed that many accounting graduates were unprepared for many elements of career success, such as managing job stress, meeting deadlines, working unanticipated overtime, preparing budgets and balancing work and family life. In short, accounting educators were not communicating sufficient information about the realities of the profession in a corporate setting and the experiences that students may encounter as they begin their careers. Conversely, it also appeared as though students were not seeking first-hand knowledge of the business world on their own. As a consequence, graduates' experiences fell short of their expectations for the "real world." AECC Statement Number 4 addressed the gap identified in the Bedford report, and the under-preparedness of students by recommending that faculty members "should acquire and maintain a high level of knowledge about *both practice issues and the nonacademic accountant's workplace* and that they *should communicate their knowledge about conditions of practice to their students*" (Siegel et al., 2007).

In summary, about twenty years ago (AAA, 1986), the academic community recognized a problem and issued recommendations (AECC, 1993) to address the problem. Unfortunately, the academic community did not develop a concrete action plan to encourage accounting educators to implement the recommendations. Thus, the accounting curriculum, particularly the undergraduate curriculum, at universities across the US remains very similar to the one that existed in 1986, and according to the Bedford Report the 1986 curriculum had changed little over the fifty previous years. A study by Albrecht & Sack (2002) confirms how slow universities have been to adapt to changes in the business world (Siegel et al., 2007).

The gap problem identified by the academic community in 1986 was recognized and addressed by the practicing profession in subsequent studies. A brief examination of these studies follows.

5.1. Public Accounting

In 1989 the eight largest public accounting firms issued a white paper to address their concerns about the quality and quantity of accounting graduates entering the profession (Big Eight White Paper, 1989). Consistent with the Bedford Report, the paper described the profession as expanding, changing and becoming increasingly complex. In the authors' opinion, these changes created a critical need to re-examine the educational process. The paper noted that while curriculum development was the responsibility of the academic community, the intention of the Big Eight authors was to inform accounting educators about the skills and capabilities needed to be successful accounting practitioners. The study concluded that "the current environment makes real curricular change essential and necessitates responses from a dynamic partnership between practitioners and academicians." To provide input into this partnership, the study provided a list of capabilities needed by entry-level accounting professionals such as communication skills, intellectual skills and interpersonal skills.

5.2. Five-year versus Four-year Accounting Programmes

Two American Institute of Certified Public Accountants' (AICPA) studies were instrumental in the creation of the 150-hour programme for the CPA certification (AICPA, 1968, 1969). These studies focused on the common body of knowledge and the suggested amount of time needed in higher education to be a successful CPA candidate (Tatikonda, 2004).

In 1988, the membership of the AICPA overwhelmingly approved an amendment to the organization's by-laws requiring membership applicants after the year 2000 to have the equivalent of 150 semester hours of education and a bachelor's degree. The AICPA is a professional membership association and not a regulatory agency; thus, binding requirements for a 150-hour education had to await passage by state and territorial legislatures. By 2001, 48 of the 54 US licensing jurisdictions had enacted supporting legislation and the law had become effective in 33 jurisdictions (Shafer & Kunkel, 2001). By 2007 the laws were effective in 47 states, with New York's effective date coming in 2009.[5]

In their study of 150 accounting education programmes Shafter & Kunkel (2001) found "… results indicate that, rather than developing integrated 5-year programmes that provide a liberal undergraduate education combined with graduate professional training, most universities have responded to the requirement by simply making master's in accounting (MA) or master's in business administration (MBA) programmes available to CPA examination candidates. This approach is inconsistent with the vision of accounting education presented by the original supporters of the extended education requirement." In 2006 Williams, in a report to the National Association of State Boards of Accountancy (NASBA), noted the last 30 hours of coursework simply focus on meeting the 150 hour requirement rather than on quality education, and thus are less integrated and more opportunistic.[6]

Other professional accounting associations that sponsor certification accept four year degree programmes as the appropriate educational requirement. To be recognized as a Certified Management Accountant (CMA) the Institute of Management Accountants (IMA) requires candidates to possess a bachelor's degree in any area, from an accredited college or university.[7] Similarly, the Institute of Internal Auditors (IIA) states that Certified Internal Auditor (CIA) candidates must hold a bachelor's degree or its equivalent from an accredited college-level institution.[8]

6. Gaps in Management Accounting Curricula

6.1. Research findings: deficiencies in traditional management accounting curricula

An indication of the deficiencies of management accounting curricula was clearly evident in the early to mid-1990s (Siegel & Sorensen, 1994) when practitioners were asked about the gap between their expectations for the academic preparation of entry-level accountants and their experience of students' job knowledge and performance. Practitioners were asked to evaluate entry level graduates on their expectation for, and their experience with, these individuals.[9] The gaps displayed in Fig. 3 are the average differences between expectation and experience scores. A positive gap indicates that the expectation for level of knowledge was higher than that employers experienced, suggesting a deficiency in preparation. A negative gap indicated the reverse, namely, preparation exceeded expectations. Executives expected entry-level accountants, for example, to be knowledgeable about strategic cost management; however, many entry-level accountants did not begin their first job with this knowledge.

Figure 3 reveals large under-preparation gaps for budgeting, product costing, strategic cost management, control and performance evaluations, information system design, working capital management, asset management and planning, internal auditing, long-term financing, consolidated statements and corporate tax. Over-preparation (or a negative gap) was identified for individual income tax, external auditing and accounting for governmental/non-profit organizations.

From a practitioner's point of view, Siegel & Sorensen (1996) helped to answer the important issue "who does what kind of work?" Significant differences were noted between industries about who does what kind of work. When comparing financial services to manufacturing, for example, manufacturing companies were more involved in activities that were expected to increase in importance in the future: customer and product profitability, financial and economic analysis and process improvement (Siegel et al., 1997, p. 45 Siegel, Kulesza & Sorensen, 1997, p. 45). The study also revealed how accounting work was carried out by varying levels of personnel. Involvement in customer and product profitability by levels of accountants

[5] www.aicpa.org/download/states/150_Hour_Education_Requirement.pdf (accessed November 11, 2007).

[6] Jan R. Williams, Report from the Campus, NASBA Annual Meeting, Atlanta, GA, November 2006.

[7] www.imanet.org.

[8] www.theiia.org.

[9] A scale of 1 to 100 points was used in the ratings.

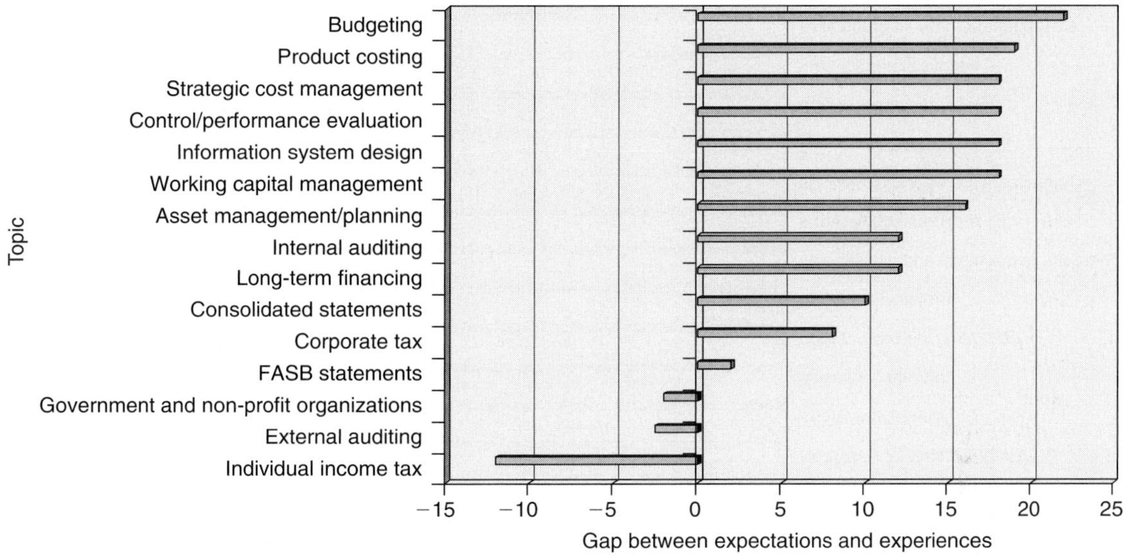

Figure 3. Academic preparation gap. *Source*: Siegel, G. & Sorensen, J. E. (1994). *What Corporate America Wants in Entry Level Accountants*. Montvale, NJ: Institute of Management Accountants.

in manufacturing showed lower-level accountants would carry out and review the work while top-level finance executives were more likely to review the work of others (Siegel et al., 1997, p. 46). However, involvement in financial and economic analysis in manufacturing was more likely to be carried out and reviewed by top-level finance executives than accountants (Siegel et al., 1997, p. 46).

More evidence about the changing professional work environment emerged in 1996 and 1999, as shown in Fig. 4 (Siegel & Sorensen, 1996). Work activities that were expected to increase in importance revealed the need for skills that placed higher and newer demands on the management accounting curricula. Twelve work activities were identified as increasing in importance. Eight of the same activities were noted in 1996, but four new ones emerged in 1999 including process improvement, long-term strategic planning, internal consulting and quality systems and controls. Looking forward from 1999 to 2002, practitioners identified five activities as becoming the most critical for success in the future:

- long-term strategic planning (ranked 1 and new in 1999);
- financial and economic analysis (ranked 2);
- customer and product profitability (ranked 3);
- computer systems and operations (ranked 4);
- process improvement (ranked 5 and new in 1999).

Structuring a management accounting curriculum to address academic gaps and changing work activities suggests curriculum revisions are likely to be happening. Long-term strategic planning and process improvement, for example, have not traditionally been viewed as management accounting topics. New and creative approaches (including working with other departments in the college) will be required to prepare students adequately for these work activities. Specific changes and how quickly these changes are occurring are addressed later in this chapter.

6.2. *Practitioner Guidance for Curricula*

How can academics develop professional accountants for the twenty-first century? What are the fissures in management accounting curricula? A management accounting academic curriculum that reflects current practice could be viewed as a practitioner-driven curriculum. A practitioner-based curriculum, such as that recommended by the Bedford report, is needed to close the gap between academic preparation and practice. Merchant & Van der Stede 2006, p. 123) observe that most "... advances to the management accounting field originated in practice" and (p. 131) "... will continue to come from practice." Empirical research insights into practice in management accounting become a compelling vehicle for improving the linkage between accounting practice and accounting education. A *2003 Survey of Management Accounting* by Ernst & Young (E&Y) and the IMA provides a glimpse of the major modern accounting tools used by current financial operating executives. The E&Y/IMA survey helps identify the tools needed to address the preparation gaps and changes in work activities cited earlier. It also attempted to identify new accounting methods that have

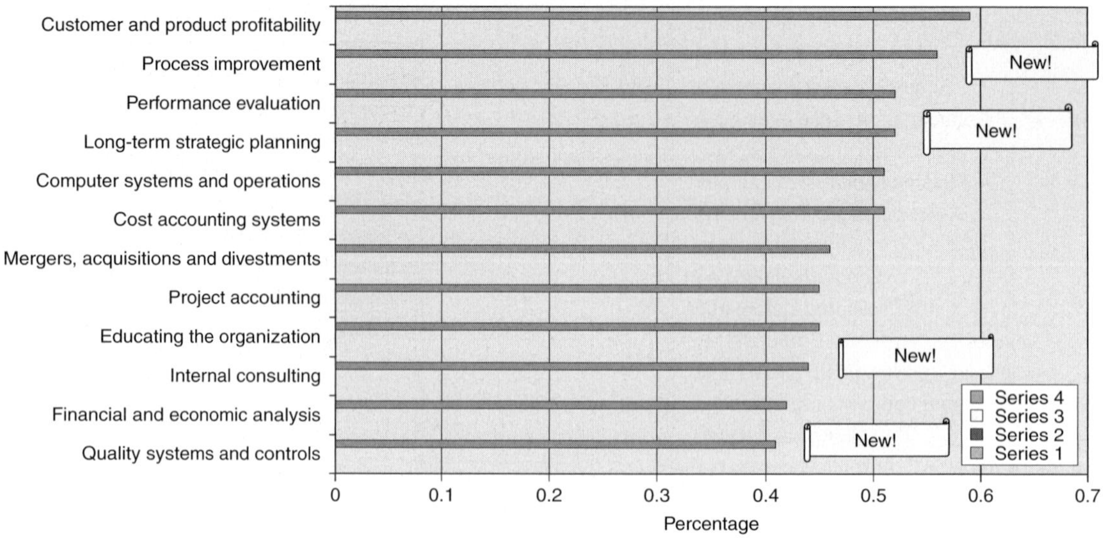

Figure 4. Work activities that will increase in importance: 1996 and 1999. *Source*: Siegel, G. et al. (1996). The Practice Analysis of Management Accounting. Montvale, NJ: Institute of Management Accountants, p. 16; Siegel, G. & Sorensen, J. E. (1999). Counting More, Counting Less: Transformations in the Management Accounting Profession. Montvale, NJ: Institute of Management Accountants, p. 17.

emerged and how fully today's companies have adopted or integrated these new management tools. The E&Y/IMA survey (hereafter referred to as the Survey in this section) is organized around four tool groups:

1. planning and budgeting;
2. decision support;
3. product costing analysis;
4. performance evaluation.

6.3. *Tools for a practitioner-driven curriculum*

The Survey analysis shows how widely the tools are used by identifying three responses: (1) extensive deployment; (2) active consideration to deploy; or (3) rejection. Combining the "extensive use" and "considering use" groupings provides a helpful perspective because it describes current and future management accounting practice. One of the research questions posed in the Survey was "Do existing tools fulfil the changing needs? If not, which tools and methods (new or traditional) are perceived as being needed or are being adopted?" The responses from the senior-level financial executives focused on how management accounting practice was developing from the position of "considering" to either "extensive use" or "rejection." (The percentages quoted later are summarized in Figs 5 and 6 for the reader's convenience.)

If accounting graduates (entry-level accountants) are expected to participate in the decision process of selecting management accounting techniques, they need to know which tools are currently applied and be knowledgeable about the advantages and disadvantages of applying these tools. Accounting graduates can participate meaningfully in this process only if they are aware of emergent tools.

6.3.1. *Planning and budgeting*

The Survey (p. 14) reports on the use of planning and budgeting tools, such as operational budgeting, activity-based management (ABM), standard budgeting and capital budgeting. Combining "extensive utilization" along with those trying to implement the tools (considering use), operational budgeting is widely used (75% + 17% = 92%) in practice. Activity-based management, along with standard budgeting, is also widely used (65% + 23% = 88%) while capital budgeting logs in at 84% (60% + 24%). A small percentage of the respondents have rejected the tools. Reasons for rejection may include failed applications, a failure to consider the tools, a genuine dislike of the tool or no perceived relevance of the tool to the issues facing the business.

6.3.2. *Decision support*

Decision support tools from the Survey (p. 15) include quantitative techniques (such as electronic spreadsheets, linear multiple regression analysis and learning curves), breakeven analysis, transfer pricing, supply chain costing and value chain analysis. Quantitative techniques are used or being considered for use by 94% of the respondents (77% + 17%). Breakeven is at 87% (62% + 25%) application, while transfer pricing is at 80% (55% + 25%). Supply chain costing has a lower level

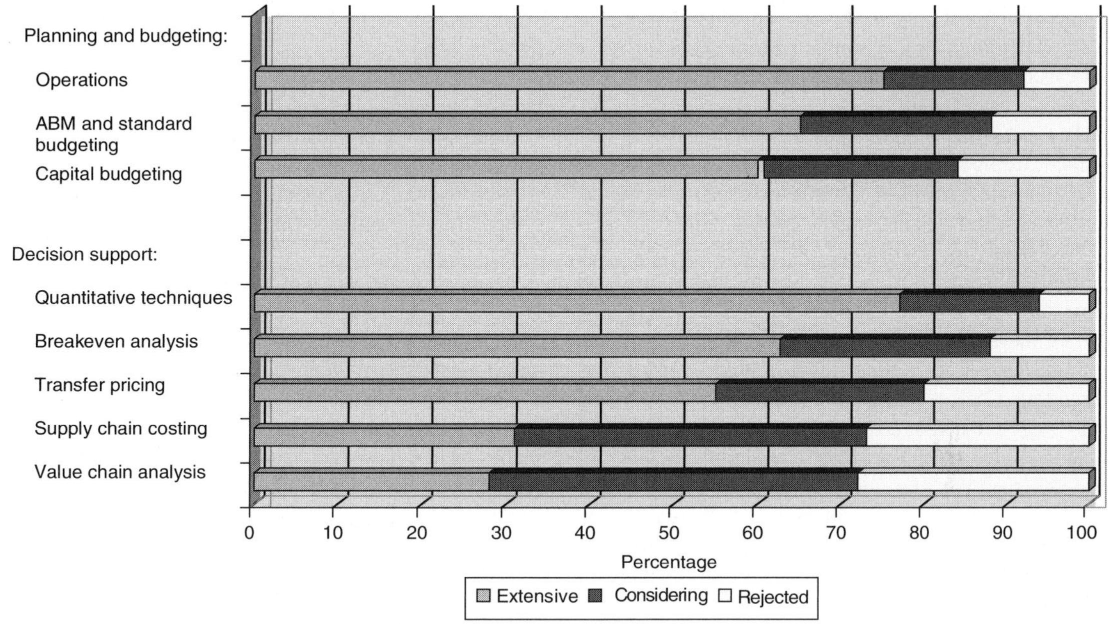

Figure 5. Summary of E&Y and IMA survey: planning, budgeting and decision support. *Source*: Ernst & Young and Institute of Management Accountants. (2003). *2003 Survey of Management Accounting.* Ernst & Young, LLP. SCORE Retrieval File No. BV0008

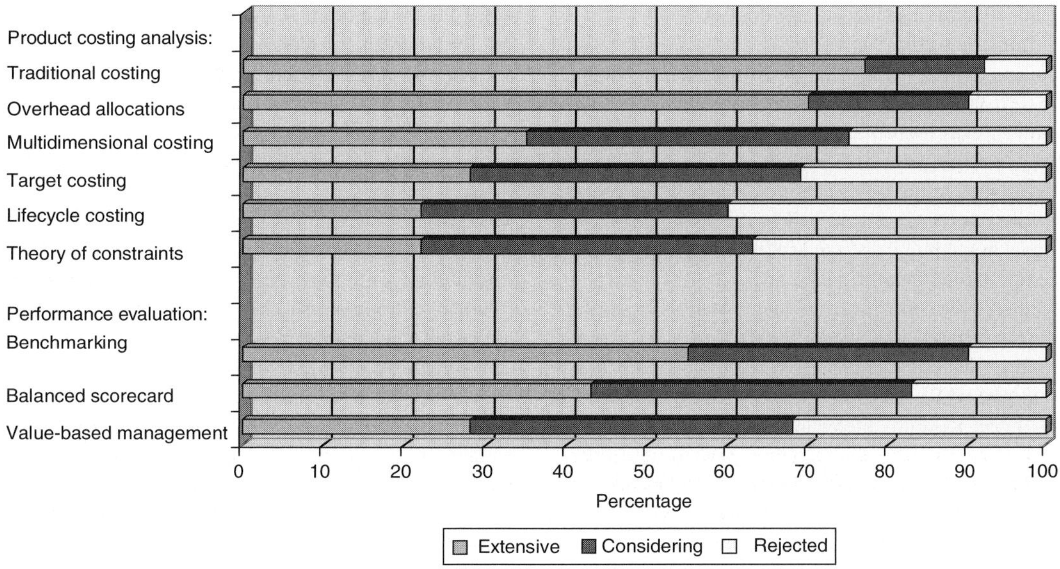

Figure 6. Summary of E&Y and IMA survey: product costing analysis and performance evaluation. *Source*: Ernst & Young and Institute of Management Accountants. (2003). *2003 Survey of Management Accounting.* Ernst & Young, LLP. SCORE Retrieval File No. BV0008

of current application (31%) with more firms trying to develop the tool (42%). A similar pattern exists for value chain analysis with 28% and 44%, respectively.

6.3.3. Product Costing Analysis

Product costing analysis tools discussed in the Survey (p. 15) include traditional costing, overhead allocations, multidimensional costing, target costing, lifecycle costing and theory of constraints. As might be expected, traditional costing (92% = 77% +15%) and overhead allocations (90% = 70% + 20%) are used by more than 90% of the respondents. Newer accounting tools, such as multi-dimension costing (35% + 40% = 75%), target costing (28% + 41% = 69%) and lifecycle costing (22% + 38% = 60%) are more in the developmental stages and also show the highest rejection rates at this point in time (25%, 31% and 40%, respectively). The theory of constraints (which would include mathematical and linear programming) has 22% with extensive use, 41% under consideration or development and 37% rejection.

6.3.4. Performance Evaluation

Performance evaluation tools included in the Survey (p. 16) were benchmarking, the balanced scorecard (BSC) and value-based management. Benchmarking is used extensively by 55% of the sample and an additional 35% are attempting to use it. A significant percentage indicate they have either fully deployed (43%) the balanced scorecard (BSC) or they are trying to use the BSC (40%), indicating BSC use by 83% of the respondents (40% + 43%). Value-based management is the lowest adopted tool at 28%, but 40% are considering its adoption.

A summary of the Survey, as shown in Fig. 5, reveals that planning and budgeting tools (operations budgeting, ABM/standard budgeting and capital budgeting) and decision-support tools (quantitative techniques, breakeven analysis, transfer pricing, supply chain costing and value chain analysis) are currently being used or are being considered for use by more than 70% of the respondents, with some tool usage being as high as 80% or 90% (operations budgeting and quantitative techniques).

Figure 6 shows that most product cost tools (traditional costing, overhead allocation, multi-dimension costing) are used or are being considered for use by 70% of the respondents, while newer tools approach or exceed 60% usage (target costing, lifecycle costing, theory of constraints). Performance evaluation tools such as benchmarking and the balanced scorecard are used or considered for use by more than 80% of the respondents, while value-based management approaches the 70% usage level.

The E&Y/IMA Survey results are supported by a KPMG study of nearly 300 senior executives (including 123 chief financial officers (CFOs)). This study showed that the five financial activities and processes most likely to improve over the next two years included (KPMG, 2006, p. 20):

- planning, budgeting and forecasting (62%);
- management reporting (60%);
- transaction processing (45%);
- enterprise-wide risk management (32%);
- regulatory compliance (30%).

Many of these activities and processes are addressed in the E&Y/IMA Survey, but the appearance of risk management represents an additional issue now surfacing at a higher level for accounting education.

Some may argue that the E&Y/IMA Survey, the KPMG study or similar organizationally sponsored studies could present a conflict of interest since these organizations may be hoping to serve as consultants to implement the tools identified in their respective studies.

7. Suggestions for Curricular Development

7.1. Curricular Guidance

Figures 5 and 6 provide powerful guidance for the formulation of practitioner-driven curricula. A group of academics or a department attempting to formulate courses that will prepare their students for success in corporate America should carefully consider the results from the 1996 IMA practice analysis, the 2003 E&Y/IMA Survey and the 2005 IBM research results. These research results provide a convenient checklist against which to compare and evaluate current course offerings. For example, there are traditional accounting tools, such as operational budgeting, traditional product cost analysis (such as full absorption costing), overhead allocations (based on direct labour), and more modern tools and techniques, such as target costing, value-based management and the theory of constraints (Siegel et al., 2007).

One emerging area, lean accounting or lean management, does not seem to be recognized explicitly in the Survey. Lean accounting and lean management propose a systematic way of eliminating waste, simplifying operations and aligning the value chain, but it challenges traditional accounting approaches (Kennedy & Brewer, 2006) and poses new measurements (Kennedy et al., 2007).

While the relative emphasis to put on topics remains an open issue, the 1996 practice analysis and other research on the work of management accountants provides strong evidence for an expanded managerial curricula with new learning objectives. Firms that have adapted new tools or are considering the use of new tools may be on the leading edge of innovation in accounting practice. What a minority of firms is doing now may be common practice in a few years as a result of increased adoptions by practitioners. Another important way it can become common practice is if we include these tools in an accounting curriculum. Firms considering or attempting to deploy tools disclose the leading edge that deserves coverage in the management accounting curriculum. This activity suggests that students need more than a single managerial accounting course to better prepare students for their first job. To assure academics select the correct topics requires a continuous surveillance of practice—a point made later about the role of management accounting research.

7.2. Other Proposals

Kahn et al. (2000, p. 2) "… offer an important first step for academic accounting programme reengineering …" using the KSAs of manufacturing and service sectors from Siegel et al. (1996). The analysis by Kahn et al. (p. 3) suggests the work activities (WAs) and KSAs for manufacturing and service businesses highlight some important similarities and dissimilarities between the two industry sectors. "The rankings of the KSAs provide useful information for assessing existing management accounting courses, revising them and developing new courses" (Kahn et al., p. 3). Table 5, adapted from Kahn et al. (p. 3), summarizes these relative emphases in manufacturing and service businesses. Armed with the analysis of KSAs by sector, Kahn et al. (2000) developed a three course block that included basic, manufacturing and service sector content courses to refocus a management accounting education for the twenty-first century (p. 4).

Cummings, Bennett & Normand (2001) outline how one university's programme core courses addressed the KSAs and work activities judged most important for work in the practice analyses of Siegel et al. (1996) and Siegel & Sorensen (1999). The revised curriculum was viewed as evolutionary, but "…a rigorous, strategically focused self-examination" (Cummings et al., p. 13). The practice analyzes (1996, 1999) "…. challenge accounting academics to design curricula that better prepare students to work productively in a constantly changing, highly-competitive global corporate environment" (Cummings et al., p. 5). The revised programme has a reduced emphasis on financial reporting and moves toward an information systems and cost management focus (p. 8). Table 6 is shown to reveal the detailed and comprehensive curricular analysis required to develop an academic accounting programme that incorporates the research findings of Siegel et al. (1996) and Siegel & Sorensen, (1999).

Sometimes the call for change has been noted by academics, but in professional journals. For example, Gabbin observes "… many accounting educators have failed to restructure accounting curriculum to equip graduates with the tools and expertise they need in today's business world" (Gabbin, 2002, p. 81). Sometimes the call is from a combination of academics and practitioners and again in a professional journal (Keith et al., 2000). An illustrative academic review comes from Howieson (2003) in the *British Accounting Review* who suggests future accountants will be knowledge workers with heavy technology, interdisciplinary and analytical orientations.

Other researchers argue for change as well. As Tatikonda observes (2004, p. 62):

> Despite significant changes in the business environment and decades of studies criticizing it, accounting curricula have remained static. Accounting (faculties) are reluctant to design alternate tracks for nonpublic accounting careers. This narrow focus undermines the needs of other industries and accounting graduates seeking nonpublic accounting careers.

In a similar vein, Clevenger, Clevenger & McElroy (2006) argue for differing accounting tracks and suggest accounting programmes should work with the various professional accounting organizations, such as the Association of Government Accountants (AGA), the IMA, the IIA and the Association of Certified Fraud Examiners, to choose the most appropriate courses for the tracks. Other illustrative authors (Brewer, 2000; Cummings, Bennett & Normand, 2001; Dosch, 2006) have proposed new curricula with less emphasis on financial reporting and more emphasis on management accounting.

7.3. Teaching methods in management accounting

Watson et al. (2007) offer a review of accounting education literature from 2003 to 2005. While broad in its scope, Watson et al. (2007) devote some space to a review of managerial and cost topics (Section 3.5.5) and a list of management accounting cases (Table A2). Some academics have offered improved teaching methodology for management accounting topics. Barsky & Catanach (2005) use a business planning model to teach introductory management accounting. The course focuses on planning, control and decision-making in a serial case, mini-cases and a simulation to emphasize the use of information in decision-making. Hoffjan (2005) employs a business game to explore relevant costs, opportunity costs and transfer prices. Van Den Brink et al. (2003) use a case-based approach to teach management accounting content while adding psychological, cultural and organizational dimensions.

Some authors propose intersections of management accounting and operations management to enable management accountants to become business partners (Kennedy & Sorensen, 2006). Wygal & Hartman (2003) suggest partnering with new stakeholders to bring new topics, such as enterprise resource planning (ERP), into the classroom. Bamber & Bamber (2006) use a publicly traded company 10-K report and a series of mini-cases to cover many of the topics covered in cost and management accounting courses, including cost–volume–profit analysis, business strategy, activity-based costing, budgeting, just-in-time,

Table 5. Relative emphasis on KSAs by manufacturing and service sectors.

Manufacturing and service had strong emphasis on	Manufacturing only had emphasis on	Service only had emphasis on	Neither sector had strong emphasis on
• Provider information for decision-making (*information needs of internal customers*) • Cost behaviour • Planning and control • Continuous improvement • Quality programmes • Performance measures	• Product costing • Variable costing • Inventory control	• Behavioural and motivational issues • Business partnering • Strategy implementation • Creation of financial models for decision-making	• Cost estimation • Regression • Benchmarking • Target costing • Economic order quantity (EOQ) • Just-in-time (JIT) • Other operations management tools

Source: Khan, A. U., Cianciolo, T. A., Peacock, E. (2000). A plan for reengineering management accounting education based on the IMA's practice analysis. *Management Accounting Quarterly*, **1**(2), p. 3.

quality costs, balanced scorecard, performance evaluation of investment centres and capital budgeting.

7.4. Inventories of Articles and Cases

Inventories of articles and cases can be of enormous value because they are an efficient way for an academic to review the available resources. For example, see Gascho Lipe (2006) and Brasel & Hentz (2006) with a database at the Iowa State University. The Iowa State database includes periodically updated bibliographic information for articles published in five accounting education journals: *Accounting Education*; *Accounting Education: An International Journal*; *Accounting Educators' Journal*; *Issues in Accounting Education* and *Journal of Accounting Education*. The active database is http://www.bus.iastate.edu/AccountingEducationPublications/ (accessed November 10, 2007).

The IMA has published cases with teaching notes on the application of management accounting for a wide range of topics (both hard and soft skills) and settings that are available to accounting educators. The early cases emerged from an initial cooperative 1985 American Accounting Association and National Association of Accountants (AAA-NAA) symposium to address a perceived lack of interaction between management accounting practitioners and educators (Hughes, 2001). (The NAA is the predecessor organization of the Institute of Management Accountants.) These materials accumulated in various ways since 1985 and are labelled the IMA Case Studies: Cases from Management Accounting Practice Volumes 1 to 17 and the IMA Case-e Journal (containing volumes 14 through 17). A new *IMA Educational Case Journal* (IECJ) is to be inaugurated in 2008 (http://www.imanet.org; accessed November 10, 2007).

Other well-known sources of management accounting cases include the Harvard Business School publishing site Harvard Business for Educators: (http://harvardbusinessonline.hbsp.harvard.edu/b01/en/academic/edu_home.jhtml (accessed November 12, 2007), the University of Virginia McIntire School of Business case centre (http://store.darden.virginia.edu/ecustomer_enu/ (accessed November 12, 2007) and Ivey publishing of the University of Western Ontario http://cases.ivey.uwo.ca/cases/pages/home.aspx (accessed November 12, 2007).

7.5. Useful References for doing Research in Management Accounting Education

Stout, Rebele & Howard (2006) identify why educational journal submissions are rejected and offer practical suggestions for future researchers. A complementary article by Howard & Stout (2006) explores why case/instructional resource submissions are rejected. Primary among the reasons for rejection are a failure to provide evidence of the educational value of the case and paltry content. Secondary reasons cited weak or poorly constructed teaching notes. Serious researchers in management accounting education should review Smith (2006), a beneficial monograph (*Reflections on Accounting Education Research*) edited by Smith and published by the American Accounting Association.

8. Suggestions for Future Management Accounting Research

8.1 Management Accountants and Management Accounting Topics

Demski & Zimmerman (2000) suggest the university education of accounting students would be at risk without a serious research component in the professional lives of accounting educators. The question then becomes "What kind of research is necessary to ensure the long-running success of our university management accounting education programmes." As established earlier, advances to the field of management accounting originated in practice, so

Table 6. How the Northern Illinois University programme addresses the KSAs and work activities judged most important for work in 1995 and 1999 practice analyses by core courses of the Northern Illinois University programme.

KSAs and work activities judged most important by survey respondents	Cost	Actg info sys	Financial 1	Assurance	Taxation	Financial 2	CFBP§	Strategic BP Ω
Long-term strategic planning							√	√
Financial and economic analysis	√		√			√		√
Customer and product profitability	√						√	√
Work ethic	√	√	√	√	√	√	√	√
Analytical/problem-solving skills	√	√	√	√	√	√	√	√
Interpersonal skills		√		√			√	√
Listening skills	√	√	√	√	√	√	√	√
Use of computerized spreadsheets	√	√					√	
Understanding (the) business	√	√		√			√	√
Understanding implications of decisions	√	√					√	√
Writing skills		√		√				√
Improvement of business processes	√	√		√			√	
Relationships of financial statements			√			√	√	
Leadership skills		√					√	√
Understanding/preparing financial statements			√			√		
Accounting system operations		√						
Computerized accounting systems		√						
Interpreting financial statements			√			√	√	
Measurement/valuation of revenues, expenses			√			√		
Accruals and deferrals, adjustments, closing		√	√			√		
Presentation skills		√		√			√	√
Information needs of internal users	√	√		√			√	

Source: Cummings, B. et al., 2001. Meeting the challenge: the university accounting program corporate America needs. Management Accounting Quarterly, **2**(2), p.10.
§ Cross-functional business problems (College of Business Course)
Ω Strategic business problems (College of Business Course)

more empirical survey and field/case research seem to be appropriate.

The E&Y and IMA Survey (2003), for example, needs to be updated. Future research is needed to understand why more than 30% of practitioners have rejected target costing, lifecycle costing, theory of constraints and value-based management (E&Y and IMA Survey, 2003). Researchers can also assess if the percentage "considering" various tools or costing systems has changed and if financial executives adopted or rejected specific tools or costing systems (E&Y and IMA Survey, 2003). In the 2003 Survey, cost estimation, cost reduction and process improvement were the top three priorities (E&Y and IMA Survey, 2003). Have these changed? How? In light of the emerging focus on risk, a review of the priorities of management accountants (E&Y and IMA Survey, 2003) may suggest a revised set.

Ittner & Larcker (2002) suggest "… accounting is fundamentally an applied research area that should ultimately provide new insights for practice … (and) … it is difficult to imagine how research in an applied discipline such as managerial accounting could evolve without the benefit of detailed examination of actual practices" (p. 788). While theories may guide and aid practice-oriented research, the results are not a mere description of management consulting practices (Zimmerman, 2001).

Field research is motivated by a quest for rich descriptions of management accounting in action (Ahrens & Dent, 1998). Despite the calls for more case and field study research, modest amounts of research have been published in the contemporary management accounting journals. A lack of knowledge on the part of researchers about how to do effective case/field study research may be part of the shortfall (Shields, 1997).

Surveys facilitate gathering data from large samples to describe practice and to test potential hypotheses (Shields, 1997). Those interested in survey research should review Young, (1996), who provides a detailed analysis of survey research in management accounting as well as suggestions on how to improve survey research.

8.1.1. Productive Examples of Empirical Management Accounting Research

An author who argues for more empirical field and survey research should identify productive examples. The following research illustrations (along with complete authorship and article title) are meant to be illustrative and not exhaustive. The instances cited chronologically are among the author's most convenient exemplars to illustrate how empirical research can advance the knowledge of management accountants in practice and accounting professors in academia.

	Content	Author (yr)	Title	Journal Reference
1.	Activity-based costing	Shields, M. D. (1995)	An empirical analysis of firms' implementation experiences with activity-based costing.	*Journal of Management Accounting Research*, **7**, 122–147.
2	Balanced scorecard	Malina, M. A. & Selto, F. H. (2001)	Communicating and controlling strategy: an empirical study of the effectiveness of the balanced scorecard.	*Journal of Management Accounting Research*, **13**, 47–90.
3	Nonfinancial measures	Said, A., Hassab Elnaby, H. & Wier, B. (2003)	An empirical investigation of the performance consequences of nonfinancial measures.	*Journal of Management Accounting Research*, **15**, 193–223.
4	Performance measurement models	Malina, M. A. & Selto, F. H. (2004)	Choice and change of measures in performance measurement models.	*Management Accounting Research*, **15**(4), 441–469.
5	Lifecycle cost	Dunk, A. S. (2004)	Product lifecycle cost analysis: the impact of customer profiling, competitive advantage and quality of IS information.	*Management Accounting Research*, **15**(4), 401–414.
6	Strategy	Naranjo-Gil, D. & Hartman, F. (2006)	How top management teams use management accounting systems to implement strategy.	*Journal of Management Accounting Research*, **18,** 21–53.
7	Organizational performance	Hyvonen, J. (2007)	Strategy, performance measurement techniques and information technology of the firm and their links to organizational performance.	*Management Accounting Research*, **18**(3), 343–366.

Atkinson et al. (1997) collaborate to offer three new directions in management accounting research that are still useful today:

1. management accounting's role in organizational change;
2. the interaction between accounting and organizational structure;
3. the role of accounting information in supporting decision-making.

No brief summary could hope to convey the richness of the Atkinson et al. (1997) review, and therefore the reader is encouraged to read the original work.

A related issue may be the number of academic management accountants available to undertake solid empirical research. In a recent American Accounting Association survey on the supply and demands for accounting PhDs in accounting, the search for PhD management accountants was about 30% of the volume sought for financial accounting (American Accounting Association, 2005, Table 2, p. 8).

8.1.2. Other Types of Empirical Research

Management accounting education needs more empirical studies to evaluate the effectiveness of optional curricular models and instructional approaches (Watson et al., 2007; Stout, Rebele & Howard, 2006; Howard & Stout, 2006).

As 150-hour programmes develop, a more systematic effort should be mounted to include advanced management accounting courses as a requirement or as an elective. As graduates enter or migrate to public accounting, corporate and governmental (and non-profit) careers, the role of more sophisticated frameworks and reasoning appears necessary as the role of management accountants as business partners emerges.

More robust reviewers of future research in management accounting should consult Luft & Shields (2003) about a perspective on the causes and effects of management accounting and suggested guidelines for future research.

8.2. Renaming the Management Accountant

Since many practicing management accountants do not identify themselves as "management accountants" (Siegel et al., 2003a), should we call ourselves accountants or should we select a new name? The Institute of Management Accountants, for example, renamed its lead practitioner journal *Strategic Finance*, dedicated its former top journal, *Management Accounting*, as the *Management Accounting Quarterly* and changed its focus to a more academic rather than a practitioner focus (www.imanet.org).

9. Conclusions

Management accounting is undergoing major changes. What management accountants need to know seems to be changing at an accelerating rate. The role of management accountants is shifting up toward the top of the organization, where they are becoming business partners—valued partners in top level decision-making. The gap between practice and education is well established and awaits bold practitioner-based educational programmes to close it. Topics deserving further research include both management accountants themselves and the tools they use, and should emphasize empirical case study, field study and survey research to broaden our consciousness of management accountants. Perhaps management accountants need to rename themselves to more clearly identify their role in the twenty-first century. As the study of management accountants gets older, our research will optimistically get wiser as well.

References

Accounting Education Change Committee (AECC). (1993). Improving the early employment experience of accountants: position and issues statements number four. American Accounting Association. Sarasota, FL. Available at http://aaahq.org/AECC/PositionsandIssues/issues4.htm (accessed November 9, 2007).

Ahrens, T. & Dent, J. F. (1998). Accounting and organizations: realizing the richness of field research. *Journal of Management Accounting Research*, **10**, 1–39.

Albrecht, W. S. & Sack, R. J. (2002). *Accounting Education: Charting the Course Through a Perilous Future.* Accounting Education Series (16). American Accounting Association. Sarasota, FL. Available at http://aaahq.org/pubs/AESv16/toc.htm (accessed November 9, 2007).

American Accounting Association (AAA). (1986). *The Bedford Report—Future Accounting Education: Preparing for the Expanding Profession.* Sarasota, FL. Available at http://aaahq.org/AECC/ (accessed November 9, 2007).

American Accounting Association (AAA). (2005). *Supply and Demand for Accounting PhDs.* Sarasota, FL. Available at http://aaahq.org/temp/phd/shortage.cfm (accessed November 20, 2007).

American Institute of Certified Public Accountants (AICPA). (1968). *Academic Preparation for Accounting Careers.* Report of the Committee on Education and Experience Requirements for CPAs. New York, NY.

American Institute of Certified Public Accountants (AICPA). (1969). *Report of the Committee on Education and Experience Requirements for CPAs.* New York, NY.

American Institute of Certified Public Accountants (AICPA). Big Eight White Paper. (1989).

Perspectives on Education: Capabilities for Success in the Accounting Profession. Available at http://aaahq.org/AECC/pdf/big8/sect3.pdf(accessed November 9, 2007).

American Institute of Certified Public Accountants (AICPA). (2006). *The Supply of Accounting Graduates and the Demand for Public Accounting Recruits—2005.* New York, NY. Available at http://ceae.aicpa.org/NR/rdonlyres/11715FC6-F0A7-4AD6-8D28-6285CBE77315/0/Supply_DemandReport_2005.pdf (accessed November 9, 2007).

Anderson, S. W. (2006). Managing costs and cost structure throughout the value chain: research on strategic cost management. In: C. S. Chapman, A. G. Hopwood & M. D. Shields (Eds), *Handbook of Management Accounting Research*, (Vol. 2). Amsterdam, The Netherlands: Elsevier, pp. 487–512.

Anderson, S. W. & Young, S. M. (1999). The impact of contextual and process factors on the evaluation of activity-based costing systems. *Accounting, Organizations and Society*, **24**, 525–559.

Ansari, S., Bell, J. & Okano, H. (2006). Target costing: uncharted research territory. In: C. S. Chapman, A. G. Hopwood & M. D. Shields (Eds), *Handbook of Management Accounting Research*, (Vol. 2). Amsterdam, The Netherlands: Elsevier, pp. 513–536.

Atkinson, A., Balakrishnan, R., Booth, P., Cote, J. M., Groot, T., Maimi, T., Roberts, H., Uliana, E. & Wu, A. (1997). New directions in management accounting research. *Journal of Management Accounting Research*, **9**, 79–108.

Baldrige National Quality Program (2008). *Why apply?* Gaithersburg, MD: National Institute of Standards and Technology. Available at www.quality.nist.gov (accessed November 9, 2007).

Bamber, E. M. & Bamber, L. S. (2006). Using 10-K reports brings management accounting to life. *Issues in Accounting Education*, **21**(3), 267–290.

Barsky, N. P. & Catanach, A. H. (2005). Motivating student interest in accounting: a business planning approach to the introductory management accounting course. *Advances in Accounting Education*, **7**, 27–63.

Berliner, C. & Brimson, J. A. (1988). *Cost management in today's advance manufacturing: the CAM-I conceptual design*. Boston, MA: Harvard Business School Press.

Boer, G. B. (2000). Management accounting education: yesterday, today and tomorrow. *Issues in Accounting Education*, **15**(2), 313–334.

Boer, G. B. & Ettle, J. (1999). Target costing can boost your bottom line. *Strategic Finance*, **81**(1), 49–53.

Brasel, K. & Hentz, B. (2006). Increasing accessibility to academic publication in accounting education: a database for research and teaching. *Issues in Accounting Education*, **21**(4), 411–416. http://www.bus.iastate.edu/AccountingEducationPublications/ (accessed November 10, 2007).

Brausch, J. M. (1994). Beyond ABC: target costing for profit enhancement. *Management Accounting*, **76**(5), 45–50.

Brewer, P. C. (2000). An approach to organizing a management accounting curriculum. *Issues in Accounting Education*, **15**(2), 211–235.

Brignall, S. & Ballantine, J. (2004). Strategic enterprise management systems: new directions for research. *Management Accounting Research*, **15**(2), 225–240.

Bureau of Labor Statistics. (2005). *Occupational Employment Statistics Survey*. Washington, DC: United States Department of Labor.

Byrne, S. & Pierce, B. (2007). Towards a more comprehensive understanding of the roles of management accountants. *European Accounting Review*, **16**(3), 469–498.

Caplan, E. H. (1966). Behavioral assumptions of management accounting. *The Accounting Review*, **41**, 496–509.

Carpenter, T. D., Fennema, M. G., Fretwell, P. Z. & Hillson, W. (2004). A changing corporate culture. *Journal of Accountancy*, **197**(3), 57–63.

CFO Research Services. (2006). *The CFO as Chief Performance Adviser.* Boston, MA: CFO Publishing Corp. Available at http://www.activeinternational.com/images/news_announcements/gspwc.pdf (accessed May 15, 2007).

Chandler, A. D. (1977). *The visible hand: the managerial revolution in American business*. Cambridge, MA: Harvard University Press.

Chapman, C. S., Hopwood, A. G. & Shields, M. D. (Eds) (2006). *Handbook of Management Accounting Research*, (Vol. 2). Amsterdam, The Netherlands: Elsevier Ltd.

Chenhall, R. H., Langfield-Smith, K. (2007). Multiple perspectives of performance measures. *European Management Journal*, **25**(4), 266–282.

Clevenger, N., Clevenger, T. & McElroy, J. (2006). Shortage of accountants: is education to blame? *The Journal of Government Financial Management*, **55**(2), 14–19.

Combes, H. (2007). The basics are still the same. *Chartered Accountants Journal*, **86**(4), 49.

Cooper, R. (1988a). The rise of activity-based costing—Part one: what is an ABC system? *Journal of Cost Management*, **2**(2), 45–54.

Cooper, R. (1988b). The rise of activity-based costing—Part two: when do I need an ABC system? *Journal of Cost Management*, **2**(3), 41–48.

Cooper, R. (1989a). The rise of activity-based costing—Part three: how many cost drivers do you need and, how you select them? *Journal of Cost Management*, **2**(4), 34–46.

Cooper, R. (1989b). The rise of activity-based costing—Part four: what do ABC systems look like? *Journal of Cost Management*, **3**(1), 38–49.

Cooper, R. (1995). *When lean enterprises collide*. Boston, MA: Harvard Business School Press.

Cooper, R. & Kaplan, R. S. (1988). Measure costs right: make the right decisions. *Harvard Business Review*, **66**, 96–103.

Cooper, R. & Slagmulder, R. (2002). Target costing for new product development: component-level target costing. *Cost Management*, **16**(5), 36–45.

Covaleski, M. A., Evans, J. H. III., Luft, J. L. & Shields, M. D. (2003). Budgeting research: three theoretical perspectives and criteria for selective integration. *Journal of Management Accounting Research*, **15**, 3–49.

Cummings, B., Bennett, R. E. & Normand, C. J. (2001). Meeting the challenge: the university accounting program corporate America needs. *Management Accounting Quarterly*, **2**(2), 4–13.

Daniel, S. J. & Reitsperger, W. D. (1992). Management control systems for quality: an empirical comparison of the U.S. & Japanese electronics industries. *Journal of Management Accounting Research*, **4**, 64–78.

Dean, J. W. & Snell, S. A. (1991). Integrated manufacturing and job design: moderating effects of organizational inertia. *Academy of Management Journal*, **34**(4), 776–804.

Demski, J. S. & Zimmerman, J. L. (2000). On "research vs. teaching:" a long-term perspective. *Accounting Horizons*, **14**(3), 343–352.

Dosch, J. (2006). A nontraditional approach to undergraduate accounting. *Strategic Finance*, **88**(1), 21–22.

Dunk, A. S. (2004). Product life cycle cost analysis: the impact of customer profiling, competitive advantage and quality of IS information. *Management Accounting Research*, **15**(4), 401–414.

Ernst & Young and Institute of Management Accountants (2003). *2003 Survey of Management Accounting*. Ernst & Young, LLP. SCORE Retrieval File No. BV0008.

Fleischman, R. K. (1996). A history of management accounting through the 1960s. In: T. A. Lee, A. Bishop, & R. H. Parker (Eds), *Accounting History from the Renaissance to the Present*. New York, NY: Garland Publishing, Inc, pp. 119–142.

Fleischman, R. K. & Marquette, R. P. (2003). The impact of World War II on cost accounting at the Sperry Corporation. *Accounting Historians Journal*, **30**, 67–104.

Fleischman, R. & Tyson, T. (2006). The history of management accounting the U.S. In: C. S. Chapman, A. G. Hopwood & M. D. Shields (Eds), *Handbook of Management Accounting Research*, (Vol. 2). Amsterdam, The Netherlands: Elsevier, pp. 1089–1107.

Fleming, P. D. (2005). The future has never looked brighter. *Journal of Accountancy*, **200**(5), 66–70.

Frank, K. E. (2003). An examination of alternative work arrangement in private accounting practice. *Accounting Horizons*, **17**(2), 139–151.

Gabbin, A. L. (2002). The crisis in accounting education. *Journal of Accountancy*, **193**(4), 81–86.

Gascho Lipe, M. (2006). Using cases published in Issues in Accounting Education: categories and topics at a glance. *Issues in Accounting Education*, **21**(4), 417–430.

Gosselin, M. (2006). A review of activity-based costing: technique, implementation, and consequences. In: C. S. Chapman, A. G. Hopwood & M. D. Shields (Eds), *Handbook of Management Accounting Research*, (Vol. 2). Amsterdam, The Netherlands: Elsevier, pp. 651–682.

Gupta, K. M. & Gunasekaran, A. (2005). Costing in [a] new enterprise environment: a challenge for managerial accounting researchers and practitioners. *Managerial Auditing Journal*, **20**(4), 337–353.

Hansen, A. & Mouritsen, J. (2006). Management accounting and operations management: understanding the challenges from integrated manufacturing. In: C. S. Chapman, A. G. Hopwood & M. D. Shields (Eds), *Handbook of Management Accounting Research*, (Vol. 2). Amsterdam, The Netherlands: Elsevier, pp. 741–765.

Harvard Business School publishing site Harvard Business for Educators: http://harvardbusinessonline.hbsp.harvard.edu/b01/en/academic/edu_home.jhtml (accessed November 12, 2007).

Hasselback, J. (2004). *The 2004–2005 Accounting Faculty Directory*. Upper Saddle River, NJ: Prentice Hall.

Heier, J. R. (2000). The foundation of modern cost management: the life and work of Albert Fink. *Accounting, Business and Financial History*, **10**, 213–243.

Hoffjan, A. (2005). Calvados—a business game for your cost accounting course. *Issues in Accounting Education*, **20**(1), 63–80.

Hopwoood, A. G. (1972). An empirical study of the role of accounting data in performance evaluation. *Empirical Research in Accounting Supplement to the Journal of Accounting Research*, **10**, 156–182.

Hoskin, K. W. S. & Macve, R. H. (1996). The Lawrence Manufacturing Company: a note on early cost accounting in US textile mills. *Accounting, Business and Financial History*, **6**, 337–361.

Howard, T. P. & Stout, D. E. (2006). Reasons accounting case/instructional resource papers are rejected for publication. *Journal of Accounting Education*, **24**(1), 1–15.

Howieson, B. (2003). Accounting practice in the new millennium: is accounting education ready to meet the challenge? *British Accounting Review*, **35**(2), 69–103.

Hughes, K. E. (2001). A descriptive index of IMA case studies (1985–2001): cases from management accounting practice. *History of cases*. Available at http://www.imanet.org (accessed November 10, 2007).

Hyvonen, J. (2007). Strategy, performance measurement techniques and information technology of the firm and their links to organizational performance. *Management Accounting Research*, **18**(3), 343–366.

IBM (2005). *The Agile CFO: A Study of 900 CFOs Worldwide*. IBM Corporation. Available at http://www-935.ibm.com/services/us/gbs/bus/html/2005_cfo_survey_gen.html (accessed November 9, 2007).

Institute of Management Accounting (IMA). (2007). IMA issues statements on management accounting. *Strategic Finance*, **89**(1), 22–22.

Ittner, C. D. (1996). Exploratory evidence on the behavior of quality costs. *Operations Research*, **44**(1), 114–130.

Ittner, C. D. & Larcker, D. (2002). Empirical managerial accounting research: are we just describing management consulting practice? *European Accounting Review*, **12**(4), 787–984.

Ittner, C. D., Nagar, V. & Rajan, M. V. (2001). An empirical examination of dynamic quality-based learning models. *Management Science*, **47**(4), 563–578.

Jarvenpaa, M. (2007). Making business partners: a case study on how management accounting culture was changed. *European Accounting Review*, **16**(1), 99–142.

Johnson, H. T. (2005). Work lean to control costs. *Manufacturing Engineering*, **18**(6), 75–84.

Johnson, H. T. & Kaplan, R. S. (1987). *Relevance lost: the rise and fall of management accounting*. Boston, MA: Harvard Business School Press.

Jones, C. T. & Dugdale, D. (2002). The ABC bandwagon and the juggernaut of modernity. *Accounting, Organizations and Society*, **27**, 121–163.

Juran, J. M. (1979/1951). *The quality control handbook*. New York, NY: McGraw-Hill Book Company.

Kaplan, R. S. & Anderson, S. R. (2004). Time-driven activity-based costing. *Harvard Business Review*, **82**, 131–138.

Kaplan, R. S. & Cooper, R. (1998). *Cost and effect: using integrated cost systems to drive profitability and performance*. Boston, MA: Harvard Business School Press.

Kaplan, R. S. & Norton, D. P. (1996). *The balanced scorecard: translating strategy into action*. Boston, MA: Harvard Business School Press.

Kaplan, R. S. & Norton, D. P. (2004). *Strategy maps: converting intangible assets into tangible outcomes*. Boston, MA: Harvard Business School Press.

Keating, P. J. & Jablonsky, S. F. (1990). *The Changing Roles of Financial Management: Getting Close to the Business*. Morristown, NJ: Financial Executives Research Foundation.

Kee, R. (1995). Integrating activity based costing with the theory of constraints to enhance production related decision making. *Accounting Horizons*, **9**(4), 48–61.

Keith, R. A., Kulesza, C. S., Albrecht, W. S. & Sack, R. J. (2000). Charting the course through a perilous future. *Management Accounting Quarterly*, **2**(1), 4–11.

Kennedy, F. A. & Brewer, P. C. (2006). *The lean enterprise and traditional accounting—is the honeymoon over? Journal of Corporate Accounting and Finance*, **17**(6), 63–74.

Kennedy, F. A., Owens-Jackson, L., Burney, L. & Schoon, M. L. (2007). How do your measurements stack up to lean? *Strategic Finance*, **88**(11), 33–41.

Kennedy, F. A. & Sorensen, J. E. (2006). Enabling the management accountant to become a business partner: organizational and verbal analysis toolkit. *Journal of Accounting Education*, **24** (2–3), 146–171.

Khan, A. U., Cianciolo, T. A. & Peacock, E. (2000). A plan for reengineering management accounting education based on the IMA's practice analysis. *Management Accounting Quarterly*, **1**(2), 1–6.

Kohler, E. L. & Cooper, W. W. (1945). Costs, prices and profits: accounting in the war program. *Accounting Review*, **20**, 267–308.

KPMG International. (2006). Being the best: insights from leading finance functions (Publication No. 302–760). United Kingdom: The Economist Intelligent United Limited. Available at http://www.kpmg.com/Services/Advisory/Other/Being+the+best.htm (accessed November 9, 2007).

Kroll, K. M. (2004). The lowdown on lean accounting. *Journal of Accountancy*, **198**(1), 69–76.

Libby, T., Salterio, S. E. & Webb, A. (2004). The balanced scorecard: the effects of assurance and process accountability on managerial judgment. *Accounting Review*, **79**(4), 1075–1094.

Lillis, A. M. & Mundy, J. (2005). Cross-sectional field studies in management accounting research—closing the gaps between surveys and case studies. *Journal of Management Accounting Research*, **17**, 119–141.

Loft, A. (1986). Towards a crucial understanding of accounting: the case of accounting in the UK, 1914–1925. *Accounting, Organizations and Society*, **11**, 137–169.

Loft, A. (1990). *Coming into the light*. London, UK: Chartered Institute of Management Accountants.

Luft, J. & Shields, M. (2003). Mapping management accounting: graphics and guidelines for theory-consistent empirical research. *Accounting, Organizations and Society*, **28**(2–3), 169–249.

Lukka, K. & Shields, M. (1999). Innovations in management accounting focus. *Management Accounting: Magazine for Chartered Management Accountants*, **77**(3), 33–34.

Malina, M. A. & Selto, F. H. (2001). Communicating and controlling strategy: an empirical study of the effectiveness of the balanced scorecard. *Journal of Management Accounting Research*, **13**, 47–90.

Malina, M. A. & Selto, F. H. (2004). Choice and change of measures in performance measurement models. *Management Accounting Research*, **15**(4), 441–469.

Marquette, R. P. & Fleischman, R. K. (1992). Government/business synergy: early American innovation in budgeting and cost accounting. *Accounting Historians Journal*, **19**, 123–145.

Merchant, K. A. & Van der Stede, W. A. (2006). Field-based research in accounting: accomplishments and prospects. *Behavioral Research in Accounting*, **18**, 117–134.

Naranjo-Gil, D. & Hartman, F. (2006). How top management teams use management accounting systems to implement strategy. *Journal of Management Accounting Research*, **18**, 21–53.

Noreen, E. W., Smith, D. & Mackey, J. T. (1995). *The Theory of constraints and its implications for management accounting*. Great Barrington, MA: The North River Press.

Previtts, G. J. & Merino, B. (1998). *A History of Accounting in the United States: The Cultural Significance of Accounting*. Columbus, OH: Ohio State University Press.

Parles-McCauley, L., O'Sullivan, S. A. & Shannon, J. H. (2007). Sarbanes-Oxley: an overview of current issues and concerns. *Review of Business*, **27**(3), 38–46.

Ratcliff, T. (2003). OCBOA Financial Statements. *Journal of Accountancy* (October). Available at http://www.aicpa.org/PUBS/JOFA/oct2003/ratcliff.htm (accessed November 9, 2007).

Said, A., HassabElnaby, H. & Wier, B. (2003). An empirical investigation of the performance consequences of nonfinancial measures. *Journal of Management Accounting Research*, **15**, 193–223.

Sedatole, K. L. (2003). The effect of measurement alternatives on a nonfinancial quality measure's forward-looking properties. *The Accounting Review*, **78**(2), 555–580.

Shafer, W. E. & Kunkel, J. G. (2001). Are 150-hour accounting programs meeting their intended objectives? *Journal of Education for Business*, **77**(2), 78–82.

Shank, J. K. & Fisher, J. (1999). Target costing as a strategic tool. *Sloan Management Review*, **41**(1), 73–82.

Shank, J. K. & Govindarajan, V. (1992). Strategic cost management: the value chain perspective. *Journal of Management Accounting Research*, **4**, 741–781.

Shank, J. K. & Govindarajan, V. (1994). *Strategic cost management*. New York, NY: The Free Press.

Sharman, P. A. (2007). A time for change. *Strategic Finance*, **89**(4), 8–10.

Shields, M. D. (1995). An empirical analysis of firms' implementation experiences with activity-based costing. *Journal of Management Accounting Research*, **7**, 148–166.

Shields, M. D. (1997). Research in management accounting by North Americans in the 1990s. *Journal of Management Accounting Research*, **9**, 3–61.

Siegel, G., Kulesza, C. S. & Sorensen, J. E. (1997). Are you ready for the new accounting? *Journal of Accountancy*, **184**(2), 42–46.

Siegel, G. & Sorensen, J. E. (1994). *What Corporate America Wants in Entry Level Accountants*. Montvale, NJ: Institute of Management Accountants.

Siegel, G. (1996). *The Practice Analysis of Management Accounting*. Montvale, NJ: Institute of Management Accountants.

Siegel, G. & Sorensen, J. E. (1999). *Counting More Counting Less: Transformations in the Management Accounting Profession*. Montvale, NJ: Institute of Management Accountants.

Siegel, G. & Sorensen, J. E. (2002). *How to Become a Business Partner*. Montvale, NJ: Institute of Management Accountants.

Siegel, G., Sorensen, J. E., Klammer, T. & Richtermeyer, S. B. (2007). *Synchronizing Accounting Education with Practice*, School of Accountancy. Denver, CO: University of Denver.

Siegel, G., Sorensen, J. E. & Richtermeyer, S. (2003a). Are you a business partner? *Strategic Finance*, **85**(3), 38–43.

Siegel, G., Sorensen, J. E. & Richtermeyer, S. (2003b). Becoming a business partner. *Strategic Finance*, **85**(4), 37–41.

Siegel, G., Sorensen, J. E. & Richtermeyer, S. (2007). *Impact of Sarbanes Oxley on Management Accountants and Business Partners*. Report in progress. Montvale, NJ: Institute of Management Accountants.

Simon, H. A., Guetzkow, H., Kozmetsky, G. & Tyndall, G. (1954). *Centralization vs. decentralization in organizing the controller's department*. New York, NY: Controllership Foundation.

Sinnett, W. M. & Heffes, E. M. (2005). Year-two section 404 compliance. *Financial Executive*, **21**(9), 31–34.

Smith, L. M. (Ed.) (2006). *Reflections on accounting education research*. Monograph of the teaching and curriculum section. Sarasota, FL: American Accounting Association.

Souissi, M. & Ito, K. (2004). Integrating target costing and the balanced scorecard. *The Journal of Corporate Accounting and Finance*, **15**(6), 57–62.

Stout, D. E., Rebele, J. E. & Howard, T. P. (2006). Reasons research papers are rejected at accounting education journals. *Issues in Accounting Education*, **21**(2), 81–98.

Tatikonda, L. U. (2004). Naked truths about accounting curricula. *Management Accounting Quarterly*, **5**(4), 62–73.

Tayles, M. (1995). Target costing: a state-of-the art review. *Journal of the Operational Research Society*, **46**(8), 10–37.

Tomkins, C. & Carr, C. (1996). Reflections on the papers in this issue and a commentary on the sate of strategic management accounting. *Management Accounting Research*, **7**(2), 271–280.

Tyson, T. N. (1992). The nature and environment of cost management among early 19th century U. S. textile manufacturers. *Accounting Historians Journal*, **19**, 1–24.

Tyson, T. N. (1998). Mercantilism, management accounting managerialism? Cost accounting in early 19th century US textile mills. *Accounting, Business and Financial History*, **8**, 211–229.

University of Virginia, McIntire School of Business, case center (http://store.darden.virginia.edu/ecustomer_enu/ (accessed November 12, 2007).

University of Western Ontario, Richard Ivey School of Business, Ivey Publishing http://cases.ivey.uwo.ca/cases/pages/home.aspx (accessed November 12, 2007).

Van Den Brink, H., Kokke, K., De Loo, I., Nederlof, P. & Verstegen, B. (2003). Teaching management accounting in a competencies-based fashion. *Accounting Education*, **12**(3), 245–259.

van der Merwe, A. & Thompson, J. (2007). The low-down on lean accounting. *Strategic Finance*, **88**(8), 26–33.

Wallin, K. I. (2003). IMA: back in the research business. *Strategic Finance*, **85**(3), 1.

Watson, S. F., Apostolou, B., Hasself, J. M. & Webber, S. A. (2007). Accounting education literature review (2003–2005). *Journal of Accounting Education*, **25**(1–2), 1–58.

Womack, J. P. & Jones, D. T. (1996). *Lean thinking—banish waste and create wealth in your corporation*. New York, NY: Simon and Schuster.

Wygal, D. E. & Hartman, B. P. (2003). Partnering for change: infusing enterprise resource planning in the accounting curriculum. *Management Accounting Quarterly*, **4**(4), 37–63.

Young, S. M. (1996). Survey research in management accounting: a critical assessment. In: A. Richardson (Ed.), *Research Methods in Accounting: Issues and Debates*. Vancouver, BC: CGA-Canada Research Foundation, pp. 55–68.

Zimmerman, J. (2001). Conjectures regarding empirical management accounting research. *Journal of Accounting Economics*, **32**(1–3), 411–427.

Management Accounting Practice Contexts

Handbook of Management Accounting Research
Edited by Christopher S. Chapman, Anthony G. Hopwood and Michael D. Shields

Accounting in and for US Governments and Non-profit Organizations: a Review of Research and a Call to Further Inquiry

Sajay Samuel[1], Mark A. Covaleski[2] and Mark W. Dirsmith[3]

[1]*Smeal College of Business Administration University Park, USA*
[2]*University of Wisconsin–Madison, USA*
[3]*Smeal College of Business Administration and the Social Thought Program, University Park, USA*

Abstract: The US government is arguably the largest organization in the world. The budget of the federal government alone runs into the trillions of dollars. From military bases and food aid in foreign countries to domestic prisons, highways and schools, the impacts of the federal, state and local governments are woven into the textures of daily life. Moreover, for at least the past 25 years, it has been the site of a far-reaching transformation. Under what has come to be called the "New Public Administration," every level of the US government is being reconfigured to lessen, if not efface, the distinctions between public and private modes of organizing and to exert greater control over public service personnel. Notably, this effort is built on the expanded use of accounting practices. A similar transformation is underway in the strategies and procedures of non-profit organizations. However, government and non-profit organizations do not receive the sustained interest of accounting scholars. In this chapter, we present a selective review of some of the main strands of management accounting research on government and non-profit organizations in the US. We identify some research questions to spark attention to this crucial substantive domain of accounting practices.

1. Introduction

The governmental and non-profit (GNP) sectors are significant aspects of everyday life in advanced industrialized countries. In the US these sectors account for a large part of the economic activity and have a direct impact on all forms of social, political and cultural life. Moreover, over the past 25 years, these sectors have become the sites of a remarkable and extensive transformation. In particular, they are being increasingly understood as predominantly commercial and economic entities, despite the absence of a profit motive. Consequently, accounting, auditing, and particularly management accounting procedures and practices, are finding their way into these sectors as techniques to ensure the better management of resources, as well as more effective achievement of organizational goals. The old staples of line item budgeting and fund accounting are now supplemented by sophisticated tools to measure performance, control and manage costs, track expenses and evaluate the effectiveness of government programmes. In the accounting literature, government and non-profit organizations are usually classified together, using the argument that neither is profit-seeking. The absence of a bottom line is considered a sufficient criterion to lump together two sectors that are, in fact, quite different. Governments, though perhaps increasingly in name only, are oriented by the public interest and carry the force of law. In contrast, non-profit organizations are non-governmental associations that aim at providing charity or ennobling civic life. Even when contested, as they have been over the past few decades, these historically-shaped purposes animate, however dimly, organizational structures, procedural patterns and types of incentives that operate in these sectors (Salamon, 1989). For reasons of space and relative expertise we focus more on the governmental sector in this review.

DOI: 10.1016/S1751-3243(07)03005-2

The structure of this chapter is as follows. In its first section, we offer a brief description of the US government and the non-profit sectors. This will substantiate the claim for the size and significance of these sectors. Moreover, we present some evidence suggesting a dire emergency in the financial condition of the US federal government and thereby underscore the need for research. In Section 2 we present and analyze data on publications in accounting journals concerning management accounting in US government and non-profit organizations. Our analysis points to the extreme paucity of management accounting research in GNP, a dearth whose significance is exacerbated by the problems concerning government finances identified in Section 1. This lack of research is particularly curious, since a number of topics typically dealt with by management accounting research in the commercial sector are also relevant to the GNP sector. This suggests a relatively low barrier to entry into GNP for future managerial accounting research. We also point to a number of open research questions concerning the division of academic labour, the structure of accounting education and research incentives that may contribute to the relative absence of accounting research into these sectors. In Section 3 we explore an important theme that has run throughout the history of attempts to reorganize and reform government towards greater efficiency and economy—that of the distinction and tensions that exist between politics and administration. The animus to reform and reorganize the practices of government has been largely, although not always, driven by the aims of improved efficiency and effectiveness. It is usually in this context of achieving administrative order that emphasis is placed on accounting, auditing and related calculative practices. From this perspective, politics is seen as both the ill to be cured and the cause for the perpetual failure of administrative order. In exploring this recurrent theme, we derive some research questions that may help bring to light the reasons for the endless failure of accounting and related managerial practices to realize its announced purposes.

2. Government and Non-profit Sectors: an Overview

Governmental organizations in the US constitute the largest organizations in the world. They include 52 state governments, tens of thousands of local governments and the federal government, which in turn is composed of numerous departments and organizations. They account for a third of the total US Gross Domestic Product (GDP), raise about $5 trillion in revenues, incur approximately $5.2 trillion in expenses and carry about $10 trillion of accumulated debt. All levels of government employ some 20 million men and women and pay out some $70 billion in monthly salaries and wages (see Table 1).

The non-profit sector in the US is similarly large. Its assets are worth $2 trillion and its annual revenue of $1 trillion exceeds all but six national economies in the world. Roughly 6% of all non-profit, tax-exempt organizations (501(c) filers) account for more than 80% of the sectors' total revenues and about 90% of its total assets. Non-profit organizations, comprising some 1.8 million registered organizations and several million other associations and support groups, contribute between 5–10% of the US GDP. This sector employs 12 million people that make up about 8% of the entire number of non-institutional civilian employees, and it further accounts for the roughly 20 billion hours of volunteer labour offered by some 109 million Americans (O'Neill, 2002, Chapter 1).

The non-profit sector has been steadily increasing in size over the last 50 years but, since the 1980s, it has increasingly had to compete with the for-profit sector for the services it provides. Since at least 1987 there has been a remarkable and sustained shift from the non-profit to the for-profit sector in all services "but nursing homes and acute care" (Salamon, 2003, p. 22). Accordingly, for-profits appear to be taking over the more profitable aspects of health and human services that were once provided through the non-profit sector, leaving such expensive services as acute care to the non-profits. It remains an open research question if such intersectoral competition

Table 1. Statistics on the US government: Financial Year 2005.

Level of government	Revenues	Expenditures	Accumulated debts (explicit)	Employment (payroll)
Federal	$2.153 trillion	$2.472 trillion	$7.918 trillion	2.70 million (Dec 05: $13.48 billion)
All state	$1.637 trillion	$1.470 trillion	$0.798 trillion	5.08 million (Mar 05: $16.06 billion)
All local	$1.307 trillion	$1.313 trillion	$1.269 trillion	11.72 million (Mar 05: $42.06 billion)
Total	$5.097 trillion	$5.255 trillion	$9.985 trillion	19.50 million

Sources: All data except federal statistics are obtained from the US Census Bureau. http://www.census.gov/govs/www/index.html. Federal government statistics obtained from the historical tables published by the Office of Management and Budget. http://www.whitehouse.gov/omb/budget/fy2008/pdf/hist.pdf

leads to improved outcomes. This explicit competition with for-profits, in addition to the general "cultural" shift towards commercialism, has also placed significant strains on the non-profits to become more "business-like." Indeed, one of the great challenges for the US non-profit sector has been identified as an "effectiveness challenge," one that demands non-profits use accounting and performance measurement systems to improve efficiency and to foster results or outcome-based management in order to compete, ironically, in the marketplace (Salamon, 2003, Chapter 3).

If fiscal pressures and ideological shifts have had a significant impact on the non-profits, forcing them increasingly to adopt such managerial practices, accounting and performance measurement systems, then these same forces have had an even greater impact on the governmental sector (Keller, 2007, p. 28). A business-like administration focused on efficiency, effectiveness and outcomes, has been the staple of attempts to reform every level of the US government since the turn of the last century (McCaffery, 1987). However, it is perhaps only since the 1990s that sustained attention has been paid to transforming the organizations and institutions comprising the US government into quasi-market entities (Hood, 1995). Accordingly, a new accent on such "administrative technologies as customer service, performance-based contracting, competition, market incentives and deregulation" began to be promoted under the broad rubric of the new public management (Denhardt & Baker, 2007, p. 139). It was during this period that "reinventing government" became a slogan animating the widespread reform of government entities (Osborne & Gaebler, 1992); that a raft of laws such as the Chief Financial Officers Act (1990), the Government Performance and Results Act (1993) and the GASB's Statement 34 (1999) requiring balance-sheets and quasi-income statements from local, state and federal governments were passed to foster increased accountability and results-based management in government operations; and that the language of managerialism and economic rationalism, exemplified in the conceit of treating citizens as "customers," took root in the domain of US public affairs (Kettl, 2002a).

Arguably, the effort to make government organizations more market-like through accountability and performance metrics is closely linked to the emerging phenomenon of the "hollow state" (Milward, 1996). The growing separation between the sources and uses of public funds lies at the heart of this development. Whether under the banner of "privatization," "contracting out," or "outsourcing," publicly-funded services are increasingly provided by the private and non-profit sectors. Since the mid-twentieth century, every major government service in the US, including Medicare, Medicaid, interstate highways and sewage treatment plants, has relied on "public–private partnerships." This hollowing out of the state is not a feature limited to the federal government, but rather affects all levels of government. Already "by the mid-1980s, the average American city contracted out 23% of its 64 common municipal services to the private sector, whereas the average American state contracted out 14% of its activities … Between 1982 and 1992 contracting out increased by 121% in the 596 cities where comparable data were available" (Prizza, 2003, p. 318). Indeed, "direct government", understood as the delivery of public services through public employees, accounts for only 5% of total government expenditures. Even when such items as interest payments, income transfers and direct payments are included within the category of direct government, third-party delivery of services still accounts for 78% of total government expenditures (Kettl 2002b, p. 4).

To grasp the historic novelty of this state of affairs, consider that as recently as the "1950s, approximately two-thirds of the budget went to pay the salaries and expenses of federal agencies" (Schick 1987, p. 9). Accordingly, the precise sense in which one can still speak of "big government" remains an open question in a time when governments function as monetary conduits channelling money from and to the private sector. For instance, the Arizona behavioural health system is comprised of five administrative layers between the provision of a federal block grant for mental healthcare and the client who receives the services. Private for-profits or non-profits not only deliver the clinical services, but also undertake such procedures as determining the eligibility of clients, choosing contractors, monitoring their performance and evaluating the outcome of programmes. Public administrator or government employees rarely, if ever, see the customer. Thus, not only are the services outsourced, but the decision to outsource services is itself outsourced (Milward, 1996, p. 193).

Moreover, the hollowing out of the government is enabled by the proliferation of a vast toolkit. These "tools of government" now extend far beyond the direct delivery of government services. Instead, through a bewildering array of tools, including grants, loans, loan guarantees, contracts, social and economic regulations, tax expenditures, insurance schemes and school vouchers, the public sector is intertwined with and enmeshed into the private sector. Some of these indirect tools of government include those that incur obligations, but nevertheless do not show up on government budgets or financial statements. For example, insurance schemes underwritten by the government for disaster relief, pension liabilities and crop failures run into trillions of dollars, but are not accounted for in budgets and financial statements. Other indirect tools of government that do appear on the financial accounts and performance assessments are explicit contracts with private entities (excluding grants, loans, insurance and direct payments) running at about 20% of the federal budget ($415 billion of $2151 billion for the financial year (FY) 2006).

Curiously, less than half of these contracts (approximately 44%) are subjected to full and open competition. More generally, all such private use of public funds entails collaboration between public and private entities, each animated by distinct and even heterogeneous purposes.

Accordingly, the discretion (decisional rights) over the use and disposition of public funds and public authority is increasingly placed in the hands of private entities (Salamon, 2002, pp. 3–5). It is this phenomenon of the separation of the sources and uses of public funds that raises the stakes in matters of accountability and performance. The demand for auditing, accounting and performance measurement has increased enormously, in large measure to address the complex private–public relationships unleashed by this "third-party government" or "hollow state." The private spending of public funds fuels the need for measures of accountability and performance, far more than what may be required in regimes of direct government. This context of a long-term project to effect a far-reaching change in the scope, scale, form and instruments of governance therefore forms the backdrop for any evaluation of research into management accounting practices in the government and non-profit sectors. In the more prosaic terms of management accounting, the phenomenon of the hollow state can be understood as the consequence of a series of make-or-buy decisions. Accordingly, a host of open research questions may be entertained:

1. What criteria govern such make-or-buy decisions—total cost, efficiency, flexibility or arms-length contracting?
2. What kinds of costs—transaction, monitoring, negotiating—are minimized through private-public relations? What kind of data is used in making these decisions?
3. Is contracting out profitable for certain services and unprofitable for others? What characteristics can help predict or describe cost saving from contracting out?
4. How are decisional rights allocated between contracting parties, whether over control of assets, delivery of service or assessment of service delivery?
5. Is there a systematic variation based on contract characteristics that explain why some contracts are fully competed and others are no-bid?
6. Do block grants by which federal monies are given to state and local governments represent a shift from the traditional line item budgeting?
7. How do accounting and performance metrics help or hinder these inter-organizational relations (between different levels of government; between government and private agents; among private agents)?

Before any systematic analysis of the production of accounting research in this setting can be conducted, it is useful to underscore, in very general terms, the grave financial condition of the US government. A fuller appreciation of this aspect of governmental finances should permit an informed analysis of the value, role and extent of accounting research in this sector. David Walker is the current Comptroller General of the US and heads the Government Accountability Office (GAO), formerly known as the General Accounting Office. The change of name in 2004 is itself significant, for it was aimed at distancing the GAO from the image of green eyeshade-clad accountants poring over the cost of paper clips to that of a professional service firm concerned with evaluating programmes, conducting analyses of social and economic policies, offering legal opinions and decisions on a host of government programmes and, of course, conducting financial and performance audits of the US government. It is self-described as the premier organization in the US government concerned with "measuring the government's performance and holding it accountable for results" (Walker, 2004).

In its newly focused activity, what the GAO has been reporting over the past years about the deteriorating state of US governmental finances is at least startling, if not downright shocking. Recently, the Comptroller General stated somewhat baldly that "the greatest threat to America's future isn't hiding in a cave in Pakistan or Afghanistan; it's right here at home" (Walker, 2006). According to its most recent report the GAO has been unable to render an audit opinion on whether the consolidated financial statements of the US government are fairly stated in conformity with US generally accepted accounting procedures (GAAP) (GAO, 2007a). This situation has persisted continuously over the past decade, ever since the federal government was required by law to present consolidated financial statements. The GAO cannot render an opinion because of material weaknesses in the financial reports of the departments of the federal government; extremely poor internal controls; its inability to track significant amounts of intergovernmental transfers; severe financial management problems at the Department of Defense; and frequent restatements by federal agencies of prior data, among other reasons (GAO, 2007a). As an example of the extent of the disarray in these accounting records, consider that the Department of Defense (DOD) has lost track of $2.3 trillion! It is not that these funds have been recorded as being misspent under the category of "waste, fraud and abuse." That is a separate category, which would include such items as the estimated $41 billion of improper payments in FY2006. Rather, the trillions missing from DOD accounts have apparently disappeared without a trace. It was spent, only nobody knows on what, why or when (CBS News, 2002). This sorry state of financial affairs, and the consequent inability to render an opinion on the financial statements of the US government, casts serious doubts on the purpose and value of such statements. The decade-long history of unverifiable financial statements raises the obvious research question of the role and purpose of US government financial statements. Are these, as often stated, intended to generate reliable information to permit efficient, economic and effective action? Or are these staged displays of supposed financial probity?

These are not the only indicators of the state of governmental financial management. The accumulated debt of the US federal government as of FY2006 was some $50.5 trillion, a 147% increase from the $20.4 trillion recorded for FY2000. This debt includes the present value of such future obligations as social security and Medicare, as well as the explicit obligation incurred on account of publicly held debt, military and civilian pensions and so on. The almost three-fold increase over six years in estimated federal debt seems to be driven mainly by changing demographics—the aging US population which will trigger future mandatory payments. At this debt level, not to mention the rate of future increase in debt, it seems unlikely that the obligations incurred by the US government will be honoured. For instance, the total US household net worth in mid-2006 was about $53.3 trillion, implying a debt-to-equity ratio of some 95%. Moreover, when divided among households, the debt burden per household in FY2006 was about $440 000 as compared to the median household income of roughly $48 200 (GAO, 2007a). Long before taxes are subtracted from personal income, and private debts such as credit cards and mortgages are added, the expected federal debt alone is more than nine times the annual income of the median household in the US. Finally, economic growth is unlikely to solve the looming fiscal crisis, for according to the GAO analyses, "closing the current long-term fiscal gap based on reasonable assumptions would require real average annual growth in the double digit range every year for the next 75 years" (GAO, 2007b). Since the average annual economic growth rate in the US over the last decade has been below 4%, it appears that the US federal government is, at this time, courting bankruptcy. At the very least, when revenues can no longer service ongoing expenses and borrowing gets too costly, the benefits promised to and already partly paid for by citizens, whether these concern social security, pensions or Medicare and Medicaid, are likely to be significantly reduced.

But this very conclusion, advanced by the GAO, suggests a number of research questions for accounting scholarship.

- Has the adoption of more business-like financial statements improved the quality of governmental financial information?
- What aspects of governmental financial accounting, if any, contribute to the prevalence of large unfunded or under-funded liabilities?
- How should federal budgets be presented? Would ten-year estimates of costs, as they once were presented, influence policy decisions? How does the presentation of unified budget figures affect policy decisions?
- Do financial reporting and performance metrics contribute to improved administrative and political decisions?
- What is the value and purpose of such ratios as the "debt burden per household" used by the GAO?
- Are the assumptions driving the present value calculations of future obligations necessary and/or valid?
- How much confidence can and should be placed on projected revenues and costs that are extremely sensitive to assumptions?

As can be seen from the list of research questions posed previously, there is much room for accounting scholarship on momentous transformation in the nature, scale, scope and size of the US government. However, it seems that accounting research has almost completely neglected this enormously important sector as a subject for systematic investigation and study.

3. Management Accounting Research in Government and Non-profit Sectors

Any review of accounting literature must contend with a paradox. A review, which purports to be a synoptic overview of a given topic, must necessarily belie itself. It is a paradox framed by the excessive production of information. For a first result of the so-called information age is "information overload." The impossibility of surveying a field comprehensively due to the excess of available information can be illustrated in the case of accounting research itself. The range and variety of accounting journals aimed at just English speaking audiences has exploded over the last two decades. Between 1988 and 1996 the number of such journals almost doubled, from 40 to 77 (Zeff, 1996). Whether this rate of increase has been sustained over the past decade, and how such increase in information contributes to relative ignorance because of "information overload," remain open research questions.

A number of recent studies have been published on the prevalence of management accounting research in accounting journals. For example, Shields (1997) examined six accounting journals to better understand the state of the literature published between 1990 and 1996 on management accounting by North American researchers.[1] He offered both a classificatory scheme and a typology of

[1]Accounting, Organizations & Society (AOS); The Accounting Review (TAR); Contemporary Accounting Research (CAR); Journal of Accounting & Economics (JAE); Journal of Accounting Research (JAR); and Journal of Management Accounting Research (JMAR).

management accounting topics that we have partly relied on in our analysis below. His results showed that while management accounting research did employ a variety of research methods and theories, only about 6.6% of the 152 articles on management accounting addressed the governmental and non-profit sectors. Hwang & Wu (2006) extended the analysis of Shield (1997) to consider not only a longer time period (1991–2000), but also to include those journals specializing in management accounting research, even if these were not considered a "leading journal." They identified three journals as specialized in management accounting: *Journal of Management Accounting Research* (JMAR), *Advances in Management Accounting* (AIMA), and *Management Accounting Review* (MAR). Their results showed that the overall percentage of articles in *The Accounting Review* (TAR), *Journal of Accounting Research* (JAR), *Contemporary Accounting Research* (CAR) and *Journal of Accounting and Economics* (JAE) on management accounting research remained constant during the 1990s, at about 10.8% of all articles published between 1991 and 2000. On the other hand, *Accounting, Organizations and Society* (AOS) reflected a higher, though more volatile, pattern of publications, with 26.3% of its articles devoted to research in management accounting (Hwang & Wu, 2006, p. 150). In contrast, rather than rely on accepted notions of leading journals, usually enforced through a pre-selected list, Lowensohn & Samuelson (2006) polled the opinions of accounting scholars in five specialized areas of accounting research to determine their perception of the highest quality journals in each field of study.[2] Between them the over 500 participating accounting scholars listed 111 different publication outlets as being of high quality in these five areas of research, and the following four journals were identified for the GNP area: *Research in Governmental & Non-Profit Accounting* (RIGNA); *Journal of Accounting & Public Policy* (JAPP); *Journal of Public Budgeting, Accounting & Financial Management* (JPBAFM); *Journal of Governmental Financial Management* (JGFM).

Based on this review of accounting journals, we selected the 12 journals as germane to a survey of management accounting in the government and non-profit settings. To the list of six journals identified by Shields (1997), we added the journals specialized in management accounting as noted by Hwang & Wu (2006). However, since MAR is an internationally-focused journal mainly aimed at non-US settings, we excluded it from our dataset. We then considered the journals identified by researchers specializing in governmental and non-profit sectors as noted by Lowensohn & Samuelson (2006). Of these four journals, we included only JAPP in our dataset. While none of these journals were thought to have a uniformly "highly favourable" outcome on promotion and tenure decisions in PhD-granting institutions, only JAPP and RIGNA were considered as at least "favourable" to such decisions (p. 232). Moreover, while accounting scholars do publish in JPBAFM and JGFM, as for example Wallace (2003), these journals nevertheless seem oriented by practicing government accountants, auditors and financial managers, and include articles by non-accounting faculty. Furthermore, we excluded RIGNA from our dataset because it was only published once (2004) between the years 2000 and 2007, the period for our analysis. Accordingly, we examined eight accounting journals to investigate the scope and depth of management accounting research in the governmental and non-profit setting.

In conducting our analyses, we first identified all articles published in these journals pertaining to GNP sectors in the US. Thus, for instance, we excluded Froud (2003) and Kurunmäki (2004) since they concerned the UK government and hospitals in Finland, respectively. Similarly, we excluded Kinney et al. (2005) despite the reference to the "US government" in the title. The substance of the article was concerned with the impact of the Sarbanes-Oxley Act regulation on auditor independence and quality of financial reports, and hence pertained primarily to the private sector. This article, and others like it, was therefore excluded from the dataset. However, we did include all articles on the US-based hospital industry, since a significant portion of this industry is composed of non-profit organizations. Thus, for instance, we included Evans, Leone & Nagarajan (2005) even though their sample of hospitals seems to be for-profit. We then classified these articles following most, though not all, of the classificatory scheme offered in Shields (1997). Accordingly, we identify the topic, theory and research methods for each article, note its specific setting (level of government and type of non-profit), and finally identify the branch of accounting research to which it belongs (see Table 4). There is considerable room for interpretative differences in this latter exercise. For instance, while using the list of management accounting topics provided by Shields (1997) as a guidepost, we erred on the side of inclusiveness when deciding whether to classify a particular article as pertaining to financial, tax or management accounting. Thus we classified Walkins (2000) as pertaining to financial accounting, since it examined the additional information over financial ratios provided by non-financial information. On the other hand, we classified Evans, Leone & Nagarajan (2005) on non-financial information as germane to management accounting, since it explored

[2]The five specialized areas of accounting research were labelled: behavioural; taxation; government & non-profit; management accounting and information systems.

the relationship between quality measures, customer satisfaction and costs. Despite such interpretative differences, our overall results are not materially affected since the publication rates in the GNP sectors are miniscule, both of accounting in general and of management accounting in particular.

The results for the quantity of articles published in these eight accounting journals on GNP settings in the US are exceedingly low (see Tables 2 and 3). Of the 1580 articles published between 2000 and 2007 so far, only 39 articles (2.5%) pertain to these sectors. This result is in some contrast to the evidence marshalled by Hwang & Wu (2006) who found about 7.8% of the 580 articles they examined pertained to the GNP sectors, and further that the area attracted greater attention during the latter half of the decade (p. 158). In our dataset, JAPP accounts for fully half of all such articles (partly due to a special issue on healthcare) and none of the other journals contain more than six articles over the eight year period. Notably, CAR has no articles at all in either the governmental or non-profit settings.

When further sieved by whether such articles pertain to management accounting, subject to the interpretations mentioned above, we note a decrease of articles on management accounting referring to the GNP sectors: the total drops by more than a third, from 39 to 24 articles, to 1.5% of all articles. While the government sector accounts for only half the number of articles devoted to the non-profit sector, much of the work in the latter concentrates on the healthcare industry. This industry is important not only because of its size and multi-faceted impact on the US economy, but also because of its significance for US politics. The field of healthcare accounting has been comprehensively reviewed both from the dominant economics perspective by Eldenburg & Krishan (2007), and from behavioural, organizational, sociological and critical perspectives by Abernathy et al. (2007). These two reviews offer a thorough analysis of the state of research understanding of accounting in the healthcare industry. However, almost all other arenas of the GNP sector remain sorely under-researched, including and not limited to education, transportation and public utilities. Overall then, the US governmental sector attracts less attention from accounting scholars when compared to the US non-profit sector, and furthermore both sectors receive little attention given their size, significance and the magnitude of recent transformations.

The paucity of research in the governmental and non-profit sectors is somewhat puzzling. There are some clues to this bias in academic scholarship. For instance, almost 20 years ago, Chan noted that "governmental accounting for a long time enjoyed (or suffered, depending on one's

Table 2. Articles in select accounting journals on US governments and non-profit organizations, 2000–2007.

Journal (1)	Total number of papers (2)	Papers on government and accounting (3)	Papers on non-profit organizations and accounting (4)	Total papers on government and non-profit organizations (5) = (3 + 4)	(3) as % of (2)	(4) as % of (2)	(5) as a % of (2)
AOS	265	4	2	6	1.51	0.75	2.26
AIMA	92	1	1	2	1.09	1.09	2.18
CAR	226	0	0	0	0.00	0.00	0.00
JAE	226	0	4	4	0.00	1.77	1.77
JAPP	177	8	11	19	4.52	6.21	10.73
JAR	222	0	1	1	0.45	0.45	0.90
JMAR	57	0	2	2	0.00	3.51	3.51
TAR	315	2	3	5	0.63	0.95	1.58
Total	1580	15	24	39	0.95	1.52	2.47

Legend:
AOS = *Accounting, Organizations and Society*
AIMA = *Advances in Management Accounting*
CAR = *Contemporary Accounting Research*
JAE = *Journal of Accounting and Economics*
JAPP = *Journal of Accounting and Public Policy*
JAR = *Journal of Accounting Research*
JMAR = *Journal of Management Accounting Research*
TAR = *The Accounting Review*

Table 3. Articles in select accounting journals on management accounting in US governments and non-profits, 2000–2007.

Journal (1)	Total number of papers (2)	Papers on government and management accounting (3)	Papers on non-profit organizations and management accounting (4)	Total papers on management accounting in government and non-profit organizations (5) = (3 + 4)	(3) as a percentage of (2)	(4) as a percentage of (2)	(5) as a percentage of (2)
AOS	265	2	2	4	0.75	0.75	1.50
AIMA	92	1	1	2	1.09	1.09	2.18
CAR	226	0	0	0	0.00	0.00	0.00
JAE	226	0	1	1	0.00	0.44	0.44
JAPP	177	4	6	10	2.26	3.39	5.65
JAR	222	0	1	1	0.00	0.45	0.45
JMAR	57	0	2	2	0.00	3.51	3.51
TAR	315	1	3	4	0.32	0.95	1.27
Total	1580	8	16	24	0.51	1.01	1.52

Legend:
AOS = *Accounting, Organizations and Society*
AIMA = *Advances in Management Accounting*
CAR = *Contemporary Accounting Research*
JAE = *Journal of Accounting and Economics*
JAPP = *Journal of Accounting and Public Policy*
JAR = *Journal of Accounting Research*
JMAR = *Journal of Management Accounting Research*
TAR = *The Accounting Review*

perspective) the benign neglect of the accounting profession and discipline" (1987, p. 1). This is a sentiment that has been shared through the years by researchers concerned with governmental accounting and auditing (Broadbent & Guthrie, 1992; Broadbent, 1999). More recently, Lowensohn & Samuelson (2006) document some evidence for their judgement that "accounting academics … in GNP may face difficulties substantiating the quality of their research" (p. 219). They report the comments of researchers in the GNP section of the AAA, one of whom said "One reviewer of TAR told me that he rejected 40 papers in the (GNP) area before reviewing a paper that was published." Another "noted that a manuscript (with the submission fee) was returned from TAR without review, because this topic is not of interest to our readers" (p. 233). In our own experience a paper examining audit processes within the GAO was rejected because "it does not concern large international public accounting firms and therefore is of little interest." Only a minority of the accounting faculty (less than 10%) belonging to the GNP section considers the usual list of top journals as representing their research or representative of their research interests.

The paucity of management accounting research in these settings is particularly surprising, given that the topics of interest to management accountants are also being discussed in the journals devoted to political science and public management. For instance, a cursory review of these journals reveals that such topics as contracting out (Choi et al., 2005); performance budgets (Aristigueta & Justice, 2006); cost control and management (Schachter, 2007); inter-organizational relations (Berry & Brower, 2005); balanced and other scorecards (Coe, 2003); strategic planning (Poister & Streib, 2005); information technologies (Roberts & Thompson, 2006) and e-initiatives to reduce costs (Ya-Ni & Bretschneider, 2007); and performance measurement (Nicholson-Crotty et al., 2006); are staples within this literature. While faculty from political science and public administration come to such topics with their own theoretical backgrounds and perspectives, it may be beneficial to understanding the government and non-profit sectors better if accounting academics were to enter into a dialogue with the scholars writing for such publications as *Public Administration Review*, *Public Productivity and Management Review* and *Public Administration Quarterly*. For instance, opportunities for

Table 4. Details of all articles on US government or non-profit organizations from selected journals, 2000–2007.

Author(s)	Journal name	Publishing information	Article title	Setting (accounting field)	Topic	Theory	Method
Core, J. E., Guay, W. R. & Verdi, R. S.	JAE	2006, **41**(3), pp. 307–333	Agency problems of excess endowment holdings in not-for-profit firms	Non-profit (M: incentives, compensation)	NPs with excessive endowments suffer agency problems	Economics	Empirical
Petrovits, C. M.	JAE	2006, **41**(3), pp. 335–362	Corporate-sponsored foundations and earnings management	Non-profit (F: earnings management)	Corporations time the contributions to their charitable foundations to manage reserves and earnings	Economics	Empirical
Sansing, R. & Yetman, R.	JAE	2006, **41**(3), pp. 363–384	Governing private foundations using the tax law	Non-profit (F: earnings management)	Tax regime changes have inconsistent effect on NP propensity for charitable distribution	Economics	Empirical
Bolton, P. & Mehran, H.	JAE	2006, **41**(3), pp. 293–305	An introduction to the governance and taxation of not-for-profit organizations	Non-profit (T: tax regimes)	NPs receive tax exemptions giving them advantages in competition with FPs	Economics	Analytical
Kallapur, S. & Eldenburg, L.	JAR	2005, **43**(5) pp. 735–752	Uncertainty, real options, and cost behavior: evidence from Washington state hospitals	Hospital industry, non-profit organizations possible (M: capital budgeting)	Increased uncertainty in revenues after PPS prompts technology investments with low fixed and high variable costs	Economics	Empirical
Yetman, R. J.	TAR	2001, **76**(3), pp. 297–311	Tax-motivated expense allocations by non-profit organizations	Non-profit (M: cost allocations)	NPs allocate expenses from tax-exempt to taxable activities to reduce tax liabilities	Economics	Empirical
Baber, W. R. Daniel, P. L. & Roberts, A. A.	TAR	2002, **77**(3), pp. 679–693	Compensation to managers of charitable organizations: an empirical study of the role of accounting measures of program activities	Non-profit (M: incentives, compensation)	Compensation to CEOs of charitable organizations reflect operational outcomes as captured by accounting-based performance measures	Economics	Empirical
Krishnan, R., Yetman, M. H. & Yetman, R. J.	TAR	2006, **81**(2), pp. 399–420	Expense misreporting in non-profit organizations	Non-profit (M: cost management, incentives)	NPs misreport fund-raising expenses as a result of managerial incentives	Economics	Empirical

(*Continued*)

Table 4. (Continued)

Author(s)	Journal name	Publishing information	Article title	Setting (accounting field)	Topic	Theory	Method
Plummer, E., Hutchison, P. D. & Patton, T. K.	TAR	2007, **82**(1), pp. 205–240	GASB No. 34's governmental financial reporting model: evidence on its information relevance	Local government (F: financial statement disclosure)	The "balance sheet" is more informative than the "income statement of the default risk." Uses school districts adopting GASB 34	Economics	Empirical
Thibodeau, N., Evans J. H. III; Nagarajan, N. J. & Whittle, J.	TAR	2007, **82**(2), pp. 483–520	Value creation in public enterprises: An empirical analysis of coordinated organizational changes in the Veterans Health Administration	Federal government (M: cost management, incentives)	Clinical costs decline and outcomes improve in VA hospitals when performance measures are combined with changes in incentives and organizational structures	Economics, Organizational theory	Empirical
Balakrishnan, R. & Soderstrom, N. S.	JMAR	2000, **12**, pp. 97–114	The cost of system congestion: evidence from the healthcare sector	Hospital industry, non-profit organizations possible (M: capacity and cost management)	Congestion in maternity wards increase C-section rates for patients "at-risk" for C-sections	Economics, Queuing theory	Empirical
Leone, A.	JMAR	2002, **14**, pp. 99–118	The relation between efficient risk-sharing arrangements and firm characteristics: evidence from the managed care industry	Hospital industry, non-profit organizations possible (M: management control systems, incentives)	Management control systems, specifically contract types vary systematically with organizational form, customer mix and environment	Economics, Organizational theory	Empirical
Mensah, Y.	JAPP	2000, **19**(1), pp. 3–7	Accounting issues in healthcare	Hospital industry, non-profit organizations possible (Review)	Review of papers published in special theme issue		
Barniv, R., Danvers, K. & Healy, J.	JAPP	2000, **19**(1), pp. 9–40	The impact of Medicare capital prospective payment regulation on hospital capital expenditures	Hospital industry, non-proprietary (M: capital budgeting)	Prospective payment scheme (PPS) influence managers to reduce capital expenditures without changing operating expenses	Economics	Empirical
Hill, N. T.	JAPP	2000, **19**(1), pp. 41–71	Adopting of costing systems in US hospitals: an event history analysis 1980–1990	Hospital industry, non-profit organizations possible (M: capital budgeting, cost systems)	Less than half the hospitals in the sample introduced costing systems after PPS	Economics, Organizational theory	Empirical

Walkins, A.	JAPP	2000, **19**(1), pp. 73–95	Hospital financial ratio classification patterns revisited: upon considering non-financial information	Hospital industry, non-profit organizations possible (F: financial statement information)	Non-financial information provided additional information over financial ratios about creditworthiness	Economics	Empirical
Eldenburg, L. & Kallapur, S.	JAPP	2000, **19**(1), pp. 97–112	The effects of changes in cost allocation on the assessment of cost containment regulation in hospitals	Hospital industry, non-profit organizations possible (M: cost allocations, incentives)	Post PPS, managers reallocate common costs from fixed fee to cost-plus lines of business. Little evidence of PPS inducing cost-control	Economics	Empirical
McLelland, A. & Giroux, G.	JAPP	2000, **19**(3), pp. 263–281	An empirical analysis of auditor report timing by large municipalities	Local government (F/Au: financial information disclosure)	External auditors take longer to submit audit reports due to regulatory burdens	Economics	Empirical
Evans J., Hwang, Y. & Nagarajan, N.	JAPP	2001, **20**(1), pp. 73–88	Management control and hospital cost reduction: additional evidence	Hospital industry, non-profit organizations possible (M: cost control, incentives)	Physicians monitored on performance manage metrics to look better without significantly reducing hospital costs	Economics	Empirical
Thorne, J., Holmes, S. A., McGowan, A. S., Strand, C. A. & Strawser, R. H.	JAPP	2001, **20**(3), pp. 189–215	The relation between audit pricing and audit contract type; a public sector analysis	Local government (M: incentives, contract design)	Audit fees for fixed-fee audit contracts are lower than that for cost-reimbursement audit contracts	Economics	Empirical
Payne, J. L. & Jensen, K. L.	JAPP	2002, **21**(1), pp. 1–29	An examination of municipal audit delay	State/local government (F/Au: financial information disclosure)	Factors driving delay of municipal audit reports include audit-firm and city characteristics	Organizational theory, Economics	Empirical
Gordon, T., Fischer, M., Malone, D. & Tower, G.	JAPP	2002, **21**(3), pp. 235–275	A comparative empirical examination of extent of disclosure by private and public colleges and universities in the United States	Education industry; Non-profit (F: financial information disclosure)	Determinants of degree and type of disclosure in financial statements include size, visibility of entity and nature of auditor	Organizational theory, Economics	Empirical
Chaney, B. A., Copley, P. A. & Stone, M. S.	JAPP	2002, **21**(4–5), pp. 287–313	The effect of fiscal stress and balanced budget requirements on the funding and measurement of state pension obligations	State government (M: cost control, management)	State employee pensions are under-funded by fiscally stressed states requiring balanced budgets	Economics	Empirical

(*Continued*)

Table 4. (Continued)

Author(s)	Journal name	Publishing information	Article title	Setting (accounting field)	Topic	Theory	Method
Cavalluzzo, K. S.	JAPP	2002, **21**(4–5), pp. 315–356	Competition, fee-for-service requirements, and government performance: evidence on the Federal Reserve	Federal Reserve Bank/ Government (M: cost management)	Competition with private sector increase productivity of services: reduced costs/ increased quality	Economics	Empirical
Johnson, L. E., Davies, S. P. P. & Freeman, R. J.	JAPP	2002, **21**(4–5), pp. 395–422	The effect of seasonal variations in auditor workload on local government audit fees and audit delay	Local government (F/Au: financial information disclosure)	Audit fees and audit report delays are related to financial year-end dates. December year-ends are worse than July and September	Organizational theory, Economics	Empirical
Mensah, Y. M. & Werner, R.	JAPP	2003, **22**(4), pp. 293–323	Cost efficiency and financial flexibility in institutions of higher education	Education industry; Non-profit (M: cost control)	Donor restrictions on use of funds do not increase cost inefficiencies. Line-item budgeting can be efficient	Organizational theory, Economics	Empirical
Phillips, J. F.	JAPP	2003, **22**(4), pp. 347–374	The dilemma of valuing not-for-profit hospitals—Is free cash flow the answer?	Hospital industry, non-profit organizations possible (F: valuation)	Acquisition price of non-profit hospitals related to operating margins and free cash flows	Economics	Empirical
Lynch, L. J.	JAPP	2003, **22**(2), pp. 151–173	The effect of Medicare capital prospective payment regulation: additional evidence from hospital financing decisions	Hospital industry, non-profit organizations possible (M: cost management)	Administrators reduced long-term debt after the introduction of PPS which refused explicit reimbursement of interest payments	Economics, Organizational theory	Empirical
Eldenburg, L. & Vines, C. C.	JAPP	2004, **23**(1), pp. 1–22	Non-profit classification decisions in response to a change in accounting rules	Hospital industry, non-profit organizations possible (F: financial information disclosure)	Administrators reclassify accounting categories from bad debts to charity care in response to new reporting regulations	Economics	Empirical

Gore, A. K.	JAPP	2004, **23**(1), pp. 23–52	The effects of GAAP regulation and bond market interaction on local government disclosure	Local government (F: financial information disclosure)	Disclosure regulations prompt managers of low debt municipalities to increase GAAP compliant disclosures	Economics	Empirical
Eaton, T. V. & Nofsinger, J. R.	JAPP	2004, **23**(3), pp. 161–189	The effect of financial constraints and political pressure on the management of public pension plans	State/local government (M: cost management, cost control)	Managers make optimistic actuarial assumptions and under-fund public pensions in fiscally stressed regions	Economics, Organizational theory	Empirical
Carpenter, B. V. L. & Feroz, E. H.	AOS	2001, **26**(7–8), pp. 565–596	Institutional theory and accounting rule choice: an analysis of four US state governments – decisions to adopt generally accepted accounting principles	State government (F: financial information disclosure; incentives)	Drivers of the decisions by four US state governments to adopt GAAP for external financial reporting	Sociology, Organizational theory	Archival
Chwastiak, M.	AOS	2001, **26**(6), pp. 501–519	Taming the untameable: planning, programming and budgeting and the normalization of war	Federal government (M: political use of MA numbers)	PPB was used to centralize resource allocation decision and to make the issue of nuclear war a matter of cost-benefit analysis	Critical theory	Archival
Cavalluzzo, K. S. & Ittner, C. D.	AOS	2004, **29**(3–4), pp. 243–267	Implementing performance measurement innovations: evidence from government	Federal government (M: performance measurement, cost management)	Organizational factors affecting greater accountability, improved decision-making and performance	Economics, Sociology, Organizational theory	Survey
Roberts, R. W. & Bobek,	AOS	2004, **29**(5–6), pp. 565–590	The politics of tax accounting in the United States: evidence from the Taxpayer Relief Act of 1997	Federal government (T: tax laws)	Corporate lobbying could influence tax laws	Political economy	Empirical, archival
Samuel, S., Dirsmith, M. W. & McElroy, B.	AOS	2005, **30**(3), pp. 249–278	Monetized medicine: from the physical to the fiscal	Hospital industry, non-profit organizations possible (M: cost management)	Economic and operations research arguments justifying HMOs and clinical practice as factory production	Sociology, Social theory	Archival

(Continued)

Table 4. (Continued)

Author(s)	Journal name	Publishing information	Article title	Setting (accounting field)	Topic	Theory	Method
Pizzini, M. J.	AOS	2006, **31**(2), pp. 179–210	The relation between cost-system design, managers' evaluations of the relevance and usefulness of cost data, and financial performance: an empirical study of US hospitals	Hospital industry, non-profit organizations possible (M: cost control)	Cost system designed with greater functionality permit improved managerial decisions and improved financial outcomes	Economics, Organizational theory	Empirical, Survey
Richardson, V.	AIMA	2004, **13**, pp. 99–142	Performance-based organizations (PBOs): the tale of two performance based organizations	Federal government: DOE; DOC (M: performance measurement)	Spotty record of implementing PBO legislation on procurement, personnel and accountability. Leadership has PB contracts tied to performance measures	Organizational theory	Interviews with key personnel
Evans, J., Leone, A. & Nagarajan, N.	AIMA	2005, **14,** pp. 1–31	Nonfinancial performance measures in the healthcare industry: do quality-based incentives matter?	Hospital industry, non-profit organizations possible (M: non-financial performance measures)	Quality measures can increase customer satisfaction without increasing costs too much. Uses FP hospitals	Economics	Empirical

Legend: M = Management accounting; F = Financial accounting; Au = Auditing; T = Tax sharing research results and knowledge could be obtained from a more detailed comparative study of the journals we excluded from this analysis (JPBAFM and JGFM) and key journals in the field of public administration. A comparison of settings, methods, theories, topics and results could be useful to establish a baseline of the similarities and differences between accounting and public administration scholarship. Such a mapping may also reveal the comparative advantages of accounting and public administration academics and thereby increase the areas of fruitful collaboration. At a minimum, it is precisely such collaboration that is suggested by the very changes occurring in the substantive domain of the GNP setting.

Even more deeply, it remains a matter for further research into the economics and sociology of knowledge production to understand why and how certain topics and settings are intensively studied to the virtual exclusion of others and how boundaries within and between academic fields are policed (Whitley, 1984, 1986). There is much research showing that the system of regulating accounting research has grown more closed and insular at precisely the moment when the volume of accounting research has grown. The presence of fewer widely recognized high-quality journals than in other business disciplines (Swanson, 2004); the dominance of a few journals among this relatively smaller list (Reiter & Williams, 2002); the predominance of a few topics—financial accounting and auditing—in these "acceptable" journals (Bonner et al., 2006); a strict policing of theories and perspectives that limit the band of what counts as "acceptable" research (Williams et al., 2006); the training of doctoral candidates along these narrowly-defined research paths (Pannozzo, 1997; Schwartz, et al., 2005); and an oligopolistic market structure in the industry of accounting knowledge production where a few universities account for the majority of authors, editors and PhD graduates (Williams, et al., 2006) contribute to this situation. However, while this body of research elucidates the mechanisms that maintain and perpetuate forms of social stratification in the accounting academy in general, it does not address the lack of GNP research in particular. More research into this question, using the insights and arguments on the incentives, mechanisms and structures of policing knowledge production, would help to clarify and potentially redress the paucity of research in the GNP setting.

Recent reviews of the future of management accounting have pointed to the plethora of topics of potential interest to both academics and practitioners (Birnberg, 2004; Selto & Widener, 2004; Baxter & Chua, 2003). These authors recommend a range of topics to extend management accounting research, though none directly address the applicability of such research to the GNP setting. However, a preponderance of accounting studies in the GNP setting, as well as most of the suggested topics for future research in management accounting, are of a technical nature. While we support the endeavour to raise the interest of accounting academics in the GNP setting, we also encourage a study of governmental accounting and budgeting within its historic and sectoral contexts, for the reasons outlined below.

4. Politics and Administration: a Dilemma or a False Choice?

In a recent review of the state of research on developments in public administration, two well-known students of public administration suggest that the field has reached its "middle age" (Hood & Peters, 2004). Contemporaneously with the emergence of "new public administration" (NPM) in the early 1980s, the research focused on a critique of public sector managerialism as articulated to neo-liberalism (see also Rose & Miller, 1992). In its second phase, research in NPM focused on examining the differences and variations in implementation. Cross-national comparative studies of NPM during the 1990s offered a descriptive map of the lines of development and dissemination of the rationales and practices that went under the NPM rubric. The authors suggest that this stream of research has now reached its third phase, one characterized by self-awareness, since it has become a standard theme in textbooks and has begun to reflect on its own history. They further argue that this maturity in the body of research on NPM is reflected by the fact that much of the new research has focused on the unintended consequences, perverse effects and paradoxes of NPM reforms. One of these is the "production paradox" according to which "the basic control routines associated with contemporary public management (originating in management accounting) involves more intensive specification of outputs, encapsulated in performance contracts and indicators" (Hood & Peters, 2007, p. 270). However, since some governmental activities are neither easily observable nor measurable, the imposition of performance and outcome metrics generate unintended effects, notably gaming (Gregory, 1995).

However, it may be that a deeper current drives the paradoxes now documented in the case of NPM. The conceptual and practical distinctions between politics and administration are founding conceits for the use and spread of the calculative practices of government. Though a contested distinction, it nevertheless is a key to unlock a persistent theme that runs through the development of metrics of accountability and performance in the government sector. From its inception and to this day, calculative procedures in government have been legitimized as necessary to forestall or mitigate the adverse consequences of politics. However, it appears that such accounting and budgeting techniques perennially fail to achieve their stated goals. Usually, it is this failure that is then offered as a justification to further improve the design and expand the scope of these techniques. Thus, it would seem that the failure of governmental accounting and budgeting to achieve its stated goal is met by calls to further increase its use. In part, this dynamic continues to fuel the growth of metrics of accountability and performance in the governmental sector. Their intensity and range are being steadily ratcheted upward, as when ABC and benchmarking are recommended as replacements for standard costing, or, as in the case of old wine in new bottles, forgotten or discarded methods are rediscovered and reemphasized as in the contemporary attention to performance measurement.

As one accounting scholar stated some three decades ago in the context of municipal accounting, "after some sixty years and numerous studies, the same problems are redefined, the same solutions rediscovered, and the same outcomes result—the reforms are ignored" (Zimmerman, 1977, p. 108). While this judgement is harsh when considering accounting and budgeting in all branches and at all levels of government, it is a useful caution tempering the excessive zeal with which administrative changes are usually heralded. As noted in a recent GAO review of cost accounting in the federal government, "few of the federal agencies we reviewed were using managerial cost accounting to make day-to-day decisions" (GAO, 2007c, p. 2; see also Cavalluzzo & Ittner, 2004). Moreover, such notions as performance measurement appear as early as 1927, and a symposium on performance budgeting was conducted in the pages of a leading public administration journal in 1960 (Gainakis, 2002, p. 37). Therefore, to better contextualize the current emphasis on metrics of accountability and performance in government we briefly review the history of these administrative practices through the lens of the contested distinction between politics and administration.

The systematic deployment of financial accounting and budgets as tools of US governments is a fairly recent development. This use was also related to, and dependent on, conceptually carving out a sphere within which such practices would make sense. As most commentators of the development of public accounting and budgeting have noted, the conceptual separation between politics and administration was a condition of the possibility for the development of public accounting and budgeting (Waldo, 1948). The emergence in the US of an "administrative state" articulated to administrative law and to attendant methods of administration are joint developments that began in the late-nineteenth century and reached maturity only in the early-twentieth century (Schiesl, 1977). Before this period, neither the bureaucratic and centralized state nor the extensive techniques of organizational calculation and management were prevalent with any of the degree of complexity or pervasiveness that has since become the norm (White, 1958).

To consider the idea of administration with its attendant methods and laws as a joint development it is important to frame the ways in which the use of metrics of accounting and performance were, and continue to be, legitimized in the governmental sector. The contrary tendency to fabricate histories of hoary accounting and related calculative procedures that began years ago can perhaps be tempered by a couple of observations. The British exchequer used tally sticks as late as 1826 to record deposits into the treasury, suggesting that modern methods of governmental record keeping are quite recent. Similarly, the idea of budgets, as a plan of future expenses and income, is also a nineteenth century notion. For instance, the very word "budget" usually meant "a collection," as in the collection of mathematical puzzles, explored by the well-known mathematician Augustus de Morgan, and published posthumously in 1915 with the title *A Budget of Paradoxes*.

The emergence of the sphere of administration as distinct from that of politics by the early-twentieth century was intended to create a politics-free bureaucratic zone. Rational bureaucratic administration, reliant preferably on numerical facts, managed by civil servants not beholden to political parties and tuned to the public interest, was thought necessary to hold back the pernicious influence of politics and to permit informed judgements by both administrators and citizens. Rational administration fostered order and organization, against messy politics—the sphere of contention, discord and disorder (Wiebe, 1967). This refurbished architecture of a polity divided into the spheres of politics and administration continues to form the ideal and idealized background of governmental accounting and budgeting. It is perhaps best described in the image of two interlocking pyramids.

> Politics–democracy proceeds upward to an apex at which the popular will is determined by law or otherwise, and then is bridged over to administration. Therefore, the will is realized downward through an organization that is hierarchical, functionally rational, professional … Responsibility, responsiveness and accountability are then brought about by the same structure, but the directions are reversed. They go up the administrative pyramid to the apex, bridge over, and go down this structure to the voters.
>
> Waldo, 1987, pp. 92–93

In the late-nineteenth and early-twentieth century, the realm of administration was intended to serve as the bulwark against the veniality and corruption of the "machines": political parties and politicians who used public office and the government coffers to distribute favours and largesse to benefit themselves and their supporters (Hofstadter 1955, pp. 257–271). Perhaps it is Woodrow Wilson who best described that founding animus behind the creation of the administrative component of the state, separated from politics.

> The field of administration is a field of business. It is removed from the hurry and strife of politics ... It is part of political life only as the methods of the counting house are part of the life of society ... Most important to be observed is the truth already so much and so fortunately insisted upon by our civil-service reformers; namely that administration lies outside the proper sphere of *politics*. Administrative questions are not political questions. Although politics sets the tasks for administration, it should not be suffered to manipulate its offices.
>
> Woodrow Wilson, 1887, p. 218 (emphasis in original)

But as Hays (1957, pp. 261–276) suggested, the reform of the political space to include a new sphere of administration illuminates not so much the content of public policy, but the nature of the resulting political structure and the types of interactions peculiar to it. Bureaucratic organizations were designed to foster impersonal types of interactions, to remove the debatable from political discussion by transforming the moral into the factual (Zucker, 1977). The newly formed science of public administration—based on rational calculation, rational organizations and expert unbiased judgements—was grounded on an unquestioned faith in "efficiency," itself thought to transcend the partisan, the sectarian and the incalculable of the political realm. "In the science of administration, whether public or private, the basic 'good' is efficiency ... efficiency is this axiom number one in the value scale of administration" (Gullick & Urwick, 1937, p. 192). Accounting and other calculative techniques of management found their place within the administrative sphere separated from, but linked to, politics and rooted in efficiency. Accounting procedures were understood as tools of administration par excellence, as unbiased, neutral and impartial reflections of socio-economic facts (Covaleski et al., 1995, 1997).

The emergence of accounting and budgetary practices in the governmental sector also entailed a vast reorganization of the relationship between the executive and legislative branches of the US federal government. The effects at the state and local levels of government were similar, although not identical (Rubin, 1988). Thus, the very nature of the US political structure was at issue in the seemingly neutral question of administrative reform. What the rise of the administrative state signalled was the beginnings of the expansion of executive powers at the expense of the Congress. Indeed, it is precisely this political reorganization that was effected through the establishment of the neutral administrative state (Arnold, 1986). Particularly in the US, it is the system of preparing executive budgets at all levels of government, as well as maintaining records of the flow of public monies according to fund accounting, that characterize the governmental accounting and budgetary practices that came to maturation in the 1920s (Potts, 1977, 1978). As noted by the Taft Commission on Economy and Efficiency in 1912, prior to the early-twentieth century:

> In the United States the Book of Estimates, our nearest approach to a budget, is rather a more or less well-digested mass of information submitted by agents of the Legislature to the Legislature for the consideration of legislative committees to enable the Legislature both to originate and to determine the policy which is to be carried out by the Executive during the budgetary period.
>
> cited in Lewis, 2007, p. 163

However, as the Commission pointed out, "the use of a budget would require that there be a complete reversal of procedure by the Government—that the executive branch submit a statement to the Legislature which would be its account of stewardship, as well as its proposals for the future" (in Lewis, 2007, p. 165). This recommendation, which became law through the Budget and Accounting Act of 1921, is understood by most students of public administration in the US as, in the words of President Harding, "the greatest reformation in governmental practices since the beginning of the Republic" (in Burkhead, 1957, p. 27). Accordingly, the birth and spread of metrics of accountability and performance in the governmental sector of the US is intrinsically related to the establishment of a government bureaucracy housed increasingly within the executive branch of the government and at one remove from the legislative political process.

The cause of administrative efficiency not only contributed to the establishment of a federal bureaucracy, but also to the growth of large-scale and relatively centralized organizations specialized in the production, accumulation, dissemination and analysis of metrics of accounting and performance to manage the administrative state. Thus, in the executive branch of the federal government, such agencies and departments as the Office of Management and Budgets, the Department of the Treasury, the General Services Administration and the Office of Personnel Management cover such matters as budget preparation, asset management, cash management including raising taxes and managing government debts, and establishing employment contracts and procedures to manage the civil service. The Congress, as political ballast to the executive, houses the Governmental Accountability Office and the Congressional Budget Office, which together provide for the independent financial oversight and programme evaluation of the administrative state apparatus. Hence, from its inception, governmental accounting and budgeting has been tied to the rise of a bureaucratic mode of governance that favoured the executive over the legislative branch of government.

The emergence of neutral and rational administration was legitimized as being heterogeneous to politics along two axes:

1. politics was understood to be rooted in the subjective, the personal, the arbitrary and the private/individual interest, whereas administration was understood as the domain of the objective, the impersonal, the predictable and oriented by the public interest;
2. politics would generate the ends for which administration would be the means of execution.

This twinned dynamic has animated the context within which government accounting and budgeting occurs. However, by the late 1940s the distinction between politics and administration was seen to be both empirically naïve and scientifically untenable. The criticisms were wide-ranging. Herbert Simon denigrated the "principles of administration" as mere folksy proverbs (Simon, 1947); the economist Kenneth Arrow cast severe mathematical doubt on the very possibility of a public good or the public interest (Arrow, 1951); and administrators were understood to be making political decisions instead of merely serving as the neutral executors of congressional laws. It was in light of this understanding that Appleby declared, in 1949, "public administration is policy-making," to mark a turning point after which "few have disputed the contention that politics, policy, and administration are inextricably intertwined" (in Fry, 1989, p. 103). Two developments, in particular, contributed to the dilution of the distinction between politics and administration. However, this dilution did not lead to a cessation of the conflict between the two, but rather to a sharpening of it.

On the one hand, economic science, predicated on the problem of allocative efficiency, cast a long shadow over both administrative science and political theory. For instance, V. O. Key laid down a gauntlet that continues to plague all attempts at devising a theory of public budgeting. He noted that, "on the most significant aspect of public budgeting, i.e., the allocation of expenditures among different purposes so as to achieve the greatest return, American budgetary literature has been singularly arid," and posed the question that remains unanswered to this day: "On what basis shall it be decided to allocate X dollars to activity A instead of activity B?" (Key, 1940, p. 1137). Similarly, politics had already absorbed the economic message and been recast as a matter of "who gets what, when and how" (Lasswell, 1936).

The homogenization of politics and administration along the plane of allocative efficiency deepened the conflict between administration and politics by diluting the distinction between them. It is a conflict that continues to bedevil the field of public administration and, by extension, governmental accounting and budgeting. Until Key brought the question into the open, public budgeting was invested with the Herculean task of being "a device for consolidating the various interests, objectives, desires and needs of all our citizens into a programme whereby they may jointly provide for their safety, convenience and welfare" (Smith, 1940, p. 72). This sentiment expressed the fervent hope and dream of solving political problems through administrative and, more generally, technological means. However, as underscored by Wildavsky, when budgeting is understood as an instrument to achieve allocative efficiency in the expenditures of government, it becomes a utopian task, never to be fulfilled (1974, p. 128–129): for when budgeting is invested with this aspiration, it implies that a calculative procedure can determine what government ought to do. Accordingly, any comprehensive theory of budgeting would simultaneously also be a comprehensive theory of politics, one that could, in fact, replace partisan political strife and struggle with cool calculations (Wildavsky, 1974, 1989). Quite apart from the wall between the positive and the normative that social scientists are congenitally loath to jump over, the question of what a government ought to do is nevertheless a political question that remains essentially contested and one that perpetually divides the people. Starting from the premises of individual preferences it is impossible to find a technical solution to the conflict over allocations. Accordingly, when both politics and administration occupy a common terrain, the very possibility of politics entails the impossibility of the administration. The distinction between politics and administration is diluted, but the conflict is deepened. And despite this high sounding argument on the limits of administrative capacities, the dream of a fully blown technical solution to politics has not abated (Dunsire, 1990).

A second source that weakened the distinction between politics and administration was the understanding that all calculative practices, including metrics of performance and accounting, were infused by political considerations. The behavioural turn in political science and public administration, no less than that in economics, accounting and finance, raised the concept of the "decision" to new explanatory heights (Lowi, 1993). The similarity of politics and administration was grounded on the concept of "the decision," whereby "if it is desired to retain the terms 'policy' and 'administration,' they can best be applied to a division of the decisional functions" (Simon, 1947, p. 58). The centrality given to the concept of decision thus unified the distinct realms of politics and administration: both politicians and administrator made decisions, and their decisions differed by the different composition of costs and benefits they faced. The calculative tools of administration were no longer understood as neutral tools that aided decisions, but rather as themselves the consequence of decisions (Beaver & Demksi, 1974, p. 170). Once cast in this manner, accounting and budgetary practices came to be seen as interested practices. Calculative practices aimed at forestalling politics in the cause of administrative efficiency would have to design the environment of costs and benefits within which decisions were supposed to be made. But that left open the question of the interests of the designer. When politics was inserted into the heart of rational practices understood as decisional outcomes, the distinction between politics and administration was diluted, but the conflict deepened.

As March & Olsen pointed out in their historical survey of administrative reorganization and reform efforts throughout the twentieth century, the rhetoric of pure administration theory and that of realpolitik are inseparable templates through which most, if not all, thinking about government is channelled. The rhetoric of administration "speaks of the design of administrative structure and procedures to facilitate the efficiency and effectiveness of bureaucratic hierarchies;" of "offices that could be abolished and … expenses that could be curtailed;" of "clear lines of authority and responsibility … and the utilization of modern techniques for management" (1983, pp. 282–283). Similarly, they argued that the other conventional rhetoric of realpolitik speaks "of a political struggle among contending interests … within the bureaucracy and outside (that) seek access, representation, control and policy benefits;" of "conflicts and inconsistencies found in statutes, authorizations and contradictory legislative mandates (that) cannot be coordinated" and of recognizing that "administrators several competing loyalties, constituencies and bosses" (pp. 283–284). Neither politics nor administration can trump the other, yet both mutually provoke each other (see also Frug, 1984).

The increased conflict between weakened enemies, as it were, has seemed to turn the founding conceit of administration to stave off politics inward on itself. Newer and more refined techniques of calculation are advanced not merely to limit politicians from distorting the rational techniques of achieving the public interest. Even more, innovative metrics of performance and accountability are devised to curtail administrators themselves from playing political games—whether the relatively benign one of protecting their turf and building empires, or the more potent one of using the letter of administrative law to subvert its spirit. Administrators were accused of adhering to, or being shackled by, outdated rules, ineffective regulations and counterproductive procedures for political reasons (Osborne & Gaebler, 1992). The general solution advanced continues to invoke a smoothly-functioning set of calculative practices that, for instance, connect "performance measurement … to strategic planning, individual performance appraisal and budgetary resource allocation," all articulated in audited financial statements that conform to GAAP (Frank, 2007, p. 237). Recently, the GAO is recommending that domestic government performance be linked to international performance indicators such as those generated by the Organization for Economic Cooperation and Development (OECD) (GAO, 2007d). The alphabet soup of budgetary innovations in the governmental sector from planning, programming and budgeting systems (PPBS) to zero-based budgeting (ZBB) and more recently to performance budgeting (PB), as well as the slew of acts from the Chief Financial Officers Act (1990), the Government Performance Results Act (1993), the Government Management Reform Act (1994) and Federal Financial Management Improvement Act (1996), can be therefore understood, in part, as aimed at generating metrics of performance and accounting to cure the disorder of politics that had invaded administration.

As if to purge itself of itself, increasingly refined techniques of measuring and recording performance are proposed to reduce the politics of administration. However, as such, there seems no end in sight: administrative practices are known to be indelibly political and yet simultaneously advanced, in the hope of curtailing the bane of politics. It is this impasse that seems, paradoxically, to fuel the incessant drive to the ever more increasing use and application of accounting and budgetary practices in government. These practices are offered as solutions to the problem of politics, but are nevertheless understood themselves as being the consequence of political machinations.

By taking measure of this background to the dynamism of governmental administrative practices, accounting scholarship could critically reflect on the growth, efficacy and necessity of the kinds of accounting and budgetary practices now underway in government.

- To what extent do such economic measures as "customer satisfaction" conflict with other public goals such as fairness and due process?
- Are all public services measurable in the manner and form required for performance measurement? If not, what aspects of services can be transformed into quantified measurements?
- At what point do metrics of performance and accountability begin to subvert the purposes for which they are designed?
- More generally, can accounting and performance measurement systems adequately monitor the private use and disposition of public funds?

Most accounting studies concerning the US government and non-profit sectors tend to focus on the technical questions of record keeping and measurement, leaving outside their purview questions of the context within which accounting practices occur (Hopwood,

1983). Obviously, there are exceptions to this generalization, notably among accounting researchers outside the US. For instance, there is a broad and deep stream of critical theorizing on NPM within its context. As noted by Cooper & Hopper (2007) in their recent review of this research stream, it has explored NPM in the context of the fiscal crises of the state; showed it to be part of a more general effort to commodify arenas of life previously thought and kept outside the logic of economic rationalism; and revealed the complex chains of competing, parallel and convergent interests that need to be stitched together with technologies and rationales in order to effect change.

The failure to account for context can be fatal, as suggested by Chwastiak (2001) who shows that such techniques as budgeting systems have been deployed to normalize issues of war and death; to transform moral questions of war into technical questions of resource allocation. The tendency to disregard the context of accounting practices impairs a nuanced understanding of the role and possible limitations of metrics of accountability and performance. For another example, consider the case of the privatization of prisons. A raft of accounting statements and performance measurements can and are being deployed to record, monitor and evaluate the efficiency with which private and public prisons are run. Yet such studies take for granted the appropriateness of private prisons, which, in essence, make profits from the loss of a person's liberty. Thus the possibility of a fundamental disjunction between achieving public peace and creating profit incentives to increase incarceration rates goes unaddressed. The increasing privatization of the US armed forces is a similar, though more politicized, context in which the increased use of outsourcing has generated the need for metrics of performance and especially accountability. Such outsourcing is promoted on the grounds of lowering the costs of war and increasing flexibility in the use of human resources, so much so that, for example, there are more private contractors in Iraq than employees of the US armed forces. However, outsourcing the war effort is not only questionable on the very grounds by which it is justified, but also at the level of policy (Singer, 2007). To take just one example, the special inspector general for Iraq reconstruction has stated that the contracting agency "does not know specifically what it received for most of the $1.2 billion in expenditure under its DynCorp contract for the Iraqi police training programme" (SIGIR, 2007).

Accordingly, a number of open questions for accounting research could constitute the background to more narrowly-framed questions about the technical efficacy of this or that accounting or performance measurement system. The continuing tension between politics and administration and the perceived perpetual failure of accounting and performance metrics suggests that accounting studies can be cast within the contexts of political theory and constitutional law, not to speak of the diverse social and political philosophies that have animated recent alternative management accounting research (Baxter & Chua, 2003).

- What are the political implications of such economic choices as outsourcing war-related activities or welfare services?
- Can and do metrics of accounting and performance capture these political "costs" and "benefits?"
- Is there a distinction that makes a difference between decisions made for the public interest and those fuelled by private interests?
- On what grounds, if any, is there a continuity of interests between the private and public sectors?
- Is there a role for the public provision of certain services to preserve the public interest?
- Is the very idea of a "public interest" one that is only of historical interest today?

5. Conclusion

In this chapter we have broadly sketched the importance of the governmental and non-profit sectors within the US economy and socio-political life. We reviewed the literature on the recent changes in the mode and manner of governmental operations to highlight two crucial features. First, a majority of the expenditures incurred by the state are spent on or through the private sector. For the collaborative mode of public–private partnerships, a renewed emphasis is placed on metrics of performance and accountability to monitor, control and manage these contractual relations. However, the state of both the accounting systems and of financial management in the US government seems to be dire enough to call for the best accounting scholars to pay attention to the causes and consequences of the looming crises. We identify a number of possible research questions to spark research in these sectors.

Secondly, we analyzed the production of accounting research in the governmental and non-profit sectors between 2000 and 2007 to establish the extreme paucity of accounting research generally, and of management accounting research in particular. Given the size, significance and modes of contemporary governmental operations that encourage bureaucracies to become more business-like and responsive to market demands, this lack of research is surprising. It is all the more so given that a number of topics that constitute management accounting are also to be found in the governmental domain. We offer some speculations on the economics and sociology of accounting knowledge production that may contribute to this blind spot in accounting scholarship, but more importantly call for research to redress this state of affairs.

Thirdly, we explore one theme that has animated the continuous call for improvements and increases in the calculative practices of government. We focus on the interplay between the ideas of administration and politics to discover that these discursive practices mutually provoke more of each other. Seen historically, the idea that administration can cure all the ills of politics is not only false, but also potentially debilitating. Currently, the only cure offered for the failures of accounting and budgeting to solve governmental problems is to offer more of the same medicine. We call for research in investigating the limits, if any, to the calculative practices of government. In effect, what are the limits of GNP accounting?

Acknowledgement
We gratefully acknowledge the research assistance of Mr Richard Krauss.

References

Abernethy, M., Chua, W. F., Grafton, J. & Mahama, H. (2007). Accounting and control in healthcare: behavioral, organizational, sociological and critical perspectives. In: C. S. Chapman, A. G. Hopwood, & M. D. Shields (Eds), *Handbook of Management Accounting Research*, (Vol. 2). Amsterdam, The Netherlands: Elsevier, pp. 805–829.

Aristigueta, M. & Justice, J. (2006). The status of performance budgeting. *Public Performance and Management Review*, **30**, 7–13.

Arnold, P. P. (1986). *Making the managerial presidency*. New Haven, CT: Princeton University Press.

Arrow, K. (1951). *Social Choice and Individual Values*. New Haven, CT: Yale University Press.

Baxter, J. & Chua, W. F. (2003). Alternative management accounting literature—whence and whither. *Accounting, Organizations and Society*, **28**, 97–126.

Beaver, W. & Demski, J. (1974). The nature of financial accounting objectives: a summary and synthesis. *Journal of Accounting Research*, **12**, 170–184.

Berry, F. S. & Brower, R. S. (2005). Intergovernmental and intersectoral management: weaving networking, contracting out, and management roles into third party government. *Public Performance and Management Review*, **29**, 7–17.

Birnberg, J. (2004). Expanding our frontiers: management accounting research in the next decade. *Advances in Management Accounting*, **13**, 1–26.

Bonner, S. E., Hesford, J. W., Van der Stede, W. A. & Young, S. M. (2006). The most influential journals in academic accounting. *Accounting, Organizations and Society*, **31**, 663–685.

Broadbent, J. (1999). The state of public accounting research: The AIPRA conference and some personal reflections. *Accounting, Auditing & Accountability Journal*, **12**, 52–55.

Broadbent, J. & Guthrie, J. (1992). Changes in the public sector: a review of recent "alternative" accounting research. *Accounting, Auditing & Accountability Journal*, **5**, 3–31.

Burkhead, J. (1956). *Government Budgeting*. New York, NY: Wiley & Sons.

Cavalluzzo, K. & Ittner, C. (2004). Implementing performance measurement innovations: evidence from government. *Accounting, Organizations and Society*, **29**, 243–267.

CBS News. (2002). *The War on Waste*. Jan 29, 2002. http://www.cbsnews.com/stories/2002/01/29/eveningnews/main325985.shtml.

Chan, J. (1987). Introduction. *Research in Governmental and Non-Profit Accounting*, **3**, 1–3.

Choi, Y-S., Cho, C. L., Wright, D. & Brundney, J. (2005). Dimensions of contracting for service delivery by American state administrative agencies. *Public Performance and Management Review*, **29**, 46–66.

Chwastaik, M. (2001). Taming the untameable: planning, programming and budgeting and the normalization of war. *Accounting, Organizations and Society*, **26**, 501–519.

Coe, C. (2003). A report card on report cards. *Public Performance and Management Review*, **27**, 53–76.

Cooper, D. & Hopper, T. (2007). Critical theorizing in Management Accounting Research. In: C. S. Chapman, A. G. Hopwood, & M. D. Shields (Eds), *Handbook of Management Accounting Research*, (Vol. 2). Amsterdam, The Netherlands: Elsevier, pp. 207–245.

Covaleski, M., Dirsmith, M. & Samuel, S. (1995). The use of accounting information in governmental regulation and public administration: the impact of John. R. Commons and early institutional economists. *The Accounting Historians Journal*, **22**, 1–33.

Covaleski, M., Dirsmith, M. & Samuel, S. (1997). A strategic deconstruction of John R. Commons' regulatory discourse. *Journal of Economic Issues*, **31**, 1–27.

Denhardt, M. & Baker, L. (2007). Five great issues in organization theory. In: Hildreth Rabin, and Miller (Eds), *Handbook of Public Administration* (3rd ed.). New York, NY: Taylor & Francis, pp. 121–148.

Eldenburg, L. & Krishnan, R. (2007). Management accounting and control in healthcare: An economic perspective. In: C. S. Chapman, A. G. Hopwood, & M. D. Shields (Eds), *Handbook of Management Accounting Research*, (Vol. 2). Amsterdam, The Netherlands: Elsevier, pp. 859–883.

Evans, J., Leone, A. & Nagarajan, N. (2005). Nonfinancial performance measures in the healthcare industry: do quality incentives matter? *Advances in Management Accounting*, **14**, 1–31.

Frank, G. (2007). Budget Theory: New perspectives for a new millennium. In: Rabin, Hildreth and

Miller (Eds), *Handbook of Public Administration* (3rd ed.). New York, NY: Taylor & Francis, pp. 227–248.
Froud, J. (2003). The private finance initiative: risk, uncertainty and the state. *Accounting, Organizations and Society*, **28**, 567–589.
Frug, G. E. (1984). The ideology of bureaucracy in American Law. *Harvard Law Review*, **97**, 1276–1315.
Fry, B. (1989). Five great issues in the profession of public administration. In: Hildreth Rabin, and Miller (Eds), *Handbook of Public Administration*. New York, NY: Marcel Dekker, pp. 1027–1075.
GAO. (2007a). FY2006, US government financial statements. Washington, DC: GAO-07-607T. http://www.gao.gov/new.items/d07607t.pdf.
GAO. (2007b). Fiscal stewardship in the 21st century. GAO-08-150CG. http://www.gao.gov/cghome/d08150cg.pdf.
GAO. (2007c). Managerial cost accounting practices: implementation and use varies widely across ten federal agencies. GAO-07-679.
GAO. (2007d). The evolving role of supreme audit institutions in addressing fiscal and other key sustainability challenges. GAO-07-1226-CG, 6.
Gianakis, G. (2002). The promise of public sector performance measurement: anodyne or placebo? *Public Administration Quarterly*, **Spring**, 35–64.
Gregory, R. (2005). Accountability, Responsibility, and Corruption: managing the public production process. In: J. Boston (Ed.), *The State under Contract*. Wellington, NZ: Bridget William Books, pp. 97–114.
Gullick, L. & Urwick, L. (1937). *Papers on the Science of Administration*. New York, NY: Augustus Kelly.
Hays, S. (1957). *The response to industrialism: 1885–1914*. Chicago, IL: University of Chicago Press.
Helden, J. G. (2005). Research public sector transformation: the role of management accounting. *Financial Accountability & Management*, **21**, 99–133.
Hofstadter, R. (1955). *The Age of Reform*. New York, NY: Vintage.
Hood, C. (1995). The "New Public Management" in the 1980s: variations on a theme. *Accounting, Organizations and Society*, **20**, 93–109.
Hood, C. & Peters, G. (2004). The middle aging of new public management: into the age of paradox. *Journal of Public Administration Research and Theory*, **14**(3), 267–282.
Hopwood, A. (1983). On trying to study accounting in the contexts in which it operates. *Accounting, Organizations and Society*, **12**, 287–305.
Hwang, R. N. & Wu, D. (2006). Has the emergence of the specialized journals affected management accounting research paradigms? *Advanced in Management Accounting*, **15**, 143–168.
Keller, L. (2007). Public administration and the American Republic: the continuing saga of management and administration in politics. In: Rabin, Hildreth and Miller (Eds), *Handbook of Public Administration* (3rd ed.). New York, NY: Taylor & Francis, pp. 3–48.
Kettl, D. (2002a). *The transformation of governance*. Baltimore, MD: Johns Hopkins University Press.
Kettl, D. (2002b). Managing Indirect Government. In: L. Salamon (Ed.), *The tools of government: a guide to the new governance*. New York, NY: Oxford University Press.
Kinney, W. R., Palmrose, Z-V. & Scholz, S. (2005). Auditor independence, non-audit services, and restatements: was the US government right? *Journal of Accounting Research*, **42**, 561–586.
Kurunmäki, L. (2004). A hybrid profession – the acquisition of management accounting expertise by medical professionals. *Accounting, Organizations and Society*, **29**, 327–347.
Lasswell, H. (1936). *Politics: Who gets what, when and how*. New York, NY: Whittlesey.
Lewis, C. (2007). The Field of Public Budgeting and Financial Management, 1789–2004. In: Hildreth Rabin, and Miller (Eds), *Handbook of Public Administration* (3rd ed.). New York, NY: Taylor & Francis, pp. 151–225.
Lowensohn, S. & Samuelson, D. (2006). An examination of faculty perceptions of academic journal quality within five specialized areas of accounting research. *Issues in Accounting Education*, **21**, 219–239.
Lowi, T. (1993). A review of Herbert Simon's review of my view of the discipline. *Political Science and Politics*, **26**, 51–52.
March, J. & Olson, J. (1983). Organizing political life: what administrative reorganization tells us about government. *American Political Science Review*, **77**, 281–296.
McCaffery, J. L. (1987). The development of public budgeting in the United States. In: R. C. Chandler (Ed.), *A Centennial History of the American Administrative State*. New York, NY: Macmillian, pp. 345–373.
Miller, P. P. & O'Leary, T. (1990). Making accounting practical. *Accounting, Organizations and Society*, **15**, 478–498.
Milward, B. H. (1996). Symposium on the hollow state: capacity, control and performance in inter-organizational settings. *Journal of Public Administration Research and Theory*, **6**, 193–195.
Nicholson-Crotty, S., Theobald, N. & Nicholson-Crotty, J. (2006). Disparate measures: public managers and performance measurement strategies. *Public Administration Review*, 101–113.
O'Neill, M. (2002). *Non-profit Nation*. New York, NY: Wiley.
Osborne, D. & Gaebler, T. (1992). *Reinventing Government*. New York, NY: Addison-Wesley.
Panozzo, F. (1997). The making of a good academic accountant. *Accounting, Organizations and Society*, **22**, 447–480.

Poister, T. & Strieb, G. (2005). Elements of strategic planning and management in municipal government: status after two decades. *Public Administration Review*, **65**, 45–56.

Potts, J. (1977). The evolution of budgetary accounting theory and practice in municipal accounting from 1870. *Accounting Historians Journal*, **4**, 89–100.

Potts, J. (1978). The evolution of municipal accounting in the US. *Accounting Historians Journal*, **4**, 99–123.

Prizzia, R. (2003). An international perspective of privatization: the need to balance economic and social performance. *American Review of Public Administration*, **33**, 316–333.

Reiter, S. A. & Williams, P. F. (2002). The structure and progressivity of accounting research: the crises in the academy revisited. *Accounting, Organizations and Society*, **27**, 576–607.

Roberts, N. & Thompson, F. (2006). "Netcentric" organization. *Public Administration Review*, **66**, 612–622.

Rodgers, J. L. & Williams, P. F. (1996). Patterns of research productivity and knowledge creation at The Accounting Review. *Accounting Historians Journal*, **June**, 51–88.

Rose, N. & Miller, P. (1992). Political power beyond the state: problematics of government. *The British Journal of Sociology*, **43**(2), 173–305.

Rubin, R. (1998). *Class, Tax and Power: municipal budgeting in the United States*. Chatham, NJ: Chatham House.

Salamon, L. (1989). The changing tools of government action: an overview. In: L. Salamon (Ed.), *Beyond Privatization: The Tools of Government Action*. Washington, DC: Urban Institute Press, pp. 3–22.

Salamon, L. (2002). *The tools of government: a guide to the new governance*. New York, NY: Oxford University Press.

Salamon, L. (2003). *The Resilient Sector: the State of Non-profit America*. Washington, DC: Brookings Institute.

Schacter, H. N. (2007). Does Frederick Taylor's ghost still haunt the halls of government? A look at the concept of governmental efficiency. *Public Administration Review*, **67**, 800–810.

Schick, A. (1987). Macro budgetary adaptations to fiscal distress in industrialized democracies. In: A. Schick (Ed.), *Perspectives on Budgeting*. Washington, DC: ASPA, pp. 218–238.

Schiesl, M. (1977). *The Politics of Efficiency*. Berkeley, CA: University of California Press.

Schwartz, B. N., Williams, S. & Williams, P. F. (2005). US doctoral students' familiarity with accounting journals: insights into the structure of the US academy. *Critical Perspectives in Accounting*, **16**, 327–348.

Selto, F. & Widener, S. (2004). New directions in management accounting research: insights from practice. *Advances in Management Accounting*, **12**, 1–35.

Shields, M. D. (1997). Research in management accounting by North Americans in the 1990s. *Journal of Management Accounting Research*, **9**, 3–61.

SIGIR. (2007). Interim review of DynCorp International, LLC, spending under its contract for the Iraqi Police Training program. www.sigir.mil SIGIR:07-016, October 23.

Simon, H. A. (1947). *Administrative behavior*. New York, NY: Macmillian.

Singer, P. (2007). *Can't win with 'em, can't go to war without 'em: Private military contractors and counterinsurgency*, Policy paper #4. Washington, DC: Brookings Institute.

Swanson, E. P. (2004). Publishing in the majors: a comparison of accounting, finance, management, and marketing. *Contemporary Accounting Research*, **Spring**, 223–255.

Waldo, D. (1948). *The Administrative State*. New York, NY: Ronald Company.

Waldo, D. (1987). Politics and Administration: on thinking about a complex relationship. In: R. C. Chandler (Ed.), *A Centennial History of the American Administrative State*. New York, NY: Macmillian, pp. 89–112.

Walker, D. (2004). GAO answers the Question: what's in a name? *Roll Call*, **July 19**. http://www.gao.gov/about/rollcall07192004.pdf

Walker, D. (2006). *America at a Crossroads*. Washington, DC: GAO-07-171CG.

Walkins, A. (2000). Hospital financial ratio classification patterns revisited: upon considering non-financial information. *Journal of Accounting and Public Policy*, **19**, 73–95.

Wallace, W. (2003). Avoding the downfall of windfalls. *Journal of Government Financial Management*, **Fall**, 18–31.

Weibe, R. H. (1967). *The Search for Order, 1877–1920*. New York, NY: Hill & Wang.

White, L. (1958). *The Republican Era: 1869–1901*. New York, NY: Hill & Wang.

Whitley, R. (1984). *The intellectual and social organization of the sciences*. Oxford, NY: Clarendon Press.

Whitley, R. (1986). The transformation of business finance into financial economics. The roles of academic expansion and changes in US capital markets. *Accounting, Organizations and Society*, **11**, 171–192.

Wildavsky, A. (1974). *The politics of the budgetary process* (2nd ed.). New York, NY: Little Brown.

Wildavsky, A. (1989). The political economy of efficiency: cost benefit analysis, systems analysis, and program budgeting. *Public Budgeting and Financial Management*, **1**, 1–41.

Williams, P. F., Gregory, J. G. & Ingraham, H. (2006). The winnowing away of behavioral accounting research in the U.S: the process of anointing academic elites. *Accounting, Organizations and Society*, **31**, 783–818.

Wilson, Woodrow (1887). The study of administration. *Political Science Quarterly*, **June**, 197–222.

Ya-Ni, A. & Bretschneider, S. (2007). The decision to contract out: a study of contracting for e-government services in state governments. *Public Administration Review*, **67**, 531–544.

Zeff, S. (1996). A study of academic journals in accounting. *Accounting Horizons*, **Sept**, 158–177.

Zimmerman, J. (1977). The municipal accounting maze: an analysis of political incentives. *Journal of Accounting Research*, **15**(supplement), 107–144.

Zucker, L. (1977). The role of institutionalization in cultural persistence. *American Sociological Review*, 726–743.

Handbook of Management Accounting Research
Edited by Christopher S. Chapman, Anthony G. Hopwood and Michael D. Shields

The Adoption and Evolution of Management Control Systems in Entrepreneurial Companies: Evidence and a Promising Future

Antonio Davila[1] and George Foster[2]

[1]IESE Business School, University of Navarra, Spain
[2]Graduate School of Business, Stanford University, US

Abstract: Management control systems have traditionally been perceived as detrimental to the entrepreneurial spirit that characterizes start-up companies. However, recent evidence suggests that the opposite holds—these systems are required for these firms to fulfil their growth potential. This chapter discusses the empirical evidence that is starting to accumulate around this research topic. These early studies have just outlined a topic that deserves better understanding and a more diverse set of theoretical lenses to understand the forces shaping the results from these studies. The chapter also presents the theories and frameworks relevant to management control systems in entrepreneurial companies. Again, these concepts are just initial efforts with a significant need for further development. The map of the field that emerges from the analysis in this chapter is a fascinating field relevant to advance our knowledge of control systems, with many research opportunities. This is a field that is not only relevant from an academic perspective, but of utmost importance for managers.

1. Introduction

The interest of management accounting researchers on entrepreneurial, high-growth start-up companies is a recent phenomenon. The traditional focus of the field had been on established organizations and stable processes. In these settings, the main role of management control systems (MCS) is to keep the organization on course to meet defined objectives. The thermostat metaphor used by Anthony (1965)—equating management accounting and control systems to a feedback mechanism that keeps the output of organizational processes close to a predetermined level—illustrates this dominant paradigm. Deviations from intended objectives are perceived as detrimental to the organization and well-designed MCS are those that minimize these deviations. Studies within this traditional paradigm often used cross-sectional research designs consistent with a static view of MCS. Early-stage companies that are constantly reshaping themselves to adapt to growth, opportunities and challenges appeared to be too removed from this paradigm to be relevant to the field. In addition, common wisdom suggested that management control systems had no role in such companies because they would jeopardize the entrepreneurial spirit and thus the potential success of the companies. Recent work has just started to explore this field. The picture that is emerging indicates that management control systems play a significant role in these companies, albeit a very different role from the traditional MCS paradigm. They provide structure to facilitate coordination and interpret fast-moving environments; they provide flexible and dynamic frames that evolve with changing conditions yet are stable enough to enable common cognitive models, communication patterns and actions. Rather than cross-sectional studies, research designs rely to a large extent on an evolutionary perspective; as Cardinal, Sitkin & Long (2004) describe it, "(traditional) research has remained centred on static typologies of control systems elements, virtually ignoring the origins and the evolution of organizational control" (p. 411). This body of work that is being built around organizational control and entrepreneurial companies identifies a field that is rich from a research perspective and of significant relevance to the large population of companies and their investors.

DOI: 10.1016/S1751-3243(07)03006-4

Management accounting is, by its nature, a field where different functions converge and has often bridged into these other functions. For instance, a rich literature has developed around the intersection between management accounting and strategy (Simons, 1987; Langfield-Smith, 2005), operations management (Gerdin, 2005), marketing (Foster & Gupta, 1994), joint ventures and strategic alliances (Dekker, 2004), supply chain management (Wouters et al., 2005) or product development and innovation (Davila, 2000; Bisbe & Otley, 2004; Booker et al., 2007). The adoption and evolution of management control systems in entrepreneurial companies is no exception, being at the crossroads of a fast-developing entrepreneurship literature. While this chapter does not review this important literature in detail, it establishes links when necessary—Shane & Venkataraman (2000) provide an interesting review of this field.

The research question is also intimately related with the evolutionary perspective in the organization theory literature (Scott, 1992; Aldrich, 1999). Aldrich defines evolutionary theory as the result of "the operation of four generic processes: variation; selection; retention and diffusion; and the struggle over scarce resources" (p. 21). It is "not a set of deductively linked law-like statements" (p. 21), but rather "a concatenated system of loose, but apparently true propositions … it poses interesting questions, provides clues to their solution and, perhaps most crucially, generates testable hypotheses" (Langton, 1984, p. 352). Rather than focusing on established mature firms, this perspective looks at the "emergence of organizations, not just their existence (and) the process through which new organizations, populations, and communities emerge" (Aldrich, 1999, p. 1). The phenomenon of MCS in entrepreneurial companies is intrinsically evolutionary. Research questions on the adoption of formal control systems, their initial development, the evolution of informal control as formal systems emerge or the sequence of systems' adoption, all require an evolutionary lens. This perspective offers significant opportunities to ground future work on various organizational theory perspectives that use an evolutionary framework: population ecology; institutional theory; interpretative; organizational learning; resource dependence or transaction cost economics.

The aim of this chapter is twofold. First, we give the reader a map of where this literature is coming from and where it stands. We focus mostly on empirical studies, although we refer to relevant concepts whenever they are needed. Secondly, we outline future opportunities to advance knowledge. Research to this date has just laid out the field; open questions are numerous and interesting. Future research promises to advance our knowledge about management control systems, but more importantly to be of interest to managers of start-up companies—a population that is growing in numbers, diversity and relevance to economic development. The applied nature of the field opens it up to teaching case studies and other teaching material as a complement to research progress in this area.

We structure the chapter around two aspects of the control illustrated in Fig. 1. The first one, where most research has been done, is the management accounting and control internal to the company. The issue addressed here is how entrepreneurial companies balance sustained growth with solving the problems of coordination (information sharing) and control (information monitoring) within the organization when informal management alone breaks down. The second aspect addresses control from a governance perspective. Boards of directors play a significantly different role in start-ups compared to established firms. While boards in larger companies have been studied in detail (although this work has been done, for the most part, outside management control literature), boards

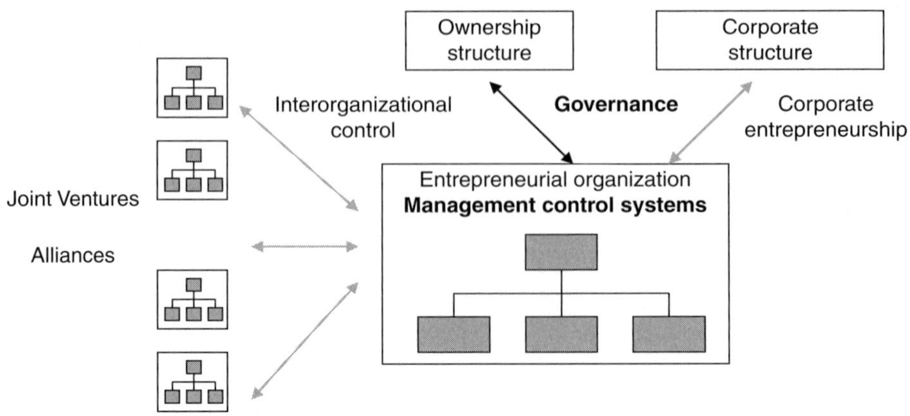

Figure 1. Management accounting and control in entrepreneurial companies.

in high-growth start-ups are a relevant control mechanism (from theoretical and practical perspectives) that only now is emerging in the literature. Figure 1 also points to two additional aspects of organizational control that are not discussed in this chapter, but are also promising to further the study of MCS and entrepreneurial companies. One of them is linked to control mechanisms associated with inter-organizational relationships (Das & Teng, 2000; Dekker, 2004). Because of the resource constraints that start-ups face, alliances, partnerships and joint ventures are often used as ways to leverage outside opportunities. So far the management control literature that has been looking at these relationships has focused on established firms; the start-up population has received attention on the strategy literature (Baum et al., 2000), although control processes in place have not been examined. Corporate entrepreneurship—an important aspect of the innovation process within established firms—is another important aspect that this chapter does not elaborate. Innovation as such has been receiving increasing attention in the management control literature (Davila, 2005); however, the particular structure of corporate entrepreneurship is still researched mostly outside this literature (Burgelman, 2002).

2. Research on Entrepreneurship

Entrepreneurs, in the most generic sense of the term, have been an essential part of the commercial world since its beginnings. Some individuals have always been more creative than others in identifying and exploiting new business opportunities. Most research, however, has focused on companies after the fruits of early-stage success have enabled them to be both sizable and publicly traded. There are multiple reasons why it is only in recent years that research on early-stage companies and their founders/starting management teams has become an exciting and growing area:

1. The short time in recent years from start-up to being an important industry player has led to heightened interest in early-stage companies. Companies like Cisco and Google have emerged so that, within a decade of their founding, they were pivotal and influential industry players. Moreover, their founders/senior managers have become well-known business names, and in some cases media personalities. There is now a high-level and broad-based interest in understanding factors associated with the emergence of these entrepreneurial companies. Researchers who examine this area experience high levels of interest in their findings. The emergence of business television networks and the high ratings of business programmes highlighting such entrepreneurs and their companies reinforce this factor.
2. The venture capital industry has been a growing and influential sector, especially in the last two decades. Although the industry has its roots in the 1950s and 1960s, it is in the 1990s and 2000s that there have been very large dollar investments by venture capital firms. Moreover, it is only in the last decade that areas outside the US (and especially Silicon Valley) have become important players in venture capital. Haemmig's research has documented sizable growth in venture capital in both Europe and Asia in recent years (Haemmig, 2007).
3. Databases covering venture capital and venture-backed companies have only recently been built up and expanded. Early-stage companies, by construction, are not publicly traded and have less information about them that researchers can readily access and analyze. In the 1990s, several US companies (including Venture One and Venture Economics) started to systematically develop databases for commercial reasons. Researchers have been able to access these databases to conduct large sample studies of the kind long since undertaken with large established and publicly-traded companies.
4. A growing number of well-trained researchers and teachers are now devoting time and resources to this area. In most universities business education, for many years, mostly focused on large established companies. Researchers with an empirical orientation had readily available databases (such as Compustat) to examine. Analysis of such companies was the low hanging fruit. Teaching cases were also heavily oriented to large companies such General Electric, Nestlé and British Petroleum. Those parts of the curriculum where early-stage or privately-held companies were discussed were often done so by practitioners or adjunct faculty. During the 1990s and 2000s there have been several important shifts. Researchers with well-developed skills/reputations have started to devote more time to topics related to entrepreneurship. Curriculum changes at leading schools in the 1990s and 2000s also started to seriously embrace entrepreneurship. This had long been an area neglected by the functional silos (economics, accounting, finance, marketing and so on) that were the hallmark of business education for many decades.
5. Respected academic journals in recent years are publishing more papers related to entrepreneurial companies. This is an important breakthrough in attracting top-level researchers to this area. For many years, research on early-stage companies was mostly found in what many viewed as less prestigious publication outlets. Much of this research had small samples and lacked rigour. Recent papers on entrepreneurship in journals like the *American Journal of Sociology*, the

Journal of Financial Economics and *The Accounting Review* are equivalent in research rigour to those on other topics in those journals. There has also been the emergence in recent years of new journals that focus on entrepreneurship. Even within these journals there has been evidence of a growing quality of research papers and higher stature researchers publishing them.

It is against this backdrop of a vital high-profile sector of the economy that is attracting the growing interest of serious researchers that we discuss research on management control systems in entrepreneurial companies.

3. Management Control Systems in Entrepreneurial Companies

Even if the field is relatively young—most articles have been published after 2000—the hint to the importance of the phenomenon goes back to 1972. Greiner (1972) used a lifecycle approach to organizational development to argue that companies grow through stages of evolution, punctuated by stages of revolution. While the article's intended audience was managers and it did not provide evidence supporting the validity of the framework proposed, its ideas have resonated with researchers as well as managers, becoming a "classic" and reproduced in 1998 as such (Greiner, 1998). Greiner identifies a "crisis of leadership" as the first revolution in the life of the company. He describes this first revolution (which comes after the initial "creativity" stage dominated by informal management) as: "Increased numbers of employees cannot be managed exclusively through informal communication and new employees are not motivated by an intense dedication to the product or organization. … New accounting procedures are needed for financial control." Greiner also predicts the rotation at the helm of the company because: "a stronger manager is needed—one who has the necessary knowledge and skills to introduce new business techniques." These descriptions suggest that this crisis of leadership is heavily linked to the adoption of management accounting and control practices.

This claim—the need to adopt management control systems—is central to Greiner's first revolution. However, while accepted at face value, it was not researched in depth for several decades. Moreover, even if the claim is intuitive, it was never confronted against the widely held assumption that MCS were unsuited for entrepreneurial companies and clan control (Ouchi, 1977) was the only control approach that would preserve the entrepreneurial spirit. From a research perspective, the study of the emergence of MCS is a recent phenomenon. While small and medium companies have been studied (Amat et al., 1994; Romano & Ratnatunga, 1994), these studies were based on traditional cross-sectional designs with a contingency theory background rather than the more dynamic aspect that the phenomenon requires. The recent build-up of this body of knowledge is associated with the increasing relevance of start-up companies in the economy that has been reflected in the organizational theory and strategy literatures and in particular the rapid growth of entrepreneurship both in terms of research and teaching.

An issue that confronts research in organizational control is to set the boundaries around this concept. This issue is even more relevant in entrepreneurship companies where, in early stages, formal controls are traditionally absent. Control mechanisms in their broadest sense exist as soon as the company is made up of two people. However, most of the studies in this field to date have looked at the transition point where formal controls—information-based routines (Simons, 1995b)—are adopted. While the focus has been on MCS, we believe that studying the evolution of informal controls (group norms, culture and socialization mechanisms) that define the bulk of organizational control during the early stages of a company is critical to fully understand the phenomenon. Understanding how informal controls evolve with growth and accommodate MCS has only started to be addressed in this literature.

3.1. Theories Used in Management Control Systems in Entrepreneurial Firms' Studies

Research in this emerging field has been empirical based on case (Section 3.2), survey (Section 3.3) and multi-method (Section 3.4) research designs. The theories that these studies are grounded on include information processing, lifecycle models, contingency theory, agency theory, psychology and signalling/legitimizing models.

Small entrepreneurial organizations require limited formal controls. Direct contact among all employees is best suited to clan control (Ouchi, 1979). However, as these organizations grow, direct interaction becomes ill-suited because:

1. information processing needs grow exponentially with the number of people and with increasing environment complexity (Miller & Friesesn, 1984);
2. the information processing capacity of clan control quickly becomes inadequate.

While formal controls become necessary to avoid control failures (Merchant & Ferreira, 1985) and ease growing pains (Flamholtz & Randle, 2000), traditional control systems are viewed as stifling the entrepreneurial spirit. An alternative to avoid this tension is to limit growth and keep organizational size within the information processing capacity of informal control—according to various chief financial officers (CFOs) of start-up companies this capacity lies somewhere between 40 and 100 employees, depending on the abilities of the manager and factors such as the geographical spread of their operations and customers (Davila & Foster, 2005). The second alternative is to manage this tension and develop non-traditional MCS that increase the information processing capacity of the organization (Tushman & Nadler, 1978). These systems fulfil the coordination and control needs while keeping the flexibility that growth demands—the concepts of enabling bureaucracy (Adler & Borys, 1996; Ahrens & Chapman, 2002) and loosely coupled systems (Scott, 1992; Lukka & Granlund, 2003) are probably closest to these systems.

The dynamic perspective embedded in the study of entrepreneurial companies leads itself to developmental and stage (rather than evolutionary) models of organizational evolution. Developmental models, such as lifecycle models, are built on the premise that organizations grow through generic stages—the most common being cycles of emergence, growth, maturity and decline (and renewal) (Miller & Friesen, 1984). For instance, the Greiner framework identifies creativity, direction, delegation and coordination. Management control systems vary as organizations evolve through these cycles. This logic is intuitively appealing and has been successfully used to associate the adoption of MCS over the life of a company (Simons, 2000). However, developmental models have been criticized as failing to predict patterns of organizational growth and not having been empirically confirmed (Levie & Hay, 1998). They are deemed as rigid where "the natural unfolding of organizational structures and processes flows from the forces that all organizations face" (Aldrich, 1999, p. 198) in contrast to an evolutionary perspective where "organizations do not follow a fixed path of development ... external events interact with an organization's own actions to drive the pace, pattern, and direction of change" (Aldrich, 1999, p. 198). This alternative perspective points to certain events as triggers of MCS adoption.

Contingency theory has shaped traditional MCS for several decades (Chenhall, 2003) and it is not surprising to have empirical studies of MCS in entrepreneurial companies grounded on it. Contingency theory is based on the premise that there is no best organizational design (and MCS in particular), but rather the best design depends on exogenous factors. Contingency theory is static in nature; it does not lead to predictions on the evolution of organizations. Rather, it predicts both (1) the best design given the exogenous factors, and (2) underperformance when the design is not optimal. Various factors have been found to affect MCS, however only the key role of strategy has been examined in entrepreneurial companies.

Agency theory also provides a useful framework to analyze the role of MCS in entrepreneurial companies. Agency issues emerge in at least two settings in these firms. First, as the number of employees grows and these people move into new locations, the company faces not only challenges associated with moving information through the organization, but also how to manage potential agency costs. MCS are relevant tools to address these costs. Performance measurement and planning systems facilitate monitoring of actions and results when direct observation is no longer possible. Compensation systems can be used to decrease agency costs associated with goal divergence. A second source of agency costs happens when these companies obtain outside investors, such as venture capitalists. At this point, potential agency issues emerge between the objectives of investors and managers. Again, MCS play an important role in decreasing potential agency costs. Within the realm of economics, signalling theory suggests that MCS can play a signalling role to identify well-managed firms and separate them from other start-up companies in the product and financial markets.

Sociology-based theories provide an important grounding for examining informal control mechanisms, the reality enacted around MCS, and the intersection between these two forms of organizational control and power. Informal control mechanisms traditionally associated with clan control include culture, group norms, values, rituals, identity formation or socialization processes (Ditillo, 2004) which play a significant role in entrepreneurial companies. Management accounting research in traditional companies has been successful in examining MCS from these different perspectives (Baxter & Chua, 2003; Oakes et al., 1998); however, in entrepreneurial companies "the links between social control and more formal system-based controls is an under-researched area, as is the evolution of those controls over time" (Collier, 2005, p. 325). For instance, institutional theory predicts roles for MCS unrelated to information or monitoring, such as legitimizing the organization in dealing with potential customers or partners.

The entrepreneurial literature has also relied on psychological explanations to analyze various questions associated with their topic. For instance, the unusually high turnover of entrepreneurs as the company reaches a certain size has been associated with psychological traits of the entrepreneur who "needs and values creative expression and is easily bored by familiar territory" (Rubenson & Gupta, 1996, p. 25). Greiner describes the first revolutionary period as "(founders) are probably unsuited to be managers" (p. 61).

The conceptual management control literature has made significant progress beyond the traditional feedback/feed-forward models (Otley, 2003). Interactive control systems (Simons, 1995b) facilitate management exploration around strategic uncertainties; the design principles of repair, internal transparency, external transparency and flexibility that characterize enabling bureaucracies

(Adler & Borys, 1996) also point to the relevance of MCS as support mechanisms to adapt to changing conditions; adaptive routines in organizational theory (Weick et al., 1999) show resilience because of their capacity to adapt to unexpected events; dynamic capabilities are MCS that redesign processes and other MCS to capture and codify knowledge (Zollo & Winter, 2002). These concepts describe MCS as flexible, to facilitate adaptation to novelty, rather than as rigid, with the objective of suppressing variation. Even if these concepts have been developed and are relevant to established companies, their underlying assumption about the relevance of MCS to uncertain environments is also applicable to MCS in entrepreneurial companies. Only the validity of this assumption explains the significance of MCS in these companies that empirical studies are documenting.

Another relevant aspect of the conceptual literature is the multiple roles that MCS have in organizations. While these roles do not directly answer why these systems are adopted (Davila & Foster, 2007b), nevertheless they offer a perspective consistent with the new theoretical concepts but closer to the phenomenon of MCS in entrepreneurial companies. These roles include: (1) making goals explicit and stable (Amabile, 1998), which in entrepreneurial companies provides direction in intrinsically dynamic environments; (2) code learning (Levitt & March, 1988) that helps liberate managers' attention from low value-added activities; (3) help coordination in start-up environments (Lundberg, 1995), MCS facilitate the development of local goals yet are consistent at the organizational level; (4) planning over time, MCS make explicit the sequence of events to execute (Cohen et al., 1996); (5) promote accountability and facilitate control, MCS liberate attention (Simons, 1995a) through performance measures that allow control by exception; (6) contract with external parties (Pfeffer & Salancik, 1978), this role becomes more important as growth firms interact with suppliers and customers and especially with external sources of funds; and (7) legitimization (Powell & DiMaggio, 1991), which is an important aspect for new firms that need to build their reputation in the market.

3.2. Case Studies

Cardinal et al. (2004) use a longitudinal case study to propose a framework of emergence and evolution of organizations' control portfolio. They collect mostly qualitative data (observations and structured, semi-structured and informal interviews with a large number of organizational members) from very early on in the life of the company ("when it had 11 employees") and over a period of 10 years, and use a grounded theory approach to analyze the data. The company's business is moving services. The authors use the traditional input, behaviour/action, and output control typology (Ouchi, 1980; Merchant, 1982) to analyze the evolution of the control portfolio over a traditional staged model with four phases that the authors identify.

- Stage 1: *founding*—relies mostly on informal mechanisms such as "personal leader supervision and feedback," except for the compensation system that is commission-based.
- Stage 2: *growth*—is driven by the need to manage culture and growth. Hiring and socialization mechanisms (input) are structured with guidelines and a value statement is developed, while behaviour and output controls are mostly informal, relying to a large extent on the founder's feedback to create the right culture. By the end of this stage the founder takes a sabbatical because of the intensity of the work.
- Stage 3: *formalization*—sees a formalization of inputs (formal application) and behaviour (middle management, business procedures, budgets, written communication, job descriptions) and a decrease of output control. The stage leads to financial problems.
- Stage 4: *rebalancing*—is characterized by the hiring of professional managers and formalized behaviour and output controls that balance discipline (standards, guidelines, pay formula) with personal interaction (quarterly meetings, beer parties, open-door policy).

The detailed study provides interesting insights. First, the stages suggest a model where controls move as a pendulum from the breakdown of informal systems to the constraints of too much formalization, before finding the equilibrium. Secondly, Stage 4 suggests the importance of professional managers, an idea that becomes more transparent in later work. Thirdly, the study details the emergence and evolution of control mechanisms and, in some cases, the phasing out of some of these mechanisms. Finally, the authors suggest that the lifecycle model identified (the four stages) might be necessary for growth: "(the company) might never have developed a balanced control system in Phase 4 if the organization had not formulated informal and formal control systems during Phases 2 and 3, respectively" (p. 426). As in any case study, the challenge is to separate which findings are idiosyncratic to the company and which ones are general. The parallel with Greiner's model and managerial evidence (Simons & Davila, 1999) suggests that the stages and revolutions—punctuated equilibrium models describe this idea of evolution punctuated by short periods of revolution (Romanelli & Tushman, 1994)—are not unique to the company; the question remains whether growth always requires going through these painful crisis and learning phases. The authors state: "because managers are unlikely to attempt rebalance until forced to by a crisis, the need for quick action is then typically perceived as urgent and reform is pushed with fervour" (p. 425). In addition, the company never grows substantially (it reaches $2 million in sales at the peak) which raises the question of whether the control problems limited growth but, more importantly, what do MCS look like in high-growth start-up companies.

Garlund & Taipaleenmaki (2005) also use a case study research design to look into the adoption of MCS in a sample of nine "new economy" start-up companies. The authors also adopt a lifecycle perspective. While the data gathering process is cross-sectional and qualitative (interviews and e-mails), the analysis of nine companies allows the authors to observe companies at different stages. The high-growth nature of "new economy" companies brings a different set of insights. First, the presence of external investors, typically venture capitalists, and scarce resources brings budgets to the forefront as "the starting point for (management control systems) in order to practice sufficient financial control" (p. 32) and requires more sophisticated financial tools "to meet the expectations … placed by external venture capitalists than requirements originating from their internal corporate evolution" (p. 43). Secondly, certain companies do not wait for crisis to set up control systems but "sought to meet the growing financial information and control needs with advanced and scalable information systems" (p. 33). Thirdly, while the authors identify variation in the importance of the finance function and management accounting tools, this variation is at least not linear with and probably even unrelated to lifecycle stages.

Collier's (2005) 10-year longitudinal case study of an Australian company looks into the evolution of informal control mechanisms. This focus makes this study unique and important, in that it opens an important aspect of early-stage company evolution. Collier reports how the entrepreneur delayed the hiring of an accountant and how problems emerged: "in contrast with the accountant's view that a growing company needed more controls, the accountant's attempts to introduce bureaucracy met resistance from (the entrepreneur)" (pp. 329–330). Information sharing and control happened through the entrepreneur's extensive travels, spending "his evenings with his employees while travelling" and when at home "barbecues and visits to pubs and restaurants" and "constant communication … while travelling around the world." Collier describes these social events as "compulsory" and the entrepreneur as "proud of knowing what projects all his employees were working on at any time" and describing his approach as "I share knowledge, I listen to people and I delegate, but I retain control. People know that the final decision is always mine" (p. 332). While the company reached 120 employees, the question remains whether this centralized and informal approach to management is scalable. As Collier describes it "the major weakness of (the entrepreneur)'s management style and the social mode of control is its complete dependence on one individual" (p. 334). Thus, the study can be characterized as looking into informal controls rather than their evolution as MCS are adopted. Yet it exemplifies the role of values, socialization and sense-making (Weick, 1995) in entrepreneurial companies.

Perren & Grant (2000) study the social enactment of management accounting systems using four small companies (less than 23 employees) through interviews with key informants. Their work is firmly grounded on a social construction perspective and interprets these systems as social artifacts to legitimize the company projecting "an appearance of rational practice towards their social environment and so maintain the support necessary for survival" (p. 395) and create shared meanings rather than taking a more functional perspective. The size of the companies researched is small enough to suggest that sharing information and monitoring is not the main functional purpose of the systems; rather they are used for personal decision-making and accounting regulation. The authors find that the accounting "microworld" that owners–managers enact comes from their previous experience, the accounting experience of other employees and the knowledge embedded in software.

The above citations to the literature do not include the various teaching cases on control systems in entrepreneurial companies found in business school case centres such as Harvard Business School and Stanford Business School. These cases were often a key stimulus to researchers obtaining exposure both to important issues facing such companies and to experiencing the high level of student interest in these companies and their entrepreneurs. Examples that illustrate this observation are Checkpoint, eBay and Salesforce.com in the Stanford system. All three cases examine the respective companies from their genesis and provide a platform for students and executives to discuss issues that research of the kind reviewed in this chapter addresses. In addition, these cases provide a rich source of potential topics of interest to research on early-stage companies.

3.3. Survey Studies

Reid & Smith (2000) use a large sample research design (150 companies interviewed) of Scottish microfirms. The study's underlying hypothesis relates certain events (cash flow crises, shortfall of finance for strategic purposes and implementation of best innovation) to the adoption of various management accounting systems. In contrast to prior studies, it does not work with a lifecycle model; rather it looks directly at the adoption of systems.

Sandino (2007), using a survey-based research design, examines the choice of MCS adoption by 131 start-up companies (32 public) in the retail industry. Her research design decision to focus on one industry allows her to keep a significant amount of potentially confounding variables constant to focus on the impact of strategy on this adoption pattern. Moreover, the retail industry offers significant variation in the variables of interest and growth comes through expansion of locations that quickly require formal systems.

The study offers various interesting findings. First, she finds that all her sampled companies adopt a set of "basic MCS" including budgets (planning and standards), pricing and inventory control. Because retail companies grow through setting up different branches, they quickly face the limits of informal management and have to complement it with basic MCS. Interestingly, the set of basic MCS are common regardless of the particular strategy and address "hygiene" control needs in the industry (needs that all companies have). This systematic approach to MCS adoption highlights (1) the importance of MCS as growth enablers (rather than inhibitors) and (2) the need for particular events or control failures (Cardinal et al.'s pendulum) to trigger adoption is not a general observation; a large number of start-ups adopt certain systems as defaults (given Sandino's sampling procedure, these companies are also likely to be the most successful ones because of survivorship bias). A second interesting finding relates strategy (a traditional contingency factor) with the variation in additional systems that companies adopt over the "basic MCS." In particular, she finds that retailers following a customization strategy adopt "revenue MCS", those following a product leadership strategy adopt "cost MCS" and those retailers offering a broader product range adopt "risk MCS." This finding also highlights the importance of strategy as a contingency variable in start-up companies. A third finding addresses the "so what" question; she finds that fit between the additional MCS adopted and strategy is associated with improved performance.

Moores & Yuen (2001) analyze lifecycle stages (Miller & Friesen, 1984) as a contingency variable within a cross-sectional, survey-based research design to explain MCS variation. Out of 49 observations, only two and four observations are classified in the birth and growth stages (those that are of interest to this chapter) while most of the observations (29) are in the maturity stage. Their findings are consistent with lifecycle as a contingency variable. The authors further conclude that "MAS formality (in terms of selection and presentation of information) across organizational lifecycle stages will increase from birth to growth" and in particular "(growth firms) pay particular attention to increasing the formality of their management accounting systems" and that "(the) results imply a longitudinal development of MAS." Cassia et al. (2005), using a similar research design with a cross-sectional survey of 501 companies, also find that management accounting systems vary across lifecycle stages; in particular their findings suggest that these systems develop ahead of organizational structure. These results are significant in highlighting the evolution of MCS over the lifecycle of a company. However, the sequential development offers an alternative view to Cardinal's pendulum-type stages, as well as Greiner's description of controls through the stages that he describes and Garlund & Taipaleenmaki who state that they do not "find support … for the observation that firms in the growth stage would rely upon a broader range of MAS tools than firms at other stages" (p. 42).

Wijbenga et al. (2007), using 93 survey responses from venture-backed Dutch companies, focus on the moderating effect of venture capital investors' attitude on the relationship between the use of cost control systems and financial performance. In particular they find that those venture capitalists that are involved beyond their monitoring role (including access to their external resource networks) have a positive effect on the relationship between cost control systems and financial performance (although they find no effect on the design of incentive and rewards systems). These findings bring a new aspect to the discussion and highlight the importance of going beyond the presence or absence of venture capitalists to consider their skills and networks.

3.4. Multi-method Studies

In a set of papers (Davila, 2005b; Davila & Foster, 2005, 2007a,b), we use a multi-method research design to examine the adoption of MCS. Consistent with Sandino (2007) and Reid & Smith (2000), we focus on the adoption and not on the evolution of these systems; therefore, the studies are not grounded in lifecycle models of MCS evolution. The databases come from two large-effort studies on start-up companies carried out at Stanford University. The first study (Stanford Project on Emerging Companies) included 95 start-up technology companies in Silicon Valley and focused on the adoption of HR practices in these companies (Baron et al., 1996; Baron et al., 1999; Baron et al., 2001). The second study (Stanford Emerging Management Accounting Systems) included 78 start-up companies (mostly technology and within the Silicon Valley) and focused on management control systems' adoption. Data include interviews and questionnaires with various managers in each company. Each interview lasted at least 45 minutes and was transcribed. The data combines cross-sectional and longitudinal information. The first study followed up each company over several years to update the information, while the second one used a retrospective approach to reconstruct the history of each company. In both cases the research effort extended over several years.

Davila (2005) focuses on the adoption of HR-related MCS and classifies them in the traditional personnel, action and results control (Ouchi, 1980; Merchant, 1982). The study examines the covariates of existence of these systems using multivariate analysis. The findings confirm various theory predictions. First, consistent with an information processing argument (Tushman & Nadler, 1978), size is associated with higher likelihood of adoption. Secondly, consistent with a learning argument (Levitt & March, 1988), where the repetition of routines (Nelson & Winter, 1982) leads to formalization, age is associated with higher likelihood of adoption. Thirdly, consistent with the argument that entrepreneurs are often ill-suited to be managers (Flamholtz & Randle, 2000; Willard et al., 1992)—they enjoy the fluidity of the early stage but are not comfortable with the structure of a company—the replacement of the founder with a new CEO is associated with a higher likelihood of adoption. Fourthly, consistent with the relevance of external investors (Robie et al., 1997), the presence of venture capital is also associated with a higher likelihood of adoption. Fifthly, strategy (coded from interview data) is also relevant in explaining adoption. These findings hold across the three types of controls, suggesting that the same variables drive their adoption. In addition, the results indicate that given size, younger firms are more likely to have adopted a larger number of MCS indicating that faster growth requires more systems—much like a faster car needs a better chassis and brakes (Simons, 2000).

Davila & Foster (2005) study the adoption of budgets in entrepreneurial companies. Their study is based on various theoretical arguments. First, the presence of venture capital is associated with faster budget adoption. Venture capital is often the first time that separation of ownership and control happens in a start-up company and agency issues become relevant to governance. The relevance of venture capital to the adoption of budgets highlights the relevance of accounting mechanisms as contracting and monitoring tools to agree on expectations and control the execution of the agreed plan. Secondly, number of employees is also highly associated with faster budget adoption. Thus it appears that budgets are effective tools in addressing the information and control needs that growth imposes on start-ups. Thirdly, CEO characteristics (experience and their perception of planning as good management practice) are also linked to budget adoption. Prior experience enhances the perceived cost–benefit trade-off. This evidence is consistent with psychological arguments that have been put forward in the entrepreneurship literature: entrepreneurs with little managerial experience are less likely to value management control systems. Fourthly, hiring of a financial manager also influences budget adoption. The concept of "import in" (where hiring a person with particular skills brings the knowledge into the company that it requires) illustrates this approach to adopting systems. Finally, the paper finds a positive association between budgets and growth—both around the adoption year and over a five-year period. Therefore, the widely held assumption that budgets are bureaucracy which inhibits the growth of entrepreneurial firms does not hold.

Davila & Foster (2007a) extend this line of research to a set of 46 MCS ranging from financial planning and evaluation, HR planning and evaluation and strategic planning to product development, marketing and partnership management. We document the importance of financial planning systems being, on average, the first ones adopted. We also document a significant difference in the pattern of MCS adoption between venture capital backed and non-venture backed firms. An important aspect of the paper is the association between company growth and the presence of MCS. Using a simultaneous equation specification, we find that growth and MCS intensity evolve together. Thus, growth cannot happen without formal control—an observation consistent with the idea that beyond a certain size, informal control alone is not enough and MCS are required—but formal control is only needed if the company grows. Another interesting aspect of the paper examines founder's tenure as CEOs. We find that MCS intensity is associated with longer tenures. While we do not get into the psychology of the entrepreneur, we document that founders that are replaced have implemented fewer systems, suggesting that these entrepreneurs have a hard time transitioning into the manager's role that growth requires.

Davila & Foster (2007b) address a different aspect of the adoption of MCS. Rather than looking into organizational covariates associated with the adoption of MCS, the study looks at why systems are adopted. In contrast to the prior studies, it is based to a larger extent on qualitative data. We find that MCS fulfil various roles, but these roles themselves are just a subset of the reasons for adoption. Certain MCS are adopted to fill specific roles, in particular to contract with external parties and to legitimize the company vis-à-vis external parties. These are external reasons for adoption. However, reasons for adoption associated with internal events are not associated with a particular role; the same reason for adoption may lead to systems that fulfil different roles. Certain reasons are proactive, such as the background of a manager recently hired (the "import in" idea) or a manager who perceives the need to adopt a certain system because the company has reached a certain stage. Other reasons are reactive, such as reacting to mistakes and chaos where a failure triggers the adoption of MCS and learning, where the constant repetition of a routine leads management to its codification. An important contribution of this study is the empirical identification of why MCS are adopted in start-up companies and clearly separating the reasons for adoption from the various roles that these systems may fulfil.

Hellman & Puri (2002) examine a different aspect of entrepreneurial company growth; using the Stanford databases they examine whether the presence of venture capital in the equity of start-ups affects their HR strategies. They find that venture backed start-up companies professionalize their management team much faster. Thus, the faster adoption of MCS in venture backed firms might be associated with faster "import in" of people with the relevant MCS knowledge and a broader effort to bring in advanced management practices more quickly.

3.5. Critical Review and Open Questions

This research stream is recent and these early papers open significant opportunities going forward. A significant question is the tension that has emerged between the "lifecycle" school and the "evolutionary" school. The former suggests and presents evidence consistent with start-up companies going through stages in their lives (Cardinal et al., 2004; Greiner, 1972; Moores & Yuen, 2001) punctuated by crisis. It suggests that the adoption of MCS is a consequence of crisis. The "evolutionary" school is less deterministic (Aldrich, 1999). Companies do not need to go through stages (Granlund & Taipaleenmaki, 2005) and adoption of MCS is not necessarily a reaction to crisis (Davila & Foster, 2007b). This latter suggestion opens up the field to exploring sociological forces as drivers of adoption.

Another question going forward is related to the perennial question of whether MCS adoption matters. Davila & Foster's (2007a) findings provide an initial affirmative answer: MCS and growth come together. However, number of employees is the growth proxy in this paper, leaving open the issue of whether this is a good enough proxy for performance. Alternative ways of identifying performance include long-term survival (that would need following start-ups over long periods of time to document failure as well as survival) or valuation. Profits in this setting are often a poor measure of performance, as they tend to be negative for significant periods of time.

Still another question is the sequencing of adoption of different types of systems. So far this literature has looked at each type of MCS in isolation, the only exception being Sandino (2007) who suggests that her "basic MCS" come earlier than the more tailored-to-strategy MCS. However, she does not go into too much depth in exploring this aspect. The question is whether having a particular system, for instance financial planning, is associated with a higher (if they are complements) or lower (if they are substitutes) likelihood of adopting a different system such as strategic planning. Addressing this question is not only interesting to start-up companies, but also to the broader MCS theory development.

So far this literature has used a limited amount of knowledge in sociology (including organizational theory and management theory), economics, psychology and other management fields—disciplines and fields that have been traditionally closely associated with MCS research. The possibilities are numerous. For instance, entrepreneurship literature has spent a significant amount of effort in understanding the psychology of the entrepreneur. This variable has had limited impact so far in the MCS in entrepreneurial companies. Other examples include contracting theory that can be important in settings where team incentives (through stock-related compensation) can be much more relevant than in larger companies; theories of motivation may also lead to interesting results on MCS design because of the passion associated with entrepreneurial companies; network theory is likely to be relevant to explain the structuring coordination and control mechanisms in resource-constrained start-ups.

4. Governance and Venture Capital

Governance and the role of the board of directors in particular, are a significant dimension of control in entrepreneurial companies. The literature on MCS in entrepreneurial companies reviewed in the previous section highlighted the relevance of venture capital investors to the development of MCS. The argument for their relevance evolves around the agency costs associated with the separation of ownership and control (Berle & Means, 1932). This argument has been detailed from a theory perspective (Admati & Pfleiderer, 1994; Bergemann & Hege, 1998; Neher, 1999; Wang & Zhou, 2002). An alternative view of venture capitalists' role in the board of directors is based on institutional theory indicating that industry practices have evolved to shape this unique role (Fried et al., 1998).

While venture capital investors' role in start-up companies has been researched in depth (Sahlman, 1990; Sapienza et al., 1996)—including their access to important networks such as financial and human capital, their experience to coach the CEO, their involvement in the strategy process or to legitimize the business—the explicit role of the board of directors has received far less attention, even if the board is the main control mechanism through which they exert control. In the same way that their presence has been shown to affect MCS (as discussed in the previous section), research on boards of directors in entrepreneurial firms has also highlighted their influence. Compared to small traditional companies and large firms, boards of venture-backed start-up companies are much more active. Based on interviews with six venture capital firms, Rosenstein (1988) describes these boards as being under outsiders' control (rather than management) and more powerful not only in terms of ownership, but also in terms of expertise and access to important resource networks; they are also smaller, with a significant proportion of outsiders and high involvement in the strategic process through more frequent meetings. In follow-up work, Rosenstein et al. (1993) survey 162 venture-backed firms to quantify these observations; they find that boards of these companies have 5.6 members with 23% to 50% of them associated with venture capital firms; they also report the perceived value (by CEOs) of outside board members to be their roles as sounding boards, interfacing with investors, monitoring operating and financial performance, recruiting and replacing the CEO and assisting in short term crisis. Clarysse et al. (2007), using a sample of high-tech start-ups, investigate the characteristics of outside board members (whether they complement or substitute management team's characteristics). Their findings suggest that start-ups with strong R&D and commercial skills and venture capital investors use outside board members with complementary skills. The presence of venture capitalists has also been associated with more independent governance and more transparent information (Sheu & Lin, 2007).

Another aspect of control is the actual instruments that venture capitalists use to exert control over the companies that they invest in. Kaplan & Stromberg (2001, 2003) use a sample of 213 venture capital investment transactions to examine these instruments. These contracts separate cash flow rights from control rights, moreover their allocation varies with company performance; poor performance shifts control rights to investors while good performance rewards management with higher control (without changing cash flow rights).

Boards of directors in small and medium enterprises (SME) are different from those in venture-backed start-ups. While SMEs are not necessarily entrepreneurial (most of them are established companies), they include some companies that have recently been founded but do not have external professional investors in their equity. Huse (2000) provides a detailed review of boards in SMEs and lines of research going forward. He highlights various issues. First, similar to venture backed companies, the presence of external board members is associated with external shareholders' control needs rather than the CEO wanting to have a sounding board or access to external resources; this result has been found to be robust in later research (additional correlates include younger CEOs, high percentage of exports and past poor performance) (Gabrielsson, 2007). Secondly, a board's working style (director knowledge and skills, preparation and commitment, behavioural independence and formality of board routines) appears to be more relevant than its structural variables. Thirdly, the attitude in family-owned SMEs (family, management or entrepreneur) leads to different approaches to structuring the board: paternal, managerial or entrepreneurial. Moreover, compared to venture-backed start-ups, SME's boards are smaller, meet less often, have a lower ratio of external members and the CEO is also more often chairman of the board (Gabrielsson & Huse, 2002). Boards of directors in these companies are more likely to be involved in strategic decisions the larger the company is and when boards have enough outside members, low CEO power, and the company is facing a transition or potential downturn (Fiegener, 2005). Finally, Kroll et al. (2007) find support for the hypothesis that, against agency theory predictions, boards with fewer outsiders perform better after IPO. Insiders have valuable tacit knowledge that the market appears to price. Consistent with prior findings, outside members are more effective when they go beyond their monitoring duties to support and advise the top management team.

This overview of the literature on boards of directors in entrepreneurial companies is devoid of any reference to both traditional and more modern control concepts, such as personnel, action and results control or interactive/diagnostic systems. Even if the board of directors is probably the most significant control mechanism in entrepreneurial companies (and board members are heavy users of MCS), the literature is developing outside research on management control systems. The opportunities for research in this topic from the MCS perspective are numerous, applying existing concepts in MCS to the functioning of these boards or developing concepts that are specific to boards.

5. Conclusions

The control function (Anthony, 1965) has evolved significantly over the last decades. But it is only recently that the traditional assumptions dissociating control from entrepreneurship have been questioned. The new paradigm views control as an integral part of the entrepreneurship; without control, entrepreneurial companies cannot fully realize their business potential. Research to date has just opened a few research lines and there are multiple opportunities going forward. This chapter highlights where the literature stands and some of the opportunities for future research. It also points out boards of directors as a neglected field in the control literature, even if this mechanism is critical in the control function of companies (and entrepreneurial companies in particular) and research on it would significantly benefit from MCS control theory.

References

Adler, P. S. & Borys, B. (1996). Two types of bureaucracy: enabling and coercive. *Administrative Science Quarterly*, **41**(1), 61–89.

Admati, A. R. & Pfleiderer, P. (1994). Robust financial contracting and the role of venture capitalists. *The Journal of Finance*, **49**, 371–402.

Ahrens, T. & Chapman, C. (2002). The structuration of legitimate performance measures and management: day-to-day contests of accountability in a UK restaurant chain. *Management Accounting Research*, **13**, 151–171.

Aldrich, H. (1999). *Organizations Evolving*. Thousand Oaks, CA: Sage Publications.

Amabile, T. M. (1998). How to kill creativity. *Harvard Business Review*. Harvard Business School Publication Corp., **76**(4), 76–87.

Amat, J., Carmona, S. & Roberts, H. (1994). Context and change in management accounting systems: A Spanish case study. *Management Accounting Research*, **5**(2), 107–122.

Anthony, R. N. (1988). *The management control function*, (revised ed., 1st ed. 1965). Boston, MA: Harvard Business School Press.

Baron, J. N., Burton, D. M. & Hannan, M. T. (1996). The road taken: origins and evolution of employment systems in emerging companies. *Industrial and Corporate Change*, **5**, 239–275.

Baron, J. N., Burton, M. D. & Hannan, M. T. (1999). Engineering bureaucracy: the genesis of formal policies, positions, and structures in high-technology firms. *The Journal of Law, Economics and Organization*, **15**, 1–41.

Baron, J. N., Hannan, M. T. & Burton, M. D. (2001). Labor pains: change in organizational models and employee turnover in young, high-tech firms. *American Journal of Sociology*, **106**, 960–1012.

Baum, J. A. C., Calabrese, T. & Silverman, B. S. (2000). Don't go it alone: Alliance network composition and startups' performance in Canadian biotechnology. *Strategic Management Journal*, **21**(3), 267–295.

Baxter, J. & Chua, W. F. (2003). Alternative management accounting research – whence and whither. *Accounting, Organizations and Society*, **28**, 97–126.

Bergemann, D. & Hege, U. (1998). Venture capital, moral hazard, and learning. *Journal of Banking and Finance*, **22**, 703–735.

Berle, A. A. & Means, G. C. (1932). *The Modern Corporation and Private Property*. New York, NY: The Macmillan Co.

Bisbe, J. & Otley, D. (2004). The effects of the interactive use of management control systems on product innovation. *Accounting, Organizations & Society*, **29**(8), 709–737.

Booker, D. M., Drake, A. R. & Heitger, D. L. (2007). New product development: How cost information precision affects designer focus and behavior in a multiple objective setting. *Behavioral Research in Accounting*, **19**, 19–41.

Burgelman, R. A. (2002). *Strategy is Destiny: How Strategy-Making Shapes a Company's future*. New York, NY: The Free Press.

Cardinal, L. B., Sitkin, S. B. & Long, C. P. (2004). Balancing and rebalancing in the creation and evolution of organizational control. *Organization Science*, **15**(4), 411–431.

Cassia, L., Paleari, S. & Redondi, R. (2005). Management accounting systems and organizational structure. *Small Business Economics*, **25**(4), 373–391.

Chenhall, R. H. (2003). Management control systems design within its organizational context: findings from contingency-based research and directions for the future. *Accounting, Organizations and Society*, **28**, 127–168.

Clarysse, B., Knockaert, M. & Lockett, A. (2007). Outside board members in high tech start-ups. *Small Business Economics*, **29**(3), 243–259.

Cohen, M. D., Burkhart, R., Dosi, G., Egidi, M., Marengo, L., Warglien, M. & Winer, S. G. (1996). Routines and other recurring action patterns of organizations: Contemporary research issues. *Industrial and Corporate Change*, **5**, 653–698.

Collier, P. M. (2005). Entrepreneurial control and the construction of a relevant accounting. *Management Accounting Research*, **16**(3), 321–339.

Das, T. K. & Teng, B. S. (2000). Instabilities of strategic alliances: An internal tensions perspective. *Organization Science*, **11**(1), 77–101.

Davila, A. (2005). The promise of management control systems for innovation and strategic change. In: C. S. Chapman (Ed.), *Controlling Strategy: Management, Accounting, and Performance Measurement*. Oxford, UK: Oxford University Press.

Davila, A. & Foster, G. (2005). Management accounting systems adoption decisions: evidence and performance implications from early-stage/startup Companies. *Accounting Review*, **80**(4), 1039–1068.

Davila, A. & Foster, G. (2007a). Management control systems in early-stage startup companies. *The Accounting Review*, **82**(4), 907–937.

Davila, A. & Foster, G. (2007b). Reasons for management control systems adoption: Insights from product development system choice by early stage entrepreneurial companies. Working paper. Stanford University.

Davila, T. (2000). An empirical study on the drivers of management control systems' design in new product development. *Accounting, Organizations and Society*, **25**(4–5), 383–409.

Davila, T. (2005b). An exploratory study on the emergence of management control systems: Formalizing human resources in small growing firms. *Accounting, Organizations and Society*, **30**(3), 223–248.

Dekker, H. C. (2004). Control of inter-organizational relationships: evidence on appropriation concerns and coordination requirements. *Accounting, Organizations and Society*, **29**(1), 27–49.

Ditillo, A. (2004). Dealing with uncertainty in knowledge-intensive firms: the role of management control systems as knowledge integration mechanisms. *Accounting, Organizations & Society*, **29**(3–4), 401–421.

Fiegener, M. K. (2005). Determinants of board participation in the strategic decisions of small corporations. *Entrepreneurship: Theory and Practice*, **29**(5), 627–650.

Flamholtz, E. G. & Randle, Y. (2000). *Growing pains: transitioning from an entrepreneurship to a professionally managed firm*, (2nd ed.). San Francisco, CA: Jossey-Bass.

Foster, G. & Gupta, M. (1994). Marketing, cost management and management accounting. *Journal of Management Accounting Research*, **6**, 43–77.

Fried, V. H., Bruton, G. D. & Hisrich, R. D. (1998). Strategy and the board of directors in venture capital-backed firms. *Journal of Business Venturing*, **13**, 493–503.

Gabrielsson, J. (2007). Correlates of board empowerment in small companies. *Entrepreneurship: Theory and Practice*, **12**(4), 271–290.

Gabrielsson, J. & Huse, M. (2002). The venture capitalist and the board of directors in SMEs: roles and processes. *Venture Capital*, **4**(2), 125–146.

Gerdin, J. (2005). Management accounting system design in manufacturing departments: An empirical investigation using a multiple contingencies approach. *Accounting, Organizations and Society*, **30**(2), 99–126.

Granlund, M. & Taipaleenmaki, J. (2005). Management control and controllership in new economy firms—a life cycle perspective. *Management Accounting Research*, **16**, 21–57.

Greiner, L. E. (1972). Evolution and revolution as organizations grow. *Harvard Business Review*, **50**(4), 37–46.

Greiner, L. E. (1998). Evolution and revolution as organizations grow. (Reprint of a 1972 article.) *Harvard Business Review*, **76**(3), 55–67.

Haemmig, M. (2007). Funding innovation through venture capital: A global perspective. In: T. Davila, M. Epstein, & R. Shelton (Eds), *The Creative Enterprise: Managing innovative organizations and people—Execution*. Westport, CO: Praeger.

Hellmann, T. & Puri, M. (2002). Venture capital and the professionalization of start-up firms: Empirical evidence. *Journal of Finance*, **57**(1), 169–198.

Huse, M. (2000). Boards of directors in SMEs: A review and research agenda. *Entrepreneurship & Regional Development*, **12**(4), 271–290.

Kaplan, S. N. & Stromberg, P. (2001). Venture capitalists as principals: Contracting, screening, and monitoring. *American Economic Review*, **91**(2), 426–430.

Kaplan, S. N. & Stromberg, P. (2003). Financial contracting theory meets the real world: An empirical analysis of venture capital contracts. *Review of Economic Studies*, **70**(243), 281–315.

Kroll, M., Walters, B. A. & Le, S. A. (2007). The impact of board composition and top management team ownership structure on post-IPO performance in young entrepreneurial firms. *Academy of Management Journal*, **50**(5), 1198–1216.

Langfield-Smith, K. (2005). What do we know about management control systems and strategy? In: C. S. Chapman (Ed.) *Controlling Strategy: Management, Accounting, and Performance Measurement*. Oxford, UK: Oxford University Press.

Langton, J. (1984). The ecological theory of bureaucracy. *Administrative Science Quarterly*, **29**(3), 330–354.

Levie, J. & Hay, M. (1998). Progress or just proliferation? A historical review of stage models of early corporate growth, Unpublished work. London,UK: London Business School.

Levitt, B. & March, J. G. (1988). Organizational learning. *Annual Review of Sociology*, **14**, 319–340.

Lukka, K. & Granlund, M. (2003). Paradoxes of management and management control in a new economy firm. In: A. Bhimani (Ed.) *Management Accounting in the Digital Economy*. Oxford, UK: Oxford University Press, pp. 239–259.

Lundberg, C. C. (1995). Learning in and by organizations: Three conceptual issues. *International Journal of Organizational Analysis*, **3**(1), 10–23.

Merchant, K. A. (1982). The control function of management. *Sloan Management Review*, **23**(4), 43–56.

Merchant, K. A. & Ferreira, L. (1985). Performance measurement and control issues in small businesses. In: B. E. Needles Jr. (Ed.) *The Accounting Profession and the Middle Market B2-The Accounting Profession and the Middle Market*. Chicago, IL: DePaul University, pp. 81–103.

Miller, D. & Friesesn, P. H. (1984). A longitudinal study of the corporate life cycle. *Management Science*, **30**(10), 1161–1183.

Moores, K. & Yuen, S. (2001). Management accounting systems and organizational configuration: A life-cycle perspective. *Accounting, Organizations and Society*, **26**, 351–389.

Neher, D. V. (1999). Staged financing: An agency perspective. *Review of Economic Studies*, **66**, 255–274.

Nelson, R. R. & Winter, S. G. (1982). *An Evolutionary Theory of Economic Change*. Cambridge, MA: Harvard University Press.

Oakes, L. S., Townley, B. & Cooper, D. J. (1998). Business planning as pedagogy: Language and control in a changing institutional field. *Administrative Science Quarterly*, **43**(2), 257–293.

Otley, D. (2003). Management control and performance management: Whence and whither? *British Accounting Review*, **35**(4), 309–327.

Ouchi, W. C. (1977). The relationship between organizational structure and organizational control. *Administrative Science Quarterly*, **22**(1), 95–112.

Ouchi, W. G. (1979). A conceptual framework for the design of organization control mechanisms. *Management Science*, **25**(9), 833–848.

Ouchi, W. G. (1980). Markets, bureaucracies, and clans. *Administrative Science Quarterly*, **25**, 129–141.

Perren, L. & Grant, P. (2000). The evolution of management accounting routines in small businesses: A social construction perspective. *Management Accounting Research*, **11**(4), 391–411.

Pfeffer, J. & Salancik, G. R. (1978). *The external control of organizations: A resource dependence perspective*. New York, NY: Harper & Row.

Powell, W. W. & DiMaggio, P. J. (1991). *The new institutionalism in organizational analysis*. Chicago, IL: University of Chicago Press.

Reid, G. C. & Smith, J. A. (2000). The impact of contingencies on management accounting systems development. *Management Accounting Research*, **11**, 427–450.

Robie, K. M., Wright, M. & Chiplin, B. (1997). The monitoring of venture capital firms. *Entrepreneurship Theory and Practice*, 9–27.

Romanelli, E. & Tushman, M. L. (1994). Organizational transformation as punctuated equilibrium: An empirical test. *Academy of Management Journal*, **37**, 1141–1166.

Romano, C. & Ratnatunga, J. (1994). Growth stages of small manufacturing firms: The relationship with planning and control. *British Accounting Review*, **26**(2), 73–195.

Rosenstein, J. (1988). The board and strategy: Venture capital and high technology. *Journal of Business Venturing*, **3**(2), 159–171.

Rosenstein, J., Albert, B. V., Bygrave, W. D. & Taylor, N. T. (1993). The CEO, venture capitalists, and the board. *Journal of Business Venturing*, **8**(2), 99–114.

Rubenson, G. C. & Gupta, A. K. (1996). The Initial Succession: A Contingency Model of Founder Tenure. *Entrepreneurship: Theory & Practice*, **21**(2), 21–35.

Sahlman, W. A. (1990). The structure and governance of venture-capital organizations. *Business Economics*, **29**, 35–37.

Sandino, T. (2007). Introducing the First Management Control Systems: Evidence from the Retail Sector. *Accounting Review*, **82**(1), 265–293.

Sapienza, H. J., Manigart, S. & Vermeir, W. (1996). Venture capitalist governance and value added in four countries. *Journal of Business Venturing*, **11**, 439–470.

Scott, W. R. (1992). *Organizations: Rational, Natural and Open Systems*, (1st ed. 1981). Englewood Cliffs, NJ: Prentice Hall.

Shane, S. & Venkataraman, S. (2000). Note: The promise of entrepreneurship as a field of research. *Academy of Management Review*, **25**, 217–226.

Sheu, D. F. & Lin, H. S. (2007). Impact of venture capital on board composition and ownership structure of companies: an empirical study. *International Journal of Management*, **24**(3), 573–581.

Simons, R. (1987). Accounting control systems and business strategy: An empirical analysis. *Accounting, Organizations and Society*, **12**(4), 357–375.

Simons, R. (1995a). Control in an age of empowerment. *Harvard Business Review*, **73**(2), 80–89.

Simons, R. (1995b). *Levers of control: how managers use innovative control systems to drive strategic renewal*. Boston, MA: Harvard Business School Press.

Simons, R. (2000). *Performance measurement and control systems for implementing strategy*. Upper Saddle River, NJ: Prentice Hall.

Simons, R. & Davila, A. (1999). ATH Technologies, Inc. Harvard Business School Case, number 9-100-017.

Tushman, M. & Nadler, D. (1978). Information processing as an integrating concept in organizational design. *Academy of Management Review*, **3**, 613–624.

Wang, S. & Zhou, H. (2002). Staged financing in venture capital: Moral hazard and risks. *Journal of Corporate Finance*, **8**, 285–306.

Weick, K. E., Sutcliffe, K. M. & Obstfeld, D. (1999). Organizing for high reliability: Processes of collective mindfulness. In: R. I. Sutton, & M. Staw (Eds), *Research in Organizational Behavior*. Stamford, CT: JAI Press.

Wijbenga, F. H., Postma, T. J. B. M. & Stratling, R. (2007). The influence of the venture capitalist's governance activities on the entrepreneurial firm's control systems and performance. *Entrepreneurship: Theory and Practice*, **31**(2), 257–277.

Willard, G. E., Krueger, D. A. & Feeser, H. R. (1992). In order to grow, must the founder grow: a comparison of performance between founder and non-founder managed high-growth manufacturing firms. *Journal of Business Venturing*, **7**, 181–195.

Wouters, M., Anderson, J. & Wynstra, F. (2005). The adoption of total cost of ownership for sourcing decisions – a structural equations analysis. *Accounting, Organizations and Society*, **30**(2), 167–191.

Zollo, M. & Winter, S. (2002). Deliberate learning and the evolution of dynamic capabilities. *Organization Science*, **13**(3), 339–351.

Handbook of Management Accounting Research
Edited by Christopher S. Chapman, Anthony G. Hopwood and Michael D. Shields

Value Creation and the Possibilities for Management Accounting Research in the Entertainment Sector: the United States Motion Picture Industry

S. Mark Young[1], James J. Gong[2] and Wim A. Van der Stede[3]

[1]*University of Southern California, USA*
[2]*University of Illinois, USA*
[3]*London School of Economics, UK*

Abstract: The management of intellectual property has become a core competence of successful enterprises. This is particularly true for firms in the entertainment and creative industries, where battles are waged for the rights to new ideas. Our focus and purpose in this chapter is to show that the US motion picture industry has the potential to provide a fruitful research field for management accounting researchers. The industry has high economic importance and is appealing to researchers because it offers rich data sets that cover the entire product lifecycle for new products and a number of challenging problems especially related to the management of talent and intellectual property. Academic research in this area, particularly in accounting, is in its infancy. In this chapter, therefore, we discuss critical management accounting and control issues faced by the motion picture industry, review cross-disciplinary literature on those issues and outline promising research directions.

1. Introduction

Information, communication and entertainment now comprise the largest sector of the US economy (Shapiro & Varian, 1999). A major category of the information sector is the motion picture industry,[1] which is America's second-largest export business after aerospace (Bureau of Economic Analysis, 2005). The motion picture industry generates revenues through selling content to consumers, licensing content to other firms or selling audience attention to advertisers. Motion pictures remain a major cornerstone of domestic entertainment, with consumers paying billions of dollars annually to watch movies in an increasing variety of formats. In 2006, consumers in the US bought about 1.45 billion movie tickets worth $9.49 billion at domestic theatres—an average of about four million tickets per day. This is just a small portion of the total revenues from movies, however, as receipts from video, television and theatres in international markets continue to increase. In 2006, worldwide consumption of US movies topped $40 billion, primarily from theatre tickets and rental or purchase of home videos (Standard & Poor's, 2007). Total spending on filmed entertainment, including box office, home video and broadcast, is one of the fastest growing media and entertainment revenue streams (Veronis Suhler Stevenson LLC, 2005).

The products supplied by the motion picture industry—movies—have the following characteristics. First, production of movies is characterized by high fixed costs of creation and low marginal costs of reproduction. The marginal costs of producing another unit of a movie with current technology (not considering distribution costs) are

[1]The information sector is a newly-created economic sector since 1998, at which time the US Census Bureau started collecting data on it. The information sector includes establishments previously classified in the Standard Industrial Classification (SIC) in manufacturing (publishing); transportation, communications, and utilities (telecommunications and broadcasting); and services (software publishing, motion picture production, data processing, online information services, and libraries) (US Census Bureau, 2006).

DOI: 10.1016/S1751-3243(07)03007-6

close to zero. Secondly, movies are experience products, meaning that it is difficult for the consumer to assess the quality of the product before purchasing it (Eliashberg & Sawhney, 1994). For suppliers, such as movie studios and exhibitors, this means that a movie's success at the box office is difficult to predict (Neelameghan & Chintagunta, 1999), partly because consumer preferences are fickle (Eliashberg et al., 2000). Thirdly, successful movies have long lives. Movies and movie franchises such as *Star Wars*, *Lord of the Rings*, *Spiderman*, *Shrek* and *Pirates of the Caribbean* can generate revenues for many years. This implies a weak contemporary link between costs and revenues and, thus, the importance of considering costs and revenues over a movie's lifecycle.

The production, distribution and retailing processes of the motion picture industry are also distinct from other consumer products industries. The production process is human–capital intensive. Movies are made by talented writers, producers, directors, technicians and actors. In addition to being highly collaborative, the production and distribution processes are based on extensive networks of individuals and organizations. At the centre of the production network are producers, who will seek out scripts, talent, financing and distribution deals. These different entities are organized on a project rather than on a permanent basis (Baker & Faulkner, 1991). Reputation and relationships are far more important in the movie industry than in other industries in the economy. Another characteristic of the industry is that business decision-making in the industry relies less on rigorous economic modelling and more on intuition and "gut feel," even though the decisions often commit millions of dollars of investment (Squire, 1992).

To structure our discussion of these unique industry features, we organize this chapter around the value chain of the industry with the major links being production, distribution and exhibition. In the context of each stage of the value chain, we discuss the most pertinent management accounting and control issues and present several opportunities for research. Part of the discussion, especially around production and distribution, involves the changes in the industry brought about by advances in digital technologies. Digital technologies not only create new content that will compete with traditional media for attention and revenue, but also create new production tools and distribution channels for traditional media and, thus, new revenue sources.

Management accounting and control research in entertainment in general, and in the motion picture industry in particular, is in its infancy. Thus, our purpose in this chapter is to provide a framework for understanding the industry that will guide our suggestions for research.

2. Value Chain of the Motion Picture Industry

Porter's (1980, 1985) value chain framework describes the activities within and around an organization, relates those activities to an analysis of the competitive strength of the organization, and evaluates which value each particular activity adds to the organization's products or services. In this chapter, we apply the value chain framework to the US motion picture industry (see Fig. 1).

Production, the first part of the chain, involves four processes: property acquisition, pre-production, production and post-production. Marketing, distribution and exhibition, as well as various channels of downstream retailing, follow next. It is these downstream retailing channels in the value chain that generate the vast majority of revenues. In today's environment, it is rarely the case that ticket sales pay for the cost of a movie; however, box office performance is still important since box office receipts brand a movie as a hit or flop, influencing the general public and determining a movie's revenue potential in other channels (Gong, Van der Stede & Young, 2007; Lehmann & Weinberg, 2000; Ravid, 1999). The downstream revenues include video sales and rentals, network and cable television rights (including syndication), independent television rights, pay-per-view and pay television rights, airline screening rights, college campus screening rights, international distribution rights, music sales for soundtracks from movies, merchandise related to the movie, potential book publishing rights, branded entertainment and product placement (products strategically shown in a movie). Table 1 shows the major sources of these revenue streams and their windows.

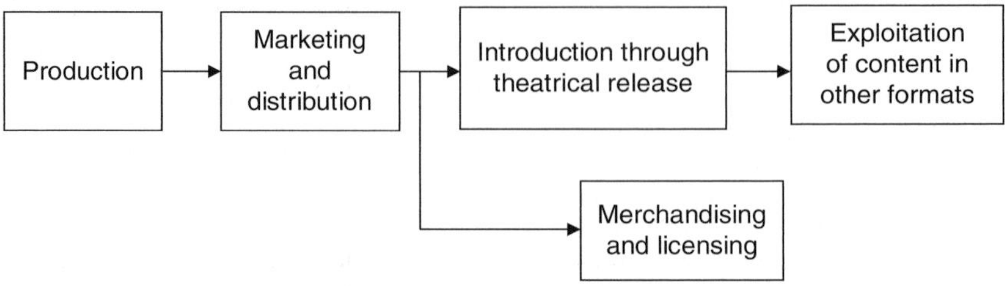

Figure 1. Movie industry value chain.

Table 1. Major sources of motion picture revenues and their windows.

Channels	Window	Beginning
Theatrical	6 months	Initial theatrical release
Home video (VHS/DVD)	7–10 years	6 months after initial theatrical release
Pay-per-view	2 months	8 months after initial theatrical release
Pay television	18 months	12 months after initial theatrical release
Network television	30 months	30 months after initial theatrical release
Pay television, second window	12 months	60 months after initial theatrical release (30 months if no network television sale)
Syndication or basic cable	60 months	72 months after initial theatrical release (42 months if no network television sale)
Syndication or basic cable, second window	60 months	132 months after initial theatrical release

Note: Omitted from the distribution channels and windows are foreign sales, the video game sector, consumer products merchandizing and theme parks. Foreign sales usually begin after the initial theatrical release in the US. Each territory has different windows for different channels. Video games based on blockbuster movies such as *Lord of Rings* and *Terminator 3* sometimes earn equivalent revenues as theatrical releases.

The chain of value creation in the motion picture industry is consistent with one of the underlying assumptions behind the wave of mergers and acquisitions in the entertainment and media industries in the 1990s. (Table 2 lists the movie studios and their parent conglomerate, as well as other downstream business units of these conglomerates.) Conglomerates realize synergies among different branches of the entertainment business by exploiting a movie—that is, the movie brand or franchise—across a number of different sectors in a coordinated manner. In other words, major studios owned by the big conglomerates are not only producing blockbuster movies, but also most importantly, brands or franchises. Further, as suggested in *The Economist* (November 19, 1998, p. S5):

> Some character or idea can be marketed in a thousand different ways. A brand is often launched with an "event" film as with Disney's *Lion King* or Sony's *Godzilla*, but brands can start a life in all sorts of ways. Viacom's *Rugrats*, which has just been turned into a film, came from a children's cable channel, Nickelodeon; Time Warner's *Batman* is an old and revered comic book character that happened to translate nicely into a live action movie and much, much more.

There have been several studies on the organization of the US motion picture industry (see Scott, 2002, for a review). An interesting phenomenon in this setting, particularly, has been the change over time from the old "studio system" to a flexible system characterized by a nexus of specialized firms, as well as individuals who operate as free agents (Christopherson & Storper, 1989). Others have studied organizational changes in this industry with respect to the rise of the "blockbuster strategy" or the era of big-budget movies, and how it led to specialization in movie production and separation of the business and artistic sides of movie making (Baker & Faulkner, 1991). However, flexible structures are not unique to the motion picture industry. As such, studies of organizational forms in the motion picture industry can draw from, or extend to, various other organizations with flexible structures, such as professional service firms (Eccles & Crane, 1988). Further, the organization theory and strategy literatures posit that organization structure, strategy and performance are intricately related (Rumelt, 1974). An interesting question, therefore, is whether and how firm characteristics in the motion picture industry affect competitive advantage and (financial) performance. As an example, Corts (2001) compared the release scheduling of movies distributed by independent studios with those by major studios, and found that major studios are not as efficient as independent studios in avoiding competition while scheduling movie releases. Obviously, many other aspects of competitive nimbleness and organizational performance associated with different organizational forms remain to be studied in this industry.

2.1. Production

2.1.1. Properties

The first step in producing a movie is the acquisition of a property. In the motion picture industry this property is either a treatment (an overview of the movie with a discussion of the characters and a brief plot synopsis) or a completed screenplay. A property may be an adaptation of an existing book or an original piece of work. Acquiring properties is a highly competitive part of the value chain where the major studios, independent producers and even actors or other investors often compete for the most promising properties. Whoever obtains the property can then develop its content into a movie, which we refer to here as the movie production process.

The movie production process often involves an extensive network of parties, as shown in Fig. 2. Among others, it includes producers, financiers, talents and their agencies and post-production firms. Below we discuss the key nodes in this network.

Table 2. The MPAA motion picture studios, major subsidiary studios, distributors, and parent corporations.

Major studios	Major subsidiary studios	Distributor	Conglomerate	Downstream businesses of the conglomerate
Twentieth Century Fox Movie Corporation	Fox Searchlight	Twentieth Century Fox International Corporation	News Corporation	Television networks (Fox News Channel), television stations, newspapers (New York Post) and magazines (Gemstar-TV Guide)
Walt Disney Pictures	Miramax Pixar Animation Touchstone Pictures	Buena Vista International, Inc.	The Walt Disney Company	Television networks (ABC), radio networks (ABC Radio), music (Hollywood Records) and consumer products (Disney Licensing)
Warner Brothers Pictures	New Line Cinema	Warner Brothers International Theatrical Distribution	Time Warner Inc.	Television networks (TBS), radio networks, music (Warner Music Group) and Publishing (Time, Inc.)
Paramount Pictures	Dreamworks Pictures Paramount Vantage	Paramount Pictures Corporation	Viacom, Inc.	Cable networks (MTV) and music (Famous Music)
Columbia Pictures	Screen Gems Sony Pictures Classics	Columbia TriStar Motion Picture Group	Sony Corporation (Sony Pictures Entertainment)	Music (Sony Music)
Universal Pictures	Focus Features	Universal International Movies, Inc.	General Electric Company	Television network (NBC)

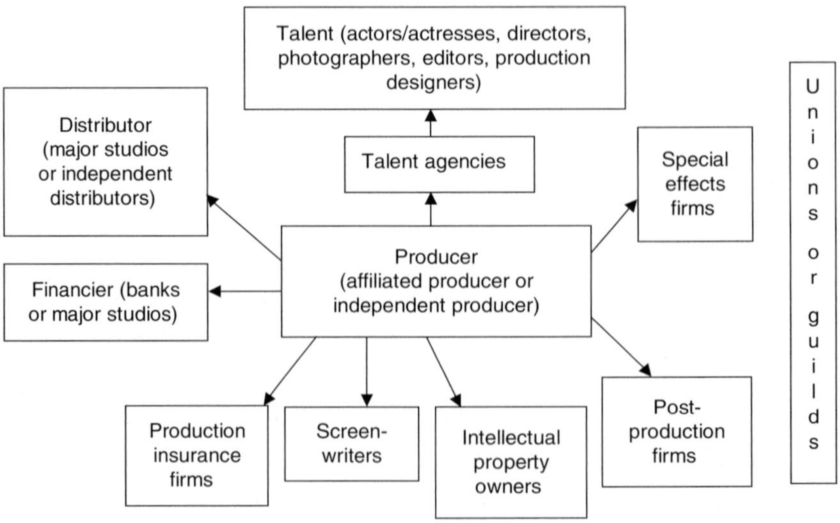

Figure 2. Network surrounding movie production.

2.1.2. *Producers*

A producer is mainly responsible for pre-production, production and post-production, but depending on the situation may also be involved in property acquisition and marketing. The whole range of activities commonly falls under the responsibility of producers who are tied to a studio, as opposed to independent producers, who are mainly focused on producing the movie. Focusing on production, the producer's key tasks are to find project financing and to hire screenwriters, actors and directors.

2.1.3. Financing

For studio-produced movies, movie greenlighting (that is, the decision to finance the production of a movie) is a critical decision characterized by an environment in which studio executives are largely unable to predict the outcome. Little is known about the process that leads to the selection of movies for production at any of the studios. Financing is an even more daunting task for independent producers. In order to obtain financing, independent producers often have to sell distribution rights to different channels (e.g., theatrical, television and video distribution) in different territories (domestic and/or international). Because there are more financing partners involved, these deals tend to involve complex arrangements for the division of costs and revenues, distribution territories, and rights to theatrical, television and video distribution. As an example, consider the case of *Terminator 3: Rise of the Machines*. An independent production company, C-2 Pictures, sold the rights to Warner Brothers, Sony Pictures and other foreign distributors. Warner Brothers contributed $55 million to production and marketing to obtain the rights for domestic theatrical distribution, video sales and rentals of the movie, but was entitled to only 50% of the revenues from these distributions (Hayes & Bing, 2004). Apart from relying on studios, financing through equity investors, bank loans and judicious use of intricate tax shelters are some of the other methods used. During the past few years, private equity firms and hedge funds have invested billions of dollars in the motion picture industry, as evidenced by Tom Cruise's deal with Morgan Stanley's hedge fund that has agreed to finance his next slate of movies. Clearly, recent private equity and hedge fund forms of funding are also having their mark in this industry.

From the studio's perspective, financing movies is risky given the high level of investment required and the wide distribution of payoffs. One way studios have dealt with the uncertainty around the success of financing movies is by turning to co-financing, risk-sharing arrangements with other studios or with smaller, semi-independent production companies. In the latter case, the large studios typically buy a substantial equity stake in the production companies, which are expected to initiate and develop movie projects that are then co-financed by both parties as part of a long-term agreement. This approach to financing has grown considerably in recent years. For instance, while there was only one multi-studio effort in 1993, eleven major releases in 2003 were co-ventures (Goettler & Leslie, 2004). In most cases, the parties involved agree to share the costs of a movie that appears to be a particularly risky proposition because of its storyline, creative talent or production budget. An example is *Seabiscuit*, for which Universal (30%), Dreamworks (30%) and Spyglass Entertainment (40%) shared the $87 million budget.

Research on the types of financing and their features, as well as the rationales of studios behind their financing decisions, is only beginning to emerge. For example, Goettler & Leslie (2004) found, perhaps surprisingly, that studios do not tend to co-finance their most risky movies. What they did find, however, was that co-financing helps soften release competition, particularly for high-budget movies. That is, studios that have co-financed a movie tend to avoid head-to-head competition with other movies in their portfolio, reducing the risk of a failed opening week for the co-financed movie. Clearly, the effectiveness of co-financing in risk management is a topic worthy of further study.

Moreover, what is largely unknown is the decision and control process that leads to the selection of movies to be produced at any of the studios. In some cases, such as sequels, the outcome is believed to be largely determined by the success of the original property (Marr, 2007). But who actually decides which movies should be greenlighted? Ultimately, a studio head has the last say in signing off on a movie, but the process is said often to come down to the tastes and preferences of a few executives. Because of the unpredictability of which movies will be successful, it is believed that studio executives choose less risky movies in order to keep their jobs (Ravid & Basuroy, 2004). Such movies often appeal to the lowest common denominator in the movie-going public. These contentions, however, must be carefully researched, as virtually no systematic evidence exists. Plausible frameworks for studying such decisions might include risk aversion, investment and employment horizon, real options and other theories.

A related question is what kind of movie projects (screenplays) have the highest box office potential and should be greenlighted? A recent study by Graser (2007) showed that original screenplay-based movies perform better than adaptations, sequels or remakes. However, studios continue to be eager to produce movie sequels, and so it remains largely unknown whether sequels lead to more favourable risk–return ratios. But perhaps not all sequels are created equal; that is, which kinds of movies are amenable to a successful sequel and which are not? Related to this, how can studios use sequels to build and sustain valuable franchises?

2.1.4. Screenwriting

Besides finding financing for the movie project, the producer needs to hire screenwriters, actors and directors. After a producer hires a screenwriter, screenplays are written. Before a script is accepted there may be numerous rewrites, sometimes involving several screenwriters. When a director is hired, he or she has his or her own vision, and when a star actor or actress is hired, he or she may have yet another opinion. Sometimes a schism develops between the screenwriter, director and actors. But, regardless of how talented directors or actors are, a poor script will overshadow their talents. Thus, obtaining a good script is often the key to retaining talent.

2.1.5. Talent

Motion pictures critically rely on talent, since the names and faces of the talent in the motion picture industry sell tickets, unlike personnel in most other industries. Moreover, in order to win financing and interest from potential distributors, producers need not only a good script, but also a reliable list of above-the-line personnel, including directors, actors and actresses. What sets the creative industries apart from, say, companies producing commodities, is the reliance on the creativity of personnel. While other industries inarguably also rely heavily on skilled individuals, the creative industries employ people many of whom are believed to have different mindsets or hard-wiring (Young & Pinsky, 2006). Although evidence is mixed, a star's presence is often believed to increase the expected revenue potential of a movie (DeVany & Walls, 1999; Ravid, 1999). Consistent with this, banks often decide how much money to lend to producers based on expected movie revenues, which they believe is a function of star power. Stars, therefore, are commonly ranked on the basis of "bankability" (Ulmer, 2000).

A complicating factor in the motion picture industry, as in the creative industries generally, is that talent is difficult to discern and the relevant credentials (such as graduation from a given acting school) are relatively unimportant (Zuckerman et al., 2003). This poses several interesting puzzles for both talent and those who hire them (in this case, talent agents who act as brokers between the talent and the producer, see below). From the talent's perspective, the question is whether they should pursue a specialist or generalist identity; that is, to be "typecast" or not (such as Sylvester Stallone being associated with an action image). And, for those who hire the talent, should they go for a proven type or run the risk that a star might fail at broadening the range of characters they can act (as Sylvester Stallone has in roles against his action image in comedies and dramas)? Zuckerman et al. (2003) is an exemplar study that examines these questions, not only because of its integrative theorizing, but also in demonstrating how studying motion picture labour markets offers unique empirical features, while allowing careful generalizations beyond just the specific industry setting (that is, theoretical generalization).

Related to the quality of talent is their compensation. In the motion picture industry, compensation of talent commonly consists of a fixed salary plus a variable component, which is either a share of gross revenue or a share of net profits. Given the presumed role of talent in a movie's success, such forms of risk-sharing compensation appear sensible (Chisholm, 1997). An important concern, however, is how to set a star's upfront fixed compensation, sometimes running in the tens of millions of dollars, given that star power sometimes fails to lead to the expected box office performance. Moreover, for the variable compensation component, the accounting of profit for net profit participants is an issue that is sometimes highly controversial and subject to litigation. All told, the motion picture industry offers an appealing setting to study compensation issues in terms of which kinds of contracts are most effective in attracting and motivating talent, considering that compensation contracts often vary from project to project, talent to talent and even over time.

Talent in the motion picture industry is comprised mostly of members of unions and guilds. The term "union" in the creative industries describes labour organizations that represent technical personnel, who are referred to as "below-the-line." The term "guild" describes labour organizations that represent the creative talent, who are referred to as "above-the-line." These designations result from their actual position on the pages of production budgets in which "creative" and "technical" costs are divided by a line. In a typical motion picture production budget, for example, below-the-line costs are considered fixed, whereas above-the-line costs are considered variable (which is, in part, because of profit participations for talent, and thus this number may vary). This labelling obviously deviates from the prescriptions in traditional cost accounting textbooks, as some of the costs related to the creative talent are clearly fixed, such as any upfront fixed compensation, whereas several of the below-the-line personnel-related expenditures are variable (such as those related to freelance services). Studies of cost treatment and behaviour in this industry therefore also offer interesting opportunities for research.

2.1.6. Pre-production

In the pre-production process, producers hire non-star actors, crews and other below-the-line personnel. Pre-production also involves the securing of equipment and locations. Since each day in movie production is very expensive, pre-production preparation is important. During pre-production, producers also prepare the production budget.

The budgeting process for motion pictures is a fertile area for research. Very little is known about it, but the process is said to require a fair amount of judgement. And because each movie can be considered a one-off project, there is little historical data to rely on. To prepare the movie production budget, every page of the screenplay is scrutinized and budgeted according to the experience of the producers, involving estimates of the number of days of shooting and the shooting sequence. Survey evidence suggests that very few certified management accountants work as "production accountants" in the motion picture industry (Neale & Allerston, 2005). These so-called "production accountants," however, play a critical role in assisting the producer in preparing the production budget and assessing the commercial viability of the movie project.

2.1.7. Production

A movie's production costs, or the costs of manufacturing the master print (called a negative, hence the term "negative costs"), have several components. These costs include any upfront payments to talent and other employees, costs of sets and other costs incurred during the production process, such as the cost of special effects. For studio movies, the production cost also includes overhead charges by the studio for use of its facilities. The studio also charges interest on the negative cost and overhead. One common problem during production is that movies tend to run over budget. Cost accountability, however, is an interesting issue due to the different parties involved; that is, there is the director who implements the production, the producer who is responsible for the budget and the financier who provides the money. Because accountability is difficult to attribute, producers often buy insurance against runaway costs. In this context, it would therefore be interesting to study how such insurance affects each of the involved parties' behaviour, as well as to understand the relevant tradeoffs and economic incentives for the parties involved in these situations.

2.1.8. Post-production

In post-production, producers aid in the editing process with the help of professional editors and the director. The editing process is critical to the form and impact of the final picture. Post-production editing can cover a myriad of production flaws. The editing sometimes takes even more time than the actual production of the movie, during which time music and sound are also added to the tape. Then the movie is rated. After the movie is cut and rated, previews are scheduled. This is similar to taking a theatrical play on the road. At a preview, producers, directors and editors learn about audience reactions, timing, laughs, tensions and the general pulse of the movie (Austin, 1989). If the reactions are not as expected, changes are made before the movie is tested again at a second preview. There may be two to four previews. Once the director and producer are satisfied, the movie is locked in and ready for release. Whereas several studies in marketing have attempted to develop pretest models for movies (e.g., Eliashberg & Sawhney, 1994; Eliashberg et al., 2000), predicting movie enjoyment and hence, movie performance, has been met with mixed success at best, causing producers to have little to go by before releasing the movie.

2.1.9. Organization

From the overview of the above process from property acquisition through post-production, the producer indisputably is the key person to manage the process. Producers fall onto a continuum ranging from being completely independent of any studio to being completely tied to a studio. The independent producers' main job is to interest distributors (studios) in their product and to obtain financing for producing the movie. Some producers, however, are under exclusive contract to a major studio. In this case, the studio finances the movie and provides production support. Some producers fall somewhere between these categories. They sign a contract with a studio, but can also work for other studios (these are so-called "first look deals"). For the latter two types of producers, finding financing is significantly easier, as the studio will often foot all, or a significant part, of the production costs. Given the crucial role of the producer in the making of a movie, various ways of organizing that role seem to each have their features and drawbacks, with potential effects on, or of, the types of movies produced, the risks assumed by the various parties, as well as the financing of the movie projects. These interrelationships stand to benefit from further study.

Movie production can be considered akin to new product development in other types of organizations. Prior studies on new product development have mainly focused on manufacturing settings (e.g., Larson & Gobeli, 1988; Hertenstein & Platt, 2000). The motion picture industry, therefore, offers a unique opportunity for research into the organization and economics of new product development, with variance in this setting ranging from what could be called "in-house" versus "outsourced" (independent, networked) modes of product development. Specifically, unlike new product development in large hierarchies like pharmaceutical firms, which consist of relatively stable new product development units, movies today are typically made by temporary organizational configurations purposely set up for developing a specific movie, which are largely disbanded upon completion of the project (Baker & Faulkner, 1991). As mentioned above, such "single-project organizations" operate largely by means of freelance contracting, which is different from the relative stability of hierarchical arrangements found in many other new product development settings (Christopherson & Storper, 1989).

The flexible approach to new product development in the motion picture industry, as well as its features, drawbacks and effectiveness, is relatively under-studied. A related question is whether financing of movies affects new product development. In the motion picture industry, creative talent and financiers are worlds apart (Caves, 2000). Movie producers essentially have the choice between using studio funds (and giving up control) or obtaining independent financing (and retaining control). Consistent with arguments in the literature on investor control, Fee (2002) finds that independent motion picture financing is more common when a filmmaker's private artistic stake in the movie is high and also for movies requiring a high level of creative effort. However, it is not clear how co-financing of a movie by several studios, which is increasingly prevalent, might affect creative control.

2.1.10. Intermediaries

Related to the choices involved in the organization of the production process, there are multiple levels of contracting issues in the creative industries. While simple agency models deal with a single principal and agent, talent in the motion picture industry often has to deal with numerous intermediaries who help them manage their careers, including managers, agents and publicists. Many intermediaries are independent or work in small firms, but others are employed by large companies such as the Creative Artists Agency or the William Morris Agency. Intermediaries match properties and talent with producers. Producers turn to agents to obtain material to be developed into movies and to identify and hire talent for production. Some intermediaries are as recognizable as the stars they represent. Who they choose to represent, and how they represent them, provides yet another interesting set of contracting issues.

Briefly:

- *Managers* play the role of chief operating officer in managing an individual. They advise their clients on every aspect of their career, such as who to sign with and what projects to accept. They also coordinate the activities of their clients' agents, publicists and attorneys.
- *Agents*' jobs involve discovering talent, matching talent to each other and locating employment opportunities.
- *Publicists* find opportunities for their clients to make personal appearances, engage in interviews and promote themselves.
- *Attorneys* represent their clients' interests by protecting their intellectual property, overseeing contracts and litigating disputes.

At the professional level in the motion picture industry, it is almost impossible for talent to succeed without a team of intermediaries working on their behalf. But stories abound in Hollywood about how the contractual process among these parties can break down, even though having the right representation is crucial for success. Since managers, agents and publicists work as a team, research on how they manage their clients' careers, as well as the myriad of contractual issues it involves, would be most intriguing.

2.2. Marketing and Distribution

Figure 3 shows the network surrounding movie marketing and distribution. As discussed above, the major movie studios serve either as both financier and distributor of movies produced by producers employed by or affiliated with them (in-house production/distribution), whereas they serve as distributors only for movies produced by independent producers. Distributors then contract with exhibitors (movie theatres) for theatrical exhibition, as well as retailers for DVD/video distribution and other retailers/broadcasters for distribution via other formats, such as satellite, pay and cable television, but also more recently, Internet distribution (web video). When a producer signs a contract with a distributor, the producer commonly yields all the distribution rights to the distributor, domestically and internationally, initial and ancillary (such as merchandising). Because marketing is done by the distributors, we discuss distribution first, including the relationship between producers and distributors, and then marketing.

2.2.1. Distribution

There are essentially four types of producer–distributor agreements when the movie is not in-house. In a production–financing/distribution agreement, the studio/distributor provides production and distribution funds to an independent producer with a fairly complete package including property acquisition and movie production, as well as a distribution arrangement that is entered into prior to the start of production.

In a negative pickup deal, the distributor makes a contractual commitment to distribute the movie if the movie meets certain pre-specified criteria. The producer then uses the contractual commitment to secure production financing from a third party lender or financier. In this arrangement, the distributor only provides distribution funds and the producer relies on the agreed share of movie revenues/profits to service the loan and earn a profit. A negative pickup deal is entered into prior to the start of the production of the movie.

An acquisition deal is similar to a negative pickup, except that the distribution deal is entered into after the movie is produced, and thus the independent producer needs to secure funding to acquire property rights, develop the screenplay and produce the movie without the commitment from a distributor.

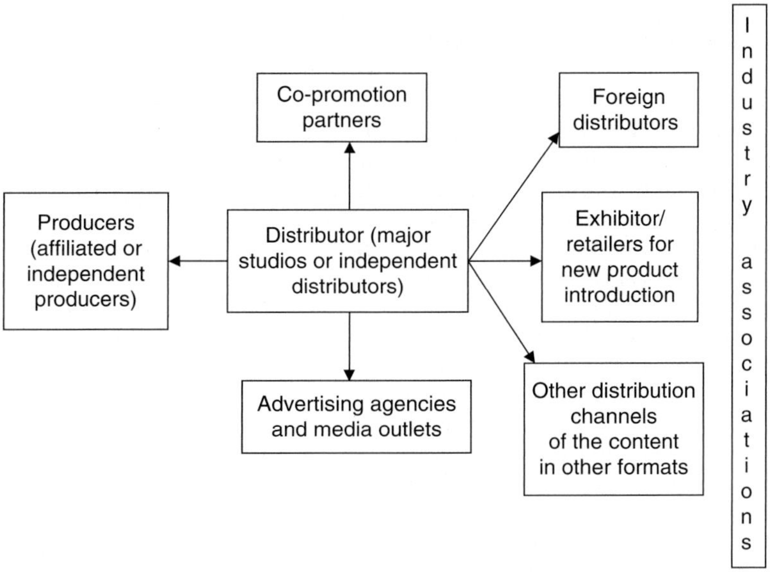

Figure 3. Network surrounding marketing/distribution and movie exhibition.

Finally, in a rent-a-distributor deal, an independent producer secures funds not only to produce the movie, but also most, if not all, of the funds to distribute it. Because the producer essentially takes on all the risks and only "rents" a distributor who does not provide any funding, the share of revenues/profits that the distributor can claim is generally at its lowest. Obviously, the rent-a-distributor deal is entered into only after the movie is produced.

The parameters of any deal between producers and distributors exhibit great variation and have evolved considerably over time. Perhaps the most important element of these deals is the specific revenue/profit sharing agreement, and there are many possible arrangements, ranging from gross to net deals and many variations of sharing for each.

In gross deals, the producer receives a share of all revenues. In first dollar gross splits, for example, the producer gets a percentage of the movie's gross revenues without any advance. Such deals impose a high level of risk on the producer, unless the movie is successful of course, in which case the deal can have a high payoff for the producer. In net deals, the distributor recoups distribution costs and sometimes other agreed amounts or fees first (such as a multiple of an advance to the producer) before splitting the remainder with the producer. Such arrangements spread the downside risk between the producer and distributor, although not necessarily equally, depending on the split and the amount of the advance. Further variations involve sliding scales, where the revenue sharing is staggered, with a different share on the first, second and so forth, slice of the revenues, and a constant share thereafter.

The specific deals brokered between producers and distributors depend on their business relationship, negotiation skills and risk preferences. For instance, in acquisition deals where the distributor acquires the right to distribute the movie only after the movie has been completed, the producer assumes all of the risk before the distributor becomes involved, which should be reflected in a revenue/profit sharing scheme that favours the producer, although that is not always so, depending on both parties' assessment of the success of the movie and, among other things, their bargaining power. Studying and understanding these agreements and their specific features represents a fertile ground for further research in the contracting, incentives or other literatures.

2.2.2. Marketing

Before a movie is released, distributors spend millions of dollars on marketing it, with marketing costs skyrocketing over the years. In 1975, the average cost of marketing a movie was \$2 million, but the movie *Jaws* changed these dynamics. The average marketing cost was \$20 million in 1996 and \$34.5 million in 2006. The vast majority of movies are marketed and distributed by a major studio's distribution arm or by speciality distributors within conglomerates. Very few movies are distributed by completely independent distributors. Studios need a regular supply of movies to fuel their domestic and international distribution operations and earn distribution fees. Distributors are responsible for the design and implementation of the marketing campaigns for the channels and territories for which they own the distribution rights.

Marketing research starts at the early stages of the development of a movie. Movie screenings, telephone surveys and trailer tests all play a role in assessing the reaction of targeted audiences which, in turn, influences and directs the positioning of the overall marketing campaign (Austin, 1989; Eliashberg et al., 2000). Nielsen NRG is a company that specializes in screening tests. The company recruits potential audiences, shows them the movies, asks them to complete questionnaires, and holds focus group discussions on the movie's weaknesses and strengths. As discussed above, several rounds of screening test results provide useful information for editing the movie and designing advertising campaigns before the movie is released. In addition to traditional marketing channels, such as in theatres, print ads and television, the Internet has also recently played an increasingly significant role in providing information about, or doing marketing for, movies, such as through streaming video of upcoming movies.

In the case of large blockbuster releases such as *Independence Day*, there is an attempt to turn the initial launch of the movie into a major event. Studio distributors spend large amounts on promoting their movies, for example on premiere events, recognizing that such efforts can substantially boost revenues. Disney spent $2 million on a lavish premiere event to promote *Pirates of the Caribbean: Curse of the Black Pearl*. The premiere was held at Disneyland and the park was closed down to the general public in the early evening for the first time since it opened in 1955. Disney received huge press coverage of this event and *Pirates* went on to gross $653 million in worldwide box office and $320 million in domestic DVD/video sales and rentals (www.the-numbers.com).

Although marketing costs have increased proportionally faster than production costs (MPAA, 2007), it is not well understood how marketing affects a movie's success (Eliashberg, Elberse & Leenders, 2006), as there are numerous examples of both blockbusters and flops. And how are marketing and production costs related? Do high production costs by themselves signal high movie quality? And, in reverse, can a studio salvage a poor movie with additional marketing? The endogeneity, as it were, between both types of cost incurrence by studios is little understood and researched.

2.3. Exhibition

Theatrical release is the most important stage in the lifecycle of a movie, given its impact on all other ancillary markets, which we discuss separately in Section 3. Nevertheless, global box office revenues (domestic and international) typically account for only about 20% of the total revenues for a movie over its entire lifecycle. Hollywood movies still dominate the theatres and are released internationally anywhere from within a couple of days to as long as six months following domestic release in the US. US studios control three-quarters of the distribution market outside the US and, in dollar terms, moviegoers in the US still account for about 44% of global box office. Geoff King (2002, p. 73) notes the following:

> Release in the cinema remains the biggest stage on which to display Hollywood's wares. It is the most prestigious part of the lifecycle of Hollywood entertainment (which) translates into the greatest levels of success further down the chain. This is why so much is often invested in initial advertising and promotional campaigns that can act as loss leaders. Their costs can be a sound investment in the longer term value of the product ... Big hits at the box office are usually the titles that fill the walls in video rental and retail outlets and earn the biggest fees for release to cable, satellite and terrestrial television.

Little is known, however, about the lifecycle of movies, either in each of its release formats ("windows") or across them, and thus, across a movie's entire life from cradle to grave. One can imagine many shapes. Some movies peak early and decay quickly, whereas others might never peak but still exhibit relatively stable "staying power" over a prolonged period. More importantly, perhaps, especially for industry participants: what are the determinants of a movie's lifecycle and/or its various shapes and what can be done to affect them? A study of the various lifetime shapes of movies, such as the one Bradlow & Fader (2001) did for *Billboard* songs, would be insightful.

Regarding a movie's theatrical life, the current business environment is tough for studios (distributors) and theatres (exhibitors). Industry observers note that box office revenues face increasing competition from television and the Internet. Tom Sherak, former head of marketing at Fox Studio, had the following comment on the theatrical release of movies (Shone, 2004, p. 238):

> The motion picture business has the shortest shelf life of any marketable product. You can spend $100 million to make a movie. You can spend another $35 million to market it, and you can be off the screen in seven to fourteen days.

With reference to the above, this suggests that many movies peak early (or do not peak at all), but decay quickly in their theatrical life.

Today, five major theatre chains control most of the movie exhibition market in the US. Independent theatres distinguish themselves by offering less publicized, independent and foreign movies. Besides sharing box office receipts with distributors, theatres also obtain revenues from concessions (i.e., sales of popcorn, sweets and drinks in the theatre), which account for roughly 35% of the revenues of theatre chains. Ironically, the high costs of concessions have caused many consumers to complain. While theatre revenues seem to be increasing, the actual number of people attending has decreased markedly. The high revenues have come about simply because ticket prices have gone up.

2.3.1. Distributor–Exhibitor Contracts

A distributor leases or licenses a movie for exhibition in theatres through direct negotiation or a bidding process. A bidding process involves a bid request from the distributor and bids from interested exhibitors. Movies are to be booked movie-by-movie, theatre-by-theatre (or by theatre chain). Thus, a licensing agreement is required for each theatre (chain). Once a bid is accepted or negotiations are completed, a distributor/exhibitor agreement is drawn up which includes the period of time that the movie will play at the theatre, advertising arrangements and how box office receipts are to be split between both parties.

The most common box office split between the distributor and exhibitor, or "rental," is 90:10, with 90% (10%) of the box office revenues for the distributor (exhibitor) for the first week, after the agreed-upon amount to cover exhibitor expenses (which is also called the "house nut"). The split ratio then typically slides down over several weeks to, say, 35:65. This creates an incentive for the exhibitor to stay with the distributor's movie and serves to keep the competition out. Current distributor–exhibitor deals often also include a minimum payment (floor) for the distributor. Just as with producer–distributor agreements, distributor–exhibitor agreements show great variation, offering a compelling research setting for studying risk and profit sharing and associated economic incentives for, and responses from, the parties involved.

Several studies, particularly in the marketing literature, have attempted to develop models to help exhibitors perform their "screens management" (e.g., Sawhney & Eliashberg, 1996; Swami, Eliashberg & Weinberg, 1999), which is viewed as a problem akin to allocating shelf space for retailers. In this regard, Swami et al. (1999, p. 352) make the following pertinent statement:

> Managing the allocation of shelf space for new products is a problem of significant importance for retailers. The problem is particularly complex for exhibitors—the retailers in the motion picture supply chain—because they face dynamic challenges, given the short lifecycles of movies, the changing demand over time, the scarcity of shelf space and the complex revenue sharing contract between the exhibitor and the distributor.

However, the extent to which such screens management models have been adopted in practice by exhibitors to replace or complement rules of thumb remains an open issue.

2.3.2. Theatrical Release

There is an obsession in Hollywood with opening box office performance. It is not uncommon for a major motion picture to open on over 3000 screens to try and recoup the large amounts invested in production, marketing and promotion. During the opening weekend, successful movies can take in between 25% and 40% of their total gross. *The Hulk* set a record with a 70% decline in ticket sales between its opening and second weekend, although the normal drop is typically around 50%. The first weekend for a "blockbuster" movie is a make-or-break proposition. A movie that fails to open strongly loses the attention of the media, audiences and exhibitors. It is therefore perhaps not surprising that most industry and academic research to date in the motion picture industry has been concerned with analyzing movie success at the box office, particularly opening box office performance (Hayes & Bing, 2004).

Given the importance of the opening box office, careful timing of the opening is critical. Decisions on when and where to release a movie are made by the distributor and are influenced by various factors, including the release dates of other competing movies and the time of year. Ideally, a movie is released on a weekend when there is no other movie competing for the same target audience. But, with so many movies released, this is difficult to accomplish. Releases also tend to be timed in particular periods, such as on holiday weekends or the Christmas season. Most research on the effects of the timing of release has focused on the role of competition and seasonality in the US market (Einav, 2003a,b; Chisholm, 2000; Krider & Weinberg, 1998).

In addition to domestic releases and their timing, the US entertainment industry's international presence is extensive. American movies typically account for the majority of box office receipts in Western Europe and Japan. Foreign demand is typically strong for the big-budget movies that are a staple of the US motion picture industry, for which the scope of a worldwide audience is also needed to support the large production, marketing and distribution budgets. Foreign box office receipts exceeded domestic box office receipts for US movies for the first time in 1993. Today, 60% of box office receipts for US movies stem from overseas for most box office hits. The foreign box office can sometimes save domestic flops. For example, *Troy*, which was considered a failure in the US, still went on to gross just under $500 million, 73% of which came from overseas.

3. Downstream Revenues

Theatrical distribution is just the first of many revenue streams, including revenues from television rights, video sales and rentals and merchandising. Blockbuster movies today aspire to be "tent-pole franchises;" that is, centrepieces for multiple spin-off products, from lunchboxes to soundtracks, comic and children's books and computer games. *Batman* earned three times as much from merchandise as it did from ticket sales. Blockbuster movies today are commercials—commercials for themselves. They also include commercials, in the form of product placement. *Tomorrow Never Dies*, the Bond movie, is a good example of such product placement, with screen time sold to Visa, Avis, BMW, Smirnoff, Heineken, Omega, Ericsson and L'Oréal.

3.1. Video

The home video market is the booming business. Consumer spending on videos and DVDs, videos for short, in 2006 was approximately $24 billion in the US, while movie ticket sales were $9.5 billion (Standard & Poor's, 2007). Videos used to be sold in two pricing tiers: a higher price to rental stores and a lower price to retail stores, to encourage purchase. The lower price was known as the "sell-through price." In the early days of home video, most movies were initially priced for rental, with a rerelease at sell-through price approximately six months to one year after the initial release. This release pattern was the norm throughout the 1980s and most of the 1990s. In the late-1990s, however, rental stores and distributors started signing revenue-sharing deals. For rental stores, revenue-sharing reduces upfront costs, allowing them to order more copies of new releases, in effect guaranteeing that every customer can get any movie at any time. This is important as consumer demand for video rentals historically peaks in the first three weeks of availability and then drops off precipitously. Distributors also benefit from revenue sharing, particularly on successful titles, considering that the marginal cost of reproduction of videos, and even more so for DVDs, is low.

The success of DVDs, however, changed the dynamics of the home viewing market again. DVDs were initially priced between $15 and $30, much lower than the $65 for video cassettes to be bought by rental stores. Since the video rental stores' upfront cost was much lower for DVDs than for video cassettes, rental stores no longer had an incentive to share the rental revenues with distributors. As a matter of fact, video rental stores now threaten not to renew revenue-sharing contracts with the distributors. At lower prices, consumers also are more inclined to purchase their own DVD, either outright, after viewing it in theatres or after renting the DVD first.

The DVD market provides the movie industry with a large new source of revenues at minimum cost, which has also led them to exploit their movie libraries more than ever before. The studios have been investing heavily in upgrading their movie libraries. For example, Sony's acquisition of MGM was fuelled in part by MGM's movie library of 4000 titles.

One of the biggest emerging markets is for the made-for-video and new-to-video categories. Made-for-video movies are those, typically with low budgets, that studios believe might garner sizable revenues on video. Some of these movies are ones that were initially set to have a theatrical release, but the studios changed their mind. New-to-video movies are those that currently exist in a studio's library, but have never been released on video.

Video has a protected window of six weeks to six months, meaning that the only place consumers can rent or buy the movie is on DVD or video. However, with pay-per-view becoming more popular, and video-on-demand a reality, some in the home video industry have argued that their window of exclusivity is too short for stores to have enough time to turn a profit.

Another issue in the video area relates to talent contracts. In the early days of home video, distributors wanted to avoid having to account for manufacturing and marketing costs when they calculated net profit for profit-participating talent. Thus, they developed a royalty structure where the distributor only considered a contractual percentage of gross home video sales as gross revenues when reporting to profit participants. The initial royalty rate set by the distributor for titles priced for the rental market was 20% of gross sales, leaving the distributor with 80% of gross sales to cover their costs and earn a profit. In the sell-through market, distributors adopted a lower royalty rate, typically 10%, because the costs of releasing home video titles to the sell-through markets were higher than to the rental market. As the distributors became more efficient and lowered their costs, their profits increased dramatically. These profits were not shared with the profit participants. As such, worldwide home video represents the widest difference between the studio's profit and the amount reported for sharing with talent in the movie. Now participants are asking a higher royalty rate. An interesting question in the video market, as well as in other profit-sharing contexts in this industry, is how to determine the contractually-agreed basis for profit sharing. Management accountants know that "true" costs can never be determined with pinpoint accuracy, but in a profit-sharing context such inaccuracies are perhaps even more contentious.

3.2. Pay-Per-View/Video-On-Demand

When the exclusive home video window closes, movies are then made available on pay-per-view or video-on-demand venues, on both cable and satellite television systems. Pay-per-view/video-on-demand is a brief window, starting eight months after theatrical release and extending for two months. (Note that the movie will always be available on video after its initial availability, so subsequent discussions of exclusivity do not include the home video window.) Typically, distributors' license pay-per-view rights to a third party, such as Viewer's Choice, which bills and collects money from the customer. For example, a customer requesting a specific movie via pay-per-view/video-on-demand at a specific time is charged a certain amount which is then split, say, 10% to Viewer's Choice, 45% to the cable operator and 45% to the studio.

3.3. Television

After the exclusive pay-per-view window expires, movies can then be shown on premium cable channels, such as HBO, Showtime or Starz. The movie is shown concurrently on both the premium cable channels and pay-per-view for approximately six weeks. Then the pay-per-view window closes, leaving an exclusive window for the premium cable channels that lasts for approximately 18 months. HBO, Showtime and Starz each have exclusive deals with the individual studios in which they agree to pay the studio for all of the movies it produces in a given year. The amount that the premium channel pays per movie is based on domestic box office revenues, and can go as high as $20–25 million for a blockbuster.

After premium (pay) television, the movie appears on network (free) television for one or two runs; this interval lasts for 12–18 months. Top-rated cable channels (USA Network, TBS, TNT) have been able to outbid traditional networks (ABC, CBS, NBC) to obtain rights to broadcast movies. For a very popular movie, the cable or network channel may even buy future runs at 5 or 10-year intervals. The network/cable channels negotiate with the studio for each movie, resulting in a fixed payment per movie ranging from $3–15 million, depending on the movie and the number of runs.

Following the broadcast premiere and second run, the movie then goes into syndication, again either on cable or network television, or both. This can continue for five years. Movies are licensed to the highest bidder on a title-by-title basis. Studios can exhibit the movies for as long as they own the copyright or the right to distribute the movie.

3.4. Merchandising

Movie studios treat their high-profile blockbusters as brands. They seek to leverage these brands to sell other products by licensing the use of the name and likeness of the movie and various characters to consumer product companies. The selection of a movie to be branded stems from its inherent popular qualities (*Shrek*, for example). Planning of merchandising deals with licensees can begin more than a year before theatrical release. Separate merchandise licenses are drawn up with companies specializing in apparel, video games, gifts, sporting goods, toys and so forth. Under these deals, upfront advances are paid to the studio, with royalties that might range from 2–3% for foodstuffs and 8–10% for apparel and toys. A related form of merchandising stems from co-promotion with fast food chains and beverage companies. For a specific event movie, such co-promoting companies can spend millions of dollars to advertise and cross-promote their products, timed with the release of the movie. From the studio perspective, such promotion campaigns can generate media awareness worth $30 to $40 million of advertising.

3.5. Web Video

Digital technology, which transmits sound and images as a series of electronic on-off signals, generally provides higher quality audio and video than older media. As audio and video recordings rely more heavily on digital technology, the personal computer has begun to loom larger in the entertainment sector. According to Standard & Poor's (2007), digital applications will remain a major driver of industry growth. It is expected that the personal computer and all of its offshoots, alongside new technology that combines computer capabilities with those of television and video, will be increasingly used to access, store and even create entertainment programming.

The web video market can be divided into two categories, based on the source of web videos. One type of web video is simply copyrighted video content posted on the web (with or without permission of the owners, which is another key issue). Another type of web video is self-made.

For copyrighted video, web video is just another distribution channel. Internet downloads currently represent a relatively small revenue source for the studios, but because electronic catalogues can house many more titles than store shelves, the Internet is expected to boost the number of titles readily available to consumers. Digital downloading via the Internet also reduces distribution costs for studios and so it is expected that the industry will see continued growth in paid Internet-based distribution of movie content. Growth in this channel is also expected to be facilitated by legal and technological restraints placed on unauthorized distribution; by growing ownership of home computing and all of its offshoots; and by access to fast broadband, high-speed Internet access services. A big unknown, however, is the extent to which distribution in non-theatrical windows, such as through the Internet and mobile phones, will substitute or complement theatrical distribution.

An interesting issue, therefore, is to examine the interdependence of revenues that studios derive from these various channels.

For self-made web video, the business model is completely different. Self-made web video is similar to network TV except that producers of web videos are often not compensated by money directly, but by affiliation. That is, distributors of self-made web videos typically claim no right to the video except that they can tag advertisements to it. This emerging phenomenon has been evolving rapidly and is currently not well understood.

Overall, interesting research questions about downstream revenues are, first, the extent to which theatrical and non-theatrical windows substitute or complement one another; that is, do they negatively or positively affect each other's revenue potentials? For example, does the availability of DVDs deter people from going to the theatre? Does the prospect of being able to see a movie on pay cable, network or syndication television deter people from renting or buying the DVD? How is owning and renting of content potentially affected by the same content being readily available online? And do the answers to the above questions differ across segments of consumers and/or across types of movies? Secondly, and from a management accounting perspective more specifically, what windowing strategies maximize studios' revenues and/or profits and what are the reasonable lifecycle revenues over the various and long-winded windows that studios should take into account when making movie production decisions? Lastly, and perhaps most fundamentally for the motion picture industry business model, what revenue windows will remain or become viable, and how and to what extent can studios best tap into or develop them?

4. Conclusions and Discussion

A distinctive feature of the creative industries is the interplay among the various parties and the complexities of the contracting process, which often takes place long before the production of the movie (Caves, 2000). It is the management and organization of the creative industries that determines how to negotiate and secure the artistic product that they then will present, market and sell to the public. In the first instance—the relationship between the creative industries and the individual artist(s)—management and organization deal primarily with rights, royalties, agents, contracts and commissions. There have been quite a few high-profile legal cases involving profit-sharing plans between distributors and the talent side of the business (Weinstein, 1998). After deducting production, distribution, advertising and other costs, including studio "overheads," any profits (if any remaining) are then divided accordingly. Given these characteristics of the industry, we believe that studies of various kinds of contracts in the movie industry constitute a promising area for management accounting researchers, particularly given our comparative advantage in costing and cost allocation methodologies. There is obviously an intricate link with research on incentives that has also become prominent in the accounting literature.

In the second instance—between the creative industries and the audience/consumer—the focus shifts to production and production costs, marketing and promotional plans, audience-building and fundraising, and consumer testing and polling. Here, too, management accounting researchers have insights to offer, such as with respect to budgeting, lifecycle costing, customer or channel profitability, and pricing methodologies and strategies.

Overall, we hope we were able to make the case that the motion picture industry provides fertile ground for research in management accounting. Because this industry is very complex and has as yet been little studied in management accounting, there should be ample room for a variety of research methods, including field research, large-sample empirical testing (for which publicly-available data are often present), as well as the development of conceptual models to systematize observed contracting and other behaviours that are common in this industry and that can be generalized to other settings. Whereas it is impossible to provide an exhaustive set of (management accounting) research opportunities in this industry setting, we hope that we have piqued the interest of researchers with diverse backgrounds and expertise in various management accounting areas (such as in cost accounting, budgeting, capital budgeting, performance measurement and incentives) and various theoretical perspectives to generate their own ideas about the many potential researchable questions in this particular industry. Although we focused on the motion picture industry in this chapter, several other industries, particularly those in the information goods sector, such as publishing, music, games and the arts, share commonalities (Werbach, 2000). And even though the motion picture industry certainly is not the only relatively unexplored sector in the management accounting literature, it is an important one given its size (sales and employment) and worldwide economic and cultural impact.

References

Austin, B. A. (1989). *Immediate Seating: A Look at Movie Audiences*. Belmont, CA: Wadsworth.

Baker, W. E. & Faulkner, R. R. (1991). Role as resource in the Hollywood film industry. *American Journal of Sociology*, **97**(2), 279–309.

Bradlow, E. T. & Fader, P. S. (2001). A Bayesian lifetime model for the "Hot 100" Billboard songs. *Journal of the American Statistical Association*, **96**(454), 368–381.

Bureau of Economic Analysis (2005). US international services: cross-border trade in 2004 and sales through affiliates in 2003. *Survey of Current Business*, **85**(10), 25–110.

Caves, R. (2000). *Creative Industries: Contracts between Art and Commerce*. Cambridge, MA: Harvard University Press.

Chisholm, D. (1997). Profit sharing versus fixed-payment contracts: evidence from the motion pictures industry. *Journal of Law, Economics and Organization*, **13**, 169–201.

Chisholm, D. (2000). The war of attrition and optimal timing of motion-picture releases. Working Paper. Lehigh University.

Christopherson, S. & Storper, M. (1989). The effects of flexible specialization on industrial politics and the labor market: The motion picture industry. *Industrial and Labor Relations Review*, **42**, 331–347.

Corts, K. S. (2001). The strategic effects of vertical market structure: Common agency and divisionalization in the U.S. motion picture industry. *Journal of Economics & Management*, **10**(4), 509–528.

De Vany, A. & Walls, W. (1999). Uncertainty in the movies: does star power reduce the terror of the box office? *Journal of Cultural Economics*, **23**, 285–318.

Eccles, R. G. & Crane, D. B. (1988). *Doing Deals: Investment Banks at Work*. Boston, MA: Harvard Business School Press.

Einav, L. (2003a). Gross seasonality and underlying seasonality: evidence from the U.S. motion picture industry. SIEPR Discussion Paper No. 02–36.

Einav, L. (2003b). Not all rivals look alike: estimating an equilibrium model of the release date timing game. Working Paper. Stanford University.

Eliashberg, J., Elberse, A. & Leenders, M. (2006). The motion picture industry: critical issues in practice, current research, and new research directions. *Marketing Science*, **25**(6), 638–661.

Eliashberg, J., Jonker, J., Sawhney, M. & Wierenga, B. (2000). MOVIEMOD: An implementable decision-support system for pre-release market evaluation of motion pictures. *Marketing Science*, **19**(3), 226–243.

Eliashberg, J. & Sawhney, M. (1994). Modeling goes Hollywood: Predicting individual differences in movie enjoyment. *Marketing Science*, **40**(9), 1151–1173.

Fee, C. E. (2002). The costs of outside equity control: evidence from motion picture financing decisions. *Journal of Business*, **75**(4), 687–711.

Goettler, R. & Leslie, P. (2004). Co-financing to manage risk in the motion picture industry. Working paper. Carnegie Mellon University.

Gong, J., Van der Stede, W. & Young, S. M. (2007). Product life-cycle costs and revenues of experience goods: the case of motion pictures. Working paper. University of Southern California.

Graser, M. (2007). How to make box-office gold: Survey says original scripts are key. *Variety Weekly*, **July 9**, 2007.

Hayes, D. & Bing, J. (2004). *Open Wide: How Hollywood Box Office Became a National Obsession*. New York, NY: Hyperion.

Hertenstein, J. H. & Platt, M. B. (2000). Performance measures and management control in new product development. *Accounting Horizons*, **14**(3), 303–323.

King, G. (2002). *New Hollywood Cinema: An Introduction*. New York, NY: Columbia University Press.

Krider, R. E. & Weinberg, C. B. (1998). Competitive dynamics and the introduction of new products: the motion picture timing game. *Journal of Marketing Research*, **35**(1), 1–15.

Larson, E. W. & Gobeli, D. H. (1988). Organizing for product development projects. *Journal of Product Innovation Management*, **5**, 180–190.

Lehmann, D. R. & Weinberg, C. B. (2000). Sales via sequential distribution channels: an application to movie audiences. *Journal of Marketing*, **64**(1), 13–33.

Marr, M. (2007). DreamWorks reboots for life beyond "Shrek". *Wall Street Journal*, **January 23**, B1.

Motion Picture Association of America. (2007). *U.S. Entertainment Industry: 2006 MPAA Market Statistics*. www.mpaa.org.

Neale, B. & Allerston, A. (2005). Financial control in the movie production and broadcasting sector. *CIMA Research Bulletin*.

Neelameghan, R. & Chintagunta, P. (1999). A Bayesian model to forecast new product performance in domestic and international markets. *Marketing Science*, **18**(2), 115–136.

Porter, M. (1980). *Competitive Strategy*. New York, NY: The Free Press.

Porter, M. (1985). *Competitive Advantage*. New York, NY: The Free Press.

Ravid, S. A. (1999). Information, blockbuster, and stars: a study of the movie industry. *Journal of Business*, **72**, 463–492.

Ravid, S. A. & Basuroy, S. (2004). Managerial objectives, the R-rating puzzle, and the production of violent movies. *Journal of Business*, **77**, 155–192.

Rumelt, R. P. (1974). *Strategy, Structure and Economic Performance*. Boston, MA: Harvard Business School Press.

Sawhney, M. S. & Eliashberg, J. (1996). A parsimonious model for forecasting gross box-office revenues of motion pictures. *Marketing Science*, **15**(2), 113–131.

Scott, A. J. (2002). A new map of Hollywood: the production and distribution of American motion pictures. *Regional Studies*, **36**(9), 957–975.

Shapiro, C. & Varian, H. (1999). *Information Rules*. Boston, MA: Harvard Business School Press.

Shone, T. (2004). *Blockbuster: How Hollywood Learned to Stop Worrying and Love the Summer*. New York, NY: Free Press.

Squire, J. E. (1992). *The Movie Business Book*. New York, NY: Simon & Shuster.

Standard & Poor's. (2007). *S&P Industry Surveys: Movies & Home Entertainment*, **March**.

Swami, S., Eliashberg, J. & Weinberg, C. (1999). SilverScreener: A modeling approach to movie screens management. *Marketing Science*, **18**(3), 352–372.

The Economist (1998). A brand new strategy: the industry used to produce movies, TV programs, books and music. Now it makes brands, **November 19**, S5–S8.

US Census Bureau. 2006. *Statistical Abstract of the United States*. www.census.gov/prod/www/statistical-abstract.html.

Ulmer, J. (2000). *James Ulmer's Hollywood Hot List*. New York, NY: St. Martin's Press.

Veronis Suhler Stevenson LLC. (2004). Veronis Suhler Stevenson Communications Industry Forecast Report.

Weinstein, M. (1998). Profit sharing contracts in Hollywood: evolution and analysis. *Journal of Legal Studies*, **27**, 67–112.

Werbach, K. (2000). Syndication: the emerging model for business in the Internet era. *Harvard Business Review*, **May–June**, 85–93.

Young, S. M. & Pinsky, D. (2006). Narcissism and celebrity. *Journal of Research in Personality*, **40**, 463–471.

Zuckerman, E., Kim, T., Ukanwa, K. & von Rittmann, J. (2003). Robust identities or nonentities? Typecasting in the feature-film labor market. *American Journal of Sociology*, **108**(5), 1018–1074.

Handbook of Management Accounting Research
Edited by Christopher S. Chapman, Anthony G. Hopwood and Michael D. Shields

Managerial Accounting in the Hospitality Industry

David A. Dittman[1], James W. Hesford[1] and Gordon Potter[1]

[1]*Cornell University, USA*

Abstract: In this chapter we review the scholarly literature on managerial accounting that is set in the hospitality industry. Despite the fact that the hospitality industry is one of the world's largest, there is very little research on its management accounting issues and practices. We conclude the chapter with a discussion of research opportunities focused on the hospitality industry.

1. Introduction and Overview

The objective of this chapter is to review managerial accounting research focused on the hospitality industry. In the first part of this chapter we lay the groundwork by defining what we mean by hospitality firms, provide summary statistics on the industry and outline the unique characteristics of these firms. We then provide information on management accounting practices in the industry. In the second part of this chapter we provide a review of the scholarly literature in managerial accounting that has been set in, or focused on, firms in the hospitality industries. We conclude with opportunities for future research.

1.1. Definition

The hospitality industry is defined here in accordance with the five industry segments of the International Council on Hotel, Restaurant, and Institutional Education (ICHRIE): lodging services; food services; recreation services; travel-related services; and convention and meeting services. Table 1 provides a listing of services within each segment.

1.2. Statistics

The hospitality industry, by many definitions, is one of the largest industries in the world. For example, in the US restaurant industry alone, annual revenues are estimated at more than $537 billion, with 12.8 million employees at 935 000 separate locations.[1] Standard & Poor's (2007) reports that dining out in restaurants comprises 49% of all US expenditures for food and that the industry is the largest private sector employer. Similarly, US statistics for the lodging industry show revenues of $122.7 billion, with employment of 1.4 million at 47 590 properties (American Hotel & Lodging Association, 2006). Finally, the US commercial airline industry employs more than 500 000 with revenues topping $141 billion. Combined, these three segments alone account for more than $800 billion in revenues and the employment of 14.7 million persons. These figures represent 5.8% of US 2007 Gross Domestic Product (Bureau of Economic Analysis, 2008) and 10.1% of the US civilian labour force (Bureau of Labor Statistics, 2008). The hospitality industry is also a diverse industry in terms of its employment. According to data by the ICHRIE (2006), there are more minority managers in the restaurant industry than in any other, 24.6% of businesses in the lodging- and food-services segments are owned by women, and 26.4% are owned by minorities other than women. On a global scale, the World Tourism Organization estimates that 3% of the total global workforce is directly employed in the hospitality industry and, if indirect jobs are considered, the figure rises to 8%. While most segments of the industry are mature and the technology is stable, ICHRIE reports significant growth in segments like gaming, senior-living care and adventure travel. Given the size and diversity of organizations in the hospitality segment, it is not surprising that we see a multitude of organizational forms. We discuss this in the next section.

1.3. Characteristics

Given the broad variety of firms that comprise the hospitality industry (see Table 1) it is not surprising that we find the full range of manufacturing, service and retail

[1]*Source*: National Restaurant Association website. Retrieved 10/22/07.

DOI: 10.1016/S1751-3243(07)03008-8

Table 1. Types of firms within the ICHRIE hospitality industry segments

Lodging services	Food services	Recreation services	Travel-related services	Convention and meeting services
• Luxury hotels • Convention hotels	• Quick-service • Family-style	• Theme parks • Marinas	• Airlines • Cruise lines	• Meeting planning • Convention centers
• All-suite hotels	• Specialty and fine dining	• Sports management	• Railroads	• Event planning
• Mid-scale hotels	• Private clubs	• Clubs (golf, etc.)	• Tour operators	• Tradeshow planning
• Budget hotels	• Banquet operations	• Campgrounds	• Travel agencies	
• Motels • Resorts • Inns • Conference centres	• Coffee shops • Pubs • Delis • Gourmet shops	• Parks • Casinos	• Tourism marketing • Wholesalers	
• Timeshares • Bed and breakfast sites • Senior-living centers • Spas	• Nightclubs • Catering companies • Food service operations*			

*Food service operations can be in companies, universities, hospitals, etc.

operations. In the lodging industry, for example, the provision of a room constitutes a pure service. A restaurant, on the other hand, is a pure manufacturer. A restaurant operates no differently than a manufacturer like General Motors (GM), the only dissimilarity being the just-in-time delivery of its outputs. A pub or bar, for example, operates as a retailer, buying stocks of liquor that are kept in stock until sold. Although there may be some mixing of drinks, it is still largely a retail operation. The only real difference with that of a clothing retailer is that the product is consumed on the premises. Finally, large hotels such as Caesar's Palace in Las Vegas illustrate the mixed example; they have, among other outputs, rooms, entertainment and gambling (pure services), restaurants (manufacturing) and shops and bars (retail) all under one roof.

The hospitality industry is both labour- and capital-intensive and operates with severe short-term capacity constraints. For example, a hotel company invests large sums of money in real estate holdings, furnishings and capital equipment. These costs are fixed over relatively long periods of time. A large firm such as Marriott or Accor will have hundreds or thousands of locations, operating on a global scale. Compare this to a very large industrial firm such as GM. While GMs investment in equipment is probably higher, it has far fewer locations (dozens or perhaps several hundred at most) and its building and land investments are chosen for their low-cost and low-tax attributes.[2] Looking at the capacity problem, a hotel once built is usually quite restricted in its ability to expand. A 40-storey hotel in New York City is not quickly, easily or cheaply expanded, as construction would probably involve adding floors on top of an existing high rise. Once again, comparing this to GM, a temporary increase in business can probably be accommodated by outsourcing some production or adding additional shifts for workers (e.g., nights and/or weekends). Permanent increases can be met by expanding physical plants (horizontally) in one of many large rural sites. Since GM has dozens of such sites, they have the added benefit of choosing to expand at a site offering the lowest overall cost and/or quickest speed. An expanded hotel in an urban setting often involves demolition and reconstruction, or relocating the property.

[2]While we specifically mention hotels, airlines and restaurants exhibit similar characteristics. The principal difference with the latter two is less frequent ownership of the real estate at each operations site.

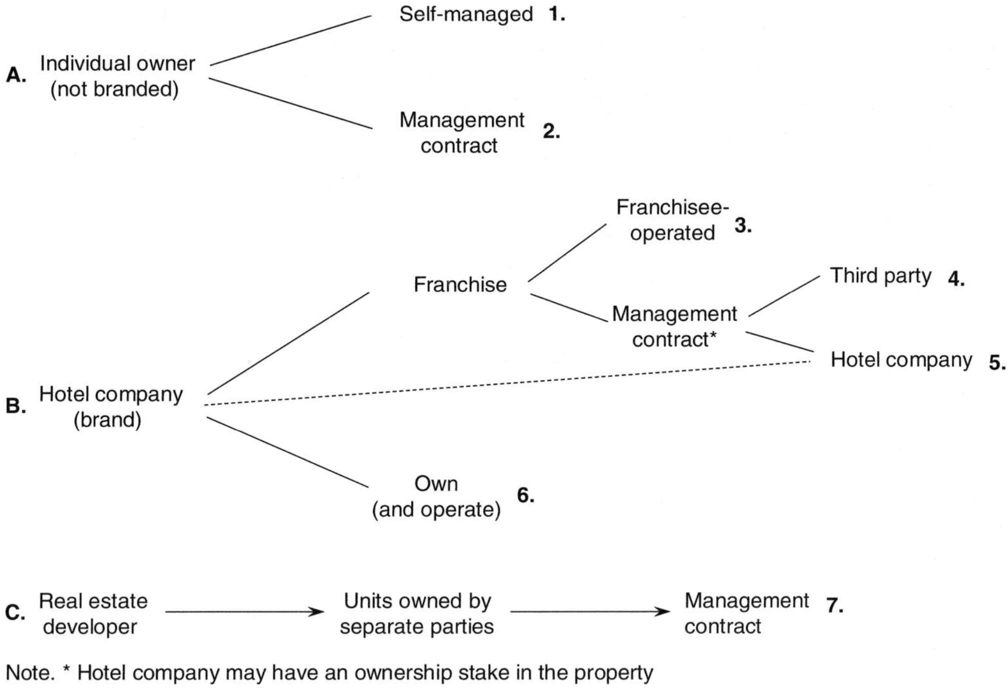

Figure 1. Organizational forms of hotels.

The hospitality industry is also characterized by a high volatility in demand. Like most businesses, there is variation with changes in the overall business climate. For example, a business hotel will see a decrease in occupancy during weak times, but may regularly sell out its rooms in a strong economy. But, unlike manufacturing firms, the perishability of outputs (e.g., rooms, meals, airline seats) means that revenue opportunities are lost forever if the product goes unsold. Combined with high fixed costs, these characteristics give rise to frequent, significant price wars. Additional fluctuation in business occurs across seasons, days of the week and within days. For example, a business hotel fully occupied during the week will often have low occupancy on weekends, giving rise to bundled "weekend getaway" packages. Within a day variation is most clearly seen in restaurants. Here we see many restaurants offering, for example, "early bird" discounts for customers who dine in advance of the normal meal hours as a means to increase capacity utilization. We see that management must make labour and capital decisions on the basis of peak demand. As we will see later, the prominence of the pricing problem has given rise to a practice known as yield management. If we contrast the hospitality industry with hospitals (another service industry) a number of similarities can be observed. A key difference, however, is these changes in demand. And manufacturers, of course, can smooth output by the appropriate use of inventory.

The broad range of firms in the hospitality industry has led to numerous modes of organizing. Figure 1 shows some representative organizational forms of hotels.[3] For example, an individual can decide to own and operate his or her own hotel unaffiliated with a brand (node 1). Alternatively, the owner can contract with a third party to manage the hotel (node 2). Another series of organizational forms begin with a hotel company (brand). They have the option of owning a hotel themselves (node 6) or franchising. If they choose to franchise, the franchisee has to decide whether to operate the hotel him or herself or to contract with another party for the management of the hotel. If self-managed, we have node 3. If the franchisee opts for a management contract, he or she has to decide whether the hotel company (brand) should run the hotel (node 5) or contract with some other third party (node 4).[4] The final form is when a real estate developer decides to build a hotel. The individual rooms are sold to investors who then choose to live in their room or enter

[3]Similar modes exist for other segments, such as airlines and restaurants.

[4]It is also possible for the hotel company to take an equity stake in the hotel, although this is not depicted in Fig. 1.

the room into a rental pool. A manager is hired according to a standard management contract (node 7). A potential problem with this organizational form is that, over time, the rooms will be in varying states of quality, possibly causing customer dissatisfaction among the hotel guests.

For nearly thirty years now, manufacturing firms have been competing on quality (Crosby, 1980). More recently service firms, including those in the hospitality industry, have also begun to compete on quality (Mene, 2000). This means that sustaining brand value requires a keen focus on quality and uniformity. In the hospitality industry, contact with customers is critical and employees directly influence the quality of the firm's output. Failures are not easily corrected prior to customer purchase/contact. This is in contrast to the manufacturing industry where employee mistakes can be corrected by inspection and rework. The challenge in the hospitality industry is more acute, since most customer contact is with employees in low-paid and low-status jobs that are characterized by high turnover.

Finally, the restaurant and lodging segments are dominated by large, branded firms that operate a large number of similar units using a variety of contractual controls. Important contractual arrangements include franchise contracts, management contracts, outsourcing contracts and facility leases. Relatively little research has been done in these important areas, despite the obvious role these contracts play as control mechanisms.

Overall, then, the characteristics of the industry give rise to some interesting forms of organization that, in turn, lead to managerial accounting issues.

1.4. Management Accounting in the Hospitality Industry

Several of the segments comprising the hospitality industry have adopted a uniform system of accounts and financial reports. Specifically, these are the:

- *Uniform System of Accounts for the Lodging Industry* (USALI). Published by the Hotel Association of New York City and the American Hotel & Lodging Association.
- *Uniform System of Accounts for Restaurants.* Published by the National Restaurant Association.
- *Uniform System of Financial Reporting for Clubs.* Prepared by the Club Managers Association of America and published by the Kendall/Hunt Publishing Company.
- *Uniform System of Accounts for Health, Racquet, and Sportsclub Industry.* Published by the International Health, Racquet & Sportsclub Association.

The first system, the USALI, was developed in 1926 by the Hotel Association of New York City to overcome the limitations of a traditional system of accounts better suited to manufacturing firms.[5] Moreover, a separation of ownership from control necessitated a formal set of accounts for contracting and valuation. The system, as it is currently formulated, stresses uniformity for the purpose of financial reporting but it has tended to become the basis for inter-property control and cost management given the lack of alternative accounting systems. In the lodging industry many firms regularly report key operating statistics to consultants, and the uniformity provided by the USALI enables managers to benchmark individual performance with a competitive set of hotels within their local markets.[6] Over the years the USALI has been updated many times to reflect changes in the industry. Although these systems provide an adaptable turnkey accounting system that has stood the test of time, adoption is by no means required or universal. A survey of controllers found approximately 75% of firms using the USALI and only a small fraction followed the system in all respects (Kwansa & Schimdgall, 1999).

2. Literature Review

In this section we review the relevant managerial accounting research. We focus primarily on the period after 1980, as new topics and several journals focusing on managerial accounting have recently emerged (Hesford et al., 2006). Due to language constraints, our search was restricted to English-language accounting journals.[7] Our search yielded only a small number of management accounting articles published in accounting journals. These articles are identified in Table 2.

In our literature review we scanned SSRN to identify pertinent working papers and we examined a variety of journals dedicated to the hospitality industry. None of the hospitality journals are focused on accounting or, more specifically, managerial accounting. In addition, many of these journals have a practitioner orientation. Thus, we identified very few of these articles for inclusion here. We also discuss some research from other academic disciplines that is directly related to managerial accounting issues within the hospitality industry.

2.1. Cost Management

2.1.1. Cost Behaviour

Cooper & Kaplan (1987, 1999) articulated the cost management arguments that product line and service channel

[5]A system of uniform accounts was established 20 years earlier for the hospital industry (Thorne, 1918), so the hospitality industry's effort was by no means a unique development.

[6]Two such examples are *Trends® in the Hotel Industry* by PKF Consulting and the *HOST Study* by Smith Travel Research.

[7]We are not aware, however, of any papers in non-English-language journals, so we have not consciously excluded any papers on the basis of language.

Table 2. Management accounting research on hospitality issues in accounting journals.

Authors	Journal*	Year	Industry	Method	Data	Topic
Ahrens & Chapman	*MAR*	2002	Restaurants	Case	Interviews, observation and archival	Central performance reports communicate strategic vision of the firm. Diversity of performance measures reflects local and central factors.
Ahrens & Chapman	*CAR*	2004	Restaurants	Case	Interviews, observation and archival	Extensive use of mechanistic controls and engaging intensive discussion and analysis provides both efficiency and flexibility.
Banker & Johnston	*TAR*	1993	Airlines	Empirical	Archival	Documents the statistical and managerial significance of operations-based drivers of overhead costs.
Banker et al.	*TAR*	2000	Hotels	Field	Archival	Nonfinancial performance measures as lead indicators. Overall financial impact of incentive plan that includes nonfinancial measures.
Behn & Riley	*JAAF*	1999	Airlines	Empirical	Archival	Nonfinancial performance measures link to current and future revenues, expenses, and profits.
Campbell	*JAR*	2008	Restaurants	Field	Archival	Nonfinancial performance measures as lead indicators. Links between outlet performance, manager pay, manager promotion and nonfinancial measures.
Collier & Gregory	*MAR*	1995	Hotels	Field	Interviews	Seeks to explain gap between theory and practice in capital budgeting. Three factors appear to influence investment appraisal technique. In this line of inquiry, survey-based research may add to confusion.
Davila & Venkatachalam	*RAS*	2004	Airlines	Empirical	Archival	Nonfinancial performance measures as a determinant of executive compensation.
Guilding	*MAR*	2003	Hotels	Field	Interviews	Finds greater formalism and greater propensity for cash forecast biasing among hotels operating under a divorced owner/operator setting. Agency conflicts.
Leidtka	*JBAF*	2002	Airlines	Empirical	Archival	The performance dimensions of financial and nonfinancial measures.
Riley et al.	*JAPP*	2003	Airlines	Empirical	Archival	Nonfinancial performance measure link to quarterly stock returns.
Sandino	*TAR*	2007	Restaurants†	Field	Survey	Identification of components of initial management control systems. Fit between initial controls components, strategy and performance.
Sharma	*MAR*	2002	Hotels	Empirical	Survey	Links between environmental uncertainty, size, decentralization and budgeting activities.

**MAR* = *Management Accounting Research; CAR* = *Contemporary Accounting Research; TAR* = *The Accounting Review; JAR* = *Journal of Accounting Research; RAS* = *Review of Accounting Studies; JAAF* = *Journal of Accounting, Auditing and Finance; JBAF* = *Journal of Business, Accounting and Finance; JAPP* = *Journal of Accounting and Public Policy.*

†A large proportion of the sample is restaurants, but retail firms are also included in the study.

variety lead to more complex operations which, in turn, may result in a disproportionate increase in costs. That is, factors other than volume drive overhead costs. To examine this notion, Foster & Gupta (1990) gathered data from 37 plants in one firm. Their analysis determined that there was not a strong association between complexity or efficiency variables and manufacturing overhead costs. However, the partial correlation analysis has been shown possibly to suffer from a biased test statistic (Banker et al., 1995) that made a rejection of the null hypothesis more unlikely. With this in mind, the pioneering study of Banker & Johnston (1993) sought to provide evidence on the drivers of indirect operating costs. The authors gathered financial and operating data from two governmental agencies, supplemented with other publicly-available data. Drawing on the previous economics and accounting literature, the panel data set is analyzed using a multivariate system of cost equations. In addition to finding significant capacity- and volume-based cost drivers, they also confirm the statistical and managerial significance of variables proxying for product diversity and process complexity. That is, they found that both volume- and operations-based variables are related to overhead costs. From the estimated equations, marginal costs are calculated to illustrate the impact of alternative strategies.

Practitioner research into the behaviour of lodging property rooms and restaurant department expenses is reviewed in Harris (1995). Generally, the early research focused on separating the fixed and variable components of costs. Although this partitioning of costs into fixed and variable components is useful for prediction and sensitivity analysis, lodging properties have a number of factors that may be impacting costs. Enz & Potter (1998) examined factors explaining differences in operating expenses for a number of properties in a full-service hotel chain. In addition to documenting that operating expenses, many of which are traditionally considered as fixed expenses, increased with occupancy rate and other control variables, they also documented that properties realize economies of scale but diseconomies of scope. Specifically, diseconomies of scope were documented because properties catering to a number of customer segments had higher operating expenses than those properties focusing on one or few customer segments. In a follow-up study, Enz, Potter & Siguaw (1999) found that the research site serving a larger variety of customer segments not only increased its operating costs, but that the cost increases were not fully compensated for by a similar increase in net revenues. Thus efforts to increase revenue sources through new customer bases may be unprofitable, a finding consistent with the cost management literature cited above.

2.1.2. Additional Cost Management Topics Pricing
The pricing problem is one that has been paid a great deal of attention in the hospitality industry. Accordingly, academics interested in the hospitality industry have also addressed this problem in a line of research known as yield management.[8] Yield management is basically a set of techniques to allocate capacity at varying prices over time, such that total revenue is maximized. Yield management, also called revenue management, originated with the airlines in the late 1970s after the industry was deregulated. The unique characteristics of the hospitality industry—high fixed costs, variable demand, perishable (i.e., non-inventoriable) output and fixed capacity—mean that a firm can optimize its profit by manipulating price to stimulate demand across different customer segments. Unlike the manufacturer that can inventory output for periods of high demand, or increase short-term output with overtime work, unsold seats or rooms represent lost profits. In recent years, yield management has been applied to a number of hospitality industry segments including hotels (Donaghy et al., 1995), restaurants (Kimes et al., 1998) and golf clubs (Kimes & Schruben, 2002), to name just a few. For a review of current research, see Chiang et al. (2007).

In building the yield management model it is critical to understand the variable cost of providing the service, as this provides a lower floor to price. However, these models assume as fixed some costs that may be adversely impacted in future periods. An example in the hotel industry would be the high cost of room renovation that will occur sooner if average occupancy rises. Another issue that receives little attention is organizational structure. For example, in the hotel segment, a management contract often pays management companies based on top-line revenue in the current year. The owner, on the other hand, is concerned with return on investment over a time horizon that is likely to differ from that of the management company. The agency issues here may be of interest to accounting researchers.

2.1.2.1. Customer profitability analysis Related to the pricing problem is the notion of customer profitability analysis (CPA). Although this topic has received little attention in the accounting literature it is of significant importance, particularly to service industries where costs are often determined by customer behaviour (Cooper & Kaplan, 1999, p. 459). In terms of the research literature, we know of only one case study. In a case study, Noone & Griffin (1999) used activity-based costing to

[8]Most of this research, however, has not been conducted by accountants or published by mainstream accounting journals.

assign costs to customer groups in a small (90-room) full-service hotel in Dublin, Ireland. They found that 38% of the revenue base generated 137% of firm profits, while the remaining customers (62%) each generated a negative contribution margin. Not surprisingly, management was unaware of the profits/losses generated by the various customer groups identified. As this was a case study, research in this area would be particularly fruitful, especially in light of interest in the topic by accounting academics engaged in research outside the hospitality industry (e.g., Niraj et al., 2001; Niraj et al., 2003).

2.1.3 Measuring Efficiency

The measurement of the productive efficiency of business units is an important issue in accounting. Analysis provides benchmark data that is useful for the determination of relative performance evaluation (RPE) measures. In the accounting literature examples include Banker et al. (1987), Mensah & Li (1993) and Dopuch & Gupta (1997). In a hospitality setting, this topic has appeared in the hospitality literature a number of times.

Morey & Dittman (1995) used allocative data envelopment analysis (DEA) to demonstrate how a hotel general manager's performance can be separated from the dynamics of the hotel's marketplace.[9] The model utilized three outputs, ten controllable inputs and four non-controllable (environmental) variables. A resource minimization approach was adopted. For each inefficient hotel, an efficiency frontier is created by a linear combination of efficient hotels which become the inefficient hotel's benchmark partners from whom "best practices" can be determined. By graphing efficiency scores versus hotel profitability, they demonstrated how this technique can be used to calculate "lost profits," the opportunity cost of inefficient operation. Hence general managers who are inefficient operators are identified, even at profitable hotels, and the cost of their inefficiencies can be determined. Additionally, it was demonstrated how this technique can be used to identify efficiently operated hotels in poor market areas which show little upside and might be candidates for disinvestment.

Morey & Dittman (2003) updates and extends Morey & Dittman (1995). In this article they give the mathematical formulation for the DEA model they used and provide a model of hotel profitability using 108 observations and a log–log regression model that explained 79.5% of the variation. They found that a 1% increase in overall service index (a combination of the hotel physical index and the customer satisfaction index) is associated with a 0.955% increase in profitability. A 1% increase in the hotel's efficiency score resulted in a 0.57% increase in profitability. A 1% increase in the hotel's competitive occupancy resulted in a 2.22% increase in profitability and a 1% increase in the hotel's competitive average daily rate resulted in a 0.565% increase in profitability, indicating that location is critical. Lastly, a 1% increase in the number of rooms resulted in a 0.823% increase in profitability.

Anderson, Fok & Scott (2000) look at overall, technical, allocative, pure technical and scale efficiencies in 48 hotels. This article does an excellent job of describing the different kinds of efficiencies that can be measured. They had two main findings. First, their results show a much higher level of inefficiency in the hotels studied compared to previous studies. They conclude that the marketplace is inefficient. Secondly, they found that the majority of inefficiency found was allocative in nature, implying that hotels are using the wrong mix of inputs, not necessarily using individual inputs inefficiently. However, the market inefficiencies measured here could result from failure to control environmental or market variables, within the DEA formulation (Sigala et al., 2005).

Sigala et al., (2005) provide a good tutorial on DEA and a good review of the literature in relating efficiency and productivity to the hospitality industry in general. They employ a stepwise DEA method to measure and benchmark productivity. They use the output augmentation approach for formulation. Their approach chooses inputs and outputs, some environmental or not controllable. They calculate DEA efficiency scores and correlate inputs and outputs with these scores. If correlations are significant they include these inputs and outputs in a new DEA model and compute the efficiency scores. They then correlate inputs and outputs not used and add those that have significant correlations to the efficiency scores to a new formulation. This procedure is continued until there are no new inputs or outputs to add. In this manner they are able to determine which inputs and outputs should be included in their model.

Wang, Hung & Shang (2006) apply the four-stage DEA procedure developed by Fried et al. (1999) to determine which environmental or non-controllable variables should be used in determining the efficiency of 54 Taiwan hotels. The environmental variables selected were location (city or resort hotel), size (<100, 100–300, 301–500 and > 500 rooms) and franchise status (chain or independent). They ran a Tobit regression with the slack of the controllable inputs as the dependent variable and the non-controllable variables as the independent variables. They then adjusted the controllable variables

[9]Two methodological approaches have been used to estimate productive efficiency: DEA, a non-parametric technique, and stochastic frontier estimation (SFE), a parametric technique.

for the effect of the environmental variables and then reran the DEA. The mean efficiency scores were compared for the initial DEA run and the adjusted DEA run. They found that city hotels were still less efficient than resorts, but that when management style and franchise status (chain versus independent) was adjusted out, no difference was found.

Johns, Howcroft & Drake (1997) look at productivity measures in the hospitality industry in general and DEA analysis in particular. Data from 15 hotels for 12 months are utilized on a quarterly basis to provide comparisons. They employ a 3-output and 4-input model with no environmental or non-controllable (i.e., categorical) variables. They used an output augmentation approach to DEA. They found inconsistency in the rankings by quarter, and little relationship between efficiency and gross profit. This is probably due to the lack of non-controllable variables and not taking seasonality into account.

Using 46 hotel brands evaluated in *Consumer Reports*, Brown & Ragsdale (2002) used DEA to estimated relative measure of market efficiency of hotel brands over four levels, from luxury to economy. They used two outputs to measure market efficiency (customer satisfaction and value) and six inputs (price per room night, problems, service, upkeep, number of hotels in brand and number of rooms in brand in the US). They found 26 of 46 hotels to have market efficiency. They then analyzed ways to improve the market efficiency of the non-efficient brands.

Other examples of DEA applied in hospitality settings are Tarim, Dener & Tarim (2000) who applied DEA to four- and five-star hotels in the Turkish Riveria–Antolya. Sigala (2003) applied DEA for measuring productivity gains in three-star hotels in the UK from investments in information and communication technologies.

2.2. *Management Control Systems*

The choice of organizational control in large hospitality firms is complex, as these companies tend to have multiple units spread over a wide geographic area. These units are expected to provide a common good or service using a similar technology (Brickley & Dark, 1987). Because the cost of search for goods and services by transient customers is high (Caves & Murphy, 1976), unit level uniformity is critical. Brand protection is critical for hospitality companies, perhaps more so than other firms because of the relative simplicity of the products and services they provide.

From an agency perspective, firms design the location of decision-making around the quality of contractible performance measures (Milgrom & Roberts 1992; Prendergast 2002; Moers, 2006). For instance Moers (2006) finds that delegation increases with the relative quality (sensitivity, precision and verifiability) of financial performance measures, in addition to the span of control and the levels of hierarchy. Abernethy, Bouwens & Van Lent (2004) find that delegation decreases with intra-firm interdependencies. They also find that the use of performance measures decreases as divisions become more interdependent, a finding similar to Keating (1997). Because hospitality firms are so dispersed and reliant on brand reputation, the decision on the extent of decentralization is crucial. We discuss the impact of the decentralization decision on the form of unit control below.

2.2.1. *Franchising Versus Ownership of Units*

One organizational form of unit control that is used extensively by hospitality firms is franchising. Franchising can help mitigate the agency problems of monitoring worker effort and quality that occur when principals have high monitoring costs. Studies by Brickley & Dark (1987), Norton (1988) and LaFontaine (1992) suggest that franchising can help reduce the costs of monitoring remote units by providing financial incentives to the local managers in the form of residual claims. For instance, after examining the franchising arrangement of 36 firms that contain some franchise units, Brickley & Dark (1987) find that the incidence of franchising increases with the distance a unit is from headquarters. Moreover, they find franchise units tend to be in less populated areas. They subscribe these results to the notion that monitoring costs are high in remote areas and thus franchising helps mitigate moral hazard problems. Interestingly, they find that hospitality-related firms, which they define as firms with fewer repeat customers, have a lower proportion of franchised units than the other franchisers in their sample. Their conjecture is that this occurs because a non-repeat customer base provides the franchisee with a greater incentive to free ride on the brand, as many restaurant and hotel customers are from distant areas.

Norton (1988) investigates the incidence of franchising in the restaurant and hotel industries using 126 observations that measure the proportion of franchising in these industries in a particular state. Key findings are that franchising increases in rural areas and for the hotel industry with the extent of travel in the state. These results are similar to Brickley & Dark (1987). The study also documents that franchising increases with labour intensity, the size of the average outlet and the variability of customer demand. These factors are similar to research by management accountants cited above on factors influencing the delegation of decision rights. Specifically, delegation increases with size and uncertainty.

Franchising can also aid organizations with innovation and uniformity problems. Bradach (1997) reports on a field study examining the structure of five restaurant chains. His inquiry concerned the organizational structure of the chains to facilitate uniformity and adaptability. He noted that a plural operating system, that is a firm operating both company-run and franchised units, was the approach these restaurant chains used to solve uniformity and adaptability issues. Company-owned units operated as a hierarchy with control over activities using budgets, internal promotions and corporate building, thus driving uniformity. Franchised units operated on a more local level, using on-site experience and monetary incentives to promote adaptability. Interestingly, he noted that most of the franchisees owned multiple units. Thus, these franchisees had incentives to profit from building their business through expansion, resulting in mini-hierarchies.

Franchising issues have recently been addressed in the management accounting literature by Campbell, Datar & Sandino (2007). These authors argue that franchising contracts can help attract local entrepreneurs who have a good sense of local conditions and have the flexibility to respond to local market dynamics. These authors document that the use of franchising is positively related to the degree of customer (market) dispersion, suggesting that franchising allows these chains to benefit from local information. These studies all highlight the potential benefits and costs of delegation of decision rights, a key issue in the design of management control systems.

2.2.2. Management Control System Use

Ahrens & Chapman (2002) examine local managers' use of performance reports and contests of accountability. Their research design is that of a case field study in a large restaurant chain. Interviews, archival data collection and direct observation were conducted over a period of two years, enabling the researchers to develop a deep understanding of the workings of the organization. In this study, the authors use structuration theory as their basis for understanding performance measurement practices. Structuration theory seeks to explain the relationship between social actors and structures. Basically structuration theory recognizes a duality between actors' behaviour within a structure that is itself moulded by their behaviour. That is, actors choose to conform or disobey and choose an effort level that determines the organization's structure, which in turn influences actors (Scott, 1998). The findings are, first, that structured, central performance reports are a means to communicate the strategic vision of the firm. Secondly, a diversity of performance measures in use by the firm reflects both local and central factors. Finally, contests of accountability are observed to be a part of routine management. This last finding is a distinct contribution compared with the prior literature, which has tended to focus on organizations in crisis and transition. Further research, the authors note, should explicitly focus on the structuring of organizational processes to performance measurement systems. This, they argue, will significantly improve our understanding of accounting practice. We certainly agree.

Ahrens & Chapman (2004) study how management control systems are used in ways that enable both efficiency and flexibility. Noting limitations to Simons' (1995) framework, the authors chose to use Adler & Borys' (1996) conceptual model of enabling and coercive bureaucracy to develop an understanding of how firms balance mechanistic controls for maintaining efficiency and organic controls that allow for flexibility. Coercive formalization seeks to deskill workers through the use of rules and procedures aimed at reducing reliance on highly-paid workers (Perrow, 1983). On the other hand, enabling formalization seeks to leverage employee skill (Adler & Borys, 1996). The research method and setting appears to be a continuation of Ahrens & Chapman (2002). Upon completion of data collection, the authors assessed their data in the context of the four features of formalization described in Adler & Borys (1996): repair; internal transparency; global transparency; and flexibility. Their choice of the hospitality setting was very helpful because it has mechanistic processes (the production of food) while the large number of local restaurants demand organic processes to successfully manage under varying circumstances. Ahrens & Chapman find that the firm makes extensive use of mechanistic management controls while also engaging in intensive discussion and analysis that reconciles local contingencies with corporate standards. This paper, then, begins to bridge the contingency and field study literatures on management control. It also provides a framework for future research that will improve our understanding of this important topic.

2.2.3. Management Control System Components

Sandino (2007) studied the implementation and effectiveness of organizational controls for early-stage companies using field-based interviews and a questionnaire. Her sample consists of 97 retail firms, about 60% of which were restaurants. The study documents four types of controls are implemented by these early stage retailers: basic; cost; revenue; and risk. Basic controls include budgeting, pricing and inventory components. Cost controls involve cost and quality measures. Risk controls include loss prevention, internal audits, credit, and policy and procedures. Quality, budgets and cost controls, among others, tend to be implemented in the first year of operations. She finds that firms following a low-cost strategy tend to adopt cost controls, whereas product differentiators tend to adopt revenue controls. Decentralized firms with more product diversity tend to emphasize risk controls. Controlling for franchising and restaurants adds little to the results, suggesting the results are representative of most hospitality organizations. Finally, the study finds that both perceived and actual performance (sales growth and store growth) is positively related to the fit between the firm's strategy and controls.

2.2.4. Performance Measures and Control

As discussed above, in recent years managerial accounting has placed considerable emphasis on the links between performance measures, incentives and the location of decision rights within an organization. Hospitality industries provide a rich setting for addressing a number of questions regarding contracting and monitoring, based on financial and nonfinancial performance measures. A number of the management accounting studies in the hospitality area have examined the role of financial and nonfinancial performance measures in organizational control.

Because financial measures of performance may be imperfect and noisy signals of a manager's effort, nonfinancial measures can add value in drawing inferences about managers' efforts and in inducing them to be long-run focused (Feltham & Xie, 1994; Hemmer, 1996). Thus, financial measures alone are not likely to be the most efficient means to motivate employees (Ittner, Larcker & Meyer, 2003), particularly when performance is needed over multiple dimensions. Nonfinancial measures are believed to complement short-run financial figures as indicators of progress towards a firm's long-term goals (American Accounting Association, 1971). Profit and other financial measures report the effects of past activities and achievements, whereas nonfinancial measures of customer satisfaction, internal processes, and the organization's innovation and improvement activities are the drivers of future financial performance (Kaplan & Norton, 1992). Consistent with this notion, Ittner, Larcker & Rajan (1997) find that the relative weight placed on nonfinancial measures increases with an innovation strategy, quality initiatives and the noise in financial measures.

Behn & Riley (1999) examined the links between accounting income measures and nonfinancial performance measures in the airline industry. Their study involved quarterly data for ten airlines over the 1988 to 1996 period. A key nonfinancial measure that they used was customer complaints. For their study, customer complaints was a fitted instrument measure constructed using Department of Transport (DOT) information concerning on-time arrivals, mishandled baggage, denied boarding and load factor. Other nonfinancial metrics included load factor, market share and available seat miles. They find that the change in complaints is negatively related to percentage changes in operating income. Moreover, they document that complaints have a negative impact on revenues and a very strong positive impact on operating expenses. Load factor is primarily related to income through its positive effect on revenues. They also find that customer complaints and load factor information is predictive of future operating profit over a one month and two month interval. Their customer related results complement work by Andersen, Fornell & Lehmann (1994) that found return on assets was positively associated with customer satisfaction measured six months earlier, and Ittner & Larcker's (1998) study examining the relation between customer satisfaction and firm performance. Using customer-level data for two large service companies, Ittner and Larcker found that customer satisfaction measures are related, albeit with some decreasing returns, to the subsequent year's customer retention, usage and profits.

Banker, Potter & Srinivasan (2000) was one of the first studies to document how a bonus plan that includes nonfinancial performance measures impacts financial performance. Two important differences between their study and prior research was the inclusion of an institution-specific long time-series of observations and detailed field interviews. Using time-series data for 72 months from 18 hotels managed by a large hospitality firm, the study documented that simple nonfinancial measures of customer satisfaction, specifically number of customer complaints and likelihood of the guest to return, were significantly associated with future financial performance after controlling for past financial performance. The analysis indicated that the positive association between future revenues and current nonfinancial performance is mainly driven by occupancy (volume effect) as opposed to room rates (price effect). More importantly, the authors found that both nonfinancial and financial performance improved at these hotels following the implementation of the bonus plan that included nonfinancial performance measures. Therefore, the study provides formal empirical evidence, limited to the fact that it is based on data from one firm, on the performance impacts of an incentive plan that includes both financial and nonfinancial performance measures. As such, it documents potential benefits of nonfinancial measures in contracting.

In a follow-up practitioner study using the same data, Banker, Potter & Srinivasan (2005) investigated the impact of the incentive plan on the hotel chain's performance. Specifically, they examined the growth in the total annual number of rooms supplied and total annual revenues under the hotel's brand. This analysis was conducted after controlling for the growth in the industry using the number of rooms supplied and revenues by up-scale and mid-scale hotel chains in the US. They found that both the number of franchised hotels and the chain's total revenues increased more than that of its competitors following the implementation of its new incentive plan. This finding provides one more rationale for the use of customer satisfaction measures in performance evaluation in the hotel industry, where such externalities are important.

Davila & Venkatachalam (2004) investigated the role of nonfinancial performance measures in explaining executive compensation in the airline industry. Their sample consisted of 246 observations from 35 US airlines over the period 1986 to 2000. The nonfinancial metric used in their study was passenger load factor, which is a common measure of capacity utilization in the airline industry (Schefczyk, 1993). Because airlines have high operating leverage, as fixed costs are a large percentage of total costs, passenger load factor is a key measure of operational efficiency. Using 15 international airlines, Schefczyk (1993) reported that high passenger load factors supported high profitability. Davila & Venkatachalam (2004) find that passenger load factor is positively related to the cash compensation of CEOs after controlling for both accounting metrics and stock returns. Moreover, the link between cash compensation and load factor is stronger when the noise in stock returns increases. This, the authors suggest, is consistent with efficient contracting, as more weight is placed on the more precise signal. The study, however, does not find a strong positive link between total CEO compensation and passenger load factor. This latter finding results because the equity portion of CEO compensation is very strongly related to the period's stock returns.

Campbell (2008) examined the links between nonfinancial measures, future financial performance and promotion and demotion decisions at a quick service restaurant chain. His sample includes 24 643 monthly observations of outlet performance for 852 managers over a 39 month period. Although all of the outlets in the study were company owned and operated, the incentive contract for the outlet manager resembled that of a franchisee, in that the manager received a large percentage of the residual claims computed net of a small percentage of sales. He finds that future financial performance is related to current and past measures of service quality and employee retention after controlling for past profit. This is interesting, because in his sample changes in manager pay are only related to changes in outlet profitability. Moreover, the study documents that promotion decisions, which result in higher pay or more responsibility, are related to both service quality and employee retention. Thus service quality, a key dimension of a branded hospitality firm, is related to future outlet performance and employee incentives.

2.2.5. Value Relevance of Nonfinancial Measures in Hospitality Industries

Little work has been done in the management accounting literature to directly link nonfinancial performance measures to stock returns in hospitality industries. Francis, Schipper & Vincent (2003) examined the relative information content of earnings and industry specific performance measures on stock returns. These authors found that, although earnings were more informative than industry specific measures in explaining stock returns in the airline industry, revenue passenger mile, cost per available seat mile and passenger load factor provided incremental explanatory power. They also found that in the restaurant industry same store sales growth was related to stock returns after controlling for earnings metrics. Again, earnings metrics dominated in the industry. No results were reported for the lodging industry, probably due to the lack of observations.

Leidtka (2002) found that nonfinancial measures of performance in the airline industry, such as customer satisfaction and safety, provided performance information that was unique from that contained in a number of financial performance measures, such as return on investment and cash flow. Riley, Pearson & Trompeter (2003) investigated the links between stock returns and financial and nonfinancial metrics in the airline industry. These authors used quarterly data on seven US airlines over the period 1988 to 1999. Quarterly returns are examined using earnings and changes in the nonfinancial variables customer complaints, load factor, market share and available seat miles. Customer complaints is a fitted instrument measure constructed using DOT information concerning on-time arrivals, mishandled baggage, denied boarding and load factor. Their key finding is that, both before and after controlling for earnings, metrics quarterly stock returns are related to nonfinancial metrics. In particular, there is a strong negative relation between complaints and returns and a strong positive relation between load factor and returns. Unlike Francis, Schipper & Vincent above, nonfinancial metrics dominate financial metrics in their study.

2.2.6. Operational Budgeting

Sharma (2002) reported that a comprehensive review of the management accounting literature found no studies examining the budget-related activities for hotels. Sharma (2002) studied factors influencing budgeting controls in 106 hotels using path analysis. Data for his analysis came from questionnaires. The study involved determining how perceived environmental uncertainty and hotel size, measured by number of rooms, impacted the extent of budgeting activities process and of decentralization. The study is unusual given that his perceived environmental construct was split into three components representing economic and technological volatility, competition and unpredictability (p. 116). With respect to the drivers of decentralization, the study finds that some measures of perceived environmental uncertainty, namely economic turbulence and competition, are related to decentralization. Unpredictability and hotel size are not. Prior accounting studies in other industries documented a positive link between size and decentralization (Merchant, 1981). With regards to budgeting activities, the paper reports that decentralization and hotel size are positively related to budgeting, a finding that is generally consistent with the management accounting literature. There are very weak links between uncertainty measures and most budgeting activities after controlling for decentralization and size.

2.2.7. Capital budgeting

Capital budgeting is a voluminous literature with a long history. For a comprehensive review, see Haka (2006). In the two decades from 1981 to 2000, 47 papers appeared in ten leading journals that publish managerial accounting research (Hesford et al., 2006). This represents 5.1% of all managerial accounting research published in those journals. Despite this level of interest, only two papers have been in the context of the hospitality industry. This is surprising to us, given the relatively homogenous nature of investment appraisal decisions and the presence of many important agency issues.

In the first paper Collier & Gregory (1995) attempt to explain the gap between investment appraisal practices and theory. For a richer understanding of this issue a field study approach was adopted. Being an exploratory study, the authors use a purposive sample of hotels in the UK, with selection based on different size and patterns of ownership. By focusing on the hospitality industry they hoped to see somewhat consistent practices. However, they were surprised to find that the techniques ranged from simple (payback) to complex (discounted cash flow analysis) methods. They concluded that three factors appeared to influence investment appraisal:

1. a hands-on management style by the CEO led to a more informal, less complex approach;
2. the tradition of the parent firm (which, we note, does not answer the study's research question);
3. communications with the group board.

In those firms that used multiple techniques, only one technique was consistently used for decision-making. Surprisingly, firm size did not appear to be related to investment appraisal choice. An important finding was that the techniques adopted by sample firms were not always consistent with standard (textbook) definitions. This, the authors suggest, means that survey-based research on the theory–practice gap may actually be adding noise and confusion, leading us away from an understanding of the problem.

The second study examines the capital budgeting implications of hotel owner and operator structures (Guilding, 2003). Like the earlier work of Collier & Gregory (1995), this is a field study. A principal difference is the level of analysis, with data collected at the hotel rather than at corporate level. And like the studies of Ahrens & Chapman (2002, 2004), the hospitality industry provides a unique setting. Guilding points out to readers that, unlike most capital budgeting practice (and research), in the hotel industry a large proportion of investment appraisal decisions involve two distinct (and legally separate) organizations; the property owner and the operating company operate under relatively long-term contracts (in some cases as long as 20 years).[10,11] Interviews with 14 senior managers (General Manager (GM) or Financial Controller (FC)) were conducted at 13 hotels on Australia's Gold Coast. Most of these hotels were operated for an owner by a management company under a long-term management contract. In these cases, GMs and FCs are employees of the management company and they initiate the capital budgeting proposals. Such an arrangement creates the potential for numerous agency conflicts. Participant responses were evaluated in terms of four typical reasons for conflicts of interest in an agency relationship (Lambert, 2001). Guilding finds both greater formalism and a greater propensity for cash forecast biasing among hotels operating under a divorced owner/operator setting (i.e., those hotels where ownership and management are separated; nodes 2, 4, 5 or 7 in Fig. 1). Many management contracts compensate the managing firm on the basis of revenues and gross profits, not on return on investment. Given the observed dysfunctionalism, one must wonder why the adoption of management contracts is so prevalent in the industry. An alternative question might be: Why do the current forms of contracting persist and, could new contracts be written that would eliminate this dysfunctionalism?

2.2.8. Outsourcing

Many large hotels have a variety of what amounts to businesses within a business. For example, a restaurant, golf course and fitness centre operating as part of a hotel all have independent competitors in the marketplace. In some cases the hotel develops these businesses to serve their hotel guests, but it is often the case that the hotel considers non-guests to be part of their customer base and a justification for having developed these "businesses." In addition to this, many of a hotel's core processes may be performed by third parties. Laundry, parking, payroll and concierge services are just a few examples. Accordingly, hotels have many opportunities to outsource, and understanding why hotels outsource is an important research question.

[10]Readers interested in management contracts may want to refer to Eyster (1988).

[11]While this issue is not unknown to academics in the hospitality industry, this important topic has failed to generate much attention (Beals, 1995; Field, 1995).

In trying to understand the different ways of organizing, Lamminmaki (2005) conducted a field study of 11 hotels in Australia. Drawing on transaction cost economics (Williamson, 1979, 1985), Lamminmaki conducted interviews with 15 managers and assessed participant responses along the lines of six dimensions of asset specificity.[12] There were two findings. First, site specificity and brand capital are the most important dimensions in the outsourcing decision. Secondly, in accordance with the theory of transaction cost economics, hotels are likely to retain a process as internal to the firm if there is high asset specificity.

2.2.9. Competitor-focused Accounting

In developing competitive strategy, Porter (1980, 1985) calls for companies to engage in competitive analysis. A key element of this process is the analysis of competitors' financial information. In the mainstream accounting literature Guilding (1999) and Hesford (2008) examine the use of accounting information for the analysis of competitors. Extending this line of inquiry, Anderson & Guilding (2006) conduct an exploratory case study of the potential for this process in the hotel industry. Based on unstructured interviews with 21 senior managers in one Australian hotel, the authors find that, while there is interest in CFA, actual practices appear quite limited, even in an informal sense.

Table 3 summarizes the articles we reviewed from hospitality and practitioner journals.

3. Hospitality-related research opportunities in management accounting

The review presented above demonstrates the minimal amount of work on hospitality firms that has been published in the accounting journals. While it is too early to ascertain the impact of the more recent articles, Banker & Johnston (1993) was one of the first papers in accounting to investigate the impact of operational complexity on operating costs. Behn & Riley (1999) was an early study on the relation between nonfinancial and financial performance measures. Banker, Potter & Srinivasan (2000) was the first study to document financial performance improvements following the adoption of an incentive plan based, in part, on nonfinancial measures.

There are many attributes of the hospitality industry that make it a rich area for management accounting researchers interested in cost management and management control systems. As noted above, the hospitality industry is labour intensive, with employee costs ranging from 30% to 40% of operating expenses. Wages tend to be low, and retention and training are critical to ensure brand consistency. Furthermore, these firms are also capital intensive and operate with significant short-term capacity constraints. This latter characteristic, combined with relatively simple production technologies and few barriers to entry, has resulted in the lodging and restaurant industries being quite competitive. To realize economies of scale and take advantage of consumer's search costs, lodging and restaurant firms tend to operate a large number of similar units using a variety of contractual controls, including those related to franchising, outside management companies and lease arrangements. This variety of control, combined with a uniformity of accounting across units of different brands and ownership structure, provides researchers with multiple observations that have similar accounts, but varying strategies and control structure. Finally, the sustained value of many of these organizations is in the overall brand image, which tends to drive the demand for nonfinancial, as well as financial, performance measures.

These attributes provide a good setting for studying issues involving cost management. As examples, we offer several suggestions:

1. the impact of capacity constraints on costs and prices;
2. the impact of variety in revenue sources and customer segments on costs, revenues and profits;
3. customer profitability; and
4. the demand and effect of cost allocation problems that is critical in these industries given the growth in centralized services.

Banker & Johnston (2006) state that there is a need for more theoretical and empirical work on value, cost, revenue and profit drivers, and hospitality industries provide a natural setting for examining these issues. With respect to strategic accounting controls, these industries provide a ripe environment for examining issues related to organization design and control which are an integral part of the agency and contingency literatures. Important issues that can be addressed include:

1. the links between the location of decision rights;
2. performance measures and incentives;
3. the determinants and effectiveness of budgets as a coordination and control mechanism;
4. the use of relative performance evaluation; and
5. the effectiveness and form of operating controls and workforce initiatives.

Nonfinancial performance measures play a key role in assessing both service quality and franchisee free riding, yet hospitality industries are reluctant to incorporate these measures in explicit contracts. Given that hospitality firms

[12]The six dimensions of asset specificity are: human, physical, site, dedicated, brand capital and temporal.

Table 3. Sampling of management accounting research in hospitality journals.

Study	Journal*	Year	Industry	Method	Data	Topic
Anderson & Guilding	*IJCHM*	2006	Hotels	Field	Interviews	Case study of customer-focused accounting. Finds interest in the concept, but no formal program and only limited informal use.
Anderson et al.	*ABR*	2000	Hotels	Empirical	Archival	DEA analysis finds that the marketplace is inefficient and that firms were using the wrong mix of inputs.
Brown & Ragsdale	*JHTR*	2002	Hotels	Empirical	Archival	In contrast to Anderson et al. (2000), more than half of the hotels have market efficiency. Ways to improve efficiency are analyzed.
Jones et al.	*PTHR*	1997	Hotels	Archival	Archival	Examines productivity measures and finds inconsistent rankings over time, probably due to a lack of non-controllable variables.
Lamminmaki	*IJCHM*	2005	Hotels	Field	Interviews	Evaluates outsourcing decisions using the notion of asset specificity. Hotels are likely to retain a process as internal to the firm if there is high asset specificity.
Morey & Dittman	*CQ*	1995	Hotels	Empirical	Archival	Using DEA, analysis demonstrates how a manager's performance can be separated from the marketplace.
Morey & Dittman	*CQ*	2003	Hotels	Empirical	Archival	Paper extends Morey & Dittman (1995) to examine factors that impact profitability.
Sigala et al.	*TSIJ*	2005	Hotels	Empirical	Archival	Illustrates a technique for identifying which inputs and outputs need to be included in the estimation of efficiency.
Wang et al.	*TSIJ*	2006	Hotels	Empirical	Archival	Develops a model using environmental and non-controllable variables to compute efficiency scores for 54 Taiwanese hotels.

**IJCHM = International Journal of Contemporary Hospitality Management; CQ = Cornell Hotel and Restaurant Administration Quarterly; ABR = American Business Review; TSIJ = The Service Industries Journal; PTHR = Progress in Tourism and Hospitality Research; JHTR = Journal of Hospitality and Tourism Research.*

have significant labour issues and a variety of owner/manager structures, we believe this industry provides one of the best settings for studying a multitude of issues regarding contract design and other control mechanisms.

References

Abernethy, M. A., Bouwens, J. & Van Lent, L. (2004). Determinants of control system design in divisionalized firms. *The Accounting Review*, **79**(3), 545–570.

Adler, P. S. & Borys, B. (1996). Two types of bureaucracy: enabling and coercive. *Administrative Science Quarterly*, **41**, 61–89.

Ahrens, T. & Chapman, C. S. (2002). The structuration of legitimate performance measures and management: day-to-day contests of accountability in a U.K. restaurant chain. *Management Accounting Research*, **13**, 151–171.

Ahrens, T. & Chapman, C. S. (2004). Accounting for flexibility and efficiency: a field study of management control systems in a restaurant chain. *Contemporary Accounting Research*, **21**(2), 271–301.

American Accounting Association (1971). Report of the committee on nonfinancial measures of effectiveness. *The Accounting Review*, **46**(Supplement), 165–211.

American Hotel & Lodging Association (2006). *The 2006 Lodging Industry Profile*. Washington, DC: American Hotel & Lodging Association.

Anderson, E., Fornell, C. & Lehmann, D. (1994). Customer satisfaction, market share, and profitability: findings from Sweden. *Journal of Marketing*, **58**, 53–66.

Anderson, R. I., Fok, R. & Scott, J. (2000). Hotel industry efficiency; an advanced linear programming examination. *American Business Review*, **18**(1), 40–48.

Anderson, S. & Guilding, C. (2006). Competitor-focused accounting applied to a hospitality context. *International Journal of Contemporary Hospitality Management*, **18**(3), 206–218.

Banker, R. D., Datar, S. M. & Rajan, M. V. (1987). Measurement of productivity improvements: an empirical analysis. *Journal of Accounting, Auditing and Finance*, **2**, 319–354.

Banker, R. D. & Johnston, H. H. (1993). An empirical study of cost drivers in the US airline industry. *The Accounting Review*, **68**(3), 576–601.

Banker, R. D., Potter, G. & Schroeder, R. G. (1995). An empirical analysis of manufacturing overhead cost drivers. *Journal of Accounting and Economics*, **19**, 115–137.

Banker, R. D., Potter, G. & Srinivasan, D. (2000). An empirical investigation of an incentive plan that includes non-financial performance measures. *The Accounting Review*, **75**, 65–92.

Banker, R. D., Potter, G. & Srinivasan, D. (2005). Association of nonfinancial performance measures with the financial performance of a lodging chain. *Cornell Hotel and Restaurant Administration Quarterly*, **46**(4), 394–412.

Banker, R. D., & Johnston, H. H. (2006). Cost and profit driver research. In: C. S. Chapman, A. G. Hopwood, & M. D. Shields (Eds.), *Handbook of Management Accounting Research*, (Vol. 2). Oxford, UK: Elsevier Ltd.

Beals, P. (1995). The Hotel Management Contract: Lessons from the North American Experience. In: P. Harris (Ed.) *Accounting and Finance for the International Hospitality Industry*. London, UK: Butterworth-Heinemann.

Behn, B. & Riley, R. Jr (1999). Using non-financial information to predict financial performance: the case of the US airline industry. *Journal of Accounting, Auditing and Finance*, **14**(1), 29–56.

Bradach, J. L. (1997). Using the plural form in the management of restaurant chains. *Administrative Science Quarterly*, **42**, 276–303.

Brickley, J. A. & Dark, F. H. (1987). The choice of organization form. The case of franchising. *Journal of Financial Economics*, **18**, 401–420.

Brown, J. R. & Ragsdale, C. T. (2002). The competitive market efficiency of hotel brands: an application of data envelopment analysis. *Journal of Hospitality and Tourism Research*, **26**(4), 332–360.

Bureau of Economic Analysis. (2008). *National Economic Accounts*. Retrieved February 1, 2008. Website: http://www.bea.gov/national/pdf/dpga.pdf.

Bureau of Labor Statistics. (2008). *Employment Situation Summary.* Retrieved February 1, 2008. Website: http://www.bls.gov/news.release/empsit.nr0.htm.

Campbell, D. (2008). Nonfinancial performance measures and promotion-based incentives. *Journal of Accounting Research*, Forthcoming.

Campbell, D., Datar, S. & Sandino, T. (2007). Franchising and control across multiple markets: the case of the convenience store industry. Working Paper.

Caves, R. E. & Murphy, W. F. (1976). Franchising: firms, markets, and intangible assets. *Southern Economic Journal*, **42**, 572–586.

Collier, P. & Gregory, A. (1995). Investment appraisal in service industries: a field study analysis of the UK hotels sector. *Managerial Accounting Research*, **6**, 33–57.

Chiang, W. C., Chen, J. C. & Xu, X. (2007). An overview of research on revenue management: current issues and future research. *International Journal of Revenue Management*, **1**(1), 97–128.

Cooper, R. & Kaplan, R. S. (1987). How cost accounting systematically distorts product costs. In: W. Bruns, & R. S. Kaplan (Eds), *Accounting and Management: Field Study Perspectives*. Boston, MA: Harvard Business School Press.

Cooper, R. & Kaplan, R. S. (1999). *The Design of Cost Management Systems*, (2nd ed.). Upper Saddle River, NJ: Prentice Hall.

Crosby, P. (1980). *Quality is Free: The Art of Making Quality Certain*. New York: Penguin Putnam.

Davila, A. & Venkatachalam, M. (2004). The relevance of non-financial performance measures for CEO compensation: evidence from the airline industry. *Review of Accounting Studies*, **9**, 443–464.

Donaghy, K., McMahon, U. & McDowell, D. (1995). Yield management: an overview. *International Journal of Hospitality Management*, **14**(2), 139–150.

Dopuch, N. & Gupta, M. (1997). Estimation of benchmark performance standards: an application to public school expenditures. *Journal of Accounting and Economics*, **23**, 141–161.

Enz, C. A. & Potter, G. (1998). The impact of variety on the costs and profits of a hotel chain's properties. *Journal of Hospitality and Tourism Research*, **22**(2), 142–158.

Enz, C. A., Potter, G. & Siguaw, J. (1999). Serving more segments and offering more products. *Cornell Hotel and Restaurant Administration Quarterly*, 54–62.

Eyster, J. (1988). *The Negotiation and Administration of Hotel and Restaurant Management Contracts*, (3rd ed.). Ithaca, NY: Cornell University.

Feltham, G. A. & Xie, J. (1994). Performance measure congruity and diversity in multi-task principal/agent relations. *The Accounting Review*, **69**, 429–453.

Field, H. M. (1995). Financial management implications of hotel management contracts: A UK perspective. In: P. Harris (Ed.), *Accounting and Finance for the International Hospitality Industry*. London, UK: Butterworth-Heinemann.

Foster, G. & Gupta, M. (1990). Manufacturing overhead cost driver analysis. *Journal of Accoungting and Economics*, **12**(1–3), 309–337.

Francis, J., Schipper, K. & Vincent, L. (2003). The relative and incremental explanatory power or earnings and alternative (to earnings) performance measures for returns. *Contemporary Accounting Research*, **20**, 121–164.

Fried, H. O., Schmidt, S. S. & Yaisawarmg, S. (1999). Incorporating the operating environment into a nonparametric measure of technical efficiency. *Journal of Productivity Analysis*, **12**, 249–267.

Guilding, C. (1999). Competitor-focused accounting: an exploratory note. *Accounting, Organizations and Society*, **24**(7), 583–595.

Guilding, C. (2003). Hotel owner/operator structures: implications for capital budgeting process. *Management Accounting Research*, **14**, 179–199.

Haka, S. F. (2006). A review of the literature on capital budgeting and investment appraisal. In: C. S. Chapman, A. G. Hopwood & M. D. Shields (Eds), *Handbook of Management Accounting Research*, (Vol. 2). Oxford, UK: Elsevier Ltd.

Harris, P. (1995). A development strategy for the hospitality operations management curriculum. *International Journal of Contemporary Hospitality Management*, **7**(5), 29–32.

Hemmer, T. (1996). On the design and choice of "modern" management accounting measures. *Journal of Managerial Accounting Research*, **8**, 87–116.

Hesford, J. W. (2008). An empirical investigation of accounting information use in competitive intelligence. *Journal of Competitive Intelligence and Management*, Forthcoming.

Hesford, J. W., Lee, S., Van der Stede, W. A. & Young, S. M. (2006). Management accounting: a bibliographic study. In: C. S. Chapman, A. G. Hopwood, & M. D. Shields (Eds), *Handbook of Management Accounting Research*, (Vol. 1). Oxford, UK: Elsevier Ltd.

ICHRIE (2006). *Guide to College Programs in Hospitality, Tourism, & Culinary Arts*, (9th ed.). Richmond, VA: International Council on Hotel, Restaurant, and Institutional Education.

Ittner, C. D. & Larcker, D. F. (1998). Are nonfinancial measures leading indicators of financial performance? An analysis of customer satisfaction. *Journal of Accounting Research*, **36**, 1–35.

Ittner, C. D., Larcker, D. F. & Rajan, M. V. (1997). The choice of performance measures in annual bonus contracts. *The Accounting Review*, **72**, 231–255.

Ittner, C. D., Larcker, D. F. & Meyer, M. W. (2003). Subjectivity and the weighting of performance measures: evidence from a balanced scorecard. *The Accounting Review*, **78**, 725–758.

Johns, N., Howcroft, B. & Drake, L. (1997). The use of data envelopment analysis to monitor hotel productivity. *Progress in Tourism and Hospitality Research*, **3**, 119–127.

Kaplan, R. S. & Norton, D. (1992). The balanced scorecard: measures that drive performance. *Harvard Business Review*, **January–February**, 71–79.

Keating, A. S. (1997). Determinants of divisional performance evaluation practices. *Journal of Accounting and Economics*, **24**, 243–273.

Kimes, S. E., Chase, R., Choi, S., Lee, P. & Ngonzi, E. N. (1998). Restaurant revenue management: applying yield management to the restaurant industry. *Cornell Hotel and Restaurant Administration Quarterly*, **39**(3), 32–39.

Kimes, S. E. & Schruben, L. W. (2002). Golf course revenue management: a study of tee time intervals. *Journal of Revenue and Pricing Management*, **1**(2), 111–121.

Kwansa, F. & Schmidgall, R. S. (1999). The uniform system of accounts for the lodging industry: its importance to and use by hotel managers. *Cornell Hotel and Restaurant Administration Quarterly*, **40**(6), 88–94.

Lafontaine, F. (1992). Agency theory and franchising: some empirical results. *The Rand Journal of Economics*, **23**(2), 263–283.

Lambert, R. A. (2001). Contracting theory and accounting. *Journal of Accounting and Economics*, **32**, 3–87.

Lamminmaki, D. (2005). Why do hotels outsource? An investigation using asset specificity. *International Journal of Contemporary Hospitality Management*, **17**(6), 516–528.

Leidtka, S. (2002). The information content of nonfinancial performance measures in the airline industry. *Journal of Business, Accounting and Finance*, **29**(7–8), 1105–1121.

Mene, P. (2000). Travel and hospitality industries. In: J. M. Juran, & A. B. Godfrey (Eds), *Juran's Quality Handbook*, (5th ed.). New York, NY: McGraw-Hill.

Mensah, Y. M. & Li, S. H. (1993). Measuring productive efficiency in a not-for-profit setting: an extension. *The Accounting Review*, **68**(1), 66–88.

Merchant, K. A. (1981). The design of the corporate budgeting system: influences on managerial behavior and performance. *The Accounting Review*, **56**(4), 813–829.

Milgrom, P. & Roberts, J. (1992). *Economics, Organization and Management*. Englewood Cliffs, NJ: Prentice Hall.

Moers, F. (2006). Performance measure properties and delegation. *The Accounting Review*, **81**(4), 897–924.

Morey, R. C. & Dittman, D. A. (1995). Evaluating a hotel GM's performance: a case study in benchmarking. *Cornell Hotel and Restaurant Administration Quarterly*, **36**(5), 30–35.

Morey, R. C. & Dittman, D. A. (2003). Update and extension to evaluating a hotel GM's performance. *Cornell Hotel and Restaurant Administration Quarterly*, **44**(5–6), 60–68.

Niraj, R., Gupta, M. & Narasimhan, C. (2001). Customer profitability in a supply chain. *Journal of Marketing*, **65**(July), 1–16.

Niraj, R., Foster, G., Gupta, M. & Narasimhan, C. (2003). Understanding customer level profitability implications of satisfaction programs. Working paper.

Noone, B. & Griffin, P. (1999). Managing the long-term profit yield from market segments in a hotel environment: a case study on the implementation of customer profitability analysis. *International Journal of Hospitality Management*, **18**, 111–128.

Norton, S. W. (1988). An empirical look at franchising as an organizational form. *Journal of Business*, **61**, 197–217.

Perrow, C. (1983). The organizational context of human factors engineering. *Administrative Science Quarterly*, **28**, 521–541.

Porter, M. E. (1980). *Competitive Strategy: Techniques for Analyzing Industries and Competitors*. New York, NY: The Free Press.

Porter, M. E. (1985). *Competitive Advantage: Creating and Sustaining Superior Performance*. New York, NY: The Free Press.

Prendergast, C. (2002). The tenuous trade-off between risk and incentives. *Journal of Political Economy*, **110**, 1071–1102.

Riley, R. A. Jr, Pearson, T. A. & Trompeter, G. (2003). The value relevance of non-financial performance variables and accounting information: the case of the airline industry. *Journal of Accounting and Public Policy*, **22**, 231–254.

Sandino, T. (2007). Introducing the first management control systems: evidence from the retail sector. *The Accounting Review*, **80**(1), 265–293.

Schefczyk, M. (1993). Operational performance of airlines: an extension of traditional measurement paradigms. *Strategic Management Journal*, **14**, 301–317.

Scott, W. R. (1998). *Organizations: Rational, Natural, and Open Systems*, (4th ed.). Upper Saddle River, NJ: Prentice Hall.

Sharma, D. S. (2002). The differential effect of environmental dimensionality, size, and structure on budget system characteristics in hotels. *Management Accounting Research*, **13**, 101–130.

Sigala, M. (2003). The information and communication technologies productivity impact on the UK hotel sector. *International Journal of Operations & Production Management*, **23**(10), 1224–1245.

Sigala, M., Jones, P., Lockwood, A. & Airey, D. (2005). Productivity in hotels: a stepwise data envelopment analysis of hotels' rooms division processes. *The Service Industries Journal*, **25**(1), 61–81.

Simons, R. (1995). *Levers of Control: How Managers Use Innovative Control Systems to Drive Strategic Renewal*. Boston, MA: Harvard Business School Press.

Standard & Poor's. (2007). *Industry Surveys: Restaurants (10-18-2007)* New York, NY: Standard & Poor's.

Tarim, S., Dener, H. I. & Tarim, S. A. (2000). Efficiency measurement in the hotel industry: output factor constrained DEA application. *Anatolia: An International Journal of Tourism and Hospitality Research*, **11**(2), 111–123.

Thorne, W. V. S. (1918). *Hospital Accounting and Statistics*, (4th ed.). New York, NY: E. P. Dutton & Co.

Wang, F. C., Hung, W. T. & Shang, J. K. (2006). Measuring pure managerial efficiency of international tourist hotels in Taiwan. *The Service Industries Journal*, **26**(1), 59–71.

Williamson, O. E. (1979). Transaction-cost economics: the governance of contractual relations. *Journal of Law and Economics*, **22**(2), 233–261.

Williamson, O. E. (1985). *The Economic Institutions of Capitalism*. New York, NY: The Free Press.

Handbook of Management Accounting Research
Edited by Christopher S. Chapman, Anthony G. Hopwood and Michael D. Shields

Management Accounting, Economic Reasoning and the New Public Management Reforms

Liisa Kurunmäki

London School of Economics and Political Science, UK

Abstract: New forms of accounting and new forms of accountability have emerged out of the set of reforms that are often referred to as "New Public Management." These changes, which are transnational even if they are not yet global, have had an impact on actors in a diverse range of settings including education, culture, policing, probation, prosecution, healthcare, social services, transport and defence. A substantial body of literature on accounting in its social and institutional context has analyzed how accounting practices affect the ways in which organizations, and the various actors that populate them and their environment, define and shape the choices available to them. It has examined how the use of accounting tools and technologies shape the ways in which activities and processes come to be articulated, debated and made operable. Accounting has been seen to possess significant potential for changing the exercise and balance of power within organizations. The roles of accounting expertise in these changes have been discussed, as has the willingness of other experts and professionals to acknowledge the influence of accounting and accountants.

This chapter, which focuses on a set of studies that have analyzed the ways in which accounting has contributed to a reshaping of existing power relations in various public sector settings, touches on three separate yet overlapping literatures: first, the relevant literature that has examined accounting in its social and institutional context, both in the public and private sector settings; secondly, the body of research on the accounting aspects of new public management reforms, including studies that go beyond the Anglo-American contexts and that focus in particular on the capacity of accounting to shift power relations in a range of public sector settings; thirdly, sociological studies of professions and professional expertise, for at the heart of the new public management reforms is not only an encounter between different types of practice, but an encounter between formally distinct and often competing professional groupings. Having reviewed briefly these three sets of literatures, this chapter considers in more detail a small number of studies that examine the shift from "financial literacy" to "hybridization," a shift that is suggested to be a central aspect of the encounter between management accounting, economic reasoning and the new public management reforms.

1. Introduction

The "New Public Management" reforms gained widespread popularity among policy makers of many Western societies during the 1980s (Hood, 1995; Hopwood, 1984). These reforms were based on a view of the public sector as a major problem with poor management identified as a primary cause (Humphrey et al., 1993). An increased use of accounting information and the introduction of competition between service providers were among key elements of proposals for remedying the alleged deficiencies, and improving the efficiency of the public sector as a whole (Humphrey et al., 1998; McSweeney, 1994; Rose & Miller, 1992; Chow et al., 2005). By the 1990s, the new public management reforms had become a transnational phenomenon (Hood, 1995; Olson et al., 1998; Guthrie et al., 2005).

The rise of managerialism—the predominance of managerial techniques, notions and expertise that abstract from the substantive domains in which they are applied—has been considered to be one of the most notable features of the socio-economic restructuring of late modernity (Giddens, 1991; Mueller & Carter, 2007). It has permeated both the public and private sectors. New informational and communication technologies are claimed to have helped modern organizations overcome the barriers of time and space, and to allow coordination

DOI: 10.1016/S1751-3243(07)03009-X

between globalized networks, as well as control over localized activities (Reed, 1996; Hopwood, 1996; Miller et al., 2008). Novel intra-organizational control technologies are argued to have enhanced the "supervisory gaze" by allowing a higher degree of visibility and transparency. And new "material technologies of control," combined with developments in "social technologies of control" are said to have allowed surveillance to penetrate even deeper into physical, social and personal areas (Willmott, 1993; Miller and Rose, 1990).

Although the actual achievements of the new managerial tools in various private and public sector settings can be debated, and no doubt vary according to national and professional contexts, it is evident that the expanding technologies of governing have brought various groups of expertise into much closer contact with accounting and accountants than previously (Bourn & Ezzamel, 1986; Broadbent et al., 1999; Chua, 1995; Harrison & Pollitt, 1994; Llewellyn, 1998; Perrin, 1988; Preston et al., 1992; Rea, 1994; Wickings, 1983; Wickings et al., 1983). This chapter reviews a set of studies that analyzes the encounters of various groups of expertise with accounting and accountants in the context of the public sector reforms and evaluates the impacts of these encounters on associated "landscapes of power".

Studies that analyze the impacts of managerialist reforms on the relations between different groups of expertise and that focus, in particular, on the capacity of accounting to alter the balance of power relations among various actors and agencies, necessarily touch on a set of distinct, yet overlapping, literatures. While these literatures can no doubt be differentiated in a variety of ways, they are categorized here under three headings: first, studies of accounting in its social and institutional context; secondly, research on the accounting aspects of the public sector reforms; and thirdly, the sociology of professions and professional expertise. The next section briefly reviews these three sets of literature. The section that follows selectively considers a small number of studies that address these partially overlapping bodies of literature, and characterizes the encounter between accounting and new public management reforms in terms of a shift from "financial literacy" to "hybridization".

2. Accounting, New Public Management and Inter-professional Encounters

First, consider those studies that have analyzed accounting in its social and institutional context (Hopwood & Miller, 1994; Miller, 2008). The papers analyzed later in this chapter draw directly and indirectly on numerous studies that have examined the roles of accounting in its organizational and social contexts, both in the private and public sectors (Ansari & Euske, 1987; Armstrong, 1987; Arnold et al., 1994; Birnberg et al., 1983; Burchell et al., 1980; Dent, 1991; Dirsmith & Jablonsky, 1979; Feldman & March, 1981; Hopwood, 1984, 1989, 1992; Jablonsky & Dirsmith, 1978; McSweeney, 1994; Meyer, 1986; Miller, 1994; Oakes et al., 1994; Pollitt, 1986; Roberts & Scapens, 1985). This literature regards accounting as constitutive of social relations, rather than secondary to them. It examines how accounting influences, and in turn is influenced by, a range of agents, entities, institutions and practices. It examines how accounting practices can affect the ways in which organizations can perceive the choices available to them, and can influence the ways in which activities and processes come to be defined and administered. It demonstrates how accounting systems can shape and form the possibilities for action within organizations.

The tripartite distinction set out by Miller (1994) concerning the distinctive contribution of this literature is relevant to the concerns of this chapter. In speaking of accounting as a technology, as based on specific rationales, and as constituting and reconstituting the economic domain, Miller draws attention to the transformative capacity of accounting, the language and meanings on which it depends, and the ways in which accounting "makes up" the financial flows through which organizations can be managed, individual choices made, and policies devised and justified. The set of articles reviewed in the next section of this chapter demonstrates the applicability of this framework by examining particular instances of introducing accounting into contexts where it has traditionally served only minor roles (Hopwood, 1992). These studies show how new accounting systems contributed to the reorganizing of social groupings in the field of education, how costing systems and the pricing of healthcare procedures enabled market principles and accounting language to be deployed throughout the hospital, how activity-based costing rendered engineering tasks calculable within the electricity industry, and how delegated financial responsibility served the ambitions of the nursing profession. The articles reviewed later in this chapter thus contribute empirically to the literature on accounting as a social and institutional practice. They also extend it theoretically by utilizing a variety of theoretical approaches, including institutional and governmentality perspectives.

Secondly, we consider studies that have examined the accounting aspects of the new public management reforms. A large volume of studies, in different disciplinary fields, have studied the objectives and impacts of new public management reforms during the past few decades. They include analyses of different models for organizing public service financing and delivery at a governmental level (Bartlett & Le Grand, 1993; Besley & Gouveia, 1994; Glennerster et al., 1994; Lapsley, 1994; Mayston, 1993; Saltman & von Otter, 1992), as well as those concerned with improving the management of public service institutions at the local level (Buxton et al., 1989, 1991; Harrison, 1988; Harrison & Pollitt, 1994).

These studies provide a basis for understanding the varying rationales for new public management reforms, the ways in which these have been articulated differently in different national and institutional settings, their implications for organizational and professional life within public service institutions and, more generally, the expanding roles for accounting that have emerged as a result (Arnold, 1991; Arnold & Oakes, 1995; Bloomfield et al., 1992; Chua, 1995; Coombs, 1987; Ellwood, 1996; Ezzamel & Willmott, 1993; Jones & Dewing, 1997; Lapsley, 1992, 1996, 1998; Lawrence et al., 1994; Marcon & Panozzo, 1998; Olson et al., 1998; Pollitt et al., 1988; Preston et al., 1992). A set of studies reviewed in the next section of this chapter focuses on the implications of the reforms in various national settings—ranging from Sweden to Canada—and their impact on the position of a variety of professionals in those contexts, ranging from healthcare to education. This extends our analysis beyond the healthcare field and the Anglo-American context that often provide the primary focus of this literature.

Finally, consider those studies that have drawn on sociological studies of the professions and professional expertise (Abbott, 1988; Ashmore et al., 1989; Engel, 1983; Jarausch, 1983; Konttinen, 1991; Perkin, 1989; Barry, 1985; Berlant, 1975; Freidson, 1975a,b; Larkin, 1983) and the accounting profession in particular (Armstrong & Jones, 1992; Loft 1986, 1990, 1994; Matthews et al., 1997, 1998; Näsi & Näsi, 1997; Pong, 1999; Walker & Shackleton, 1995, 1998). Changes in organizational forms and organizational practices arising from the new public management reforms have brought questions of the position, power and legitimacy of various professions to the fore. Some have viewed these reforms as purposeful attempts to redistribute power and control in those public sector settings where suspicion or hostility towards professional power is prevalent (Kurunmäki, 1999; Reed, 1996). Often, the consequences of this redistribution have been considered as disadvantageous to the professionals, insofar as the reforms have aimed to shift the emphasis from professional standards towards more explicit and measurable performance standards, often through extensive use of accounting practices (Hood, 1995; Blomgren, 2003; Abernethy & Vagnoni, 2004). Professional logics have been depicted as giving way to administrative–managerial logic and professionals have been depicted as resisting the reforms, trying to protect their core activities and key values (Broadbent & Laughlin, 1998; Robbins, 2007). Yet, evidence provided by accounting studies shows that the encounter between the reforms and the different professional groups that they come into contact with, may produce a variety of responses, ranging from fierce resistance to willing adoption. The next section of this chapter considers in particular those studies that analyze and aim to explain these different responses by various groups of experts in their specific national, institutional and professional contexts.

In contrast to the early studies of professions and professionalization, which focused typically on individual professions, the set of articles reviewed here examines the interrelated development of two or more bodies of expertise. Abbott's injunction to examine the professions as an interdependent system is thus taken into account, as is his insistence that effective analysis of such phenomena should begin with case studies of jurisdictions and jurisdictional disputes (Abbott, 1988, p. 2). Accordingly, these studies analyze the transformations in accounting and other expertises at their margins (Miller, 1998). They extend the scope of such research empirically by reporting findings from a variety of contexts and national settings. To this extent, they contribute to a growing body of comparative studies of accounting and other expertises (Ahrens, 1996; Ahrens & Chapman, 2000; Armstrong, 1985, 1987; Dezalay, 1995, 1997; Jacobs, 2005; Jacobs et al., 2004; Kurunmäki et al., 2003; Matthews et al., 1997, 1998). The results highlight the difficulties of referring to the "accounting profession", as well as other professions, as if they were homogeneous entities across, or within, different national contexts. A comparison of different national settings brings out the fundamental variation in the institutional and pedagogic location of expertises in different countries, and the importance of focusing on the location and transferability of their associated techniques, rather than only the abstract knowledge that may define some professions. Whereas the image of jurisdictional disputes and interprofessional rivalry provides a fruitful starting point, and may describe accurately a system in which the competitive instinct is deeply embedded, it may not be a universal phenomenon. Besides competition, a hybridization of expertise may take place in some contexts, and to the extent that it does this process of hybridizing may have profound implications for the development of one or more professions in a particular field. The importance of case studies of particular encounters within the "system of professions" is demonstrated in this chapter, as are the benefits of extending the scope of such studies beyond the Anglo-American contexts most often addressed. Accordingly, the following section examines this issue, and considers how the encounter between the new public management reforms and accounting can be characterized in terms of a shift from "financial literacy" to "hybridization".

3. From Financial Literacy to Hybridization

The increasing managerialism of public services has been widely regarded as providing career and earning opportunities for business experts, such as accountants. A study by Samuel, Dirsmith & McElroy (2005) explores the improved fortunes of the accounting profession within the US healthcare industry since the early 1980s, when hospital administration and medical practice were reorganized under the banner of "cost-containment" (Preston, 1992). According to Samuel et al., it was the industrial engineers who took advantage of their historical jurisdiction over factory productivity to construct products, called DRGs, out of medical practice. Economists, for their part, built on this development and came to insist on medical service as a market phenomenon replete with producers, consumers and commodities. By conceptualizing patients as demanding consumers, and doctors and hospitals as self-interested suppliers, economists made plausible a market for a commodity called "care." Labouring in a grove seeded by engineers and cultivated by economists, accountants are depicted by Samuel et al. as picking the fruits of the growing healthcare market. Together with other business experts, accountants have come to offer healthcare producers in the US and elsewhere an increasing range of services, such as the audit of diagnostic codes to analyze and maximize hospital revenues, case-mix accounting to manage product costs and the designing of e-commerce solutions to manage hospital supply chains.

Accountants and other managerial experts selling business advice and tools in the US healthcare market have clearly benefited from the commercialization of health care, even if they have not solved the problem of rising medical costs. However, studies of the managerialist reforms elsewhere, in a wide variety of national and institutional contexts, have not produced uniform accounts concerning the consequences of managerial reforms. This section reviews a small number of studies that have analyzed, in differing contexts, the reactions of a range of actors to the managerial reforms, their implications for power relationships within organizations, as well as in the broader social fields, and the impacts of these reforms on different groups of experts, especially accountants.

A study by Neu (2006) contributes to our understanding of these issues. It analyzes the relationship between accounting and public space in the context of educational reforms in Alberta, Canada, in the mid-1990s. Drawing on the works of both Bourdieu and Foucault, it focuses on the constitutive role of accounting, and asks how accounting is implicated in the constitution of social spaces, what roles accounting plays in organizing and ordering public spaces, and how accounting facilitates the reordering and reorganization of a particular field. It examines how financial, accounting and accountability changes reconstituted the field of education, shifted economic and social capital, contributed to the reorganizing of social groupings, and encouraged changing ways of saying and doing in a particular field at a particular time.

A starting point for Neu's study is a mapping of the educational field during pre- and post-reform periods in terms of financial, accountability and interactional flows among field participants. The reforms analyzed include various funding, accounting and accountability changes. These reforms centralized educational funding at the provincial level and introduced new accountability practices, including the publication of school district financial statements and student achievement test results. The sector also saw a substantial reduction in education funding over the four year period that followed the reforms, and an emergence of the term "financial" in the public discourse in the domain of education. Financial representations and accounting techniques were observed to have become an important part of the vocabulary of education during the post-reform period.

Neu's analysis highlights how the financial and accountability mechanisms introduced by the reforms facilitated changes in the types and amounts of capital of certain field participants, thus altering the landscape of power. The findings of Neu's study, in this respect, are similar to the findings of Oakes, Townley & Cooper (1998), who studied the introduction of business planning in the museums and cultural heritage sites in Alberta, Canada in the early 1990s. According to Oakes et al., business planning had significant implications for the field studied. It was found to redefine the field by changing the capitals and positions within this field. In the educational field, funding changes were also found to have significant implications for the positions of power and influence. These changes liquidated the economic capital and also reduced the symbolic capital of the School Board of Trustees. Trustees were elected during municipal elections for a term of three years and, until the reforms, possessed a significant influence over both the resource inflow and use of funds. However, the reforms centralized economic and informational capital at the level of provincial government, thereby increasing the influence of the politicians and bureaucrats and their allies, such as the business community. According to Neu's analysis, accounting and other numbers came to be intrinsic to the form of justification used by government spokespeople to justify their actions, and they also influenced the ways of acting and talking within schools. Field participants came to talk about education differently, focusing more on the financial aspects. They spent more time on accounting and reporting activities and they viewed internal social relations differently.

Financial literacy thus emerged as a form of cultural capital within the field. The reforms increased the value of accounting literacy in this particular field and "restricted" the groups who could participate in various discussions inside and outside the schools. However, although accounting numbers facilitated the creation of a space where numbers became central to public discourse, it appears that the position of accountants was not significantly enhanced. According to Neu, most of the participants in various discourses were not accountants and tended to use numbers in non-technical ways. While some degree of financial literacy was necessary to participate in the discussions and to use the financial numbers, the debate was not limited to accountants and other technical experts. This is what is meant here by "financial literacy," the diffusion of a vocabulary drawn from accounting and financial management, but which is accessible to all.

A field study by Kurunmäki (1999) contributes similarly to the literature on accounting in its social and institutional context, as well as to the literature on the accounting aspects of the public sector reforms. It also uses Bourdieu's concepts of field and capital. The study focuses on the introduction of market forces in the Finnish healthcare field in the early 1990s. The aim of the paper is to analyze whether these market-based reforms, and the introduction of the accounting systems that were so central to these reforms, succeeded in altering the relations of power in the hospital field. Enhancing the value of economic versus professional capital in the field of healthcare and, accordingly, increasing the power of healthcare financiers over that of service providers is analyzed as one of the main objectives of the Finnish healthcare reforms.

However, the process of marketization in the Finnish healthcare field encountered limits. The view of those involved with health service production was that conditions favourable to competition were absent, due in large part to the small number of service providers. Local authorities were also reluctant to set up competition for political reasons and there were difficulties in creating purchaser–provider relationships between health service professionals. A further problem was considered to be the limited and unreliable nature of information provided to those responsible for service purchasing. Contrary to the aspirations of healthcare reformers, the monetarization of health service transactions through the price and market mechanisms was regarded as having failed to reveal unambiguous differences in health service providers' cost efficiency or quality. As a result, political decision-makers were regarded as unable to augment the value of their financial capital and unable to challenge the professional capital of the medical experts.

A further paper analyzing the Finnish healthcare market reforms contributes to the literature of professions and professional expertise by focusing on the encounter between medical professionals and the calculative practices of managerial accounting (Kurunmäki, 2004). This paper similarly reveals the continuing dominance and autonomy of medical professionals in the Finnish hospital settings, despite the aspirations of the reformers to diminish the power of this group. These two papers on Finnish healthcare reforms do not, however, imply a static picture of medical expertise and its power base, nor do they suggest that the new public management reforms had been without effect. Although these reforms failed to reorganize relations of power within this field as intended, the process of marketization none-the-less had substantial consequences. A "hybridization" of the medical profession in Finland was one such consequence of the encounter between medical professionals and the practices of managerial accounting (Kurunmäki, 2004; Lehtonen, 2007). The term "hybridization" is used to characterize the outcome of the process by which medical professionals acquired much of the calculative skills often regarded as the preserve of management accountants, an outcome which is significantly different from the spread of "financial literacy." An appropriation and use of basic accounting tools by medical professionals enabled them, for example, to prepare budgets, calculate costs and set prices, resulting in a profound change in the organizational life of the hospitals studied. Economic reasoning was observed to play an important role in healthcare settings, even if it was employed differently in different types of hospitals (Kurunmäki, 1999). To make themselves heard and believed, health professionals had started to inform their various proposals with economic rationality, rather than in purely medical terms, and—as in the context of Canadian educational reforms discussed by Neu—the competence to speak and argue using accounting language had come to be regarded as a highly valued capital in the field. The requirement of medical professionals to translate their terms of calculation from medical to financial had not only changed the form of augmentation in hospitals. In the process, health professionals had been urged to think about their activities in new ways and according to changed norms. Altered ways of talking were regarded as having contributed to new ways of acting in healthcare settings.

Mueller & Carter (2007) continue with the themes of managerialism and hybridization. Their analysis focuses on the impacts of the organizational changes that took place in the British electricity supply industry in the period following the sector's privatization in the early 1990s. In a case study of one regional electricity company, Mueller & Carter analyze the de-legitimation of the extant mode and logic of organization—that of the centrality of professional engineering—and the creation of the conditions for managerialism to prosper and carve out jurisdictional control. Their study has commonalities with findings by Dent (1991), whose study focuses on the managerial reorganizations within a British nationalized railway company. Like the study of Mueller & Carter, the analysis by Dent investigates the gradual displacement of the dominant organizational culture, one that centred on the engineering and production concerns, by a new preoccupation with economic and accounting concerns in its particular institutional setting.

Mueller & Carter describe how engineers had enjoyed full professional jurisdiction over the domain of regional electricity companies in the UK since the nationalization of the industry in the late 1940s. The dominance of professional engineers was manifested through their virtual monopoly of managerial positions. While the internal arena of work organization was dominated by engineering considerations, the external arena was dominated by economists and economic forecasting. Treasury economists, responsible for macroplanning and the governance of the industry as a whole, set relatively modest financial expectations, reinforcing the culture of "non-interference." There was a loose coupling between the two groups of experts—professional engineers and treasury economists—with the implication that the regional electricity companies had very little engagement with the broader social world, especially the world of management thought.

The idea according to which electricity companies (just like railway companies) were most efficiently run by engineers by virtue of their knowledge and expertise came to be challenged by the ideals of the new Thatcherite government elected in 1979. The privatization of the electricity supply industry that followed contributed to a "seismic shift in the balance of power" in the industry. Integral to this privatization was the establishment of a new regulator. While the new regulator was run by an economist, accountants also played important roles. An operationalization of monetarist economic theories was accompanied by a panoply of contemporary management accounting techniques which, according to Mueller & Carter, amounted to a "hybridization" of economics and management accounting. Instead of two dominant groups—engineers and economists—occupying semi-autonomous spheres, there was "the interpretation of accounting and economics into the sphere of engineering." Monism was replaced by dualism, and loose coupling was replaced by tight coupling of the external industry environment and internal work organization. In distinct contrast to the nationalized past, external expectations came to be translated directly into internal actions. Performance measures instituted by the regulator reshaped perceptions of what constituted the critical issues. Notions of customer service and financial performance came to replace notions of engineering excellence. Cost and price targets imposed by the regulator led to the use of activity-based costing to create "market rates" for different tasks, and total quality management was applied as a means of delivering improved services and reduced costs. The application of such new managerial tools was also seen as serving the purpose of conveying positive messages about the organization to the regulator.

Changes introduced in the electricity sector from the early 1980s onwards led to new ideas entering the organization that ultimately exposed the vulnerability of the engineering profession. In the space of seven years following the privatization of the industry, professional engineers went from being a dominant group in the organization to almost being removed from the organization. Engineers, who in this specific national and industry setting did not possess a tradition of having to defend themselves, became the objects of reorganization and control. Managerial tools increased the transparency of what it is that the engineering profession does, and activity-based costing rendered engineering tasks calculable. Activities that were once the preserve of a profession came to be carried out by semi-skilled workers with the help of step-by-step guides. Senior engineers, many of whom came to see themselves as corporate executives, largely internalized and embraced the practices and languages of managerialism. For a vast majority of engineers, however, job redesign projects and work process reengineering—facilitated by accounting technologies—amounted to a reduction in the task autonomy, skill level and task significance or, at its most extreme, the loss of a job.

If increased transparency with respect to work tasks contributed to the loss of autonomy, status and jurisdiction of professional engineers in the UK electricity industry (Mueler & Carter, 2007), the "invisibility" of caring work is exactly what has long been considered as the problem for the professional status of nursing experts (Bowker & Starr, 1999). A study by Blomgren (2003) contributes to the set of studies of managerial reforms and the broader literature of professionalization by addressing the issue of the responses to, and the handling of, managerial reforms by nurses in the context of Swedish healthcare reorganization in the 1990s. The study analyzes two campaigns launched by the Swedish nursing association as a response to these reforms. Although these campaigns indicate seemingly contradictory responses—swaying from optimistic to pessimistic stance—Blomgren warns against interpreting these differences in reaction as evidence of the nursing association changing its mind. The paper argues that the two contradictory responses have their roots in the profession's internal constitution, which is heterogeneous and which has incorporated attempts at making nurses into mini-doctors and administrative leaders, as well as experts of caring. Overall, Blomgren calls into question the view of a profession as a coherent, stable and complete entity, arguing that the two distinct responses demonstrate how a profession that is internally heterogeneous and embraces varying ideas of professional identity simultaneously may actively try to translate reforms and their effects in ways that would further its divergent ambitions.

The optimistic campaign by the Swedish nursing association towards the managerial reforms is analyzed by Blomgren against the background of decades of jurisdictional disputes over the administrative leadership responsibilities of Swedish doctors and nurses. The expectation that the new public management reforms would bring about a more decentralized healthcare organization where head nurses would be given greater financial responsibility—and thus more freedom, autonomy and authority within the hospital hierarchy—led to a campaign that encouraged the membership of the association to fight to fulfil this expectation in their local workplaces. The reforms were seen to provide an important opportunity to make administrative leadership a possible career choice for nurses at the ward level, in a context where the latest development in the contest between physicians and nurses had been to accord administrative leadership within clinical units to physicians.

Whereas the segment of the nursing profession that already worked in administrative leadership roles was contented, feeling that their positions as head of their wards had been vindicated and that their relation to the medical professionals had strengthened as a result of the reforms, the segment of the profession that promoted the ideal of nurses as experts of caring were struggling. These nurses argued that they had problems protecting the integrity of their caring work in a context where the increased cost-consciousness and patient turnover rate had become important principles. It was these reactions that produced the pessimistic "No way!" campaign, directed at the wider public with the aim of standing up for the kind of healthcare that required a lot of nursing and caring. Interested in protecting the quality of caring, nurses had a reason to argue for the establishment of quality assurance programmes. From the professionalization viewpoint, systems of quality assurance that relied on extensive documentation highlighted this aspect of nurses' work and thereby gave visibility to caring work.

Blomgren's paper discusses the extensive impact of the increased managerialism in her case study context, including the ways in which increased cost-consciousness came to be accepted as an organizing principle among nurses in the hospital studied. Her paper also acknowledges the perceived importance of the location of financial responsibility in the power struggles within the overall organizational hierarchy, as well as between different groups of expertise. However, her paper, as many of the other papers reviewed above, does not discuss how accounting skills were acquired by different groups of expertise, or the implications of this on the roles, positions or numbers of accounting experts. A hybridization of medical and nursing expertise in administrative roles, with at least some basic skills of managerial accounting acquired, is assumed rather than analyzed.

The studies reviewed above demonstrate the variety of responses and the range of implications of accounting-based managerial reforms. They show how, from the viewpoint of specific groups of actors, the effects vary from developing some forms of basic financial literacy to a much more profound appropriation of accounting ideas and tools. These studies show not only how new uses of accounting potentially influence the position of accountants, but also how accounting may make other forms of expertise vulnerable and possibly contribute to their decline in particular settings, or how accounting may be appropriated by non-accountants in ways that reinforce the position of these new types of hybrid expertises. The concluding section of this chapter discusses some gaps in the literature. It raises questions concerning the roles of account*ants*—as distinct from the roles of account*ing*—in the public sector reforms, the roles of different types of accounting expertise, as well as the transferability of accounting tools and skills to other groups of experts, focusing on the implications of these for the position and future of management accountants.

4. Discussion and Conclusions

We already know much about the encounter between management accounting, economic reasoning and the new public management reforms. The studies reviewed above share a number of features and offer a reasonably consistent picture. They all demonstrate the constitutive and transformative potential of accounting that Hopwood (1987), Hines (1988), Dent (1991) and others have identified. They show how accounting, when entering new organizational and institutional settings, is capable of imposing particular rationalities for organizational action, new ideas of legitimate behaviour, and new patterns of authority and influence. They show how accounting may contribute to remarkable shifts in positions of power and how the introduction of accounting systems may change the knowledge bases of different groups of experts. Besides similarities, however, these studies also highlight possible differences. They show how accounting systems are implicated in various settings in different, possibly unique ways. And they highlight how the effects of accounting cannot be understood without appreciating the specifics of the field, as the particular changes and outcomes always reflect, at least to some extent, the local conditions. In terms of the encounter between accounting and various expertises, these studies illustrate how we can expect a variety of responses from groups ranging from nurses to engineers. These differences in responses have been analyzed and explained by the factors concerning the particular reforms, such as their design, implementation and specific context. They have also been analyzed by considering the professions in question, including their history, position and knowledge systems. We have characterized the variation in outcomes in terms of a distinction between "financial literacy" and "hybridization," albeit schematically.

In this concluding section, rather than summarizing the findings of the papers reviewed above, we wish to pose a few key questions which, it is hoped, will allow us to investigate further the nature of the encounter between management accounting, economic reasoning and the new public management reforms. Despite the significant interest of researchers from both accounting and other disciplines, our understanding of the implications of these reforms remains surprisingly limited. The following questions seek to highlight some of these gaps in our knowledge and to identify some avenues for further research.

First, we ask whether it is important to draw a distinction between the roles of account*ing* and the roles of account*ants* in the managerial reforms. Is it the case that, while the central position of accounting technologies and language have been widely noted by accounting researchers examining these reforms and their impacts, the accountants themselves may not have played equally significant roles? Studies of the managerial reforms in the accounting literature often discuss the roles played by accounting, yet they seldom address the roles played by accountants. Research into the roles and tasks of management accountants itself has been fragmented, and there is a need to extend our knowledge of management accounting to include a more cohesive body of knowledge about management accountants (Byrne & Pierce, 2007; Chapman, 1997, 1998). For example, we know little about how accountants contributed to, or what happened to the accountants as a result of, the managerial reforms in the educational field or in museums and cultural heritage sites in Alberta, Canada (Neu, 2006; Oakes et al., 1998). We know equally little about the impact of the managerialist reforms on accountants in the UK electricity and railway companies (Mueller & Carter, 2007; Dent, 1991). Finally, the roles of accountants during, and subsequent to, the reorganization of the Swedish healthcare system remain unaddressed (Blomgren, 2003). We need to know more about how accounting language and technologies were introduced in these and other comparable settings, and the roles played by accountants in these processes. We also need to know more about the impacts of these reforms on the numbers, roles and positions of accountants.

Secondly, we ask who wins and who loses in this process. Or, to put it in rather more nuanced terms: Who has benefited most from the managerial reforms within the accounting profession? While the study of Samuel et al. (2005) emphasizes the positive and significant impacts of the US health system changes on the earnings of accountants and other business experts, their discussion focuses on those professional accountants who provide their services through large accountancy and professional services firms. We wish to draw a distinction here between those accounting experts who sell their services as management consultants and those who work as management accounting experts within organizations affected by the reforms. We propose that these two distinct groups of accounting experts have different characteristics and may have benefited in differing ways and to different extents from the new public management reforms. The various managerial reforms within the public sector since the 1980s should have offered new earning and career opportunities for accountants, both within the consultancy industry and across the organizations reshaped by the diffusion of new managerialist ideals. The timing of these reforms coincided with the heavy promotion of new costing and cost management tools and the strong encouragement to managerial accountants to move from the "number cruncher" or "bean counter" role to the role of "business partner" (Johnson & Kaplan, 1987; Granlund & Lukka, 1989). The extent to which this has occurred, however, has varied according to many factors, not least the ability and eagerness of accountants to capitalize on the new business or career opportunities (Clarke, Hill & Stevens, 1999; Marriott & Marriott, 2000).

Overall, accounting experts within the professional services industry—equipped with relatively standardized tools, technical knowledge and expertise, as well as experience in selling their "customized solutions" to the client organizations—appear to have been relatively successful in exploiting the "new" accounting tools and the various financial management reforms. This is in contrast to their counterparts working in managerial accounting roles within service provider organizations. The efficient codification and dissemination of "value creating" technical expertise and knowledge systems within professional service organizations is regarded as crucial for their success (Morris & Empson, 1998). Globalized professional service firms have come to occupy a powerful position—amongst other actors such as academics, professional associations, software publishers and media—in disseminating the latest fads and fashions (Alcouffe, Berland & Levant, 2008; Bjørnenak, 1997; Malmi, 1999), and they have actively created new business opportunities for themselves, for example, by becoming major funders of various political campaigns (Empson, 2007). By participating in the organizing, administering and executing of the neo-liberal agenda, the professional service firms have taken the lead in reshaping public services in many developed and developing economies (Arnold & Cooper, 1999).

In comparison with their colleagues practising in the globalized professional service industry, the skill-set of those management accountants employed in various service–delivery settings within different national contexts is much more variable. The level of professionalization of management accountants—including the availability of, and access to, the professional associations, as well as requirements for continuing education—varies across countries, as does the training of these experts, their location within the academy, the availability of practitioner journals, etc., (Clarke, Hill & Stevens, 1999; Ahrens & Chapman, 2000; Kurunmäki, 2004). Evidence so far suggests that management accountants in different national and organizational settings have shown unequal enthusiasm towards the prospects provided by the new accounting tools, as well as various managerialist reforms. The findings of those studies that cover, but also extend beyond, the Anglo-American contexts highlight the dangers of referring to the "profession" as if it was a homogenous entity across, or even within, different national contexts (Blomgren, 2003). More needs to be known about the diversity of accounting expertise across organizations, industries and national settings, as well as the impacts of these differences on the status, position and earnings of different segments within the profession.

Finally, our third question relates to the future of management accounting expertise. It asks how readily transferable are the core terminology and techniques of accounting, and—to the extent that this is a variable—what are the implications for the future of accounting expertise. The evidence so far has demonstrated not only varying degrees of eagerness on the part of different segments of the accounting profession to capitalize on the managerialist reforms, but also varying levels of interest in the transferability of accounting language, skills and tools amongst potentially competing groups of expertise. Hybridization—facilitated by the mobility or transferability of accounting techniques and their associated knowledge basis, combined with the readiness in some contexts of other groups of experts to appropriate the core skills and language of accounting—poses significant risks to the future of the profession. For accounting is itself a hybrid that was formed and reformed at the margins of other practices and disciplines, which, in the case of management accounting, included engineering and economics (Miller, 1998). Skills and tasks that have, over the years, come to be regarded as the preserve of accountants, may increasingly come to be carried out by other groups of experts. In this process, tools introduced by accountants to facilitate organizational control, and often assumed to lead to an improved position for accountants, may be taken over by other groups, making accountants themselves the objects, rather than agents, of reorganization and control. More needs to be known about the mobility of accounting techniques across the systems of knowledge within various groups or sets of experts, as well as the likely impacts of these skills and knowledge transfers on management accountants.

References

Abbott, A. (1988). *The system of professions: an essay on the division of expert labor*. Chicago, IL: University of Chicago Press.

Abernethy, M. A. & Vagnonib, E. (2004). Power, organization design and managerial behaviour. *Accounting, Organizations and Society*, **29**(3–4), 207–225.

Alcouffe, S., Berland, N. & Levant, Y. (2008). Actor-networks and the diffusion of management accounting innovations: A comparative study. *Management Accounting Research*, **19**(1), 1–17.

Ahrens, T. (1996). Styles of accountability. *Accounting, Organizations and Society*, **21**(2–3), 139–173.

Ahrens, T. & Chapman, C. S. (2000). Occupational identity of management accountants in Britain and Germany. *European Accounting Review*, **9**(4), 477–498.

Ansari, S. & Euske, K. J. (1987). Rational, rationalizing, and reifying uses of accounting data in organizations. *Accounting, Organizations and Society*, **12**(6), 549–570.

Armstrong, P. (1985). Changing management control strategies: the role of competition between accountancy and other organizational professions. *Accounting, Organizations and Society*, **10**(2), 129–148.

Armstrong, P. (1987). The rise of accounting controls in British capitalist enterprises. *Accounting, Organizations and Society*, **12**(5), 415–436.

Armstrong, P. & Jones, C. (1992). The decline of the operational expertise in the knowledge-base of management accounting: an examination of some post-war trends in the qualifying requirements of the Chartered Institute of Management Accountants. *Management Accounting Research*, **3**(1), 53–75.

Arnold, P. J. (1991). Accounting and the state: consequences of merger and acquisition accounting in the U.S. hospital industry. *Accounting, Organizations and Society*, **16**(2), 121–140.

Arnold, P. J. & Cooper, C. (1999). A tale of two classes: The privatisation of Medway Ports. *Critical Perspectives on Accounting*, **19**(2), 127–152.

Arnold, P. J., Hammond, T. D. & Oakes, L. S. (1994). The contemporary discourse on health care cost: conflicting meanings and meaningful conflicts. *Accounting, Auditing and Accountability Journal*, **7**(3), 50–67.

Arnold, P. J. & Oakes, L. S. (1995). Hospitals in the United States: a study of the entity assumption in accounting. *Critical Perspectives on Accounting*, **6**, 105–123.

Ashmore, M., Mulkay, M. & Pinch, T. (1989). *Health and efficiency: a sociology of health economics*. Milton Keynes, UK: Open University Press.

Barry, J. (1985). Piety and the patient: medicine and religion in eighteenth century Bristol. In: R. Porter. (Ed.), *Patients and practitioners: lay perceptions of medicine in pre-industrial society*. Cambridge, UK: Cambridge University Press.

Bartlett, W. & Le Grand, J. (1993). The theory of quasi-markets. In: W. Bartlett & J. LeGrand (Eds),

Quasi-markets and social policy. London, UK: The MacMillan Press Ltd.

Berlant, J. (1975). *Profession and monopoly: a study of medicine in the United States and Great Britain*. Berkeley, CA: University of California Press.

Besley, T. & Gouveia, M. (1994). Alternative systems of health care provision. *Economic Policy*, **October**, 200–258.

Birnberg, J. G., Turopolec, L. & Young, M. S. (1983). The organizational context of accounting. *Accounting, Organizations and Society*, **8**(2–3), 111–129.

Bjørnenak, T. (1997). Diffusion and accounting: the case of ABC in Norway. *Management Accounting Research*, **8**(1), 3–17.

Blomgren, M. (2003). Ordering a profession: Swedish nurses encounter New Public Management reforms. *Financial Accountability and Management*, **19**(1), 45–71.

Bloomfield, B. P., Coombs, R., Cooper, D. J. & Rea, D. (1992). Machines and manoeuvres: responsibility accounting and the construction of hospital information systems. *Accounting, Management & Information Technologies*, **2**(4), 197–219.

Bourn, M. & Ezzamel, M. (1986). Organizational culture in hospitals in the National Health Service. *Financial Accountability & Management*, **2**(3), 203–225.

Bowker, G. C. & Star, S. L. (1999). *Sorting things out, classification and its consequences*. Cambridge, MA: The MIT Press.

Broadbent, J., Jacobs, K. & Laughlin, R. (1999). Comparing schools in the UK and New Zealand: individualizing and socializing accountabilities and some implications for management control. *Management Accounting Research*, **10**(4), 339–361.

Broadbent, J. & Laughlin, R. (1998). Resisting the "New Public Management" absorption and absorbing groups in schools and GP practices in the UK. *Accounting, Auditing and Accountability Journal*, **11**(4), 403–435.

Burchell, S., Clubb, C., Hopwood, A. G. & Hughes, J. (1980). The roles of accounting in organizations and society. *Accounting, Organizations and Society*, **5**(1), 5–27.

Buxton, M., Packwood, T. & Keen, J. (1989). Resource management: process and progress – monitoring the six acute hospital pilot sites. Interim report of the Brunel University evaluation team. Uxbridge, UK: Health Economics Research Group, Brunel University.

Buxton, M., Packwood, T. & Keen, J. (1991). Final report of the Brunel University evaluation of resource management. Health Economics Research Group, Research Report No. 10.

Byrne, S. & Pierce, B. (2007). Towards a more comprehensive understanding of the roles of management accountants. *European Accounting Review*, **16**(3), 469–498.

Chapman, C. S. (1998). Accountants in organisational networks. *Accounting, Organizations and Society*, **23**(8), 737–766.

Chapman, C. S. (1997). Reflections on a contingent view of accounting. *Accounting, Organizations and Society*, **22**(2), 189–205.

Chow, D. S. L., Humphrey, C. G. & Miller, P. (2005). Financial Management in the UK Public Sector: Historical Development, Current Issues and Controversies. In: J. Guthrie, C. Humphrey, L. R. Jones, & O. Olson (Eds), *International Public Financial Management Reform*. Greenwich, CT: Information Age Publishing.

Chua, W. F. (1995). Experts, networks and inscriptions in the fabrication of accounting images: a story of the representation of three public hospitals. *Accounting, Organizations and Society*, **20**(2–3), 111–145.

Clarke, P. J., Hill, N. T. & Stevens, K. (1999). Activity-based costing in Ireland: barriers to, and opportunities for, change. *Critical Perspectives on Accounting*, **10**(4), 443–468.

Coombs, R. W. (1987). Accounting for the control of doctors: management information systems in hospitals. *Accounting, Organizations and Society*, **12**(4), 389–404.

Dent, J. F. (1991). Accounting and organizational cultures: a field study of the emergence of a new organizational reality. *Accounting, Organizations and Society*, **16**(8), 705–732.

Dezalay, Y. (1995). "Turf battles" or "class struggles": the internationalization of the market for expertise in the "professional society". *Accounting, Organizations and Society*, **20**(5), 331–344.

Dezalay, Y. (1997). Accountants as "new guard dogs" of capitalism: stereotype or research agenda? *Accounting, Organizations and Society*, **22**(8), 825–829.

Dirsmith, M. W. & Jablonsky, S. F. (1979). MBO, political rationality and information inductance. *Accounting, Organizations and Society*, **4**(1), 39–52.

Ellwood, S. (1996). Full-cost pricing rules within the National Health Service internal market—accounting choices and the achievement of productive efficiency. *Management Accounting Research*, **7**(1), 25–51.

Empson, L. (2007). Professional Service Firm. In: S. R. Clegg & J. Bailey *International encyclopedia of organization studies*. Thousand Oaks, CA: Sage.

Engel, A. (1983). The English universities and professional education. In: K. H. Jarausch (Ed.), *The transformation of higher learning 1860–1930*. Chicago, IL: The University of Chicago Press.

Ezzamel, M. & Willmott, H. (1993). Corporate governance and financial accountability: recent reforms in the UK public sector. *Accounting, Auditing and Accountability Journal*, **6**(3), 109–132.

Feldman, M. S. & March, J. G. (1981). Information in organizations as signal and symbol. *Administrative Science Quarterly*, **26**(2), 171–186.

Freidson, E. (1975a). *Professional dominance: the social structure of medical care*. Chicago, IL: Aldine Publishing Company.

Freidson, E. (1975b). *Profession of medicine: a study of the sociology of applied knowledge*. New York, NY: Dodd, Mead & Company.

Giddens, A. (1991). *The consequences of modernity*. Cambridge, UK: Polity Press.

Glennerster, H., Matsaganis, M., Owens, P. & Hancock, S. (1994). *Implementing GP fund holding: wild card or winning hand?* London, UK: Open University Press.

Granlund, M. & Lukka, K. (1998). Towards increasing business orientation: Finnish management accountants in a changing cultural context. *Management Accounting Research*, **9**(2), 185–211.

Guthrie, J., Humphrey, C., Jones, L. R. & Olson, O. (Eds) (2005). *International Public Financial Management Reform*. Greenwich, Connecticut: Information Age Publishing.

Harrison, S. (1988). *Managing the National Health Service: shifting the frontier?* London, UK: Chapman and Hall.

Harrison, S. & Pollitt, C. (1994). *Controlling health professionals: the future of work and organization in the National Health Service*. Buckingham, UK: Open University Press.

Hines, R. (1988). Financial accounting in communicating reality. We construct reality. *Accounting, Organizations and Society*, **13**(3), 251–261.

Hood, C. (1995). The "New Public Management" in the 1980s: variations on a theme. *Accounting, Organizations and Society*, **20**(2–3), 93–109.

Hopwood, A. G. (1984). Accounting and pursuit of efficiency. In: A. G. Hopwood & C. Tomkins (Eds), *Issues in public sector accounting*. Oxford, UK: Philip Allar.

Hopwood, A. G. (1987). The archeology of accounting systems. *Accounting, Organizations and Society*, **12**(3), 207–234.

Hopwood, A. G. (1989). Organizational contingencies and accounting configurations. In: B. Fridman, & L. Östman (Eds), *Accounting development—some perspectives—in honour of Sven-Erik Johansson*. Stockholm, Sweden: Blackwell Publishing.

Hopwood, A. G. (1992). Accounting, calculation and the shifting sphere of the economic. *The European Accounting Review*, **1**(1), 125–143.

Hopwood, A. G. (1996). Looking across rather than up and down: On the need to explore the lateral processing of information. *Accounting, Organizations and Society*, **21**(6), 589–590.

Hopwood, A. G. & Miller, P. (1994). *Accounting as social and institutional practice*. Cambridge, UK: Cambridge University Press.

Humphrey, C., Miller, P. & Scapens, R. W. (1993). Accountability and accountable management in the UK public sector. *Accounting, Auditing and Accountability Journal*, **6**(3), 7–29.

Humphrey, C., Miller, P. & Smith, H. (1998). Financial management in the UK public sector: ambiguities, paradoxes and limits. In: O. Olson, J. Guthrie & C. Humphrey (Eds), *Global warning! Debating international developments in New Public Financial Management*. Oslo, Norway: Cappelen Akademisk Forlag as.

Jablonsky, S. F. & Dirsmith, M. W. (1978). The pattern of PPB rejection: something about organizations, something about PPB. *Accounting, Organizations and Society*, **3**(3/4), 215–225.

Jacobs, K. (2005). Hybridisation or polarisation: doctors and accounting in the UK, Germany and Italy. *Financial Accountability & Management*, **21**(2), 135–161.

Jacobs, K., Marcon, G. & Witt, D. (2004). Cost and performance information for doctors: an international comparison. *Management Accounting Research*, **15**(3), 337–354.

Jarausch, K. H. (1983). Higher education and social change: some comparative perspectives. In: K. H. Jarausch (Ed.), *The Transformation of Higher Learning 1860–1930*. Chicago, IL: The University of Chicago Press.

Johnson, H. T. & Kaplan, R. S. (1987). *Relevance lost: The rise and fall of management accounting*. Boston, MA: Harvard Business School Press.

Jones, C. S. & Dewing, I. P. (1997). The attitudes of NHS clinicians and medical managers towards changes in accounting controls. *Financial Accountability and Management*, **13**(3), 261–280.

Kesteloot, K. & Penninckx, F. (1993). The costs and effects of open versus laproscopic cholecystectomies. *Health Economics*, **2**, 303–312.

Konttinen, E. (1991). *Towards modern in a traditional way—the social birth of professions in Finland* (Perinetieseti moderniin—professioiden yhteiskunnallinen synty Suomessa). Tampere: Vastapaino.

Kurunmäki, L. (1999). Professional vs. financial capital in the field of health care – struggles for the redistribution of power and control. *Accounting, Organizations and Society*, **24**(2), 95–124.

Kurunmäki, L. (2004). A hybrid profession – the acquisition of management accounting expertise by medical professionals. *Accounting, Organizations and Society*, **29**(3–4), 327–347.

Kurunmäki, L., Lapsley, I. & Melia, K. (2003). Accountingization vs. legitimation: A comparative study of the use of accounting information in intensive care. *Management Accounting Research*, **14**(2), 112–139.

Lapsley, I. (1992). Reforming financial controls in the NHS – or is the NHS a "deviant" organization? In: M. Ezzamel & D. Heathfield (Eds), *Perspectives on financial control: essays in memory of Kenneth Hilton*. London, UK: Chapman & Hall.

Lapsley, I. (1994). Market mechanisms and the management of health care: the UK model and experience. *International Journal of Management*, **7**(6), 15–25.

Lapsley, I. (1996). The puzzle of hospital doctors decision-making: an exploratory case study. *International Association of Management Journal*, **8**(2), 1–19.

Lapsley, I. (1998). Reforming the public sector: demon accountants at work? *Irish Accounting Review*, **5**(1), 115–131.

Larkin, G. (1983). *Occupational monopoly and modern medicine*. London, UK: Tavistock Publications Ltd.

Lawrence, S., Alam, M. & Lowe, T. (1994). The great experiment: financial management in the NZ health sector. *Accounting, Auditing and Accountability Journal*, **7**(3), 68–95.

Lehtonen, T. (2007). DRG-based prospective pricing and case-mix accounting: Exploring the mechanisms of successful implementation. *Management Accounting Research*, **18**(3), 367–395.

Llewellyn, S. (1998). Boundary work: Costing and caring in the social services. *Accounting, Organizations and Society*, **23**(1), 23–47.

Loft, A. (1986). Towards a critical understanding of accounting: The case of cost accounting in the UK, 1914–1925. *Accounting, Organizations and Society*, **11**(2), 137–169.

Loft, A. (1990). *Coming into the light: a study of the development of a professional association for cost accountants in Britain in the wake of the First World War*. London, UK: CIMA.

Loft, A. (1994). Accountancy and the First World War. In: A. G. Hopwood & P. Miller (Eds), *Accounting as social and institutional practice*. Cambridge, UK: Cambridge University Press.

Malmi, T. (1999). Activity-based costing diffusion across organizations: an exploratory empirical analysis of Finnish firms. *Accounting, Organizations and Society*, **24**(8), 649–672.

Marcon, G. & Panozzo, F. (1998). Reforming the reform: changing roles for accounting and management in the Italian health care sector. *The European Accounting Review*, **7**(2), 185–208.

Marriott, N. & Marriott, P. (2000). Professional accountants and the development of a management accounting service for the small firm: barriers and possibilities. *Management Accounting Research*, **11**(4), 475–492.

Matthews, D., Anderson, M. & Edwards, J. R. (1997). The rise of professional accountant in British management. *Economic History Review*, **50**(3), 407–429.

Matthews, D., Anderson, M. & Edwards, J. R. (1998). *The priesthood of industry: the rise of the professional accountant in British management*. Oxford, UK: Oxford University Press.

Mayston, D. (1993). Principals, agents and the economics of accountability in the New Public Sector. *Accounting, Auditing and Accountability Journal*, **6**(3), 68–96.

McSweeney, B. (1994). Management by accounting. In: A. G. Hopwood & P. Miller (Eds), *Accounting as social and institutional practice*. Cambridge, UK: Cambridge University Press, pp. 237–269.

Meyer, J. W. (1986). Social environments and organizational accounting. *Accounting, Organizations and Society*, **11**(4–5), 345–356.

Miller, P. B. (1994). Accounting and objectivity: The invention of calculating selves and calculable spaces. In: A. Megill (Ed.), *Rethinking objectivity*. London, UK: Duke University Press.

Miller, P. B. (1998). The margins of accounting. In: M. Callon (Ed.), *The laws of the markets*. Oxford, UK: Blackwell Publishers.

Miller, P. B. (2008). Calculating economic life. *Journal of Cultural Economy*, **1**(1), 51–64.

Miller, P., Kurunmäki, L. & O'Leary, T. (2007). Accounting, hybrids and the management of risk. *Accounting, Organizations and Society*, doi: 10.1016/j.aos.2007.02.005.

Miller, P. & Rose, N. (1992). Political power beyond the state: Problematics of government. *British Journal of Sociology*, **43**(2), 173–205.

Morris, T. & Empson, L. (1998). Organisation and expertise: An exploration of knowledge bases and the management of accounting and consulting firms. *Accounting, Organizations and Society*, **23**(5–6), 609–624.

Mueller, F. & Carter, C. (2007). "We are all managers now": Managerialism and professional engineering in UK electricity utilities. *Accounting, Organizations and Society*, **32**(1–2), 181–195.

Neu, D. (2006). Accounting for public space. *Accounting, Organizations and Society*, **31**(4/5), 391–414.

Näsi, S. & Näsi, J. (1997). Accounting and business economics traditions in Finland—from a practical discipline into a scientific subject and field of research. *The European Accounting Review*, **6**(2), 199–229.

Oakes, L. S., Considine, J. & Gould, S. (1994). Counting health care costs in the United States: A hermeneutical study of cost benefit research. *Accounting, Auditing and Accountability Journal*, **7**(3), 18–49.

Oakes, L., Townley, B. & Cooper, D. J. (1998). Business plans as pedagogy: Bourdieu and institutional change. *Administrative Science Quarterly*, **43**(2), 257–292.

Olson, O., Guthrie, J. & Humphrey, C. (Eds) (1998). *Global warning! Debating international developments in New Public Financial Management*. Oslo, Norway: Cappelen Akademisk Forlag as.

Perkin, H. (1989). *The rise of professional society: England since 1880*. London, UK: Routledge.

Handbook of Management Accounting Research
Edited by Christopher S. Chapman, Anthony G. Hopwood and Michael D. Shields

Management Accounting in Financial Services

Kim Soin[1] and Tobias Scheytt[2,3]

[1]*Department of Management, King's College London, UK*
[2]*School of Management, Innsbruck University, Austria*
[3]*Helmut-Schmidt University, Hamburg, Germany*

Abstract: This chapter focuses on the changing role of management accounting and control in the financial services sector over the last 25 years. It identifies two key phases that impacted the use and nature of management accounting systems. The first phase relates to the (global) deregulation of the industry and shows how, as a result of increased competition, a new emphasis on efficiency and effectiveness emerged. Management accounting techniques (such as activity-based costing (ABC) and the balanced scorecard) became the primary devices to manage costs and performance. The chapter then highlights how, during the second phase of reregulation and the resulting changes in the industry, management accounting was replaced by risk as the central issue in internal control. The chapter concludes that management accounting and control systems have had a short career in financial services, yet might again attain more relevance for practice and research once the limitations of risk management, like the neglect of strategic risks and the difficulties of grasping operational risks, are fully realized.

1. Introduction

This chapter focuses on the changing nature of management accounting practices in the financial services sector over the past 25 years. It provides a comprehensive review of the literature in order to illustrate how cultural aspects of this sector influenced the path of change in a specific way. It highlights the reasons for the introduction of more sophisticated management accounting techniques from the 1980s to the mid-1990s and the way in which these systems were implemented. It also highlights the impact of these changes on organizational practices and demonstrates that not only does management accounting have technical effects, but also social, organizational and political effects (Soin et al., 2002). In addition, the chapter addresses the seeming decline of the relevance of management accounting systems since the 1990s, and how this decline can be traced to changes in the regulatory framework and market forces in the financial services sector.

The first section provides an overview of the changing environment for financial services institutions during the first phase outlined above. It focuses on the effects of deregulation of the financial services sector, the impact of increased competition and hence the pressure on margins. This is followed by a consideration of specific studies in this area. First, and most significant, the changing regulatory and market framework led to an emphasis on management accounting systems that focused on overhead costs and allocation of costs. Several related studies which study management accounting change, and particularly the implementation of activity-based costing systems, are discussed. This was followed by the implementation of systems that focused on qualitative aspects of financial services organizations management, such as customer orientation, service quality and the performance of management. Studies of the use of several concepts, such as the balanced scorecard, TQM and budgeting, are discussed in this respect. In the third section the chapter goes on to consider the changes that have occurred in the second wave of regulatory shifts, and highlights the growing significance of risk-based approaches to the regulation of financial services institutions and the subsequent diminishing relevance of management accounting systems. For this, we refer to studies that discuss the relationship between risk management and management (accounting) practices in financial services institutions. Some concluding remarks in Section 4 of this chapter emphasize the—questionable—future of management accounting for financial services organizations.

DOI: 10.1016/S1751-3243(07)03010-6

2. The 1980s: Deregulation of Financial Services and the Efficiency Focus

The development and use of management control/ management accounting systems[1] in financial services institutions is inextricably linked to the changes that have taken place in the social, economic and political environment. Although management accounting played an important role in the early twentieth century in facilitating local banking practices (Jaecle & Walsh, 2002), in more contemporary times it was not given a pivotal role in the day-to-day management of financial services institutions. It was only when the effects of the profound changes in the financial regulatory framework started to emerge in the 1980s that interest shifted to management accounting and control practices. The change of regulatory regimes, however, was not only an economic endeavour, but was the outcome of a shift in the political agendas over time. As Morgan & Knights (1997, p. 1) put it:

> Led by the free market enthusiasms of Reagan in the USA and Thatcher in the UK, a range of initiatives were taken throughout the world to remove the hand of government from direct intervention in the market system and replace state control with various forms of indirect regulation.

The effects of the ideology of the free market on the financial services sector have had an ongoing impact up to the present day and are reflected in two clear cultural shifts that impacted financial services organizations around the globe.

The first shift took place in the 1980s, spurred by the growth of global money markets, when financial services institutions embarked upon an intensive reorganization, both at a global and national level. The consequences of this cultural shift for the management of financial services institutions in the 1980s can be understood as an outcome of the neo-liberal political discourse of "market freedom." Generally, deregulation resulted in new entrants into the financial markets and accelerated dynamics of institutional change not previously seen (see Merton, 1995). Controls on lending limits and conditions for credit were loosened, and in many cases removed. Companies were allowed to develop new products for personal and corporate customers, like derivatives, which promised new ways for profit making, but also raised new forms of risk. Barriers that restricted the banks' ability to diversify were also lifted. New information technologies, and finally a globalization of trading practices in the dimensions of time and space, augmented the scope for doing business.

[1]The terms management accounting (MA) and management control systems (MCS) are used interchangeably in this chapter.

Internally, an increase in compensation schemes and an intensified profit-orientation occurred in financial services institutions, leading to a pressure for subunits and employees to perform. These changes triggered a process of consolidation, mainly driven by mergers and acquisitions, with the aim of forming all-financial conglomerates and thereby realizing economies of scale. Whereas the efficiency gains could not be identified in many cases (Berger et al., 1999; Amel et al., 2003), and although there were early warnings that managers should not forget the opportunity costs of organizational growth and diversification (Clark, 1996), the consolidation process was based on the idea of, and resulted in, an industry-wide focus on cost management and new forms of managerial control. Drawing on Middaugh (1988), Vieira & Hoskin, 2005 (p. 9), highlight that:

> … the US has been a conspicuous mover of change … key structural changes in the US banking sector were based around (de)regulation and competition. In the 1980s the US congress disassembled much of the regulation that had governed financial services since the Great Depression. Changes in the competitive environment came via technological and monetary developments and changes in consumers' financial awareness, all of which impacted on business practices. An important step in this development was the final revocation in the 1980s of laws passed in the 1930s following the 1929 Wall Street Crash, setting regional limits to banking conglomerates.

For the UK context, Soin (1996) and Soin et al. (2002) describe a similar situation. This research emphasizes that the UK banking sector, for example, has been subject to dramatic changes in their regulatory and competitive environments in the last three decades. Progressive deregulation, beginning with the introduction of the Competition and Credit policy in 1971, followed by government regulation (capital adequacy requirements) and government deregulation (Financial Services Act 1986 and Building Societies Act 1986) led to new competition from overseas banks and building societies in the banks' traditional markets. Furthermore, banks have had to meet the more stringent capital requirements of the Basle agreement. The banking environment has itself become more unpredictable. The combined effects of deregulation, the capital adequacy requirements and the harmonization of the EC have made the banking environment very competitive, resulting in increased uncertainty (Soin, 1996). Similar trends can be observed in other European countries, for example, Italy (Euske & Riccaboni, 1999) and Portugal (Vieira & Hoskin, 2007) and more generally, globally. More recently, pressure on margins has led to banks finding more inventive ways to innovate, leading to some risky, and some could argue reckless, lending resulting in some serious consequences, as evidenced by the US subprime loans market and its consequences for the 2007 run on Northern Rock in the UK, and the large lending losses experienced by Merrill Lynch, Credit Suisse and Citicorp, to name but a few casualties.

While the fundamental effects of deregulation are most visible in the Anglo-Saxon countries, these developments have, however, taken place globally. Euske & Riccaboni (1999) for example, presented an in-depth, longitudinal study on the interaction of the regulatory forces, forms of governance and the management accounting (MA) and management control systems (MCS) in an Italian context. It provides a rich insight into the role of MA and MCS in dealing with changes in internal and external dependencies in the domains of strategy and structure of the organization. Internal interdependencies (II) are categorized as relating to controlling the relationship of management and workers, the separation of ownership and control, and the division of labour among different levels of management. External interdependencies (EI) relate to a wide range of relationships such as with the state, customers and suppliers (Fligstein & Freeland, 1995).

The research was undertaken in an Italian bank which needed to adapt its MCS to changing internal and external interdependencies in the privatization process. There are two aspects to the story. The first relates to the role of MCS in the privatization process and, in particular, how the MCS evolved to ensure the success of the process. The second aspect relates to the role of the MCS in an organization that was changing to meet a new and different competitive environment. Not only was the bank being privatized, but the state was also redefining the parameters of the market. The authors draw on Fligstein's (1991) framework (based on institutional theory) and focus on the actors that fashion the organizational field and the role of actors in influencing change.

The internal bank's changes were a response to the changes that the Italian government was imposing on the competitive environment. As it turned out, however, "becoming more efficient and increasing the legitimacy of the bank meant that the banking regulators would have less reason to intervene in the operations of the bank (for example, replace top management)" (Euske & Riccaboni, 1999, p. 466). Hence, four new types of costing systems were introduced: budgeting, cost, compensation and reporting systems. These were seen as being similar to the types of systems one would expect to find in competitive organizations.

Turning to the specific phases of change that are presented in this case, the first phase, or "the beginnings of the change" occurred in the 1960s. In the past, given the tightly controlled market for Italian banks, there was little reason to focus on efficiency and effectiveness. The focus was on managing risk within the bureaucratic process defined by the regulatory body in Rome. The information system was geared to external reporting. At the time, regulatory reporting requirements were a major factor in the design of the information systems down to branch level. The use of the information by the regulatory body also influenced the structure of the reporting system within the bank.

The second phase of change, "the mid-years" was around the 1970s and 1980s. During this time new competition was introduced, particularly with foreign banks opening branches in Italy. With them came financial innovation and new competitors. At this time, there was also a squeeze on margins due to the Italian government offering short-term government bonds at relatively high interest rates. This encouraged banks to develop new systems to identify the cost of various products and services.

The final phase, "the years of privatization" took place in the 1990s. The key change influences were:

- Market globalization, with new competitors and the need to support clients in their international activities;
- Deregulation by the Bank of Italy, thereby eliminating some administrative constraints and controls;
- A new banking law giving banks the authority to operate in any financial sector.

These changes made survival of a financial institution much more performance-based than it had been in the past.

The redefined environment made it imperative to use reliable cost of services information. Knowing which products generated the profits and losses made it crucial to the banks survival. The emphasis was no longer just on the clients but on "the clients and shareholders" (Euske & Riccaboni, 1999, p. 475). Shareholders, particularly the larger ones, were concerned with bottom line results. A key feature of the change process was the chief executive officer (CEO), during his time in office he delineated the changes and defined the context—bringing a redefinition of the interdependencies including, for example, a focus on the reduction of personnel costs and the increase in loans to public entities.

The MA/MCS also dealt with changes in the internal and external interdependencies in the domains of strategy and structure of the organization, the organizational field and the state. Addressing strategy and structure, the new branch budgeting system was designed to emphasize specific budgetary goals. The accounting system shifted from one that focused on providing information for regulatory control to one that focused on measuring success, defined in terms of returns to stockholders. Cost and profit reporting systems were developed to meet the new market and owner focus. The control system was also used to reduce/minimize the dependence on the regulatory body and to demonstrate the adaptability of the organization in meeting the evolving competitive environment.

3. The (Short) Career of Management Accounting Systems in Financial Services Institutions

Most relevant for the implementation of advanced management accounting systems in the 1980s and 1990s, however, was the resulting effect of pressure on margins resulting in a new focus on profitability, cost control, efficiency, effectiveness and performance.

In an early analysis of these changes, Middaugh (1988) identifies, as consequences of deregulation in the US financial services sector, changes in budgetary control practices; the establishment of independent profit centres; changes in transfer pricing, revenue sharing and compensation. Likewise, Seal & Croft (1997) observe that, with respect to the UK context, until the mid-1980s there was very little management accounting in banks and that the dominant control technologies tended to be based on administrative practices and personnel controls rather than management accounting (Cobb, Helliar & Innes, 1995; Morris, 1986; Munro, 1995; Soin, 1996; Soin et al., 2002). As Seal & Croft (1997, p.74) put it, one reason for this historic lack of management accounting in traditional banking activity:

> ... may have had a technically contingent basis. Being a service industry, there was no need to value stocks via costing systems, nor was there an underlying engineering model of the labour process, which is generally found in manufacturing.

However, with deregulation of the sector, the banking industry became more similar to manufacturing companies. The disintegration of front- and back-office services and the subsequent distinction between idiosyncratic, consulting-intensive activities and pure administrative activities—which are repetitive and can therefore be standardized—allowed financial services institutions to implement several management tools derived from other sectors that had a longer tradition in process analysis, cost control and the use of management accounting concepts. Hence changes occurred, for example the use and introduction of business process reengineering (BPR), total quality management (TQM), activity based costing/management (ABC/M) and the balanced scorecard (BSC). The emphasis shifted to the "bottom line," customer focus, value-added and non value-added activities and customer profitability. Prior to this, costs had not been a focus for banks and, in particular, there had been very little attempt to allocate costs to products. In addition, these changes were pushed through fairly fast.

Seal & Croft (1997, p. 77) argue that the trigger for change and the subsequent emphasis on cost control techniques was a response to a severe profits crisis at the end of the 1980s, stating that:

> ... the response from the banks was to curtail lending and introduce more careful analysis of the sources of operating income ... this meant that more sophisticated information was required on the costs of particular—and mainly manufacturing-like—repetitive bank activities like cheque clearing.

Added to this, there were dramatic changes in the structure and locus of decision-making, branches were increasingly being seen primarily as sales outlets and corporate lending decisions were made at large regional business centres. As Soin (1996) and Soin et al. (2002) illustrate in their case study, as a result of deregulation the great factory-like cheque clearing centres began to tender competitively for clearing contracts from building societies and develop a new level of cost-consciousness.

Although there is still relatively little research on the implementation of management accounting techniques in the financial services sector in comparison to other sectors, the main line of arguments in favour of an intensified use of management accounting systems are similar. For example, Davis & Albright (2004, p. 2) in their paper on the effects of the balanced scorecard on financial performance, observe that since the 1980s, and as a result of the criticisms of traditional management accounting practices levelled by Johnson & Kaplan (1987), researchers have:

> ... described the increasing irrelevance of traditional control and performance measurement practices. Weaknesses included failure to link performance measurement to strategic initiatives of organizations, an emphasis on accounting for external reporting rather than on accounting reports useful for internal decision making and a failure to account for advances in technology ...

While many of these criticisms were directed at the manufacturing sector, these issues are seen as equally important in research on service sector industries such as banks.

A further effect of increased competition and thinner interest spreads meant that banking became defined about marketing financial products according to the degree of profitability. As the drive for market share led to bad debts and poor cost–income ratios, the trend in the 1990s became more focused on the cost and profitability of the various bank services and products, with a shift in emphasis to cost identification. It is at this point that activity-based costing (ABC) gained pre-eminence. Innes & Mitchell (1991) highlighted that ABC is well-suited to the financial sector, as many service costs are process- rather than volume-related. In addition, the main characteristics of financial services institutions are very similar to those required for the successful application of ABC in the manufacturing industry: first, a highly competitive market; secondly, diversity of products, processes and customers; thirdly, significant overhead costs not easily assigned to individual products; and finally, demands on overhead resources placed by individual products and customers not proportional to volume. This is supported by Sephton & Ward (1990) and Mabberley (1992), who suggest that ABC can be used as part of the strategic management process through understanding cost behaviour and analyzing the profitability of customers and the newly-created products.[2] It is, however, worth noting that the basic assumption underlying the ABC system, namely that the cost of non-volume drivers are understated in traditional costing systems, has been criticized in the light of empirical research on the US banking industry (see Banker, Ou & Potter, 1997).

A variety of theoretical approaches have been adopted to understand the role of activity-based costing/management (ABC/M) in banks, with much of the research focusing on implementation and organizational change-related issues. The study by Cobb et al. (1995) developed Innes & Mitchell's (1990) model to study a UK-based division of a multinational bank. Soin (1996) studied the change process in a UK clearing bank by drawing on Laughlin's (1991) theoretical framework, followed by Soin et al. (2002), which drew on institutional theory (Burns & Scapens, 2000). Norris (2002) considered factors related to the successful implementation of ABC using grounded theory. More recently, Vieira & Hoskin (2007) have drawn on the work of Foucault to look at the effects of ABC implementation in a Portuguese bank.

The study by Soin et al. (2002) uses institutional theory to interpret the role of management accounting in organizational change. The paper reports on a longitudinal empirical study of the implementation of an activity-based costing (ABC) system in the clearing department of a UK-based multinational bank. The focus here is on the processes and the actors involved in management accounting change (Burns, 2000; Burns & Scapens, 2000). This research interprets the interplay between management accounting and other agents of organizational change that drew on rationalities and legitimations from spheres such as scientific management and human resource management. Given that the ABC project team in the focal organizations was operating at the same time as other change agents (productivity consultants and human resource engineering), their inter-relationships are explored through the displacement/establishment of routines and institutionalized practices. The extent and nature of organizational change is evaluated by drawing on the dichotomies of formal versus informal change, revolutionary versus evolutionary change and regressive versus progressive change (Burns & Scapens, 2000). Tensions were identified between the need to establish ABC as an organizational routine, thereby ensuring its reproduction with the less routinized but more revolutionary aspirations of activity-based management (ABM). The ABC team succeeded in institutionalizing a less radical version of ABC that revealed new links between costs and products, but did not go so far as to transform the strategic thinking of the bank's senior management.

The study undertaken by Vieira & Hoskin (2005, 2007) focuses on the development and implementation of an ABC system in a Portuguese bank, the aim of which was to improve the economy, efficiency and effectiveness of employee activity. In common with the other cases discussed here, the culture of banking in Portugal had changed significantly since the 1980s but some of the older traditions remained strong. Another significant factor was that the bank had been reprivatized in the early 1990s. Drawing on a Foucault inspired framework developed by Hoskin & Macve (e.g., 1986, 1988, 1994, 2000), and on research into the financial sector undertaken by Morgan & Sturdy (2000), the research highlights the increase in visibility and perceived importance of accounting, and how accounting is significant beyond its technical roles. It also illustrates how the management accounting practices, along with other organizational systems, play an important role in questioning, visualizing, analyzing and measuring implemented strategies. Furthermore, it demonstrates how, as the language and practice of management have shifted toward strategy and marketing discourses, patterns of work, organization and career are being restructured by accounting practices.

The use of "accurate" cost information delivered by ABC systems and other cost accounting practices in financial services organizations coincided with an emphasis on budgetary practices. Similar to the co-development of standard costing and budgetary systems in the manufacturing industry in the 1930s and the resulting increased potential to control the behaviour of subunits and individuals (see Miller & O'Leary, 1987), budgeting became a central governing mechanism in financial services organizations. The research by Lau & Tan (1998), for example, analyzes the impact of budgetary control systems on the performance of Australian and Singaporean managers in financial services. In particular, they look at the impact of performance evaluative styles on subordinates behaviour, attitudes and performance by considering contingency factors: participation, task uncertainty, strategy, and task difficulty. This study examines whether the three-way interaction between budget emphasis, budgetary participation and task difficulty affecting managerial performance

[2]See Soin, (1996) and Soin et al. (2002) for a more comprehensive review of why ABC is suited to financial services firms.

found in the manufacturing sector can be generalized to the financial services sector. The study also extends across national culture, with reference to Hofstede's (1980) cultural dimensions of power distance and individualism and Harrison's (1992, 1993) cultural theoretical framework. Their findings indicate that budget emphasis has a significant and positive main effect on performance for financial sector managers, while budgetary participation interacts significantly with task difficulty to affect performance. However, no cultural effects on the relationship between evaluative styles and performance were found.

A third, and most recent, development in the use of management accounting systems in financial services institutions relates to comprehensive performance measurement and management systems. Interest in performance measurement in financial services has grown over a number of years, with a particular emphasis on nonfinancial performance measures (NFPM), for example, market share, customer satisfaction, efficiency productivity, product quality and employee satisfaction (Lynch & Cross, 1991; Kaplan & Norton, 1996, 2001; Otley, 1999). This is evidenced by the growing interest in benchmarking, total quality measures and balanced scorecards.

This development can be understood as a consequence of a stronger orientation towards market development, service quality and customer relationships, particularly in retail banking. However, in some empirical contributions it is doubted that these developments have resulted in a broadening of the cost and efficiency focus. Davis & Albright's (2004) research assesses whether new management initiatives, such as the balanced scorecard, are better or just different. They analyze whether an improvement in financial performance incurred after implementing a balanced scorecard and whether the change in financial performance is significantly greater than performance observed in a similar setting where a traditional performance measurement system using only financial measures is employed. Their results suggest that the inclusion of nonfinancial performance measures (NFPMs) in a performance measurement system is associated with improved financial performance. These findings contrast with Ittner, Larcker & Randall (2003) who found a negative association between balanced scorecard usage and return on assets (ROA), and Ittner, Larcker & Meyer's (2003) empirical findings that balanced scorecards that are linked to bonus plans are often modified or utilized, respectively, by managers according to their personal advantage. What can be taken from this critique is that the occupational culture in financial services institutions has changed dramatically over time. Accordingly, Kominis & Emmanuel (2007) argue that there is now an increasingly strong link between performance measurement techniques, reward systems and the individual motivation of managers in financial services institutions. Furthermore, Knights & McCabe (1997) highlight how TQM is an attempt to control costs (and employees) while espousing the importance of the customer.

However, it is still the case that external factors play an important role for the design of management control systems. Hussain & Hoque (2002) draw on new institutional sociology to look at performance management practices, with a particular emphasis on NFPMs in four Japanese banks. Their study focuses on how various institutional forces (both internal and external) affect the design and use of nonfinancial performance measurement systems in the banks. Their findings indicate that several institutional forces influenced the banks to implement a particular performance measurement system. Of these, economic constraints increased pressure on financial performance measures rather than NFPMs and, in a more competitive environment, increased use of NFPMs such as customer satisfaction and quality. Other institutional forces that impacted on choice of performance measures were regulatory control, accounting and financial legislation, strategic focus of management and bank size. Building on these findings, Hussain (2003) looked at the impact of economic conditions on management accounting performance measures in banks in Finland, Sweden and Japan, and found that greater economic uncertainty increases the importance of financial performance measures, and management tries to improve management accounting practice for performance measurement. These findings are similar to the earlier findings of Hussain & Hoque, (2002). In another study, Hussain (2005) looked at management accounting and performance measurement in four Swedish banks. Once again, the emphasis was on financial performance rather than NFPM and none of the banks studied used techniques such as the balanced scorecard.

4. The 1990s: Regulation of Financial Services and the Risk Focus

The second phase of the use, or arguably the superseding of management accounting practices, relates to efforts to reregulate the (global) financial services sectors and the associated shift in emphasis from efficiency and effectiveness to the introduction of risk-based approaches since the mid-1990s. At that time it was clear that the impact of deregulation was more complex than originally expected and that freedom from one set of constraints might indeed require the construction of new forms of regulation (Morgan & Knights, 1997; Morgan & Soin, 1999). The increased amount of risk that banks were, and are, taking has become the over-arching topic. Consequently, attempts have been made to reregulate the business of these institutions and, more importantly, to impact on their internal management accountability and responsibility structures. Legislation in the form of the Sarbanes-Oxley

Act of 2002 was established in the US. In the UK context there is the Turnbull Guidance and the COSO framework, and similar frameworks have been created in other countries. These frameworks have resulted in enforced internal control mechanisms that focus on issues of risk and risk management—rather than on efficiency and effectiveness.

A number of serious scandals, as well as a gradual shift in the nature of their business, led to a rethinking of the guidelines and regulations for financial services institutions. In the UK, for example, the senior management of the clearing banks was criticized for their lax lending policies during the 1980s; there were also large losses on the wholesale markets culminating in the bankruptcy of Barings Bank in 1995. In 2007, the world has witnessed the repercussions of lending decisions related to the US sub-prime loans market, most visibly in the case of the UK-based Northern Rock Bank. The response to these and other incidents has been to introduce a "risk-based" approach to regulation, with heavy reliance on the internal control system. As Power (2004b, p. 27) notes, "the risk based internal control system has become an increasingly significant regulatory object, particularly with the passing of the Sarbanes-Oxley Act management in the USA".

However, it would be too easy to ascribe the reasons for the scandals and the subsequent attempts to reregulate financial markets solely to the increased pressure on employees to perform, and hence to single individuals' mistakes and weak control procedures. Rather, studies on the sociology of finance and management studies (see, for example, Knorr-Cetina & Preda (2004), and, respectively, Fenton-O'Creevy et al., 2003, 2004; Willman et al., 2002, 2006) argue that a cultural shift has taken place in the financial services sector. This shift, supported by new technologies, an increased "futurization" of financial markets, and a growing proportion of profit gained by financial services institutions by trading their own positions on financial markets, has reduced the emphasis on cost and enhanced the focus on risk. However, and paradoxically, it was not the reduction of risk that became the cornerstone for the management of financial services institutions; rather it is an increasing "risk appetite" of those institutions that is the guideline for internal management and hence for the actions and decisions of their managers.

The background and effects of this risk-based approach to regulation and management have been documented extensively (see, for example, Power, 1994, 1997a,b, 1999, 2002, 2004a,b, 2007; Holzer & Millo, 2005; Kalthoff, 2005). In the following discussion we will therefore concentrate on the effects this development has on management control within financial services institutions and the role management accounting has—or indeed, has not—in this context.

In an exploratory research project undertaken for the Chartered Institute of Management Accountants (CIMA) Soin (2004) attempted to identify, evaluate, assess and analyze the role, or potential role, of management accounting and control in relation to the introduction of the risk-based approach to regulation in the UK financial services sector. A key aspect is the Financial Services Authority's ARROW[3] risk assessment approach. The emphasis is on how risk is analyzed, controlled, communicated and monitored and is based upon the Turnbull guidance (see Financial Report Council, 2005) which aims to link risk and internal control with business objectives. The nature of the risk-based approach suggests that there might be implications for the management accounting and control systems within financial services organizations, or that at least considerations of efficiency should be combined with considerations on the risks of single business operations. In addition, the demands of regulation also raises questions about whether or not the costs of these risk management systems (and more generally, regulatory compliance systems) are being taken into account and whether, for example, budgetary control and monitoring mechanisms exist with respect to regulatory costs.

The tensions between the "costs of compliance" and meeting regulatory requirements can have significant consequences, as is demonstrated in the case of Allied Irish Banks Plc where the treasurer permitted a weakening or elimination of key controls under his responsibility as part of a cost cutting exercise (Dunne & Helliar, 2002). In addition, anecdotal evidence suggests that risk management is finding its way into the overall performance measurement systems of banks; some banks (for example, Deutsche Bank) are introducing a risk dimension on the balanced scorecard. As Williamson (2004, p. 3) highlights:

> Measuring performance towards objectives for an organization is familiar territory to management accounting. It may now be seen as supporting risk management as well as control, whether by quantifying objectives, estimating the consequences of potential outcomes from risk events, analyzing the costs and benefits of risk management processes, or comparing actual performance to risks faced.

The research, however, demonstrates that despite the obvious potential for the use of management accounting and control techniques and practices within risk management, these techniques are not being utilized. Soin (2004) suggests that the problem occurs in relation to the

[3]ARROW—assesses firms on the basis of the risks they pose to the FSA's four statutory objectives (market confidence; public awareness; consumer protection and reduction of financial crime)—not directly on the traditional basis of credit, operational or market risk.

understanding of management accounting and control systems in financial services organizations. As mentioned above, previous research has highlighted the historical lack of emphasis on management accounting systems in this sector (Cobb et al., 1995; Soin et al., 2002), or as management accounting by another name, for example, "global expense managers" (Ahrens & Chapman, 2000, p. 477). Much of the emphasis has tended to focus on the very traditional role of management accounting, namely, budgeting, cost control and performance measurement, as opposed to the broad range of management tasks that management accounting encompasses.

In relation to the risk-based approach—and despite the fact that risk management thinking in this area has emerged from professional views on control (Williamson, 2004)—management accounting professionals are, however, not highly thought of in this context, and, as highlighted by Collier, Berry & Burke (2004), are being marginalized in relation to risk management. Consequently, management accounting practices are no longer seen as an integral part of management tasks; rather, there is very little integration between management accounting and risk management.

The data gathered in this exploratory research suggests that much of the thinking is still geared towards a very traditional role of management accounting, as opposed to the very diverse nature of what management accountants actually do in organizations (see Ahrens & Chapman, 2000). Hence, in financial services institutions there is a lack of understanding about how a risk-based approach can actually profit from what management accounting can offer. This is reinforced by work that highlights the nature of competition between different types of expertise in organizations: professionals may find themselves competing not just with rival professionals, but also with other actors within the organization itself for new activities (Abbott, 1991). This "professional rivalry" and marginalization of management accountants comes as no surprise and is another example of what has been highlighted in the literature by other researchers (see, for example, Armstrong, 1985; Jönsson, 1988).

5. Concluding Remarks

We argued in this chapter that management accounting systems have had a short career in financial services institutions. It was only for a short period of time, from the mid-1980s to the mid-1990s, that the practice of management accounting generated a similar level of interest as in the manufacturing industries. As a response to the first wave of (de)regulation of financial markets, the increasing competitive markets and the subsequent quest for reengineering services, cutting costs, customer orientation, performance-based rewards, etc., traditional management accounting practices proliferated in this industry. However, by the second wave of (re)regulation and the resulting risk-based approach, the "genetic code" of financial services institutions has again been fundamentally changed. Considerations of efficiency and effectiveness have been superseded by the requirements of balancing risk and performance in an ever-accelerating technologically and managerially more complex environment.

While this chapter cannot predict the future of management accounting systems in financial services institutions, we suggest that there are still a number of related issues that should be pursued in further research. First, why is it that there is so little research on management accounting in the financial services sector? Although it has had a very short career, it is surprising that management accounting scholars show so little engagement in the analysis of management accounting practices in financial services, given the importance of this sector to the global economy. Secondly, one has to ask, what does the above-mentioned focus on a risk-based approach mean for the role of management accounting—and the profession of management accountants. For example, given the complexities of operational risks (see Power, 2007) that result in problems to conceptualize it with the usual quantitative methods of risk management, and given that frameworks like Basle II explicitly exclude strategic (and reputational) risks from risk management frameworks, it seems that there is still an agenda for risk-related analyses provided by management accountants. An analysis of these issues, however, presumes an answer to a third question, namely, how these professional jurisdictions emerged, how has management accounting being marginalized from the process of risk management in financial services organizations and what, if any, are the possibilities for management accountants as a profession in the future in relation to risk management?

To summarize, therefore, the history of management accounting systems in financial services institutions is a short one; its presence is that of a bulk of techniques and tools that are seemingly more a necessary evil than a central management issue; and its future can be seen as uncertain, given the fast changing regulatory and market-related environments of financial services institutions. However, as contributions to the "sociology of finance" show, the intra- and trans-institutional context of financial services institutions and their development over the last 25 years promises to be an interesting field for management accounting research as long as the social and institutional context of this economically and societally important sector is considered in such research.

References

Abbott, A. (1991). *The System of Professions*. Chicago, IL: University of Chicago Press.

Ahrens, T. & Chapman, C. S. (2000). Occupational identity of management accountants in Britain and Germany. *European Accounting Review*, **9**(4), 477–498.

Amel, D., Barnes, C., Panetta, F. & Salleo, C. (2004). Consolidation and efficiency in the financial sector. *Journal of Banking and Finance*, **28**(10), 2493–2519.

Armstrong, P. (1985). Changing management control strategies: the role of competition between accountancy and other organizational professions. *Accounting, Organizations and Society*, **10**(2), 129–148.

Berger, A. N., Demsetz, R. S. & Strahen, P. E. (1999). The consolidation of the financial services industry: causes, consequences and implications for the future. *Journal of Banking and Finance*, **23**(2–4), 135–194.

Burns, J. (2000). The dynamics of accounting change: inter-play between new practices, routines, institutions, power and politics. *Accounting, Auditing and Accountability*, **13**(5), 566–596.

Burns, J. & Scapens, R. W. (2000). Conceptualising management accounting change: an institutionalist framework. *Management Accounting Research*, **11**(1), 3–25.

Carmona, S. & Gutiérrez, I. (2003). Vogues in management accounting research. *Scandinavian Journal of Management*, **19**(2), 213–231.

Clark, J. E. (1996). Economic cost, scale efficiency and competitive viability in banking. *Journal of Money, Credit, and Banking*, **28**(3), 342–364.

Cobb, I., Helliar, C. & Innes, J. (1995). Management accounting change in a bank. *Management Accounting Research*, **6**(4), 155–175.

Collier, P., Berry, T. & Burke, G. (2004). Risk and control: drivers, practices and consequences. Paper presented to the *Sixth International Management Control Systems Conference*, Edinburgh, July 2004.

Davis, S. & Albright, T. (2004). An investigation of the effect of balanced scorecard implementation on financial performance. *Management Accounting Research*, **15**(2), 135–154.

Dunne, T. M. & Helliar, C. V. (2002). The Ludwig Report: Implications for corporate governance. *Corporate Governance: The International Journal of Effective Board Performance*, **2**(3), 26–31.

Euske, K. J. & Riccaboni, A. (1999). Stability to profitability: managing interdependencies to meet a new environment. *Accounting, Organizations and Society*, **24**(5–6), 463–481.

Fenton-O'Creevy, M., Nicholson, N., Soane, E. & Willman, P. (2004). *Traders: Managing Risks and Decisions in Financial Markets*. Oxford, UK: Oxford University Press.

Fenton-O'Creevy, M., Nicholson, N., Soane, E. & Willman, P. (2003). Trading on illusions: Unrealistic perceptions of control and trading performance. *Journal of Occupational and Organisational Psychology*, **76**(1), 53–68.

Financial Reporting Council (2005). *Internal control: Revised guidance for directors on the combined code (Turnbull Guidance)*. London, UK: FRC.

Fligstein, N. (1991). The structural transformation of American industry: An institutional account of the causes of diversification in the largest firms, 1919–1979. In: P. J. DiMaggio, & W. W. Powell (Eds), *The New Institutionalism in Organizational Analysis*. Chicago, IL: University of Chicago Press, pp. 311–336.

Fligstein, N. & Freeland, R. (1995). Theoretical and Comparative Perspectives on Corporate Organization. In: Annual Review of Sociology, (21). Palo Alto, CA: AnnualReviews Inc, pp. 21–43.

Harrison, G. L. (1992). The cross-cultural generalizability of the relation between participation, budget emphasis and job related attitudes. *Accounting, Organizations and Society*, **17**(1), 1–15.

Harrison, G. L. (1993). Reliance on accounting performance measures in superior evaluative style: the influence of national culture and personality. *Accounting, Organizations and Society*, **18**(4), 319–339.

Hofstede, G. (1980). *Culture's Consequences: International Differences in Work-Related Values*. Beverly Hills, CA: Sage.

Holzer, B. & Millo, Y. (2005). From risks to second order dangers in financial markets: unintended consequences of risk management systems. *New Political Economy*, **10**(2), 223–245.

Hoskin, K. & Macve, R. (1986). Accounting and the examination: A genealogy of disciplinary power. *Accounting, Organizations and Society*, **11**(2), 105–136.

Hoskin, K. & Macve, R. (1988). The genesis of accountability: The West Point connection. *Accounting, Organizations and Society*, **13**(1), 37–74.

Hoskin, K. & Macve, R. (1994). Writing, Examining, Disciplining: The Genesis of Accounting's Modern Power. In: A. G. Hopwood & P. Miller (Eds), *Accounting As Social and Institutional Practice*. Cambridge, UK: Cambridge University Press, pp. 67–97.

Hoskin, K. & Macve, R. (2000). Knowing more as knowing less? Alternative histories of cost and management in the USA and UK. *Accounting Historians Journal*, **27**(1), 91–149.

Hussain, M. M. (2003). The impact of economic condition on management of accountign performance measures: experience with banks. *Managerial Finance*, **29**(2–3), 23–41.

Hussain, M. M. (2005). Management accounting performance measurement systems in Swedish banks. *European Business Review*, **17**(6), 566–589.

Hussain, M. M. & Hoque, Z. (2002). Understanding non-financial performance measurement practices in Japanese banks. *Accounting, Auditing and Auditability Journal*, **15**(2), 162–183.

Innes, J. & Mitchell, F. (1995). A survey of activity-based costing in the UK's largest companies. *Management Accounting Research*, **6**(2), 137–153.

Innes, J. & Mitchell, F. (1997). An application of activity-based costing in the UK's largest financial institutions. *The Service Industries Journal*, **17**(1), 190–203.

Innes, J., Mitchell, F. & Sinclair, D. (2000). Activity-based costing in the UK's largest companies: a comparison of 1994 and 1999 survey results. *Management Accounting Research*, **11**(3), 349–362.

Ittner, C. D., Larcker, D. F. & Randall, T. (2003). Performance implications of strategic performance measurement in financial service firms. *Accounting, Organizations and Society*, **28**(7–8), 715–741.

Ittner, C. D., Larcker, D. F. & Meyer, M. W. (2003). Subjectivity and the weighting of performance measures: evidence from the balanced scorecard. *The Accounting Review*, **78**(3), 725–758.

Jaecle, I. & Walsh, E. J. (2002). From moral evaluation to rationalization: accounting and the shifting technologies of credit. *Accounting, Organizations and Society*, **27**(8), 737–761.

Johnson, H. T. & Kaplan, R. S. (1987). *Relevance Lost: The Rise and Fall of Management Accounting*. Boston, MA: Harvard Business School Press.

Jönsson, S. (1988). *Accounting regulation and elite structures: forces in the development of accounting policy*. Chichester/New York, NY: Wiley.

Kalthoff, H. (2005). Practices of calculation: economic representations and risk management. *Theory, Culture & Society*, **22**(2), 69–97.

Kaplan, R. S. & Norton, D. P. (1996). *The Balanced Scorecard: Translating Strategy into Action*. Boston, MA: Harvard University Press.

Kaplan, R. S. & Norton, D. P. (2001). Transforming the balanced scorecard from performance measurement to strategic management: Part 1. *Accounting Horizons*, **15**(1), 87–104.

Knights, D. & McCabe, D. (1997). How would you measure something like that? Quality in a retail bank. *Journal of Management Studies*, **34**(3), 371–388.

Knorr-Cetina, K. D. & Preda, A. (Eds) (2004). *The Sociology of Financial Markets*. Oxford, UK: Oxford University Press.

Kominis, G. & Emmanuel, C. R. (2007). Developing an extended model of managerial motivation. *Management Accounting Research*, **18**(1), 49–75.

Lau, C. M. & Tan, M. (1998). The impact of budget emphasis, participation and task difficulty on managerial performance: a cross-culture study of financial service sector. *Management Accounting Research*, **9**(2), 163–183.

Lynch, R. L. & Cross, K. F. (1991). *Measure Up! Yardsticks for Continuous Improvement*. London, UK: Blackwell.

Mabberley, J. (1992). *Activity-Based Costing in Financial Institutions*. London, UK: Pitman.

Mabberley, J. (1997). *Managing the Future in Financial Institutions: Meeting the Challenge with Better Information*. London, UK: Pitman.

Merton, R. C. (1995). Financial innovation and the management and regulation of financial insitutions. *Journal of Banking and Finance*, **19**(3–4), 461–481.

Middaugh, J. K. (1988). Management control in the financial-services industry. *Business Horizons*, **31**(3), 79–86.

Miller, P. & O'Leary, T. (1987). Accounting and the construction of the governable person. *Accounting, Organizations and Society*, **12**(3), 235–265.

Morgan, G. & Knights, D. (Eds) (1997). *Regulation and Deregulation in European Financial Services*. London, UK: Macmillan.

Morgan, G. & Soin, K. (1999). Regulatory Compliance. In: G. Morgan, & L. Engwall (Eds), *Regulation and Organizations*. London, UK: Routledge, pp, pp. 166–190.

Morgan, G. & Sturdy, A. (2000). *Beyond Organizational Change: Structure, Discourse and Power in UK Financial Services*. London, UK: Macmillan.

Morris, T. (1986). *Innovations in Banking: Business Strategies for Employee Relations*. Beckenham, Kent, UK: Croom Helm.

Munro, R. (1995). Managing by ambiguity: an archaeology of the social in the absence of management accounting. *Critical Perspectives on Accounting*, **6**(5), 433–482.

Norris, G. (2002). Chalk and cheese: grounded theory case studies of the introduction and usage of activity-based information in two British banks. *British Accounting Review*, **34**(3), 223–255.

Otley, D. T. (1999). Performance management: a framework for management control systems research. *Management Accounting Research*, **10**(4), 363–382.

Power, M. (1994). *The Audit Explosion*. London, UK: Demos.

Power, M. (1997a). *The Audit Society*. Oxford, UK: Oxford University Press.

Power, M. (1997b). From risk society to audit society. *Soziale Systeme*, **3**(1), 3–21.

Power, M. (1999). *The Audit Implosion: Managing Risk from the Inside*. London, UK: Institute of Chartered Accountants in England and Wales.

Power, M. (2002). Standardization and the regulation of management control practices. *Soziale Systeme*, **8**(2), 190–203.

Power, M. (2004a). Enterprise risk management and the organization of uncertainty in financial institution. In: K. Knorr-Cetina & A. Preda (Eds), *The Sociology of Financial Markets*. Oxford, UK: Oxford University Press, pp. 250–268.

Power, M. (2004b). *The Risk Management of Everything*. London, UK: Demos.

Power, M. (2005). The invention of operational risk. *Review of International Political Economy*, **12**(4), 577–599.

Power, M. (2007). *Organized Uncertainty: Designing a World of Risk Management*. Oxford, UK: Oxford University Press.

Seal, W. B. & Croft, L. (1997). Professional rivalry and changing management control approaches in UK clearing banks. *Accounting, Auditing and Accountability Journal*, **10**(1), 60–84.

Sephton, M. & Ward, T. (1990). ABC in Retail Financial Services. *Management Accounting (UK)*, **April**, 29 & 33

Soin, K. (1996). *Organizational Change and the Introduction of Activity Based Costing in a UK Clearing Bank*. Unpublished PhD thesis Sheffield Hallam University.

Soin, K. (2004). *Management Accounting, Risk and Regulation: A Pilot Study of Compliance Practices in UK Financial Services*. Unpublished report funded by the Chartered Institute of Management Accountants (CIMA).

Soin, K., Seal, W. & Cullen, J. (2002). Activity based costing and organizational change: an institutional perspective. *Management Accounting Research*, **13**(2), 249–271.

Vieira, R. & Hoskin, K. (2005) *Accounting practices and discourses change: The implementation of activity based costing in a Portuguese bank*. Paper presented to the *Workshop on the Changing Roles of Management Accounting as a Control System*, Antwerp, Belgium.

Vieira, R. & Hoskin, K. (2007). *Power, discourses and accounting change: the implementation of activity based costing in a Portuguese bank*. Paper presented to the *APIRA 2007 Conference*, Auckland, July 2007.

Williamson, D. (2004) *A call for management accounting and control research into risk management*. Paper presented to the *Sixth International Management Control Systems Conference*, Edinburgh, July 2004.

Willman, P., Fenton-O'Creevy, M., Nicholson, N. & Soane, E. (2002). Traders, management behaviour and loss aversion in investment banking: a field study. *Accounting, Organisations and Society*, **27**(1–2), 85–98.

Willman, P., Fenton-O'Creevy, M., Nicholson, N. & Soane, E. (2006). Noise trading and the management of operational risk; firms, traders and irrationality in financial markets. *Journal of Management Studies*, **43**(6), 1357–1374.

Management Accounting Around the World

Handbook of Management Accounting Research
Edited by Christopher S. Chapman, Anthony G. Hopwood and Michael D. Shields

Management Accounting in India

Sanjay Kallapur[1] and Ranjani Krishnan[2]

[1]*Indian School of Business, Hyderabad, India*
[2]*Broad School of Business, Michigan State University, USA*

Abstract: This chapter surveys the history, evolution and current status of accounting systems and practices in India. Tracing the roots of Indian accounting systems to the ancient civilization of the Indus Valley, we discuss the accounting contributions of historical writings such as the *Smritis* and the *Arthashastra*. We also discuss the accounting system used by the East India Company. Next we provide an overview of contemporary Indian accounting systems and institutions, and accounting education and curricula. We discuss the prevalence of modern management accounting practices in Indian companies. We conclude with a discussion of future research opportunities provided by India's current status as an emergent economic power.

1. Introduction

Over the last couple of decades India has witnessed considerable economic change, including privatization of state-held monopolies, deregulation in many important sectors, and the emergence of outsourcing as an important economic force. India has especially emerged as an attractive destination for outsourcing of accounting functions such as payroll, general ledger, financial management and tax. It has been estimated that 50% of Fortune 500 companies outsource to Indian information technology (IT) companies, and a large proportion of these companies are exploring the outsourcing of their accounting and finance operations to India (Patankar, 2005). This trend is likely to continue because India produces over 50000 English-speaking accounting graduates every year (Valanju, 2005), while other countries such as the US face a shortage of accountants (Clevenger et al., 2006).

In spite of its current status as a rising economic power (Kirkland, 2007) there are surprisingly few academic papers that review accounting practices in Indian companies or the status of accounting education in India. Exceptions include Anderson & Lanen (1999), who use a contingency theory framework and examine a broad range of management accounting practices in 14 Indian firms, and Joshi (2001) who examines the extent of new management practices in 60 Indian firms and compares their use with that in a sample of Australian firms.

The purpose of this chapter is to review accounting in India from three perspectives. First, we discuss the history of accounting in India dating back from the ancient civilizations to the post-independence period. Second, we examine the evolution of accounting as an academic discipline and the structure of accounting curriculums. Third, we review management accounting practices that are prevalent in Indian firms and compare and contrast the prevalence of these practices with that in US and UK firms.

2. History of Indian Accounting

2.1. Pre-colonial Accounting

Thousands of years before British occupation, which occurred from 1858 to 1947 (Roy, 2000), free trade thrived in India. The Indus Valley civilization was the oldest civilized human urban settlement, and had an advanced commercial and trade system that included not only intra-city trade and commerce, but also trade across the major cities of Harappa and Mohenjo-daro. It is believed that writing originated in Mesopotamia in the fourth millennium BC from archaic record-keeping, and that it spread from there to the Indus Valley (Schmand-Besserat, 1992).

The earliest documented evidence of accounting rules in India have been found in the "*Smriti*" literature which dates to 700 BC (Choudhury, 1983). The *Smritis*, which were written in Sanskrit, essentially dealt with

DOI: 10.1016/S1751-3243(07)03011-8

interpretation of religion, religious rituals and the Vedas, and the rules that should govern human conduct. In addition, the *Smritis* were also the law books of ancient India and prescribed the rules that governed transactions and commercial exchange. The *Smritis*, for example, included definitions of partnerships, rights, duties and liabilities of partners, and mechanisms for resolving disputes.[1]

The formalization of the Indian accounting system is credited to Vishnugupta Chanakya Kautilya (usually referred to as Chanakya). Kautilya was the author of *The Arthashastra* (*The Science of Wealth and Welfare*), which was published during the fourth century BC (between 321–297 BC). *The Arthashastra* comprised 15 volumes and 150 chapters classified by topic. The main topics included:

1. national security and foreign policy;
2. administration of justice;
3. rules governing economic development, taxation and accounting.

Sihag (2004) provides a comprehensive discussion of Kautilya's contribution to accounting, which we summarize below.

Kautilya's *Arthashastra* developed and made detailed contributions to four areas of accounting and control systems. First, the *Arthashastra* developed principles of modern accounting. Second, it specified the scope and methodology of accounting, including ways and means to deal with "false accounting." Third, the *Arthashastra* contained a codification of financial rules and regulation and development of an organizational structure to reduce conflicts of interest, which laid the foundation for the auditing profession. Finally, the *Arthashastra* specified the important role of ethics in accounting. Kautilya proposed a formal theory of accounting as an integral part of economics. He developed formal links between accounting and other macroeconomic systems. He also developed a comprehensive department-level accounting system, including accounting for revenues, expenditures and cash flows.

Kautilya proposed governance and control systems that are remarkably modern. For example, he proposed a two-pronged governance system for the state: the treasurer and the comptroller. The treasurer was responsible for managing assets, whereas the comptroller's office maintained the records. Thus, a separation of duties and responsibility could be achieved. Finally, Kautilya believed that accountants should hold themselves to very high ethical standards.

Another unique feature of the Indian mercantile community dating back hundreds of years was the use of the hybrid system of accounting under which income was recognized using a cash system and expenditures were recognized via an accrual system for expenditure accounting (Ramanujam, 2005).

2.2. *The British Colonial Period*

The colonization of India by Britain began with the establishment of the East India Company in the early 1600s. The East India Company (EIC) was the first publicly-traded company in the world. During the 250 year period between 1600 and 1850, EIC was not just a company, but also an imperial power which ruled a fifth of the world's population (Lawson, 1993). It had a private army of a quarter of a million soldiers and generated revenues higher than the entire gross domestic product (GDP) of Britain. It has been estimated that, by 1833, the EIC controlled half a million square miles of Indian territory with a population of 94 million people, who paid over £23 million a year in taxes to Britain (Bowen, 2006).

The governance and accounting system of the EIC was remarkably sophisticated. The company had an established system of consultation books, account books and communications between Britain and India. The consultation books stipulated how decisions would be made, i.e., the chain of command to be followed, reporting guidelines, due processes to be followed, and also recorded past decisions (Ogborn, 2006).

Accounting systems at the EIC included both accounting for internal decision-making, as well as external reporting. Factories of the EIC were required to use uniform accounting systems for comparability purposes. Relative profitability of factories was reported and made publicly available, and efficiency-increasing practices used by high-performing factories were made visible to other factories. In addition, the accounting system was designed to enable the factory accounts to be combined into a hierarchical set of accounts, so that at the end of the year the London office could receive a uniform, legible and combined set of accounts that provided a comprehensive picture of the economic performance of the EIC (Ogborn, 2006). Factory accountants were required to have training in accounting, literature and writing. The accounting rules also specified how to ensure continuity from year to year and in the event of personnel changes. The communication between London and the EIC offices occurred about six times a year and included details of performance and performance summaries. The company auditors in London audited the books with the objective of identifying unwarranted charges, errors, fraud and poor bookkeeping (Ogborn, 2006). Overall, the accounting system at the EIC was sophisticated in both cost and financial accounting, as well as governance and reporting.

[1]Jha (1930) provides details of the Smritis, and Choudhury (1983) describes *Smriti* rules regarding partnerships.

2.3. Post-independence

2.3.1. Industrial Organization

After attaining independence in 1947, India was faced with poverty, unemployment, weak formal capital markets and inadequate resources. The environment was therefore not suitable for the growth of private enterprise, especially in the capital-intensive manufacturing sectors. Thus, under the leadership of the first Prime Minister, Jawarhal Nehru, India followed an economic strategy of planned development. Key manufacturing industries such as metals, railways, cement, food processing and distribution, fertilizers, oil and gas, and chemicals, as well as service industries such as banking and insurance, were set up to be government owned and managed—this was referred to as the "public sector." The objectives of the public sector organizations were to build infrastructure, provide employment and promote balanced regional growth (Raman & Singh, 2005). The government imposed strict controls over public sector organizations in all areas of governance, including production, price setting and distribution.

Public sector organizations enjoyed substantial market share in most major industries until the mid-1980s. By this time, most public sector organizations suffered from inefficiencies, high costs and rampant corruption. During the late 1980s and the 1990s, industrial policy shifted toward privatization and deregulation. In 1999, the Ministry of Disinvestment (a division of the Department of Finance) was established to supervise the controlled reduction of government shares in 247 state-owned companies to a 26% stake. For example, in early 2000, 51% of the stake in Bharat Aluminum Company Limited was sold to a private company named Sterlite Limited. In May 2002, the governance of India's top carmaker, Maruti Udyog, which had a 60% market share of the Indian automobile market, was transferred to the Suzuki Motor Corporation (SMC) of Japan.

While the public sector continues to have a large market share in many industries, such as banking, insurance and oil and gas, the share of the private sector has been increasing steadily. Despite regulatory barriers and a "license Raj" environment, the market share of private sector organizations and their contribution to the GDP has been significant. For example, in 1960 the private sector contributed 87% of the GDP of the country (Asian Development Bank, 2003). The primary contributor to the large GDP share of the private sector has been the agricultural sector. The agricultural sector contributes about 70% of the GDP and is largely unorganized and privately-owned. Since the 1980s, however, capital investment in the private sector has been significantly higher than in the public sector (72% versus 28%).

2.3.2. Accounting Systems and Institutions

Accounting systems in public sector organizations are regulated and governed by the federal or state governments in a manner similar to that of other government departments. The public sector organizations obtain budget allocations from the appropriate administrative departments (such as the department of telecommunication for telecom firms, or the ministry of health for public hospitals). The revenues of public sector organizations accrue to the consolidated fund of the respective state or union where they are domiciled, and the responsibility for their audit vests with the Comptroller and Auditor General of India (Khumawala, 1997).

Soon after India's independence in 1947, two statutory bodies were created to regulate the professions of auditing the financial and cost accounting systems of public and private sector companies, namely the Institute of Chartered Accountants of India (ICAI), and the Institute of Cost and Works Accountants of India (ICWAI). In addition, the Indian Audit and Accounts Service was established when the Indian Constitution came into effect in 1950; its responsibility was to perform the accounting and audit of the federal and state governments, government companies and companies receiving substantial state and federal government revenues. The following sections describe these institutions in greater detail.

2.3.2.1. The Institute of Chartered Accountants of India (ICAI). The ICAI was established via the Chartered Accountants Act, passed on May 1, 1949 with the purpose of regulating the statutory auditing profession in India. To gain membership to the institute, the applicant must pass three levels of exams: an entrance exam (common proficiency test), a professional competency exam conducted in two groups, and a final exam in two groups. The curricula in the exams include financial accounting, managerial accounting, auditing, tax, management information systems, management control systems, economics, business law, business mathematics and quantitative aptitude. The pass rate in these exams is low (34% and 32% in Groups I and II of the professional competency exam, and 38% and 39% in Groups I and II of the final exam (*The Chartered Accountant*, February 2007, p. 1275). In addition to passing all three exams, a candidate must complete three and a half years of practical training with a licensed chartered accountancy firm. After completing the practical training (commonly referred to as "articleship"), the candidate can obtain a license to practice as a chartered accountant (CA). While most CAs serve as public accountants, similar to a certified public accountant in the US, they are also trained to serve as tax accountants, company accountants or investment bankers.

Chartered accounting firms in India primarily consist of small partnerships (less than five partners). All the major US accounting firms have affiliate offices in India. CA firms are regulated via the Chartered Accountants Act of 1949 and the Companies Act of 1956. Some of these regulations are quite stringent and include restrictions on CA firms advertising either in India or in other countries, limiting the total number partners to less than 20, limiting the number of audits that can be accepted and prohibiting auditors from holding shares in their client companies.

2.3.2.2. The Institute of Cost and Works Accountants of India (ICWAI). The ICWAI was formally established in 1959 as professional body for the purposes of training cost and management accountants in India. Under the Indian Companies Act, government companies (public sector companies) and other companies in strategic industries such as metals, chemicals and pharmaceuticals are required to have an audit of their cost and management accounting systems and effectiveness of cost control. This cost audit has to be conducted by a cost auditor who is a member of the ICWAI.

To obtain a license as a cost auditor, the candidate is required to pass two levels of exams. The areas tested include financial accounting, cost accounting, management accounting, business laws, auditing, business mathematics, financial strategy and reporting, financial management, international finance, strategic management, marketing, cost audit and management audit. While the curriculum is similar to the CA exam, the ICWAI syllabus places greater emphasis on cost accounting, quantitative methods and business knowledge.

2.3.2.3. The Indian Audit and Accounts Service (IA&AS). The IA&AS is headed by the Comptroller and Auditor General of India and it has responsibility for auditing the accounts of federal and state government organizations. Its role is similar to the US GAO and the UK National Audit Office (http://www.naaa.gov.in/iaas.htm).

Article 149 of the Indian Constitution prescribes the duties and responsibilities of the Comptroller and Auditor General of India as follows:

> The Comptroller and Auditor-General shall perform such duties and exercise such powers in relation to the accounts of the Union and of the States and of any other authority or body as may be prescribed by or under any law made by Parliament and, until provision in that behalf is so made, shall perform such duties and exercise such powers in relation to the accounts of the Union and of the States as were conferred on or exercisable by the Auditor-General of India immediately before the commencement of this Constitution in relation to the accounts of the Dominion of India and of the Provinces respectively.

Officers of the IA&AS are selected via a rigorous multi-step examination (The Civil Services Examination), which includes general aptitude questions, as well as subject matter questions. Selected candidates undergo a two-year training programme at the National Academy of Accounts and Audit in India.

3. Accounting Education

The first Indian Universities were set up in Bombay (now Mumbai), Calcutta (now Kolkata), and Madras (now Chennai) in 1857. They were modelled on the framework of the University of London, i.e., the teaching was done in affiliated colleges. As of 2003–2004, India had 389 degree-granting institutions (universities, "deemed universities," "institutes of national importance" such as the Indian Institutes of Technology, and research institutions) and 14 169 colleges affiliated to the universities (source: Ministry of Human Resource Development, Division of Higher Education web site). About 10 million students were enrolled in these institutions, of which 1.6 million were in commerce and management degree programmes. During 2001–2002, about 88 000 Indian students were enrolled in degree programmes in foreign countries (of whom 67 000 were in the US).

Colleges typically offer undergraduate degrees, although some also offer master's degrees. The enrolment ratio, percent of college-enrolled students divided by the population of 18–24 year-olds, was 9.23% as of 2003–2004. Government expenditures on education are 3.76% of GDP, of which 18% is spent on higher education. The vast majority of the universities are public, while the majority of colleges are private. The Universities Grants Commission (UGC) specifies standards that have to be adhered to by universities and colleges. Specifically, it conducts a National Eligibility Test (NET) for master's degree-holders; it is required as a qualification for appointment of lecturers in universities and colleges (PhD holders are exempted from NET, and MPhil degree holders are exempted from NET for undergraduate teaching).

The UGC model curriculum for bachelor's degree programmes in commerce and related fields is provided in Table 1. The courses described in the model curriculum run all year long. Each course usually meets for three hours of classroom teaching each week. Autonomous colleges (numbering 138 in 2005) conduct their own assessments and typically have semester-long courses in which grading is based on performance in mid-term and final exams and other components such as term papers, but in most other colleges common exams are administered by the university for all its affiliated colleges.

UGC norms stipulate about 16 hours per week of classroom contact time for college lecturers and about

Table 1. UGC model curriculum for undergraduate business programmes.

No	BC	BAF	BM	BIB	BBI	BeC
			First year			
1	Business communication	Business communication	Business communication	Business communication	Business communication	Business communication
2	Mathematics	Mathematics	Mathematics	Mathematics	Mathematics	Mathematics
3	Financial accounting	Financial accounting	Financial accounting	Financial accounting	Financial accounting	Financial accounting
4	Business regulatory framework	Business regulatory framework	Business regulatory framework	Business regulatory framework	Business regulatory framework	Business regulatory framework
5	Business economics	Business economics	Business economics	Business economics	Business economics	Business economics
6	Business environment	Business environment	Business environment	Business environment	Business environment	Business environment
			Second year			
1	Corporate accounting	Corporate accounting	Corporate accounting	Corporate accounting	Corporate accounting	Business statistics
2	Company law	Company law	Company law	Company law	Company law	Principles of business management
3	Business statistics	Business statistics	Business statistics	Business statistics	Business statistics	Company law
4	Cost accounting	Cost accounting	Cost accounting	Cost accounting	Cost accounting	Cost accounting
5	Principles of business management	Principles of business management	Principles of business management	Principles of business management	Principles of business management	Information technology and its implications in business
6	Income tax	Income tax	Income tax	Income tax	Income tax	Internet and worldwide web
7	Fundamentals of entrepreneurship	Fundamentals of entrepreneurship	Fundamentals of entrepreneurship	Fundamentals of entrepreneurship	Fundamentals of entrepreneurship	Fundamentals of entrepreneurship
			Third year			
1	Information technology and its implications in business	Information technology and its implications in business	Information technology and its implications in business	Information technology and its implications in business	Information technology and its implications in business	Corporate accounting
2	Money and financial systems	Management accounting	Principles of marketing	Principles of marketing	The Indian banking system	Income tax
3	Management accounting	Financial management	International marketing	International marketing	Fundamentals of insurance	Indirect taxes
4	Auditing	Financial market operations	Personal selling	International business environment	Merchant banking and financial services	Management accounting
5	Indirect taxes	The Indian financial system	Advertising and sales promotion	India's foreign trade and policy	Insurance management	Essentials of e-commerce

Table 1. (Continued)

No	BC	BAF	BM	BIB	BBI	BeC
6	Either comb.-I* 3.61, 3.71	Security analysis and portfolio management	Agriculture and rural marketing	Export–import procedures and documentation	Commercial bank management	Principles of e-marketing
				Third year		
7	Or comb.-II* 3.62, 3.72	Financial statement analysis	Distribution and retailing	International finance	Legislative insurance framework	Fundamentals of m-commerce
8	Or comb.-III* 3.63, 3.73	BCom (BC) courses in comb I, II, III, IV I. BC 3.61 Financial management and BC 3.71 Financial market operations II. BC 3.62 Principles of marketing and BC 3.72 International marketing III. BC 3.63 Fundamentals of insurance and BC 3.73 The Indian banking system IV. BC 3.64 Internet and worldwide web and BC 3.74 Essentials of e-commerce				
9	Or comb.-IV* 3.64, 3.74					

Degree legend: BC = Bachelor of Commerce; BAF = Bachelor of Accounting and Finance; BM = Bachelor of Marketing; BIB = Bachelor of International Business; BBI = Bachelor of Banking and Insurance; BeC = Bachelor of e-Commerce.

14 hours per week for readers/professors. They also specify a minimum of 180 teaching days in a year (30 six-day weeks). In contrast, faculty in most research oriented universities in the US teach an average of 12 credit hours per year, which translates to about six hours of classroom contact time per week. This leaves little time for research for faculty in Indian universities compared to US universities.

The exams conducted by the Institute of Chartered Accountants of India and the Institute of Cost and Works Accountants of India were described earlier. These Institutes conduct "postal coaching," i.e., distance education through mail. They also conduct, and have accredited private institutes for conducting, "oral coaching" in major cities.

4. Management Accounting Practices

4.1. Evidence from Surveys

There is limited academic research examining management accounting practices in Indian companies. One paper by Anderson & Lanen (1999) uses a contingency theory framework and examines the evolution of management accounting practices in 14 firms. The authors use a survey and personal interviews to examine differences in the use of management accounting practices by firms based on two factors. The first factor is the experience and exposure of a firm to international markets. The second factor is the competitive strategy of the firm. They compute a firm's exposure to international markets and classify their sample firms as domestic or international, based on its response to seven survey questions. These include the percentage of purchased parts and raw materials as a fraction of total direct material costs provided by domestic suppliers, percentage of sales and the total unit volume sold in domestic markets, domestic and international market shares of their lead product, and strategic alliances with Western or Japanese suppliers. Also based on survey responses, Anderson & Lanen assess competitive strategy of the firm using the Miles & Snow (1978) typology of defenders and prospectors. Defenders are firms that operate in relatively more stable environments and compete through low cost. Defenders use routine technology and economies of scale for efficiency. Prospectors, on the other hand, are firms that operate in an uncertain and rapidly changing environment and use flexible and non-routine technologies. A synopsis of the main results of Anderson & Lanen is provided in Table 2. The results indicate that, consistent with the predictions of contingency theory, the extent of use of specific management accounting practices varies as a function of the firm's strategy and international orientation.

In addition to the results presented in Table 2, Anderson & Lanen also found that all the firms in the sample indicate that their planning process has become more decentralized since 1991, managers have a better understanding of strategic objectives and involvement in strategic planning, and customer satisfaction and expectations are used as inputs in the decision process. In addition, while firms in their sample had been using budgets for a long period, these budgets have become more meaningful than they were in the past. Performance measurement practices have also become more expansive and use quantitative information.

Table 2. Summary of key results from Anderson & Lanen (1999).

Management accounting/ Control issue	Prospector (P) versus defender (D)		Domestic (D) versus international (I)	
	P vs D	Potential explanation	D vs I	Potential explanation
Involvement of mid-level managers and line workers in strategic planning	P > D	Prospectors have higher levels of decentralization		
Use of market share growth data for strategic planning	P > D	Prospectors operate in higher uncertainty markets		
Use of competitor performance data for strategic planning	P > D	Prospectors operate in higher uncertainty markets		
Use of customer satisfaction data for strategic planning	P > D	Prospectors need to be more nimble in identifying market opportunities		
Use of external agencies to assess quality			I > D	Important to maintain higher quality standards in international markets
Use of cost data in developing budgets	D > P	Defenders place greater importance on cost data when preparing budgets	D > I	International firms may have deeper pockets that loosen budget constraints
Plant managers participate in setting budgets	D > P	Defenders place priority on cost management and plant managers are the first line of cost control	D > I	Domestic firms have capital constraints
Use of employee surveys to obtain cost reduction opportunities	P > D	Prospectors make more intensive use of methods to obtain ideas	D > I	
Firm's information system provides accurate data	P > D	Prospectors more likely to view information system as accurate	D > I	Domestic firms more likely to view information system as accurate

Another paper by Joshi (2001), examines management accounting practices based on a survey of 60 large- and medium-sized (sales revenue exceeding US $25 million) manufacturing companies in India and contrasts the results with a similar study of Australian firms by Chenhall & Smith (1998). The survey instrument was adapted from Chenhall & Smith (1998) and Miller, De Meyer & Nakane (1992). An extract of the results from Joshi's survey is presented in Table 3. Joshi finds that Indian companies use traditional management accounting practices, such as budgeting, for operational planning and cost control, and performance evaluation based on return on investment and divisional profit extensively. Some management accounting practices, such as supplier evaluation and product profitability, were used to a moderate extent. However, the use of recent management accounting practices such as activity-based costing (ABC), activity-based management, balanced scorecard, benchmarking and target costing is less frequent. The companies in his sample did not place much emphasis on nonfinancial performance measures and instead placed heavier emphasis on financial measures. Joshi also found evidence that larger companies were significantly more likely to use recent management accounting practices such as ABC.

To better understand the diffusion of management accounting practices in India, a team of three authors representing two management institutes in India and the SEC (Anand, Sahay & Saha) conducted a comprehensive survey of Indian companies in 2003, with the objective of understanding the prevalence of managerial accounting practices such as cost management, ABC and the balanced scorecard. Their survey instrument was mailed to the chief financial officers of 579 companies and they received a response from 53 companies. The findings from their survey are summarized in a series of three published papers. In the following paragraphs, we summarize their major findings. A summary of the key findings of Anand et al. regarding the extent of usage of cost management tools in India is also provided in Fig. 1 (reproduced from their 2004 study).

Table 3. Summary of key results from Joshi (2001).

Management accounting technique	Adoption rate %
Budgeting to plan day-to-day operations	100
Performance evaluation—ROI	100
Performance evaluation—divisional profit	100
Budgeting for planning cash flows	95
Budgeting for controlling costs	93
Performance evaluation—ongoing suppliers evaluations	88
Product profitability analysis	82
Performance evaluation—customer satisfaction surveys	80
Long-range forecasting	58
Cost–volume–profit analysis	65
Product life cycle analysis	45
Performance evaluation—balanced scorecard	40
Target costing	35
Benchmarking with outside organizations	32
Value chain analysis	25
Activity-based costing	20
Activity-based management	13
Activity-based budgeting	7

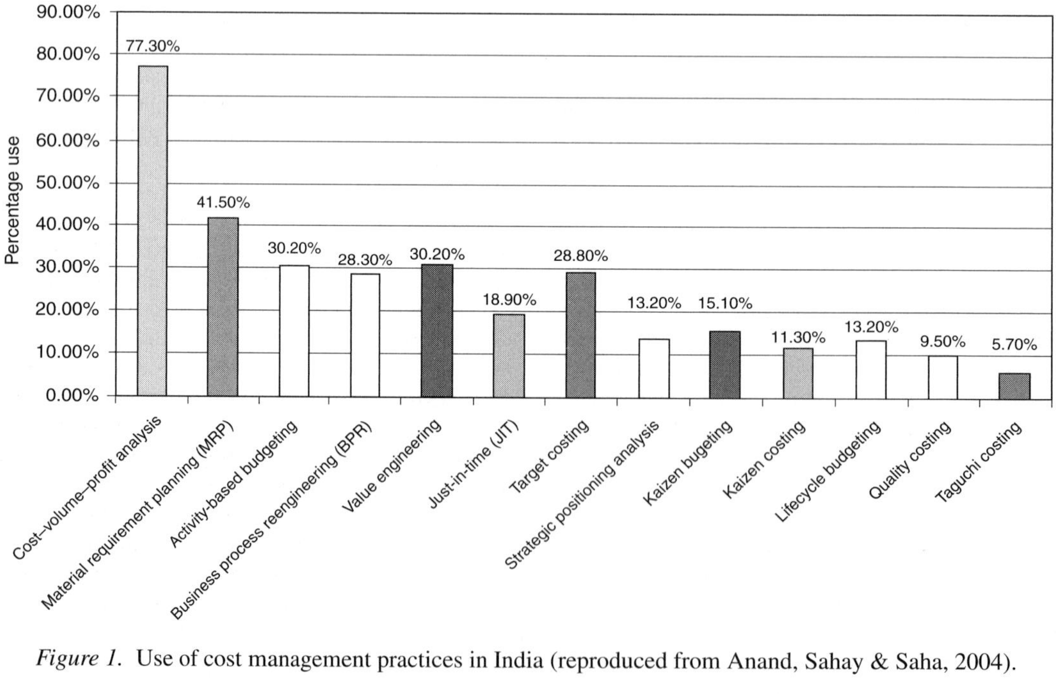

Figure 1. Use of cost management practices in India (reproduced from Anand, Sahay & Saha, 2004).

In a paper published in *Vikalpa* in 2005, Anand, Sahay & Saha examine the extent of adoption of the balanced scorecard by Indian companies. They also examine the following:

1. the extent to which Indian firms use all the four perspectives in the balanced scorecard, i.e., customer, financial, internal business, and learning and growth;

Table 4. Summary of major findings from Anand, Sahay & Saha (2005).

Balanced scorecard issue	% of firms responding as "very important"
Objective of performance measurement and control system: balancing profit, growth and control	65.2
Motivation for implementation of balanced scorecard: initiating change in the organization	50.0
Perspectives considered important in the balanced scorecard: financial perspective	87.5
Key performance measures in the customer perspective:	
Customer satisfaction	83.4
On-time delivery	83.3
Key performance measures in the internal business perspective: unit cost	75.0
Key performance measures in the innovation perspective: market share	79.2
Key performance measures in the financial perspective: return on Investment	62.5
Key performance measures in the shareholder perspective: EVA	58.3
Problems faced during the implementation of the balanced scorecard:	
Difficulty in assigning weightage to different perspectives	45.8
Difficulty in establishing cause–effect relationships amongst the perspectives	41.7
Impact of balanced scorecard on different areas: cost reduction opportunities	60.9

2. companies' motivation for implementing the balanced score card; and
3. the key performance measures used for each perspective in the balanced scorecard.

They use data from a survey of 53 Indian companies, conducted in 2003, and find that 24 of the sample of 53 firms (45.28%) have adopted a balanced scorecard as a strategic tool. The most important motivations for implementing a balanced scorecard were specified as:

- initiating change
- broadening performance measures
- facilitating integration of business plans with financial plans.

Regarding the importance of each of the four perspectives, a majority of the respondents (87.5%) ranked the financial perspective as the most important, followed by the customer perspective. The respondents indicated that the key performance indicators used for the customer perspective was customer satisfaction with quality and on-time delivery. For the internal business perspective, the most important key performance indicator was unit cost. Respondents indicated that the most important performance indicator for the innovation and growth perspective was market share. For the financial perspective, ROI and days of working capital were the most frequently used performance measures. Of the respondents, 58.3% indicated EVA as the most important key performance indicator in the shareholder perspective. Respondents were asked to indicate the problems that they faced in the implementation of the balanced scorecard; 45.8% indicated that difficulty in assigning appropriate weights to the different perspectives was the most difficult of the implementation challenges. Difficulty in establishing cause–effect relationships amongst the different perspectives was the hardest challenge according to 41.7%. Key findings from the study are summarized in Table 4.

Using the data from the same survey, Anand et al. (2005) examine the extent of adoption of ABC in Indian companies in an article published in the *Decision* journal. They also examine whether firms using ABC systems are more likely to have accurate cost and profit information for managerial decision making. Of the 53 firms that responded, 26 firms (49%) reported that they used ABC systems either as a supplementary/offline system (11 firms) or as a fully integrated accounting and ERP system (15 firms). The adopting firms were predominantly from the manufacturing sector (20 firms, or 76.92%). The factors mentioned as the most important management motivations for the introduction of ABC were: to have detailed information on value-added and non value-added activities; to be competitive in the industry in terms of price quality and performance; and for budgeting. The survey also enquired about the problems faced during the implementation of ABC systems. Respondents indicated that difficulties in implementation arose because of the inability of traditional costing systems to capture the informational needs of an ABC system (42.3%), difficulty in developing an activity directory (34.6%) and a lack of review of the implementation process (30.8%).

The prevalence of advanced management accounting techniques such as ABC and balanced scorecard in Indian companies is likely to grow in the future for several reasons. First, with the growth in outsourcing and the emergence of India as an economic partner, Indian companies will be under pressure to adopt modern management accounting techniques to improve efficiency and for benchmarking and performance evaluation. Second, there has been a growth in international joint ventures, which will facilitate the diffusion of refined accounting techniques. Third, accounting and MBA curriculums in most universities expose students to modern management accounting techniques. Fourth, educational institutions such as the Indian Institutes of Management, Indian School of Business, and the Indian Institutes of Technology have actively recruited faculty trained in the US and Europe in permanent, as well as visiting, faculty positions, which is accelerating the dissemination of modern accounting techniques.

4.2 Recent Trends: Managing the Outsourcing Function

Over the last few years, India has emerged as an attractive destination for outsourcing of information technology (IT) and other business processes, such as back-office transaction processing and vendor and customer contact centres. A report issued by NASSCOM (National Association of Software and Services Companies, a trade association) and the consulting firm McKinsey notes that India accounts for 65% of the global industry in offshored IT and over 46% of the global market in business process outsourcing. Outsourcing gives rise to a number of control and incentive problems. The governance and management of the outsourcing function in India and the types of performance measures and other control systems used to mitigate opportunity costs and to ensure that performance standards are met is of interest to management accounting researchers. However, there is paucity of academic research in this area, an exception being Nicholson, Jones & Espenlaub (2006), which uses a transaction cost approach and a case study methodology to examine the practices and controls governing offshored accounting and finance activities. The authors use field data using semi-structured interviews from eight firms, including three subsidiaries of multi-national companies, five independent outsourcing vendors and one client firm. They qualitatively analyze the types of transaction costs incurred by clients and vendors during three stages of the relationship, i.e., contact stage, contract stage and control stage, and methods of mitigating them.

The *contact* stage in an offshoring relation consists of gathering information, site visits and assessing the capabilities of the vendor firm. Nicholson et al. (2006) find that many customers offshoring to India make use of intermediary firms, whose main function is to provide information, reduce search and uncertainty costs and help in negotiation of the initial contract. These intermediary firms also help subsequently in dispute resolution at later stages of the relationship. Many firms look for accreditation status of the vendors (such as ISO certification), as well as their legal status. Although there are a large number of smaller and less well-known firms, there are also an increasing number of larger and well-established firms such as Tata Consultancy Services (TCS) and Infosys, which have an international presence.

At the *contract* stage, Nicholson et al. (2006) find that the comprehensiveness of the actual service arrangements differed within the companies in the sample, largely based on the extent of work outsourced. They find that larger or more complex outsourcing tasks used more comprehensive contracts, and such contracts included detailed provisions for dispute resolution, safeguards against opportunism, intellectual property management, confidentiality and mechanisms for gain sharing.

There were several mechanisms used for ongoing *control* of the outsourcing relationships. The controls used at this stage included boundary controls such as the types of work that were outsourced, process controls such as operating procedures required to maintain privacy and secrecy, and physical office arrangements that minimized security leaks.

The governance of outsourcing relations is an interesting and important issue that has potential for future research. For example, future research could examine the differences in performance measurement systems used when firms offshore work to India instead of outsourcing to firms within the same country. The management and governance of international inter-firm contractual relations is also a rich area for future study.

4.3 Influence of Ownership on Firm Ownership Managerial Accounting and Control Systems

Research in strategy, accounting and economics indicates that ownership type influences a firm's goals, objective functions, strategic decisions and accounting and control systems (Lambert & Larcker, 1995; Roomkin & Weisbrod, 1999; Eldenburg & Krishnan, 2007). The Indian landscape is populated by firms representing a variety of ownership types such as family owned, public (government) owned, professionally owned and foreign owned. Gollakota & Gupta (2006) examine the evolution of ownership types in India and discuss the implications of different ownership types on corporate governance. They conclude that there is greater need for research that examines the effects of ownership differences on economic outcomes, as well as control system effects. Prior research has also shown differences in financial performance based on ownership. For example, Majumdar (1998) examines the differences in financial performance between state-owned, privately-owned and mixed state- and private-ownership firms and finds evidence that privately-owned firms were the most profitable, followed by mixed ownership, and that state-owned enterprises exhibited the worst performance. Khanna & Palepu (2005) find that of the 2600 publicly listed firms in India in 1993, half were non-family group affiliated. While the group affiliated firms had much higher sales revenues, there were no differences in financial performance across the two groups. Future research on the impact of ownership on corporate governance and control systems in a transitional economy such as India is warranted.

5. Conclusions

This chapter summarizes the history, evolution and current status of management accounting and control systems in India. We trace the evolution of accounting systems dating from Mesopotamia in the fourth millennium BC, the British occupation from the seventeenth to the twenthieth century, the public sector and license Raj era of the mid-twentieth century, to the current modernization and market oriented economy that India has evolved into in the twenty-first millennium. There is a dearth of research that examines the prevalence and use of management accounting and control systems in India. The few existing empirical studies document that modern management accounting and control techniques such as ABC and the balanced scorecard are used, but not widely prevalent. Indian firms continue to use traditional management accounting techniques, such as standard costing, to a greater extent. In view of India's current status as an emergent economic power, future research that examines the use of management accounting, control and contracting systems from alternative theoretical lenses would be a useful research endeavour.

References

Anand, M., Sahay, B. S. & Saha, S. (2004). Cost management practices in India: An empirical study. *ASCI Journal of Management.*, **33**(1–2), 1–13.

Anand, M., Sahay, B. S. & Saha, S. (2005). Balanced scorecard in Indian companies. *Vikalpa*, **30**(2), 11–25.

Anand, M., Sahay, B. S. & Saha, S. (2005). Activity-based management practices in India: An empirical study. *Decision*, **32**(1), 123–152.

Anderson, S. W. & Lanen, W. (1999). Economic transition, strategy and the evolution of management accounting practices: The case of India. *Accounting, Organizations and Society*, **24**(5–6), 379–412.

Asian Development Bank. (2003). Private sector assessment—India. (www.adb.org/documents/CSPs/IND/2003/appendix3_private_sector_assessment.pdf).

Bowen, H. V. (2006). *The Business of Empire: The East India Company and Imperial Britain*. Cambridge, UK: Cambridge University Press.

Chenhall, R. H. & Smith, K. L. (1998). Adoption and benefits of management accounting practices. *Management Accounting Research.*, **9**, 1–19.

Choudhury, N. (1983). Vedic partnership rules. *The Accounting Historians Journal.*, **10**(2), 129–138.

Clevenger, N. N., Clevenger, T. B. & McElroy, J. (2006). Shortage of accountants: Is education to blame? *The Journal of Government Financial Management*, **55**(2), 14–19.

Eldenburg, L. & Krishnan, R. (2007). The influence of ownership on accounting information expenditures. *Contemporary Accounting Research,* **25**(3).

Gollakota, K. & Gupta, V. (2006). History, ownership forms, and corporate governance in India. *Journal of Management History*, **12**(2), 185–198.

Joshi, P. L. (2001). The international diffusion of new management accounting practices: The case of India. *Journal of International Accounting, Auditing & Taxation*, **10**, 85–109.

Jha, G. (1930). *Hindu law and its sources,* (Vol. 1). Allahabad, India: The Indian Press Ltd.

Khanna, T. & Palepu, K. (2005). The evolution of concentrated ownership in India: broad patterns and a history of the Indian software industry. In: R. Morck (Ed.), *The history of corporate governance around the world: family business groups to professional managers*. Chicago, IL: University of Chicago Press.

Khumawala, S. (1997). Public sector accounting in India: a historical review and an analysis since independence to the economic reforms of the nineties. *Journal of Public Budgeting, Accounting, and Financial Management*, **9**(2), 305–330.

Kirkland, R. (2007). The greatest economic boom ever. *Fortune*, **156**(2), 120.

Lambert, R. A. & Larcker, D. F. (1995). The prospective payment system, hospital efficiency, and compensation contracts for senior-level administrators. *Journal of Accounting and Public Policy*, **14**, 1–31.

Lawson, P. (1993). *The East India Company: A History*. London, UK: Longman.

Majumdar, S. K. (1998). Assessing comparative efficiency of the state owned, mixed, and private sectors in Indian Industry. *Public Choice*, **96**, 1–24.

Miles, R. & Snow, C. (1978). *Organization structure, strategy, and process*. New York, NY: McGraw-Hill.

Miller, G., De Meyer, A. & Nakane, J. (1992). *Benchmarking Global Manufacturing*. Homewood, IL: Irwin.

Nicholson, B., Jones, J. & Espenlaub, S. (2006). Transaction costs and control of outsourced accounting: case evidence from India. *Management Accounting Research*, **17**, 238–258.

Ogborn, M. (2006). Streynsham master's office: accounting for collectivity, order, and authority in 17th century India. *Cultural Geographies*, **13**, 127–155.

Patankar, K. (2005). Financial outsourcing: the next big thing. *Knight Ridder/Tribune Business News*, **February 12**, 1.

Raman, K. & Singh, U. (2005). Transition in human resources function in public sector enterprises in India—in the context of economic reforms. *The Business Review, Cambridge*, **4**(2), 106–113.

Ramanujam, T. C. A. (2005). The now-buried cross-breed. *Financial Daily*, Saturday Dec 10.

Roomkin, M. J. & Weisbrod, B. A. (1999). Managerial compensation and incentives in for-profit and nonprofit hospitals. *Journal of Law, Economics, and Organizations*, **15**(3), 750–781.

Roy, T. (2000). *The Economic History of India 1857–1947*. Delhi, India: Oxford University Press.

Schmandt-Besserat, D. (1992). *Before Writing: from counting to cuneiform*. Austin, TX: University of Texas Press.

Sihag, B. S. (2004). Kautilya on the scope and methodology of accounting, organizational design, and the role of ethics in ancient India. *The Accounting Historians Journal*, **31**(2), 125–148.

Valanju, S. (2005). Site unseen? *Financial Management*, **July–August**, 16.

Author Index for Volumes 1, 2 and 3

Page numbers not in brackets refer to the reference lists; those in brackets refer to the citations in the text.

Subject Index for Volumes 1, 2 and 3

OVERVIEW OF VOLUMES 1, 2 AND 3

THE SCOPE OF THE MANAGEMENT ACCOUNTING RESEARCH LITERATURE

THEORETICAL PERSPECTIVES

RESEARCH METHODS

MANAGEMENT ACCOUNTING PRACTICES

MANAGEMENT ACCOUNTING PRACTICE CONTEXTS

MANAGEMENT ACCOUNTING AROUND THE WORLD